D0162128

CANIDS OF THE WORLD
Wolves, Wild Dogs, Foxes, Jackals, Coyotes, and Their Relatives

José R. Castelló

Foreword by
Claudio Sillero-Zubiri

PRINCETON UNIVERSITY PRESS
PRINCETON AND OXFORD

Published by Princeton University Press,
41 William Street, Princeton, New Jersey 08540
In the United Kingdom: Princeton University Press, 6 Oxford Street,
Woodstock, Oxfordshire OX20 1TR
nathist.princeton.edu

Requests for permission to reproduce material from this work should be sent to
permissions@press.princeton.edu

Library of Congress Control Number : 2017963961
ISBN 978-0-691-18372-5
ISBN (pbk.) 978-0-691-17685-7

British Library Cataloging-in-Publication Data is available

Production and design by José R. Castelló, Madrid, Spain
This book has been composed in Helvetica Neue
Printed on acid-free paper ∞
Printed in China

10 9 8 7 6 5 4 3 2 1

CONTENTS

FOREWORD

While most people would know what a Fox, Wolf, Jackal or Wild Dog may look like, and we can agree that they all share an easily distinguishable Dog morph, some members of the family Canidae are not so well known, even to the most dogged Dog enthusiast. Let alone the rich and diverse social structure and behavior displayed by Canid species distributed worldwide, and their ability to occupy most habitats. The typically tall, lithe Canid body, bushy tail and long limbs with digitigrade four-toed feet are adaptions to the cursorial pursuit of prey in open environments. This is matched up with a flexible diet—from an almost exclusive emphasis on frugivory or insectivory, to omnivory to strict carnivory—and an opportunistic and adaptable behavior, and there is a complex social organization with much variation within and between species.

To understand them fully, and thereby to appreciate their wonder, one must know several snippets of Canid natural history. Perhaps most revealing in this quest are the many long-term studies in which field biologists have often spent half a lifetime, burrowed deep into the intricate detail of the behavior of a particular species in the wild. As a fun alternative to a scholarly sabbatical in a library, this field guide presents many interesting facts and vignettes of the ecology and behavior of these animals, guaranteed to engage the reader—whether an enthusiast or a scholar—in getting to the gist of what it means to be a wild Canid.

Wolves and their canine relatives have always held a fascination to humankind. Dogs are surely our first domestic animals. The history regarding the location of their transformation from Wolves, and the peoples responsible for it, has been intriguing but also confusing, with recent genetic evidence pointing to Europe, the Far East and places in between. A tribute to that is the close connection that persists between Domestic Dogs, wild Canids and culture, with many examples in the arts and literature. Genetically and behaviorally, the closeness between Domestic Dogs and some *Canis* species is such that they may even interbreed, although these events may be rarer than previously thought.

Wild Canids seem to have an exceptional capacity to evoke strong feelings of charm, affinity or loathing in human onlookers. People are especially attuned to Canid communication signals and use of extensive postural, vocal and olfactory signals because we are so frequently their recipient from our Domestic Dogs. Although domestication has affected the Dog's repertoire, the barks, growls, whines and howls of Wolves are ever present in our daily lives.

Partly due to this fascination, wild Canids command attention that is disproportionate to their species diversity or abundance, chiefly because they so frequently and successfully challenge human interests. They will often compete with humans as predators, since they find human-raised livestock irresistible prey, and often prey on game species. Rarely, a few of the larger species may occasionally even maul or kill people. And more recently, their role as vectors of diseases that can be harmful to people and their domestic animals has been highlighted. For those reasons Canids have borne a high proportion of the conflict between humans and carnivores. The more prolific and adaptable Canids, like Red Foxes, Jackals and Coyotes, have fared well despite this competition.

The contemporary Canidae is the most widespread family of extant Carnivora, with at least one species present on all continents except Antarctica. They range from deserts to ice fields, from mountains to swamps or grasslands, and from rain forests to urban "jungles." To do this they may travel home ranges as small as the Island Fox (0.5 km²) or as large and non-defensible as the African Wild Dog (up to 2,000 km²).

Those familiar with taxonomy will not be surprised to know that even the question of the exact number of Canid species remains unresolved, but we tend to agree that there are at least 37 living Canids in 13 genera. These include three ancient Wolves recently recognized as species in their own right, namely the African, Himalayan and Indian Wolves. Recognition of the Eastern Wolf *Canis lycaon* in North America would add another. Overall the main clades within the Canidae are well resolved, although there are still a few loose ends, as exemplified by unresolved African Jackal taxonomy and the species status of the Red Wolf. Intriguingly, the ability of *Canis* species to hybridize would suggest an important role for genetic admixture in lupine Canid evolution.

The distribution of Canidae species may be highly restricted, and a species may be endemic to one country or even a small fraction of one—almost the entire Darwin's Fox population occurs only on

Chiloé island off the Chilean mainland, Island Fox subspecies occur on one island each, and Ethiopian Wolves are found only above 3,000 m a.s.l. in a few mountain enclaves in the Ethiopian highlands. At the other end of the spectrum other Canid species span several continents; for instance the Gray Wolf was until a century ago the most widely distributed terrestrial mammal. Its successor to the throne is the wily and thriving Red Fox, covering nearly 70 million km^2 across the entire Northern Hemisphere and introduced to Australia in the 1800s.

Somewhere in the middle in terms of size, and almost as numerous, we find the more prolific and adaptable Canids. Coyotes rule in North America, *Lycalopex* zorros are ubiquitous in the southern cone of South America and Jackals command vast areas of Africa and Asia. These meso-carnivores have fared well despite competition, while the larger mob operators or pack hunters—e.g., African Wild Dogs and Dholes—and the more specialized members of the family, like the Ethiopian Wolf, Bat-Eared Fox and Darwin's Fox, have become rarer and are often threatened with extinction.

Almost all Canids live together in territorial groups, either as monogamous pairs or as larger units enhanced by the delayed dispersal of offspring. These larger packs share a common territory, tend to engage in cooperative breeding, have more than one breeding female, and include non-reproductive adults, which may benefit the breeders' fitness through allosuckling, babysitting, feeding the pups or through territorial defense.

What is not up for debate is that the Canids, from the largest Gray Wolf to the puny Fennec Fox or Blanford's Fox, comprise a fascinating and beautiful assortment of animals, with many intriguing adaptations and social behaviors. José R. Castelló has brought out the most interesting facts about these animals, and illustrated this guide with wonderful photographs and artwork. By depicting them against the white page he achieves the same effect of field-guide illustrations, but gives the reader the extra excitement of looking at an actual live animal.

This is a wonderful field guide, which will satisfy different users, from the amateur enthusiast trying to learn more about the Canids of the world, to the more systematic mammal "ticker", who will find here an excellent check list, to the scholar mining information for a comparative study. The wealth of information crammed into this guide should also be of use to those planning and implementing relevant conservation actions, and help the survival of all these intriguing species encompassed in the family Canidae.

Claudio Sillero-Zubiri
Associate Professor of Conservation Biology
University of Oxford, Wildlife Conservation Research Unit
Chair, IUCN SSC Canid Specialist Group
Author of "Family Canidae" *in* Handbook of the Mammals of the World, Volume 1: Carnivores

ACKNOWLEDGMENTS

First, I would like to thank my wife, Beatriz, for her love and support. She has been my companion during the years of work on this project. I could not have completed this book without her. I also thank my son Alejandro and my daughter Bea for their support. Also, I need to thank my parents, who taught me the value of hard work and an education.

A special thanks to Claudio Sillero-Zubiri for his expert and gracious assistance in preparing this book, and for sharing his vast knowledge of Canids. Claudio is a conservation biologist at the University of Oxford, Chair of the IUCN Canid Specialist Group, and the Head of Conservation for the Born Free Foundation, an international NGO. He is a major reference in the behavioral ecology of wild Canids.

Many experts and wildlife photographers have greatly contributed to the contents of this book. I would like to thank all of them for their expertise and dedication to this field. Special thanks to Benjamin N. Sacks, Associate Adjunct Professor at the Center for Veterinary Genetics, University of California, for his advice on North American Canids. Thank you also to Jan F. Kamler, from the Wildlife Conservation Research Unit, University of Oxford, and member of the IUCN Canid Specialist Group, for his assistance. I would like to express my very great appreciation to Colin Groves, Professor of Biological Anthropology at the Australian National University, for his valuable and constructive suggestions during the development of this work. Thanks to Nils Christian Stenseth, Research Professor of Ecology and Evolution, and Anagaw Atickem, researcher from the Department of Biosciences, University of Oslo, for their advice on the taxonomy of the rediscovered African Wolf. Appreciation is extended to Abi Tamim Vanak, Associate Professor at the Suri Sehgal Centre for Biodiversity and Conservation in India, for his advice on Asiatic Canids. Thank you to James K. McIntyre, Director of Field Research at the New Guinea Wild Dog Foundation, for sharing the findings from his recent expedition confirming the presence of New Guinea Singing Dogs in their native habitat for the first time in over 50 years. Thank you also to Bill Leikam from the Urban Wildlife Research Project for his research on the behavior of the Gray Fox. I am particularly grateful for the assistance given by Agustín Iriarte Walton, General Manager at Flora and Fauna Chile, Estela Luengo Vidal, from the Mammal Behavioural Ecology Group, Universidad Nacional del Sur, Argentina, Julio C. Dalponte from the Department of Zoology at the Universidade de Brasília (Brazilian Canids), Joares A. May, Professor at the Universidade do Sul de Santa Catarina and President of Panthera Brasil, and Rogério Cunha de Paula from the Centro Nacional de Pesquisa e Conservaçao de Mamíferos Carnivoros in Brazil, for their help and knowledge of South American Canids. My grateful thanks are also extended to Angel J. España Baez, a Spanish biologist and co-author of the book *Lobos Ibericos*.

I wish also to acknowledge the help provided by Klaus Rudloff, Curator Emeritus at Tierpark Berlin, for his help with the German names, and Pierre de Chabannes, a photographer specializing in animal conservation, for his help with the French names. Assistance provided by Alex Kantorovich, curator of Hai Park Kiryat Motzkin, and Jonas Livet, a French biologist and consultant in zoology, was greatly appreciated.

A very special thanks goes also to my friend Sergey Chichagov, a Latvian biologist and passionate photographer, who has shared his profound knowledge of Canids and hundreds of photographs with me.

Finally, many thanks also to Nayer Youakim, Alexander Meyer, Ulrike Joerres, Pascale Delalandre, Emmanuel Keller, Puch Corinne, Maxime Frechette, Fariborz Heidari, Jim Cumming, Jan Reurink, Scott Lamont, Markus Lilje, Tomoko Ichishima, Gabriel Enrique Levitzky, Jem Babbington, Stuart Reeds, Steven Metidi, Heather Paul, Phil Myers, Mark Piazzi, Graham Ekins, Joe McKenna, Leon Molenaar, David Beadle, Allan Drewitt, Steven Metildi, Craig Salvas, Mark Dumont, Max Waugh, Pascale Ménétrier Delalandre, Heather Paul, Carlo Galliani, Arno Meintjes, Arjan Haverkamp, Frida Bredesen, Karen McCrorey, Ken Behrens, Lindell Dillon, Rob Sall, Jem Babbington, Liora Levin, Fariborz Heidari, Andrey Kotkin, Robert Gould, Gerard W. Beyersbergen, Scott Martin, and to all the great photographers for their enormous generosity in sharing their photographs; without them, this work would not be possible. I want also to acknowledge and thank Flickr and ZooChat, and their community of wildlife photographers.

RECOGNITION

The Canid family is a lineage of terrestrial carnivorans, adapted for swift running, which includes Wolves, Coyotes, Jackals, Foxes, Dogs, Dingoes, Dholes and other Dog-like mammals, with a total of 13 genera and at least 37 extant species. They are mostly social animals, living together in family units or small groups and behaving cooperatively. Most are seasonal breeders producing a single litter each year. They exhibit many reproductive and behavioral traits uncommon in other mammals, such as monogamy with paternal care, long-term incorporation of young adults into the social group, alloparenting, inhibition of reproduction in subordinate individuals, monoestrus, and a copulatory tie. They inhabit temperate and tropical forests, savanna, tundra and deserts throughout the world, with the exception of some oceanic islands and Antarctica. Most Canids feed on mammalian prey, but vegetable matter, carrion, and invertebrates are also an important source of food in many species.

Size and body shape (fig. 1): Canids vary widely in size, from the Gray Wolf, which may be up to 160 cm long, and can weigh up to 80 kg, to the diminutive Fennec Fox, which may be as little as 24 cm in length, and weighs less than 1 kg. Most Fox species weigh 1.5 to 9.0 kg, while most other species are 5 to 27 kg. Body lengths (without tail) range between 35 and 160 cm, and tail lengths are approximately 12 to 56 cm. In most Canids, body size is attributed as a response to food availability: very small Canids (e.g., Fennec Fox) are usually associated with arid and poor habitats in which only a small body mass can be supported year-round, while large Canids (e.g., African Wild Dog) are often associated with habitats in which prey is abundant. Sexual dimorphism, when present at all, is minimal, with males slightly larger than females. The body forms of Canids are similar, typically having long muzzles, upright ears, teeth adapted for cracking bones and slicing flesh, lightly built bodies, and long legs adapted to running down prey or foraging on the trot, and bushy tails. Most Canids are isomorphic; that is, proportions are constant (e.g., Wolves have bigger heads because they have larger bodies, but if shrunk they would just look like Coyotes or Jackals).

Figure 1. Variety of size and body shape in Canids: (1) Gray Wolf (*Canis lupus*); (2) Maned Wolf (*Chrysocyon brachyurus*); (3) African Wild Dog (*Lycaon pictus*); (4) Red Fox (*Vulpes vulpes*); (5) Gray Fox (*Urocyon cinereoargenteus*); (6) Bush Dog (*Speothos venaticus*); (7) Fennec Fox (*Vulpes zerda*). Sizes compared to an adult human.

Coat (figs. 2 and 3): Pelage is usually relatively short, with dense underfur mixed with longer guard hairs. The fur is thicker and lighter colored in the winter and in low-temperature zones. Males and females are indistinguishable in terms of pelage. Color varies significantly, tawny brown or gray in most cases, but black, white and shades of ocher also occur. Most species are uniformly colored or speckled, but some may have stripes on the sides of the body (e.g., Side-Striped Jackal), or may be covered with blotches (e.g., African Wild Dog). The underparts are usually paler than the rest of the body. The tail is usually bushy, often with a contrasting white or black tip and a darker, bristly patch covering the dorsal supracaudal scent gland near the root. Desert and Arctic Canids are usually very pale in color. There may be considerable variation in coloration through the range of a species and

silver-gray
color phase

white
color phase

gray/brown
color phase

black
color phase

Figure 2. Variations in pelage color in Wolf (*Canis lupus*): Coat color varies more in the Wolf than in almost any other wild species, with colors from white through cream, buff, tawny, reddish, and gray to black (melanistic). Such variation occurs throughout its range, although gray predominates. The occurrence of colors other than gray seems to increase in the higher altitudes. Several of the color phases may be found in a single litter. Photo credits: *Nicolas Grevet,* Mercantour National Park (France), *Josef Pittner,* Parc Omega, Quebec (Canada), *Sergey Chichagov,* Chapultepec Zoo (Mexico) and Riga Zoo (Latvia).

some Canids may exhibit different color morphs. Melanism, a mutation producing excessive synthesis of the melanin pigment, results in black or dark brown morphs, often accompanied by a white pectoral spot and white on the feet, and is frequently observed in some North American Canids, such as Gray Wolves, Red Wolves, Red Foxes, and less frequently in Coyotes, but rarely occurs in Europe and Asia. On the contrary, leucism and albinism (partial or total lack of the synthesis of melanin) is rare among wild Canids as they lack evolutionary adaptive significance in nature (except in snow-covered regions), and are therefore usually eliminated from the natural populations. Most Canids molt, naturally losing dead hair at certain times of the year. The most obvious molt takes place in the spring, when the heavier winter coat is shed, with the underfur growing back slowly from the late summer onward.

Skeleton (fig. 4): The skeletal structure of Canids is remarkably consistent, reflecting the lack of specialization in terms of lifestyle. Like other carnivores, they have 7 cervical, 13 to 14 thoracic, 6 to 8 lumbar, and 3 to 4 sacral vertebrae. The greatest variation of the vertebral column occurs in the tail area, varying from 14 to 23 total vertebrae. The neck has strong muscle attachments, being adapted to pull down prey while running. The rib cage is large to accommodate the lungs and heart, and the

summer
coat

winter
coat

summer coat
(desert form)

Figure 3. Variations in pelage length in Red Fox (*Vulpes vulpes*): Pelage characteristics undergo seasonal variations. Intraspecies variation of pelage characteristics can occur according to location and habitat characteristics. Middle East Red Foxes (left) are adapted to desert life, being smaller in size, with much larger ears and shorter pelage, while North American Red Foxes (right) are larger, with longer and fuller fur.

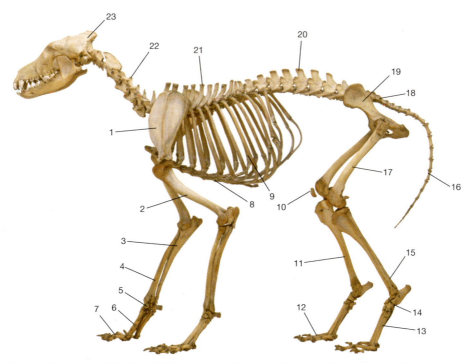

Figure 4. The skeleton of the Gray Wolf (*Canis lupus*): (1) scapula; (2) humerus; (3) ulna; (4) radius; (5) carpus; (6) metacarpus; (7) phalanges; (8) sternum; (9) ribs; (10) patella; (11) tibia; (12) phalanges; (13) metatarsus; (14) tarsus; (15) fibula; (16) caudal vertebrae; (17) femur; (18) sacral vertebrae; (19) pelvis; (20) lumbar vertebrae; (21) thoracic vertebrae; (22) cervical vertebrae; (23) skull. Photo credit: *Colin Keates*.

sternum is not completely ossified, enabling the chest to expand as the animal breathes. The relatively long tail of most Canids helps with balance when they are running and turning at speed. Males have a well-developed grooved penis bone (baculum).

Skull (figs. 5 and 6): The skull is long and narrow, giving the head an elongated shape with a long tapering muzzle, in contrast to the relatively short face of Felids and Mustelids. The zygomatic arches are wide and the bony orbits never form a complete ring. The temporal ridges may be either wide or fused to form an interparietal crest. Canids are recognized by three aspects of cranial anatomy: the type of auditory bulla, the location of the internal carotid artery, and specific features of dentition, such as the possession of carnassial teeth, used to slice their prey's flesh. The Canid inner ear has a large entotympanic bulla (large round bone that holds the eardrum) and a septum between the inner ear bones. They have also completely lost the stapedial artery, which connects inner ear muscles in fetuses of other mammals. The placement of the carotid arteries is also different from that in other mammals, being closer to the brain. These basicranial characteristics have remained more or less stable throughout the history of Canids, allowing easy identification in the fossil record when these structures are preserved.

Dentition (figs. 5, 6 and 7): Most Canids have 42 teeth, with a dental formula of I 3/3, C 1/1, P 4/4, M 2/3. The Bush Dog has only one upper molar with one or two below (M 1/1-2), the Dhole has two above and two below (M 2/2), while the Bat-Eared Fox has three or four upper molars and four lower ones (M 3-4/4), which is more than any non-marsupial mammal. As in other members of Carnivora, the upper fourth premolar and lower first molar are adapted as carnassial teeth for slicing flesh (the Bat-Eared Fox differs in this respect, being largely insectivorous). The molar teeth are strong in most species, allowing the animals to crack open bone to reach the marrow. The canine teeth are long and more or less sharply pointed but unspecialized. The deciduous, or baby teeth, formula in Canids is I 3/3, C 1/1, P 3/3, molars being completely absent. Dhole, African Wild Dog, and Bush Dog have a trenchant heel, a unique meat-cutting blade, on their lower carnassial teeth.

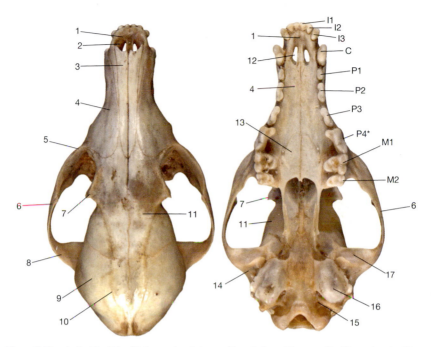

Figure 5. The skull of Red Fox (*Vulpes vulpes*), top and basal views: (1) premaxilla; (2) nasal cavity; (3) nasal; (4) maxilla; (5) jugal; (6) zygomatic arch; (7) postorbital process; (8) squamosal; (9) parietal; (10) sagittal crest; (11) frontal; (12) incisive foramen; (13) palatine; (14) temporal; (15) occipital; (16) auditory bulla; (17) glenoid fossa; (I) incisors; (C) canine; (P) premolars; (M) molars; (*) carnassial. Photo credit: *Phil Myers*, Museum of Zoology, University of Michigan-Ann Arbor (USA).

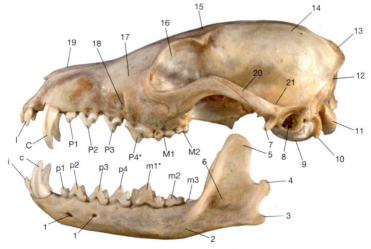

Figure 6. The skull of Red Fox (*Vulpes vulpes*), side view: (I) Incisors; (C) canines; (P) premolars; (M) molars; (*) carnassials; (1) mental foramina; (2) mandible; (3) angular process; (4) condyloid process; (5) coronoid process; (6) masseteric fossa; (7) retroauricular process; (8) external acoustic meatus; (9) auditory bulla; (10) paraoccipital process; (11) occipital condyle; (12) occipital; (13) sagittal crest; (14) parietal; (15) frontal; (16) orbit; (17) maxilla; (18) infraorbital foramen; (19) nasal; (20) zygomatic arch; (21) temporal. Photo credit: *Phil Myers*, Museum of Zoology, University of Michigan-Ann Arbor (USA).

Figure 7. Dentition in the Red Fox (*Vulpes vulpes*): The generalized Canid dental formula is (I 3/3, C1/1, P 4/4, M2/3) x 2 = 42. Incisors are moderately large and used with the canines for gripping and tearing. The canines are large but not necessarily very sharp, often used as a killing device. Carnassial teeth (the last upper premolar, P4, and the first lower molar, m1) are specially adapted to cutting flesh with a scissor-like action. Their occlusal surfaces are sloped to allow them to slide past one another when the jaw closes. Jaw articulation allows open and shut movements, but not side to side. Photo credits: *Gorpie, Lisa Clarke.*

Limbs (fig. 8): Canids are digitigrade, and tarsal and carpal regions never touch the ground during walking. Limbs are long and slender and adapted for swift running. There are four functional digits on each limb, and the two middle digits are considerably longer than the rest. On the forelimb the first digit is vestigial and is represented by a claw and small pad higher up on the foot than the four functional pads (in the African Wild Dog this digit is totally absent). In the Domestic Dog and Dingo a vestigial first digit may also be present on the hind limb as well. The pads on the soles of the feet are naked, with hairs growing between the pads (in the Arctic Fox and some desert Foxes, the sole of the foot is densely covered with hair at some times of year). Unlike in the Felidae, the claws are not protractile and are relatively blunt and not sharply compressed laterally. The last phalanges are not capable of flexing far back and upward and have normal articulating surfaces. Other adaptations to running include fusion of scaphoid and lunar bones in the wrist, and locking of radius and ulna in the front leg to restrict rotation.

CLASSIFICATION

The Canidae belong to the order Carnivora, a monophyletic group comprising 16 extant families. Carnivorans have teeth and claws adapted for catching and eating prey. The order Carnivora is characterized by functional specializations for shearing in the fourth upper premolar and the first lower molar. These teeth, called carnassials, have a blade-like morphology and are the central character complex that unites members of the order Carnivora. Other features shared by all carnivores include the fusion of certain bones in the foot (scaphoid, lunar and central bones) to form the scapholunar, an ossified auditory bulla, a relatively undeveloped clavicle, and a penis containing an elongated bony structure known as the baculum (lost in hyenas).

Carnivora are grouped into two suborders (fig. 9): Caniformia (Dog-like carnivorans) and Feliformia (Cat-like carnivorans). The former includes two major groups that share a close genetic relationship: superfamily Cynoidea, which includes Canidae (Dogs, Wolves, Coyotes, Jackals and Foxes), and superfamily Arctoidea, which includes Ursidae (bears), Ailuridae (red panda), Mephitidae (skunks and stink badgers), Procyonidae (raccoons and relatives), Mustelidae (weasels, badgers and otters) and three marine mammal families: Phocidae (true seals), Otariidae (seals and sea-lions), and Odobenidae (walruses). Feliformia includes Felidae (cats), Nandiniidae (African palm civet), Prionodontidae (linsangs), Viverridae (civets and genets), Hyaenidae (hyenas), Eupleridae (fossa), and Herpestidae (mongooses).

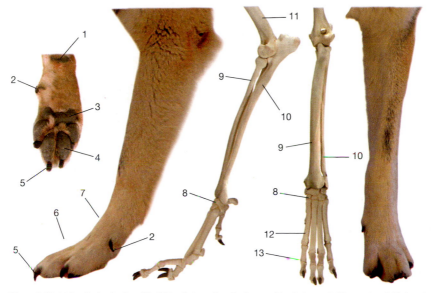

Figure 8. Right forelimb of a Gray Wolf (*Canis lupus*) and a Coyote (*Canis latrans*): (1) carpal pad; (2) dewclaw; (3) metacarpal pad; (4) digital pad; (5) non-retractable claw; (6) paw; (7) pastern; (8) carpus; (9) radius; (10) ulna; (11) humerus; (12) metacarpus; (13) phalanges. Photo credit: *Sergey Chichagov*, *Dr. Ray Whalen*, College of Veterinary Medicine and Biomedical Sciences (Colorado State University), and *Gerry Wykes*, Naturespeak.

The Canidae family is currently recognized as comprising three major subfamilies: the extant Caninae, and two others known only from fossil specimens: Borophaginae and Hesperocyoninae.

Subdivision of the Canids has been a field rich in conflicting hypotheses. The exact organization of the living Canid phylogeny has long been contested in the scientific literature, probably due to its relatively recent radiation and the close genetic similarities between all members. Most molecular phylogenetic analyses have found four distinct groups within the Canidae family (fig. 10): Wolf-like Canids, Red Fox-like Canids, South American Canids, and Gray Fox-like Canids.

The Wolf-like Canids are a monophyletic group that consists of Wolves (Gray Wolf, Red Wolf, Eastern Wolf, African Golden Wolf and Ethiopian Wolf), Coyotes, Eurasian Jackals (genus *Canis*), Black-Backed and Side-Striped Jackals (genus *Lupulella*), and the Dhole (genus *Cuon*), as well as the African Wild Dog (genus *Lycaon*), basal to *Canis* and *Cuon*.

The Red Fox-like Canids include a monophyletic group of true Foxes, the Vulpini, closely related to the Red Fox (genus *Vulpes*): Indian Fox, Corsac Fox, Tibetan Fox, Rüppell's Fox, Arctic Fox, Kit Fox, Swift Fox, Blanford's Fox, Fennec Fox, Cape Fox and Pale Fox. The phylogenetic position of the distinct Raccoon Dog (genus *Nyctereutes*) and the Bat-Eared Fox (genus *Octocyon*) is highly uncertain, but they are considered to form successive sister taxa to the remaining Vulpini.

The South American Canids also probably form a monophyletic group. The Maned Wolf (genus *Chrysocyon*) and Bush Dog (genus *Speothos*), previously grouped as sister taxa and more closely related to the Wolf-like Canids, share a common ancestor with the other South American Canids: the Fox-sized Canids such as the Pampas Fox, Hoary Fox, Darwin's Fox, Sechuran Fox, Chilla and Culpeo (genus *Lycalopex*), and the more basal Crab-Eating Fox (genus *Cerdocyon*) and Short-Eared Dog (genus *Atelocynus*).

Finally, the Gray Fox-like Canids are formed by a monospecific genus (*Urocyon*), with two species, the Gray Fox and the Island Fox. They appear as the most primitive lineage, being closest to the ancestors of all *Canis*.

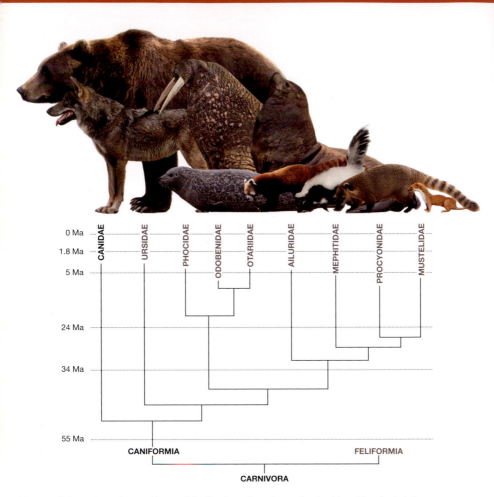

Figure 9. Schematic phylogenetic tree of the Carnivora, based on molecular data, with estimated divergence times, and illustrations of representative taxa (from left): Canidae: Gray Wolf (*Canis lupus signatus*); Ursidae: brown bear (*Ursus arctos*); Phocidae: gray seal (*Halichoerus grypus*); Odobenidae: walrus (*Odobenus rosmarus*); Otariidae: Steller sea lion (*Eumetopias jubatus*); Ailuridae: red panda (*Ailurus fulgens*); Mephitidae: striped skunk (*Mephitis mephitis*); Procyonidae: ring-tailed coati (*Nasua nasua*); Mustelidae: least weasel (*Mustela nivalis*) (Modified from Nyakatura and Bininda-Emonds, 2012). Photo credits: *Robert Gould, Rick Ruppenthal, Simon Goldsworthy, Eric Isselee, James Linnell.*

Chromosome number and structure vary widely among Canid species, from 36 (Red Fox) to 78 (Wolves, Coyotes and Jackals). This degree of variation contrasts sharply with most other carnivore families in which chromosome number and structure are well conserved.

TAXONOMY

The taxonomy of Canids is somewhat controversial. There are some uncertainties regarding the use of some generic names, with some disagreement regarding the use of the genus name *Pseudalopex* or *Lycalopex* for the South American genera. Phylogenetic studies tend to place the distinctive African Wild Dog and the Dhole into a monophyletic clade alongside the *Canis* genus, while the more basal Black-Backed Jackal and Side-Striped Jackal are excluded from it, with the subgenus *Lupulella* and *Schaeffia* being proposed respectively. *Fennecus* (Fennec Fox) and *Alopex* (Arctic Fox) are no longer considered valid by most authors, and are now included in the *Vulpes* genus.

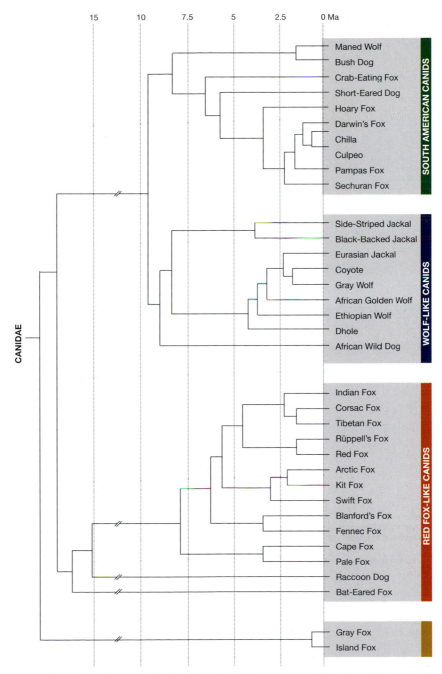

Figure 10. Phylogenetic tree of the Canidae, based on molecular data, with estimated divergence times. Modified from Nyakatura and Bininda-Emonds, 2012.

While major clades within the Canidae seem to be partly resolved, many doubts still remain concerning the more recent splits. In North America, controversy exists regarding the current taxonomic status of the Eastern Wolf and the Red Wolf, which seem to have a mixed ancestry as a result of past admixture between Coyotes and Gray Wolves, and currently hybridization still occurs between these four Wolf-like Canids. A recent extensive global phylogenetic study of Red Foxes has found that Red Foxes in North America are genetically distinct from Eurasian Red Foxes and merit recognition as a distinct species. Mainland Raccoon Dogs and Japanese Raccoon Dogs are considered different species by some authors, as they have different karyotypes (54 and 38 respectively), and significant phenotypic, craniometric and behavioral differences. Golden Jackals from Africa and Eurasia have been recently found to represent distinct monophyletic lineages separated for more than one million years, sufficient to merit formal recognition as different species: Eurasian Golden Jackal and African Golden Wolf. In India, two small endangered populations of Wolves, the Himalayan and Indian Wolves, have recently been shown to be genetically distant from other Wolves, and some have proposed to treat them as separate species, although this is not widely accepted. Dingoes and New Guinea Singing Dogs have been considered a distinct taxon in some studies, as they differ from Wolves in many behavioral, morphological and molecular characteristics, although most authors now consider them feral derivatives of ancient breeds of Domestic Dogs that were carried to Australia and New Guinea during prehistoric times by humans. Domestic Dogs have been treated either as a species of their own, or as a subspecies of the Gray Wolf. Some authors treat Kit Fox and Swift Fox as being conspecific, but genetic and morphological studies support the recognition of the two as separate species.

There is a clear need for taxonomic research on the Canids below the species level, and unraveling the validity of subspecies is a much more complex task. Definitions of subspecies are a source of considerable disagreement, and listing subspecific taxa has become increasingly controversial. There is also a general concern about the great number of subspecies designations, which varies widely according to different authors. Canids can travel great distances and overcome topographic obstacles, and high rates of gene flow may stifle genetic differentiation among even widely separated populations (e.g., Gray Wolves have been observed to disperse over 1,000 km during their lifetime). Additionally, many Canids are habitat generalists, so they can easily cross even the most highly anthropogenic areas. So it is common to find weak patterns of intraspecific differentiation even between geographically distant regions. In many cases subspecies were defined long ago on very few specimens, or based solely on pelage or skeletal morphology, and may reflect rapid evolution of specific ecotypes through selection, or differences in food supply. The molecular genetic evidence suggests that these phenotypic differences do not necessarily signify a long history of genetic isolation, and numerous subspecies defined for many taxa are unlikely to be valid. For instance, molecular analysis of Gray Wolves and Coyotes in North America has shown low levels of genetic divergence among populations, and probably only the Mexican Wolf and the Alaskan Wolf are distinct. In contrast, Wolves from the Old World, where populations are highly fragmented and small in size, show that most populations had single genotypes not found elsewhere. In the African Wild Dog, the Rift Valley lakes may effectively interrupt gene flow between the eastern and southern African populations, and there seems to be no gene flow across this barrier. The mobility of small Canids is much less, which may lead to more subspecific differentiation. In Kit Foxes, the San Joaquin Valley Kit Foxes form a distinct clade and Arizona populations to the east of the Colorado River may also be distinct. Little is known about genetic subdivision within small Old World Foxes such as the Fennec Fox, the Pale Fox, the Bengal Fox and Blanford's Fox. Species such as the Bat-Eared Fox or the Cape Fox, although abundant, may be composed of genetically distinct subpopulations.

Hybridization and introgression are probably more dramatic in the Canidae than in any other group of carnivores, and may potentially threaten the genetic integrity of several species. All species in the genus *Canis* can interbreed and produce fertile offspring (with the exception of Side-Striped and Black-Backed Jackals, and Dholes). Other members of the Canidae family, are less closely related to and cannot hybridize with the Wolf-like Canids. However, the Domestic Dog may hybridize with the Crab-Eating Fox and Pampas Fox, both of which belong to the South American Canids, and with two *Vulpes* species. The Red Fox also hybridizes with the Gray Fox. There are numerous reports of wild or domestic Canids hybridizing with rare or endangered species, although research is needed to determine the importance of hybridization in wild populations. For example, the Ethiopian Wolf is threatened by hybridization with Domestic Dogs. Red Wolves may hybridize with Coyotes in the wild, and Gray Wolves and Coyotes interbreed in the Great Lakes region of North America. In Italy and Russia, Gray Wolves occasionally interact and may interbreed with semi-feral populations of Domestic Dogs, although recent studies provide evidence that natural hybridization between Wolves and Dogs is a much rarer event than previously thought. The Dingo breeds freely with other Domestic Dogs and in some areas Dingoes are now mostly mixed-breed dogs.

BEHAVIOR

Social organization: Almost all Canids are social animals and live together in groups. In general, they are territorial or have a home range and sleep in the open, using their dens only for breeding and sometimes in bad weather. The most common social structure is a monogamous pair where both parents raise their mutual offspring, but other social formations have also been recorded, such as cooperative breeding, additional non-reproductive adults, plural breeding females, and several non-reproducing individuals that share the same territory. Additional group members can bring benefits such as increased cub guarding, territorial defense, assistance in food delivery or securing the survival of older offspring in the absence of vacant territories. The smaller Canids, like Red Foxes and Bat-Eared Foxes, are usually solitary animals that create temporary bonds only during the breeding season, and the male and female stay together only for four to five months to bring up offspring; they are usually monogamous, but are on occasion polygynous, and have a sex ratio biased toward females, with male dispersal. Medium-sized Canids, like Jackals and Coyotes, are strictly monogamous, and offspring stay with their parents until the next breeding season; their adult sex ratios are equal, and their male and female helping behavior and dispersal are equivalent. The largest Canids, like the African Wild Dog or the Gray Wolf, are the most social, and have a monogamous mating system with a tendency toward polyandry. There is usually only one monogamous breeding pair, along with non-breeding adults who also care for the young and provision the mother and pups. Adult sex ratio is biased toward males, male helpers, and female emigration. Among large Canids cooperative hunting is common, while smaller Canids tend to be solitary hunters.

Feeding behavior and diet: Most small-sized Canids are opportunistic omnivores, having a wide-ranging diet, from mammals to birds, eggs, reptiles, insects, fruits, berries, and carrion, with large seasonal fluctuations. Medium-sized species, such as Coyotes and Jackals, are opportunistic, generalist predators, eating a variety of food items ranging from fruit and insects to prey larger than themselves, including both wild and domestic ungulates. Large cooperative hunting Canids, as Gray Wolves, Dholes and African Wild Dogs, are more strictly carnivorous, preying on medium to large-sized mammals that often exceed their own body size. Pack hunting allows tackling prey that is many times the size of any individual predator. Anthropogenic food sources such as garbage or domestic animals are also used by most Canids in areas close to humans. Most species readily scavenge. Canids are uniquely adapted to cursorial pursuit, which they often combine with group efforts to achieve high hunting success, although they lack any specialized way to kill their prey, unlike Felids. Larger prey is usually run to exhaustion, and pack members grab at the hindquarters and soft rear areas. They generally prey on injured, sick, young or otherwise vulnerable animals. Most Canids employ a characteristic "mouse leap" behavior to capture rodents and other small mammals hidden in the grass or under deep snow (fig. 11). This is followed by a violent shaking with rapid side-to-side movements of the head to kill the prey. Canids are unique among mammals in that they are able to regurgitate food for their offspring. This behavior is important in the provision of food for pups before, during and after weaning, and sometimes for the mother during the first weeks. Most Canids also bury surplus food in well-hidden caches.

Figure 11. Coyote hunting pounce sequence. Most Canids employ a characteristic "mouse leap" behavior to capture rodents and other small mammals hidden in the grass or under deep snow. Photo credit: *Kenneth Canning.*

Reproduction: Canids exhibit several reproductive traits that are uncommon among mammals: they are typically monogamous, provide paternal care to their offspring, have reproductive cycles with lengthy proestral and dioestral phases and have a copulatory tie during mating (fig. 12). They also retain adult offspring in the social group, suppressing the ability of these to breed while making use of the alloparental care they can provide to help raise the next generation of offspring. Breeding is seasonal and, with the exception of the Bush Dog, occurs annually, beginning at one to two years of age. During the long proestral period, which ranges from one to three weeks, there is an increase in the frequency of scent marking and vocalizing in both sexes, and in the frequency of agonistic encounters between males, which occasionally result in the infliction of wounds. Female estrus generally lasts for two to five days and during this period only one or two copulations per day are observed. The copulatory tie (fig. 12), which is very uncommon in other carnivores, is observed in all matings and lasts for 5-20 minutes. The back-to-back position, which is seen after intromission has been achieved and the male has dismounted from the female, occurs in all ties except those of the Bush Dog and the Raccoon Dog. Gestation takes 49 to 72 days. Preceding parturition there is often an increase in burrowing and digging activity. The size of a litter varies, from 1 to 16 or more pups. The young are born small, blind and helpless and require a long period of parental care. Young are relatively incompletely developed: the eyes of newborn pups are still closed, the ears do not yet function and temperature regulation is still far from perfect. The young of the Canidae are typically altricial, passing the early stage of their life in a den or burrow and being unable to survive without the constant care of the parents. Females generally have three to seven pairs of mammae.

Visual communication: In social Canids visual communication is more commonly used, where compound facial expressions (fig. 13), tail movements and ear positions can be enhanced by coloration of the coat. In most Canids, the sides of the face or cheeks are white, and the lips are black, which accentuates facial expressions. Aggressive emotion causes the hair to bristle, increasing apparent size, and longer hair along the spinal column and tail amplifies the effect. The tail is erected or arched when the animal is aroused and lowered in submissive animals. It may be loosely wagged for greeting, or stiffly in aggression. Tail movement may also enhance olfactory inspection of the glands in the anal region. Eye contact can be used as a friendly greeting, but a direct stare is a threat, whereas subordinate Wolves or Coyotes avoid eye contact when they meet the direct look of a dominant individual. In Foxes and Coyotes a wide jaw-gape is seen as a component of threat expression, while dominant Wolves or Dogs may grasp the muzzle or neck of a subordinate in an inhibited bite. Ears have been incorporated into facial expression, being shifted up and forward in the alert or dominant Canid; in submission, fear, or apprehension the ears may be flattened backward, and in submission and greeting ears may be flattened sideways. Confident Canids display a rigid posture with head and tail up, while submissive individuals approach with the hind end lowered, the back arched in a "C" posture, the head lowered, and the tail tucked between the legs. In active submission they may lick the corner of the mouth of dominant animals in greeting. In passive submission they may lie down and roll over, exposing the belly, and additionally may urinate.

Figure 12. The mating procedure in most Canids includes a copulatory tie. Male Canids have a locking bulbous gland (a spherical area of erectile tissue at the base of the penis). During copulation, it becomes engorged with blood and locked in the contracted vagina. The two animals remain attached by their genitals for 15 minutes or more, during which time they stand or lie rump to rump. It is characteristic of mating in most Canids. Photo credit: *JudiLen*.

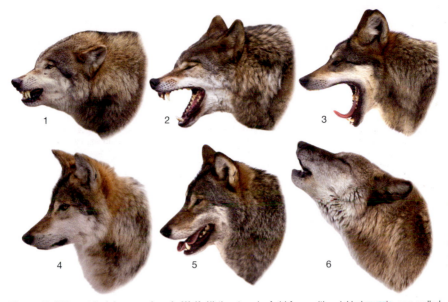

Figure 13. Different facial expressions in Wolf: (1) threatened, afraid face, with wrinkled muzzle, ears pulled back, eyes narrowed, and bared teeth; (2) aggressive, threat face, with erect ears, and open mouth; (3) yawning face, usually signaling a tired Wolf; (4) alert or neutral face; (5) relaxed face; (6) howling face. Photo credits: *Jan Rose, Andreas Baumgartner, Matthew James, Lwp Kommunikáció, Steve Harris, Jeff Goldberg.*

Olfactory communication: Canids have a remarkable sense of smell, and olfactory communication has a variety of forms, being used for individual recognition, territory marking, and as a way to leave messages. Olfactory signals include urine and fecal droppings, ground scratching, anal sac secretions, general body odor, rubbing certain body areas on a specific object, and rolling in noxious-smelling substances. Marks may be made on objects, territory, or scent marks of other individuals, or the animal may mark itself. Urination and defecation have evolved into a complex behavior of territorial marking, through which packs or individuals leave a message about themselves and acquire information about other packs or individuals in a given region. Male urination is considered scent marking and it is frequently accompanied by the leg-raised pattern. Dominant Wolves may urinate more frequently and may display leg-raised urination, while subordinate males may urinate in an infantile crouch position. Estrous females may urinate more, leaving long-distance messages for males. All Canids possess paired small glands on each side of the anal sphincter (perianal glands), which release some of their contents when defecation occurs. After urination or defecation, some Canids may scratch the ground, as a visual display that attracts attention of conspecifics or provides an additional territorial signal. General body odor is a product of glands on the feet, head, anal region, the upper surface of the base of the tail and between the hind legs. The violet gland on the upper tail surface, present in all Canids (except the Dog and the Wild African Dog), secretes most actively during the denning season. Mutual sniffing, first the head and then the anogenital region, is characteristic between Canids.

Vocal communication: Most Canids vocalize during the first weeks of life, but subsequently there is an inhibition of that behavior outside the home den, probably due to the dangers for young animals outside the den. Adult Canids may howl or bark and different kind of barks may be distinguished. They are individually specific and therefore may serve for individual recognition. Howling is a loud form of vocalization, and it is employed to affect companions over greater distance. It serves to bring individuals together, to inform rivals of pack presence, and may indicate an animal's size and aggressiveness, and thus have a function in defense of territory. As a form of communication, howling is present in social but not solitary Canids. Barking in Wolves may serve as an alarm call for the entire social group, when they have to defend the group territory. Barking may be used as a part of dominance/submission display. Some Canids may bark when they are aroused, to defend territory or a piece of meat, while barking may be preceded with a growl. Barking is used in many different situations, and may presumably serve to draw attention, while information that follows can be received through other sensory channels, i.e., visual and/or olfactory. Domestic Dogs are more vocal than all other Canidae and their barking can be considered hypertrophied in comparison with wild relatives. Vocal communication among different species varies greatly, especially between the different social structures. Various sounds have been described: whines, yips, howls, growls, clicks, yelps, screams, barks, coughs, coos, mews and grunts; depending on the species, these sounds may vary in time, pitch and frequency, and the same sound emitted by different species can mean different things. For example, Foxes only bark when there is a threat and scream as a greeting, whereas Domestic Dogs bark for many reasons, and growl for a threat. Domestic Dogs are the only species to yelp, a shorter whine used for greeting. This sound is seen to be analogous to the yip of Coyotes and the scream of Foxes. Foxes produce higher-pitched sounds such as screams and coos, a trilly, cackling sound with unknown meaning. Foxes display minimal social sounds due to general lack of sociability. The Wolf-like Canids produce lower sounds such as coos and guttural vocalizations. The high-pitched yipping sounds are only made by Coyotes and Jackals. Mixing of these sounds is used in more complicated emotional portrayal generally in the more social Canids. "Yowling" a combination of the yelp and bark, is seen in Domestic Dogs, a social sound analogous to the Wolves' group howl. Other extremely social species, such as the African Wild Dog, have been known to mix many sounds, creating sounds unique to them such as twitters and rumbles, and also have a range of barks that almost rivals that of Domestic Dogs, thus showing the extent to which social structures affect vocalization variability.

DISTRIBUTION AND HABITAT

Canids are the most widespread carnivoran family that occurs throughout the world from the Arctic to tropical forests with at least one species present in every continent except Antarctica. Many Canids have distributions that span over a whole continent. Red Foxes and Gray Wolves have the most extensive natural range of any land mammal, with the exception of humans and perhaps some commensal rodents. Red Foxes are the only Canid present in five continents, recorded in a total of 83 countries. Gray Wolves occur naturally in North America, Europe and Asia, their range spanning over 62 countries. The Red Fox and Dingo have reached Australia and Oceania with assistance from humans. Most countries have Canids, except some island states (e.g., Caribbean islands, Madagascar, Malta and most Australian islands). Africa, Asia and South America support the greatest diversity of Canids. There are five species endemic to a single country. Not surprisingly, most are also threatened: Red Wolf (USA), Ethiopian Wolf (Ethiopia), Darwin's Fox (Chile), Island Fox (USA), Hoary Fox (Brazil), and the Sechuran Fox is a near-endemic to Peru.

Their habitats are as diverse as their prey, including deserts, mountains, forests and grasslands. Only two species live permanently in closed-canopy forests, the Raccoon Dog in East Asia, and the Bush Dog in South America; both have short legs and a comparatively compact body to negotiate tangled pathways. Forests typically support a lower density of ground-living rodents and lagomorphs than more open areas. "Edge" habitats with a mixture of woods and open country are favored by many Canids. Only a few species are arboreal: the North American Gray Fox and the Raccoon Dog. Several species, notably the Red Fox and the Coyote, have benefited from the human conversion of forests into cropland. Several Fox species live in deserts. The large pack hunting species, due to their mobility and prey habits, have the widest ranges of habitats used: the Gray Wolf's enormous range includes tundra, ice floes, boreal forest, and the deserts of the Sinai and northern Mexico. However the African Wild Dog may be even more extreme, from deep in the Sahara to the montane forests of Ethiopia, or above the snowline on Mount Kilimanjaro.

EVOLUTION AND FOSSIL RECORD (fig. 14)

The Canidae family possesses a well-sampled fossil record spanning approximately the past 40 million years, with more than 120 fossil taxa. The Canidae is represented by two extinct subfamilies (Hesperocyoninae and Borophaginae) and one living one (Caninae). The first two subfamilies were endemic to North America and have been extinct since the middle Miocene and early Pleistocene respectively. The sole surviving subfamily, the Caninae, arose in the early Oligocene (30 million years ago [Ma]) in North America. The first recognized member of this subfamily is the Fox-sized *Leptocyon*. They coexisted with larger Hesperocyonines and the more vigorously evolving Borophagines during most of the Miocene.

In the middle Miocene (10 Ma), a Jackal-sized Canid emerged, *Eucyon*, with the presence of the frontal sinus, a characteristic feature that is retained in the descendants of this clade. *Eucyon* reached Europe through the Beringian land bridge by the end of the Miocene (6 Ma) and was evidently present in Asia

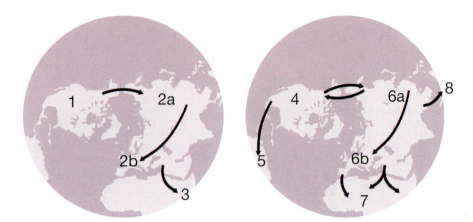

Figure 14. Canidae dispersal through time: (1) Evolutionary radiation in North America at the end of the Miocene, resulting in the appearance of early members of all the major clades: *Eucyon/Canis*, *Vulpes*, *Urocyon*, *Cerdocyon* and *Chrysocyon*. (2) Dispersal and evolution in Eurasia in the latest late Miocene-early Pliocene, resulting in the appearance of new species of *Eucyon* and *Vulpes*, and *Nyctereutes*; fossil evidence suggests that they entered first Europe (2b) and then the Far East (2a). (3) In the late Miocene they entered Africa, represented by *Vulpes* and *Eucyon/Canis*. (4) During the late Pliocene-Pleistocene, North America continued to be a center of Canid evolution, with the appearance of several new *Canis* species. (5) They entered South America after the establishment of the Panama Isthmus, and during the early Pleistocene, diversity increased with species of *Lycalopex*, *Chrysocyon*, *Theriodictis*, *Protocyon* and *Canis*. (6) During the late Pliocene *Nyctereutes* was distributed throughout Eurasia, and during the Plio-Pleistocene, new *Canis* species, and *Cuon* and *Xenocyon* appeared (6a). The earliest record of *Canis* in Europe is from latest Pliocene (6b). During the Pleistocene, several Eurasian species (*Vulpes, Canis, Cuon* and *Xenocyon*) entered North America. (7) During the late Pliocene, *Nyctereutes* was present in Africa, and during the Pleistocene Jackals and *Lycaon* appeared. (8) Dingoes originated in East Asia, and traveled to Australia 5,000 years ago. Modified from Lyras, 2009.

in the early Pliocene (4 Ma). During the transitional period from the Miocene to Pliocene (5-6 Ma), North America also gave rise to the first members of the *Canis* genus, mostly Jackal-sized species displaying evidence for hypercarnivory. In the early Pliocene they arrived in Europe and diverged in the Old World during the late Pliocene and Pleistocene (1.5-2 Ma), colonizing Europe, Asia and Africa. The typical cooperative hunting in packs and social behavior are thought to have arisen at this time, linked to the increase in brain size within this group. This radiation gave rise to Canid forms such as Wolves, Dholes and African Wild Dogs. The Eurasian *Canis etruscus* and its descendant *Canis mosbachensis* are regarded as the ancestors of Wolf-like Canids. Wolves emerged by 130,000-300,000 years ago and extended their habitat to North America by crossing at the Bering Strait 100,000 years ago. Coyotes represent the only surviving endemic species in the New World, originating from the extinct *Canis lepophagus* (1-2 Ma). Canid lineages arrived in South America much later, in the late Pliocene (2.5-4 Ma), after the rise of the Panama Bridge, generating a great diversity of species. At the end of the Pleistocene, all large Canids, with the exception of *Chrysocyon*, became extinct in South America. Another parallel event was the evolution of the Vulpini in the late Miocene (10 Ma); all extant Foxes are the descendants of this clade.

DOMESTICATION

Among Canids, the Dog is the only member to have been domesticated, although the Red Fox and the Raccoon Dog have been bred for their fur. The Dog was probably the earliest domesticated animal, and predated the advent of agriculture and the domestication of other animals, and it is currently the most widespread and phenotypically diverse domestic animal. Although there have been many debates concerning the origin of the Dog, most authors consider the Gray Wolf to be the principal if not the unique Dog ancestor. This process of domestication might have covered a period lasting 15,000 years, between 30,000 and 15,000 years before the present.

Bones of Wolves and hominids have been found together at several locations in Asia and Europe, dated 300,000-150,000 years before the present. These associations suggest that humans and Wolves

Figure 15. Phenotypic heterogeneity in Domestic Dog (*Canis lupus familiaris*): Dogs are the most phenotypically diverse mammal, and more than 400 Dog breeds are recognized nowadays. Morphologic and behavioral diversity among Dog breeds exceeds that among wild Canids. (1) German Shepherd; (2) Doberman Pinscher; (3) Irish Setter; (4) Basenji; (5) Dalmatian; (6) Great Dane; (7) Dachshund; (8) Pug; (9) Pomeranian. Photo credits: *Eric Isselee, Yurikr, Wenzhi Lu, Pfluegler, Iakov Filimonov.*

probably shared the same territories and lived in close contact. The oldest Dog skull, showing a clear differentiation from Wolves, is dated at 31,700 years before the present. During this period, there is little evidence for a concerted effort to domesticate animals, and it is believed that Wolves in search of food were attracted by human camps where they could find some leftovers and thus became progressively accustomed to human presence. Human hunters also probably killed Wolves looking for food and used their skins for clothing. They may have carried around live pups that would occasionally become tamed. These tamed Wolves were many generations away from the true Domestic Dogs, but were undoubtedly their precursors. Fifteen thousand years ago, humans started to use arrows, and predomesticated Dogs may have helped them track and bring back wounded animals, enhancing a new partnership between hominids and Dogs. From the following prehistoric period (11,000-7,000 years before the present), a large number of Dog remains have been found in many parts of the world, including the earliest case of Dog burial in the Americas, at about 11,000 years ago.

Dogs are the most phenotypically diverse mammal, and more than 400 dog breeds are recognized nowadays (fig. 15). The difference in cranial and skeletal proportions among Dog breeds exceeds that among wild Canids, and considerable differences in behavior and physiology also are evident. The origin of this diversity is uncertain and began more recently, 3,000-4,000 years before the present. These many different breeds were created along the centuries, being adapted to purposes such as herding, guarding, hunting or just companion pets. All these breeds show a wide range of phenotypes unmatched by any other species. For example, Great Dane is up to 100 times heavier than Chihuahua, and Greyhound is eight times larger than Pekingese. The Middle East is considered the primary source of genetic variations in the Dog, with potential secondary origins from Europe and East Asia. Across all breeds, levels of sharing between Dogs and North American Wolves are substantially lower than levels of sharing between Dogs and Old World Wolves. Humans who colonized America 12,000-14,000 years before the present probably brought multiple lineages of Domestic Dogs with them.

CONSERVATION STATUS

According to the International Union for Conservation of Nature (IUCN) Canid Specialist Group, at least 25% of Canid species are threatened and in need of urgent protection. Others are rare and even declining or too common for their own good, and thus involved in major wildlife management issues (such as disease transmission, predation on livestock, sport hunting, fur trade).

The Gray Wolf, formerly the most widely distributed terrestrial mammal, was extirpated from many areas in Eurasia during the past century. Several subspecies or races of Wolf that occupied the American west and Europe have also vanished, being able to survive in quite small areas of uncultivated land and in frequent contact with humans. The Red Wolf was declared Extinct in the Wild by 1980, but has been reintroduced into eastern North Carolina, although hybridization with Coyotes poses a threat. African Wild Dogs remain in as little as 7% of their former range, being extinct in 22 countries that they formerly inhabited, with fewer than 5,000 free-ranging remaining. Dholes, formerly living throughout Asia, inhabit a fraction of their former range, and are thought to be extinct in 11 of 20 countries that they formerly inhabited. As in other pack-living carnivores such as African Wild Dogs and Wolves, only one pair usually breeds in each pack, so that the number of animals contributing genes to the next generation is a fraction of the total population size. Pure Dingoes occur only as remnant populations in central and northern Australia, and they are threatened by cross-breeding with Domestic Dogs. In general, the large pack hunters have been excluded from areas of settled agriculture and now survive only in wilderness.

Among the intermediate and smaller species, the forms that are most endangered have very restricted ranges. The Ethiopian Wolf, with about 500 survivors, is the most vulnerable species. This species is endemic to the Ethiopian highlands, found only in Afroalpine heath and grasslands at altitudes above 3,000 m. Continuous loss of habitat due to high-altitude subsistence agriculture; the presence of Domestic Dogs, with disease transmission, hybridization and direct competition threatening wolf survival; and rabies outbreaks represent the major threats. The Bush Dog, despite a supposedly widespread distribution in South American forests, is rarely seen, and threatened by habitat conversion and human encroachment. Islands restrict the range and hence population size of two other endangered species: Island Fox exists only on an archipelago off the coast of southern California, while Darwin's Fox lives almost exclusively on Chiloé Island off the coast of Peru.

One species of Canid has gone extinct in recent times: the Falkland Island Wolf (*Dusicyon australis*), declared extinct in 1876. This large, Coyote-like animal was common on the Falkland Islands, nearly

500 km from the South American mainland. Due to being tame and curious and unafraid of humans, it was particularly susceptible to culling, and was hunted to extinction by settlers and fur traders.

As natural wild Canid populations become increasingly threatened, self-sustaining ex situ populations become essential to securing species persistence. For unknown reasons, zoo populations of some wild Canids, including the Maned Wolf, African Wild Dog, and Bush Dog, breed poorly. Several threatened Canids, such as the Mexican Gray Wolf, the Island Fox, and the Red Wolf, have recently been saved through captive-breeding efforts in partnership with reintroduction programs.

Many Canid species are viewed as pests to humans, and populations of many species have been decimated. Coyotes, Jackals, Foxes and Wolves are persecuted by ranchers, who blame them for losses to sheep and cattle herds. Other species have been targeted as carriers of rabies (many of the Foxes) and likewise have been the target of hunting. Some Foxes are valued for their pelts, which have been used in the fashion industry.

HOW TO USE THIS BOOK

The main purpose of this guide is to enable the observer to identify all known species of wild Canids from all over the world. Information is presented in the same format throughout, with maps showing geographic ranges, and photographs highlighting the specific identification criteria in each case. We have packed as much detail into this volume as possible, but also worked hard to keep it concise and efficient, so that it is not unwieldy in the field. All the information for a given taxon is displayed on two facing pages.

Most Canids can be identified from field sightings by using the photographs and descriptions in this guide. Look through the color plates and determine what type of animal you saw. Turn to the text page for the species that most resembles your sighting and look at the distribution map. If the map is not shaded for your area, then return to the color plates and try another similar species or subspecies. Keep in mind that many species may vary in color from one region to another and that not all color morphs can be illustrated in a guide. When you find a species that resembles your sighting and occurs in the correct geographic area, read the text to see if the description fits the habitat that you are in and any behavior you may have observed. Also check the Similar Species section for other possibilities.

The overall structure of this guide is based on the taxonomic classification of the family Canidae into four recognized groups, and is organized to provide the maximum ease of use for its readers. Each account in this book is organized as follows (fig. 16):

(1) **Classification**: To help the reader grasp the scientific arrangement, the pages for each group have a distinctive color on their top margin. This organization helps also to clarify the relationship between species in the same group. When trying to identify an unfamiliar Canid, it can often be helpful to first place it into a group, which will reduce your search.

(2) **Name**: The most common name as well as the scientific name is included for each entry. There is no official list of vernacular names for Canids, and common names have developed through long usage. They are convenient labels but they carry no deeper meaning, and some are actually inappropriate. Some species are named for people (Rüppell's Fox), for geographic locations (Pampas Fox), for habitats (Arctic Fox), or for an external feature (Short-Eared Dog). Furthermore, common names differ widely around the world. The scientific names, although less accessible, are much more valuable, since they impart real information about relationships among species. The scientific names are governed by rules of nomenclature and are standardized worldwide so that they transcend language barriers. The first word of the scientific name (always capitalized) is the genus. The second word, in lowercase, is the species name. For polytypic species (species with two or more subspecies), the third word, also in lowercase, is the subspecies name.

(3) **Description**: The identification section begins with a list of external measurements and weight, recorded in centimeters and kilograms, respectively. Measurements and weights are given as averages or ranges. They are intended to aid in identification and to give a clearer impression of the animal. Keep in mind that many Canids may exhibit tremendous variability in size and weight, and that males and females may differ in size. Where applicable, differences between the sexes are outlined. Explanations of the most common standard measurements for Canids are as follows: Body length (BL) is measured from the tip of the muzzle to the base of the tail. Tail length (TL) is measured from its junction with the body to the end of the vertebrae. Shoulder height (H) is measured from the base of the foot to the top

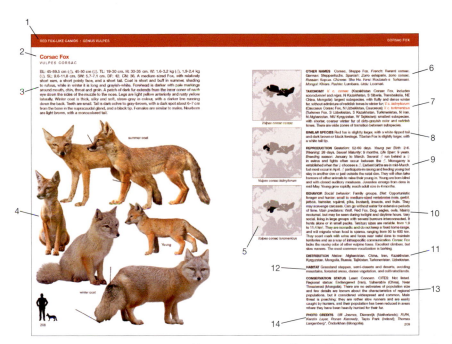

Figure 16. Understanding a page layout: (1) phylogenetic group; (2) scientific and common name; (3) measurements and description; (4) color plates and silhouette comparing size with a human figure; (5) distribution maps; (6) other names, including foreign and local names; (7) subspecies and taxonomy; (8) similar species or subspecies; (9) reproduction biology; (10) behavior; (11) distribution; (12) habitat; (13) conservation status and estimated population; (14) photo credits.

of the shoulder. Weight (W) is expressed in kilograms (weight is influenced by seasonal changes and body conditions). Skull length (SL) is the condylobasal length of the skull, measured from the anterior points of the premaxilla to the posterior surfaces of the occipital condyles. Skull width (SW) is the zygomatic width of the skull, the maximum width across the zygomatic arches. Dental formula (DF) is the number of teeth. Chromosome number (CN) is the diploid number of chromosomes. Descriptions in this guide concentrate on external features that can be observed in a live animal, and will assist the reader in species or subspecies identification, including pelage characteristics and colorations, and notable morphological traits.

(4) **Color plates:** The color plates, which are based on real photographs, are the core of this guide and will be the most useful component for identification. The illustrations show each species described. Occasionally, coat variations and young forms are also illustrated. Features that are most important for identification are indicated by bars. Silhouette drawings illustrate the species on each page to a common scale in order to relate its size to a human figure 180 cm tall.

(5) **Distribution maps**: The black parts of the maps represent the approximate area within which a species or subspecies occurs at present, although within this area it would not be found in unsuitable habitat. The gray parts of the maps represent the species distribution when a subspecies is depicted. Areas of hybridization between subspecies may occur. Former distribution has not been taken into account. A glance at the range map will give a quick indication of species or subspecies distribution. It should be remembered that the scale of the maps is such that only general distribution patterns can be given. Always consult the Distribution section to obtain a more detailed indication of range.

(6) **Other names**: Following the English and scientific names in each species account, this section lists alternative and colloquial English names, and French, German, Spanish, Russian, and local names are added where appropriate.

(7) **Taxonomy**: This section lists the subspecies for a polytypic species. The identification of subspecies can be a rewarding and exciting challenge. However, the differences between subspecies are usually

25

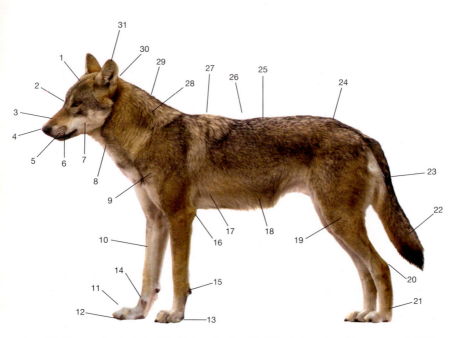

Figure 17. Topography of a typical Canid: Eurasian Gray Wolf (*Canis lupus lupus*), summer coat: All Canids have a similar basic form, although the relative lengths of muzzle, limbs, ears and tail vary considerably between species. (1) Forehead; (2) stop; (3) muzzle; (4) nose; (5) whiskers; (6) lip; (7) cheek; (8) throat; (9) shoulder; (10) forearm; (11) forefoot (paw); (12) toes and nails; (13) pads; (14) dewclaw; (15) carpal pad; (16) elbow; (17) brisket; (18) abdomen; (19) thigh; (20) hock; (21) pastern; (22) tail; (23) supracaudal (violet) gland; (24) rump; (25) loin; (26) back; (27) withers; (28) neck; (29) crest; (30) nape; (31) ear. Photo credit: *Ulli Joerres*, Zoo Osnabrück (Germany).

less distinct than the differences between species. When a subspecies may be identified based on external features that can be observed in a live animal, a short description with their distinguishing features is included. Sometimes subspecies may be identified based only on their geographic range, which is also described in this section and illustrated in the distribution map. Keep in mind that some authors may disagree over the validity of certain subspecies, or whether a certain population is a subspecies or a full species. Additionally, animals that belong to different subspecies of the same species may be capable of interbreeding and producing fertile offspring.

(8) **Similar species**: This section lists those species or subspecies that are similar, have a similar range, or could be confused with another, and their distinguishing features are mentioned. Before you finalize your decision on the species identity, check this section.

(9) **Reproduction**: A brief description of breeding biology is given, including gestation duration, litter size, weaning time, sexual maturity and maximum life span (generally in captivity).

(10) **Behavior**: This section includes information on group composition and structure, range size, diet and diet preferences, predators, daily and seasonal activity patterns, and social interaction. Behavioral characteristics that may aid in identification are given preference, but other aspects of interest are also mentioned.

(11) **Distribution**: This section describes the actual countries in which a species is native and the general geographic space that it occupies. Distribution and habitat must be considered together to determine if a given animal is likely to be found in a given area.

(12) **Habitat**: Includes the local conditions of climate, vegetation, soil types, water availability, elevation and terrain. Some animals have very specific habitat requirements, while others may occupy just about any habitat within their range.

(13) **Status**: This section indicates the species' relative abundance and lists its conservation status in cases where the species is threatened or endangered. When available, estimated population of a species is also given. The conservation status is based on up-to-date information published in the IUCN Red List of Threatened Species. The IUCN (International Union for Conservation of Nature) is a global conservation group that researches threatened species and coordinates practical conservation plans. Listed statuses in this guide are adapted from the IUCN Red List of Threatened Species (Categories & Criteria, version 3.1). The IUCN Red List of Threatened Species places species into one of the following categories: Extinct: There is no reasonable doubt that there are no remaining individuals alive. Extinct in the Wild: A species is known to survive only in captivity or as a naturalized population well outside the past range. Critically Endangered: A species has an extremely high risk of extinction in the wild or is already likely to be extinct, but confirmation is required. Within this category, it is often difficult to be certain that a species is extinct, as the last few individuals may still be holding on and in need of conservation attention. Endangered: A species has a high risk of extinction in the wild. Near Threatened: A species is likely to become vulnerable in the near future and has been evaluated against the criteria but does not qualify for Critically Endangered, Endangered or Vulnerable now, but is close to qualifying for or is likely to qualify for a threatened category in the near future. Least Concern: A species is widespread and abundant. Data Deficient: There is not enough information to assess the risk of extinction. Not Evaluated: A species has not yet been evaluated. Domesticated: This is not an official category of the IUCN Red List; this category overlaps Least Concern but has been applied to domesticated animals, for which the IUCN criteria are not valid. *CITES* listings are also included. *CITES* (the Convention on International Trade in Endangered Species of Wild Fauna and Flora) is an international agreement between governments, aimed to ensure that international trade in specimens of wild animals and plants does not threaten their survival. *CITES* Appendix I lists species that are the most endangered and for which international trade is prohibited, except when the purpose is not commercial. Appendix II lists species that are not necessarily threatened with extinction but that may become so unless trade is closely controlled; international trade may be authorized by the granting of an export permit or re-export certificate. Appendix III is a list of species included at the request of a party that already regulates trade in the species and that needs the cooperation of other countries to prevent unsustainable or illegal exploitation.

(14) **Photo credits**: The contribution of every photographer is gratefully acknowledged, and their name and the place where the photograph was taken appear in each entry. Copyright rests with the individual photographers. Some photos have been enhanced through the use of graphics editing programs to highlight identification marks and remove distracting background features.

ABBREVIATIONS

The following abbreviations, contractions and symbols have been used in the book to make it simpler for the reader to access the information.

ca.: circa (approximate date)

cm: centimeters

g: grams

kg: kilograms

m: meters

km: kilometers

km²: square kilometers

ha: hectares

kmph: kilometers per hour

BL: body length (without tail)

TL: tail length

H: shoulder height

W: weight, west, western

SK: skull length (condylobasal length)

SW: skull width (zygomatic width)

CN: chromosome number

DF: dental formula

Ma: million years ago

N: north, northern

NE: northeast, northeastern

NW: northwest, northwestern

S: south, southern

SE: southeast, southeastern

SW: southwest, southweastern

E: east, eastern

♂: male, males

♀: female, females

†: extinct

South American Canids

MANED WOLF, BUSH DOG, SHORT-EARED DOG, SOUTH AMERICAN FOXES

RECOGNITION South American endemic Canids form a phylogenetically independent group. It includes the Maned Wolf, Bush Dog, Short-Eared Dog, Crab-Eating Fox and the six species of *Lycalopex* (South American Foxes). This group is more closely related to Wolf-like Canids than to Foxes. Most South American Canids can be described as Fox-like, but vary considerably in size and morphology. There is little size dimorphism between males and females. Several species are morphologically atypical, compared to most Canids, such as the extremely long-legged Maned Wolf, or the short-legged Bush Dog. They exhibit the typical Canid dental formula, I 3/3, C 1/1, P 4/4, M 2/3 = 42, except Bush Dogs, which have 38 or 40 teeth and trenchant heel dentition. Chromosome number is 2n=74, except for the Maned Wolf and Short-Eared Dog (2n=76), and there are no"marker chromosomes," a generalized characteristic in the Carnivora and an ancestral character in other Canids.

PHYLOGENY After being confined to North America for a period of about 30 million years, Canid lineages spread across the world, invading the Old World in the late Miocene (ca. 10 Ma) and arriving in South America much later, in the late Pliocene (ca. 4-2.5 Ma). This migration to South America generated a great diversity of species, represented by six living genera, mainly small to medium-sized omnivorous Canids, and several extinct species that included large hypercarnivorous forms. The large hypercarnivorous taxa were particularly well represented in the past, with two endemic genera (*Theriodictis* and *Protocyon*) and three species that have been included in *Canis*. Phylogenetic and molecular studies, as well as some fossil records, suggest that at least three or four independent lineages of the South American clade invaded South America after the rise of the Panama Bridge (ca. 4–2.5 Ma), pointing to an origin outside SouthAmerica for this group. Canids from other clades, *Urocyon* and *Canis dirus,* invaded this continent at least during the late Pleistocene, and Domestic Dogs (*Canis lupus familiaris*) were introduced by aborigines in the Holocene.

BEHAVIOR Most South American Canids are solitary animals, forming pairs only during the breeding season, but the Bush Dog forms social groups. *Lycalopex* and the Maned Wolf are monoestrous, while the Bush Dog is polyestrous. Crab-Eating Fox females produce two litters annually. The reproductive status of the Short-Eared Dog is unknown. This group has omnivorous habits, but the Bush Dog is strictly carnivorous.

DISTRIBUTION This group is endemic to South America. Maned Wolves are found in S Brazil, Paraguay, Peru and Bolivia east of the Andes. Bush Dogs are found from S Panama through much of South America E of the Andes, as far S as central Bolivia, Paraguay, and S Brazil. Short-Eared Dog is endemic to the Amazon basin. Crab-Eating Fox is endemic to the central part of South America. Hoary Fox is endemic to the cerrado biome and adjacent areas in central Brazil. Sechuran Fox occurs on the Pacific coast of Peru and Ecuador. Darwin's Fox is endemic to coastal Chile. Pampas Fox is currently thought to range from E Bolivia and W Paraguay to central Argentina and S Brazil. Chilla Fox is widespread in areas of plains and mountains on both sides of the Andes, from S Peru and N Chile south to the Strait of Magellan, and was introduced by humans onto the island of Tierra del Fuego in 1953. Culpeo Fox is distributed along the Andes and hilly regions of W South America, from S Colombia to Tierra del Fuego. South American Canids are found in every habitat on the continent, from the coastal deserts, to the open savanna, rain forests, and coastal and lowland forests.

CONSERVATION Nearly every species in this group requires careful monitoring and individual consideration. Little is known about the abundance and distribution of most species. The Maned Wolf is Near Threatened and already extinct in Uruguay; conservation interest has resulted in legal protection in Brazil and Argentina, but specific action has yet to be implemented, and significant population declines are expected to occur because of continuing habitat loss and degradation. The poorly known Short-Eared Dog is also listed as Near Threatened, and is known to be at risk from diseases transferred from Domestic Dogs and habitat loss; no comprehensive ecological research has been carried out on this species. The status of the Bush Dog is difficult to determine because of its natural rarity and elusive, nomadic nature; it is a social predator that requires healthy populations of small and mid-sized vertebrate prey, and its persistence depends on the protection of large, connected areas of grassland, woodland, and shrub-dominated lowland where Domestic Dogs and vehicle traffic are minimal. Darwin's Fox is Endangered, with only two small remnant populations containing fewer than 250 individuals; the initial assumption that it was a subspecies of the Chilla Fox contributed to a lack of conservation or captive breeding efforts. The Crab-Eating Fox and *Lycalopex* Foxes seem tolerant of habitat degradation and remain widespread and common. The Pampas Fox, however, is heavily persecuted because of its perceived predation on livestock.

Maned Wolf
Chrysocyon brachyurus, 30

Bush Dog
Speothos venaticus, 32

Short-Eared Dog
Atelocynus microtis, 34

Crab-Eating Fox
Cerdocyon thous, 36

Hoary Fox
Lycalopex vetulus, 42

Sechuran Fox
Lycalopex sechurae, 44

Darwin's Fox
Lycalopex fulvipes, 46

Pampas Fox
Lycalopex gymnocercus, 48

Chilla
Lycalopex griseus, 54

Culpeo Fox
Lycalopex culpaeus, 62

Maned Wolf
CHRYSOCYON BRACHYURUS

BL: 95-125 cm. TL: 30-45 cm. H: 74-91 cm. W: 20-25 kg. SL: 24.8 cm. SW: 13.3 cm. DF: 42. CN: 76. A large and very distinctive Canid, with extremely long legs. It is the largest South American Canid. Coat is thick and soft, orange brown to reddish golden on the back and sides, lacking underfur. Throat is white. Mouth, base of the neck, and legs are black. Head is small in proportion to the body, with a long, Fox-like muzzle. Ears are large, straight and tent-shaped, white inside. Eyes are large and slanting, brown in color, with round pupils. Visible erectile black mane on the nape of the neck and back. Limbs are exceptionally long and thin. Tail is proportionally short and wide, ending in a white tuft. Females are similar in appearance to males. Young are brownish gray or black.

Young

Chrysocyon brachyurus

OTHER NAMES *French*: Loup à crinière. *German*: Mähnenwolf. *Spanish*: Boroche, lobo de crin. *Russian*: Гривистый волк. *Portuguese*: Lobo guará. *Guaraní*: Aguaraguazú.

TAXONOMY Monotypic. Includes *campestris*, *cancrosa* and *jubatus*, which are not considered valid. It is most closely related to the genus *Lycalopex*. Despite its name, it is not related to other Wolves.

REPRODUCTION *Gestation*: 62-66 days. *Young per birth*: 2-5. *Weaning*: 105-180 days. *Sexual maturity*: 1-2 years. *Life span*: 12-16 years in captivity. *Breeding season*: Mating between April and June in Brazil, with most births occurring from June to September, in dens made in tall grass or thickets. From July to August in Paraguay, and from October to February in Europe and North America, in captivity. ♀ are monoestrous and may copulate several times during an estrus of about 5 days. ♀ provide milk and later regurgitated food for the growing pups. ♂ play an important role in pup care.

BEHAVIOR *Social behavior*: Solitary, monogamous pairs sharing a territory but only meeting during the breeding season. *Diet*: Omnivorous generalist, including the lobeira fruit (*Solanum lycocarpum*), and small to medium mammals (paca, rabbits, armadillo, rodents), but also birds, reptiles, amphibians, fish and invertebrates. *Main predators*: Cougar, jaguar. Crepuscular or nocturnal, spending a great deal of the day asleep hidden in vegetation; increased daytime activity is seen in areas with low levels of human disturbance. They are territorial, with little tolerance for conspecifics outside their breeding pair. Unlike other large Canids, they do not hunt cooperatively. Large home ranges (25 km² to over 80 km²). Scent marking and roar-bark vocalizations are used to communicate and keep boundaries. Their call is a long deep-throated bark, which is repeated at intervals of around 7 seconds. Deposits of feces are used as markers to deter intruders. When individuals do have encounters, they circle one another warily and each tries to intimidate the other. They raise the long darker fur on their shoulders and neck to give an impression of greater size. Their long legs enable them to see above the tall grass, an adaptation that helps them hunt for food and avoid predators.

DISTRIBUTION *Native*: Argentina, Bolivia, Brazil, Paraguay, Peru. *Possibly extinct*: Uruguay. Past range extended from the N tip of Brazil, along the edge of the Amazon Basin, S into the N parts of Paraguay, Argentina, Bolivia and Uruguay. Today, it is more restricted and can be found in central and E Brazil, NE Argentina and Paraguay. It is extinct or surviving in very low numbers in E Bolivia and Uruguay.

HABITAT Tall grasslands, shrubs, woodlands with open canopy (cerrado) and wet fields (Pantanal), which may be seasonally flooded. Also present in cultivated lands and where the rain forest has been cut down and replaced by conifer and *Eucalyptus* plantations. Not found at high altitudes or in rain forest.

CONSERVATION STATUS Near Threatened. *CITES*: Appendix II. *Regional status*: Vulnerable (Brazil), Endangered (Argentina). Found in low densities throughout the range. Estimated population of 15,000 animals in 2012, mostly in Brazil.

PHOTO CREDITS *Emmanuel Keller*, Zoo d'Amnéville (France); *Anan Kaewkhammul*, Chiang Mai Night Safari (Thailand); *fraxprax*; *Thomas-Uwe Maassen*, Dortmund Zoo (Germany). Young: *Janice Sveda*, Smithsonian's National Zoo (USA); *Arjan Haverkamp*, Diergaarde Blijdorp (Netherlands).

Bush Dog

SPEOTHOS VENATICUS

BL: 57-75 cm. TL: 11-15 cm. H: 20-30 cm. W: 4-10 kg. SL: 12.4 cm. SW: 7.6 cm. DF: 38-40. CN: 74. A small to medium-sized, very distinctive Canid, with an elongated body, short limbs and short bushy tail, interdigital membranes and small rounded ears. Coat color ranges from uniform dark brown to yellowish red, with lighter color on neck, nape of neck and ears. Underparts and limbs are darker. Head is broad, bear- or mustelid-like, with a lighter reddish tinge, and no facial markings. Eyes are small, brown in color, with elliptical pupils. Muzzle is short and broad. Front feet broad with partial webbing between the toes. Tail is dark brown in color, very short and well furred but not bushy, often held upright. Young are uniformly black.

Young

Speothos venaticus venaticus

Speothos venaticus panamensis

Speothos venaticus wingei

OTHER NAMES Vinegar Dog, Savannah Dog. *French*: Chien des buissons. *German*: Waldhund. *Spanish*: Zorro vinagre, perrito venadero, cachorro vinagre, guanfando, perrito de monte, perro de agua, perro grullero, umba, zorro pitoco. *Russian*: Кустарниковая собака. *Portuguese*: Cachorro-do-mato. *Guarani*: Jagua yuyguy.

TAXONOMY *S. v. venaticus*: darker subspecies, found in S Colombia and Venezuela, Guyana, French Guiana and Suriname, most of Brazil, E Ecuador and Peru, Bolivia, N Paraguay; *S. v. panamensis*: smaller subspecies, found in Panama, N Colombia and Venezuela, W Ecuador; and *S. v. wingei*: S Brazil and Paraguay, NE Argentina.

SIMILAR SPECIES Short-Eared Dog has larger legs and tail, darker pelage around head and neck, and a Fox-like head.

REPRODUCTION *Gestation*: 63-83 days. *Young per birth*: 1-6. *Weaning*: 30-48 days. *Sexual maturity*: 10 months (♀), 12 months (♂). *Life span*: 10 years in captivity. *Breeding season*: Probably throughout the year, with most births occurring during the wet season; estrus lasts up to 12 days, and occurs every 15 to 44 days. Mating includes a copulatory tie, during which the animals are locked together. Only the alpha ♀ breeds successfully, and all other group members guard the young. Young are born blind and helpless, the eyes opening after 14-19 days, and the pups first emerge from the den shortly thereafter. Pack members help raise pups by provisioning mothers at the den during nursing.

BEHAVIOR *Social behavior*: Small packs from 2 to 12 animals, consisting of a mated pair and their immediate young; they sleep in groups. *Diet*: Exclusively carnivorous: small mammals (paca, agouti, capybara, armadillo); reptiles and birds are also taken. *Main predators*: Cougar, jaguar. The most social South American Canid. Urine marking may be important for maintenance of pair-bonds. Although they can hunt alone, they are usually found in small packs. Mostly diurnal, sleeping in burrows overnight, but may hunt at night; they use hollow logs and cavities such as armadillo burrows for shelter. Home ranges from 3.8 to 10 km². They have partially webbed toes, which allow them to swim more efficiently. They are more reliant on olfactory communication than visual communication due to their morphology and habitat. Vocalizations facilitate communication in dense vegetation, and include whines, grunts, growls and barks.

DISTRIBUTION *Native*: Argentina, Bolivia, Brazil, Colombia, Ecuador, French Guiana, Guyana, Panama, Paraguay, Peru, Suriname, Venezuela. Found from extreme E Central America and N South America, S to Paraguay and NE Argentina (Misiones). Isolated subpopulations may also still occur in Ecuador and Colombia, W of the Andes. It may still survive in Costa Rica.

HABITAT Habitat generalist, occurring generally near small water streams (semi-aquatic). Observed in lowland, primary and gallery forest, semi-deciduous forest, and seasonally flooded forest.

CONSERVATION STATUS Near Threatened. *CITES*: Appendix I. *Regional status*: Vulnerable (Brazil), Critically Endangered (Argentina). Although widespread, it is rare throughout its range, and hard to observe in the wild. Estimated population of fewer than 15,000 mature individuals.

PHOTO CREDITS *Ulli Joerres*, Randers Tropical Zoo (Denmark); *John R. Chandler* and *Martyn Richardson*, Twycross Zoo (UK); *Cherri Sample*, Zoo Atlanta (USA); *Russell Harvey*, Sequoia Park Zoo (USA); *Lukas Blazek*, Zoo Praha (Czech Republic).

Short-Eared Dog
ATELOCYNUS MICROTIS

BL: 61-100 cm. TL: 25-35 cm. H: 25-36 cm. W: 6.5-10 kg. SL: 14.7 cm. SW: 8.9 cm. DF: 42. CN: 74-76. A medium-sized Canid, with short and slender limbs, stocky and compact body, and short and rounded ears. Coat is short and uniformly colored, ranging from black to brown to rufous gray, often darkest in a dorsal line from head to tail. Inconspicuous narrow black collar. Reddish individuals have been observed, and it is not clear whether color varies with age, habitat or molt. Underparts are the same dark color as the body, except for the inguinal region where the hair is lighter. Head is Fox-like, with a long, slender muzzle. Ears are a rufous color both internally and externally, rounded and relatively short. Paws are partly webbed. Tail is bushy, compared to the short pelage on the rest of the body, with a dark mid-dorsal band of thick erectile hairs and light-colored underside. Females may be larger than males.

Atelocynus microtis

OTHER NAMES Short-Eared Fox, Small-Eared Dog. *French*: Renard á petites oreilles, chien des buissons aux oreilles courtes. *German*: Kurzohrfuchs, Kurzohrhund. *Spanish*: Zorro de orejas cortas, perro de monte, perro selvático, zorro negro, zorro ojizarco. *Italian*: Volpe dalle orecchie corte. *Russian*: Малая лисица. *Portuguese*: Cachorro-do-mato-de-orelhas-curtas, raposa-de-orelhas-pequenas. *Guaraní*: Aguerau. *Ayoreo*: Divequena. *Yucuna*: Uálaqua. *Huitoto*: Urúbui. *Carijona*: Kerejuqué. *Okaima*: Juhxuutsoona. *Barasana*: Buyaíro.

TAXONOMY Monotypic. Two subspecies have been traditionally described: *A. m. microtis* (Brazil, Colombia, Bolivia), and *A. m. sclateri* (Patagonia, S Chile, Argentina), but this distinction is not generally recognized. Formerly placed in the genera *Lycalopex*, *Cerdocyon* and *Dusicyon,* but phylogenetic analysis has shown it to be a distinct taxon most closely related to another monotypic Neotropical Canid, the Bush Dog.

SIMILAR SPECIES Bush Dog also inhabits lowland Amazonian forest, is smaller, light colored, with a very short muzzle, legs and tail, lives in packs, and is seldom seen alone. Crab-Eating Fox, Culpeo Fox and Domestic Dog could potentially be mistaken, but none of these have the combination of a slender, long snout, short ears, and a bushy tail. Tayra (*Eira barbara)* are also brownish and have bushy tails, but differ in their much smaller ears, yellowish throat and mostly arboreal habits. Jaguarundi (*Herpailurus yaguarondi*) may be similar in color, but is smaller, more delicate, and has a very slender tail.

REPRODUCTION *Gestation*: Unknown. *Young per birth*: Unknown. *Weaning*: Unknown. *Sexual maturity*: Probably 1 year. *Life span*: 9-11 years in captivity. *Breeding season*: From April to December, with births occurring in May or June in Peru.

BEHAVIOR *Social behavior*: Mainly solitary. *Diet*: Generalist carnivore: fish, insects, small mammals (agouti, marsupials, small rodents), birds, frogs and fruits. Very little is known of its behavior in the wild, and most observations of this species have been made in captivity. Both diurnal and nocturnal activity have been observed. It hunts alone and in pairs. It is partly aquatic, as suggested by its sleek, thick coat and the partial interdigital membrane; it has been observed hunting in waterholes and swimming after prey. Its short limbs facilitate movement in dense forests. It moves with feline lightness unparalleled among the other Canids. Excited ♂ spray a musk produced by the tail glands. Agitated ♂ will raise the hairs on their backs.

DISTRIBUTION *Native*: Bolivia, Brazil, Colombia, Ecuador, Peru. Found in scattered sites from Colombia to Bolivia and Ecuador to Brazil. Its presence in Venezuela is not confirmed.

HABITAT Undisturbed rain forest in the Amazonian lowlands, including terra firme forest, swamp forest, stands of bamboo, and primary succession along rivers, up to 1,200 m. They avoid areas near towns and agricultural areas.

CONSERVATION STATUS Near Threatened. *CITES*: Not listed. *Regional status*: Vulnerable (Brazil), Data Deficient (Ecuador). It is uncommon across its range. Major threats include habitat loss, prey-base depletion from hunting, and diseases spread by feral Dogs.

PHOTO CREDITS *Santiago Fernando Burneo Núñez*, Parque Amazónico "La Isla" (Ecuador); *Asociación para la Conservación de la Cuenca Amazónica (ACCA),* (Brazil); *Carlos Boada*, Fauna Web Ecuador; *Galo Zapata Ríos*, Yasuni National Park (Ecuador).

Eastern Crab-Eating Fox

CERDOCYON THOUS THOUS AND AZARAE

BL: 59-76.5 cm. TL: 24.3-41 cm. H: 40 cm. W: 3.6-7.9 kg (♂). SL: 12.2 cm. SW: 7.4 cm. DF: 42. CN: 74. A small to medium-sized Canid, with a short muzzle, and short and strong legs. Coat is short and thick, coloration is variable, generally dark gray to gray brown, grizzled with buff, with an indistinct median band of black hairs extending from the nape of the neck to the base of the tail. Head is finely grizzled with whitish. Lower jaw is black grizzled with white. Throat and underparts are whitish gray to dull ochraceous buff. Ears are wide and round, relatively short, tawny on the posterior surface, with whitish hairs inside. Legs are usually blackish brown grizzled with white above, buffy beneath. Tail is long and narrow, not bushy, of the same color as the back, black above and at the tip. No sexual dimorphism. Young are charcoal gray with a buff patch in the inguinal region.

dark form

Cerdocyon thous thous

Cerdocyon thous azarae

OTHER NAMES Savanna Crab-Eating Fox, Crab-Eating Zorro, Savannah Fox, Common Zorro, Azara's Crab-Eating Fox. *French*: Renard crabier, renard des savanes. *German*: Savannen-Maikong, Azara-Maikong, Waldfuchs, Savannenfuchs. *Spanish*: Zorro perruno, zorro baya, perro de monte, perro sabanero, zorro lobo, perro zorro, zorro gris, zorro cangrejero, zorro sabanero, perro cenizo. *Russian*: Майконг северо-восточный (*thous*), восточный (*azarae*). *Portuguese*: Raposa, lobinho, cachorro-do-mato, guaraxaim.

TAXONOMY Five subspecies traditionally recognized: *C. t. thous* (Savanna Crab-Eating Fox), *C. t. azarae* (Azara's Crab-Eating Fox), *C. t. entrerianus* (Southern Crab-Eating Fox), *C. t. aquilus* (Northern Crab-Eating Fox), *C. t. germanus*. The validity of these subspecies has not been confirmed by genetic analysis and is based on differences in fur color, which shows wide intraspecific variation. Phylogeographic analyses have revealed two main phylogenetic clades: a northern group (Colombia, French Guiana, Guyana, Suriname, Venezuela and N states of Brazil), and a southern group (Argentina, Paraguay and S states of Brazil). Includes *brachyteles*, *lunaris*, *rudis*, *savannarum*, *vetulus*, *angulensis*, *cancrivorus*, *guaraxa* and *robustior*.

REPRODUCTION *Gestation*: 52-59 days. *Young per birth*: 3-6, with 1 or 2 litters per year. *Weaning*: 90 days. *Sexual maturity*: 12 months. *Life span*: 11-13 years in captivity. *Breeding season*: Begins in November or December, and again in July and August. Births occur typically from January to March, and then in September to October. They occupy the abandoned burrows of other animals, and do not excavate their own. Pups are born with the eyes and ears closed and without teeth, weighing 120 to 160 g. Both parents share in pup care and den guarding. Young disperse at about 5-8 months of age.

BEHAVIOR *Social behavior*: Solitary or mated pairs; monogamous. *Diet*: Omnivorous opportunist: small mammals (rodents), fruits, invertebrates (insects, snails, land crabs), lizards, frogs, birds, bats; it may also eat carrion. It shifts its food seasonally in accordance with availability. Depredations on domestic fowl are reported by ranchers. *Main predators*: Cougar, Domestic Dog. Mainly nocturnal; its daytime retreat is usually a burrow dug by some other animal. Moderately social; they travel in pairs, but may hunt individually or in pairs; rarely cooperative. Mutual grooming, sniffing, and licking the mate's head are common. Territories are not strictly defended or observed, with home ranges overlapping with neighboring pairs. Range size averages 2.2 to 5.3 km².

DISTRIBUTION *Native*: Brazil, French Guiana, Guyana, Suriname, Venezuela. *C. t. thous* occurs in SE Venezuela, Guyana, Suriname, French Guiana, and N Brazil, with the exception of the Amazon Basin lowlands. *C. t. azarae* is found SE, N, NW and central Brazil.

HABITAT Forest and forest edges, open woodlands, wooded savannas, from elevations of 1 to 2,200 m.

CONSERVATION STATUS Least Concern. *CITES*: Appendix II. It has no direct commercial value due to the unsuitability of the fur, which is coarse and short.

PHOTO CREDITS *Irmaos Mello*, Poconé, Mato Grosso (Brazil), *Margareta Wieser*, Bahia de Cata, Aragua (Brazil), *Adriana Füchter,* Campina Grande (Brazil); *Hermann Redies*, Mãe-da-lua Reserve, Itapajé (Brazil).

Northern Crab-Eating Fox

CERDOCYON THOUS AQUILUS AND GERMANUS

BL: 59-76.5 cm. TL: 24.3-33.5 cm. H: 40 cm. W: 3.6-7.9 kg (♂). SL: 10.9 cm. SW: 6.8 cm. DF: 42. CN: 74. A small to medium-sized Canid, with a short muzzle, and short and strong legs. The smallest subspecies of Crab-Eating Fox. Coat is short and thick, coloration is dark gray to gray brown, with a darker band along the back reaching the tail. Front of the neck, breast, belly and inner side of the legs are dull ochraceous buff. Ears are wide and round, relatively short, brownish black, dull tawny around edges, nearly naked inside. Sides of the neck behind the ears are tawny. Lower legs brownish black. Tail is long and narrow, not bushy, of the same color as the back, black above and at the tip, dull clay color below. No sexual dimorphism.

Cerdocyon thous aquilus

Cerdocyon thous germanus

OTHER NAMES Crab-Eating Zorro, Savannah Fox, Common Zorro. *French*: Renard crabier, renard des savanes. *German*: Nördlicher Maikong. *Spanish*: Zorro perruno, zorro cangrejero, zorro de monte, zorro sabanero. *Russian*: Майконг северный (*aquilus*), колумбийский (*germanus*). *Guahibo*: Namo. *Tukano*: Oá. *Chaké*: Perupa. *Chimila*: Uá-kua. *Puinave*: Yu. *Chibcha*: Fo, fu. *Tunebo*: Vescura. *Piaroa*: Awari. *Cubeo*: Macadwini. *Cuna*: Taimi. *Arhuaco*: Gagaru. *Kogui*: Maktu. *Chimila*: Kiisoué. *Wakú*: Uarir.

TAXONOMY Considered a subspecies of Crab-Eating Fox (*C. thous*), but its validity has not been confirmed by genetic analysis. These subspecies belong to the northern phylogenetic clade. Includes *apollinaris* (Coachi in Colombia), and *aquilus* (Santa Marta Mountains in Colombia), with the former having preference.

SIMILAR SPECIES Gray Fox (*U. cinereoargenteus*) is smaller, with a larger and bushier tail, larger ears, a redder coloration in the shoulder and legs, and a more contrasted white throat. Culpeo Fox is larger, with ears, legs and sides having a lighter tawny to reddish-brown coloration.

REPRODUCTION *Gestation*: 56 days. *Young per birth*: 3-6, with 1 or 2 litters per year. *Weaning*: 90 days. *Sexual maturity*: 12 months. *Life span*: 12 years in captivity. *Breeding season*: Begins in November or December, and again in July. Births occur typically from January to March, and then in September to October.

BEHAVIOR *Social behavior*: Solitary or breeding pairs, with yearlings and pups. *Diet*: Opportunist, omnivore. It feeds preferentially on small vertebrates, insects and fruits; the diet composition varies in the dry and wet seasons. Mainly nocturnal and also active at dusk, but may be seen during the day. Hideouts and dens are found in bushes and in thick grass, with multiple entrance holes per den. Despite being capable of tunneling, it uses dens made by other animals. It hunts individually or in pairs. It is easy to domesticate and farm. Territorial during the dry season; during rainy seasons, when there is more food, they pay less attention to territory. Vocalizations include barking, whirring and howling, which often occurs when pairs lose contact with one another.

DISTRIBUTION *Native*: Colombia, Ecuador, Panama, Venezuela. Relatively common throughout its range. Found in the coastal and montane regions of N Colombia, N Venezuela (N of the Orinoco River), E Panama (Darién region), and N and Amazonian Ecuador. *C. t. germanus* is restricted to the high savannas of central Colombia.

HABITAT It has a clear preference for open habitats, but occurs in most habitats, including marshland, savanna, cerrado, caatinga, chaco-cerrado-caatinga transitions, shrubland, woodlands, dry and semi-deciduous forests, gallery forest, Atlantic forest, *Araucaria* forest, isolated savanna within lowland Amazon forest, and montane forest. There are records up to 3,690 m in Colombia. It adapts well to deforestation, agricultural and horticultural development. It has been seen near urban areas.

CONSERVATION STATUS Least Concern. *CITES*: Appendix II. It has no direct commercial value due to the unsuitability of the fur, which is coarse and short. Population is stable. Not protected.

PHOTO CREDITS *Juan Gonzalo Ochoa Zuluaga* and *Jorge Johnson*, Santuario de Fauna y Flora Otún Quimbaya (Colombia); *Nick Athanas*, Reserva El Dorado (Colombia); *Alex Kantorovich*, Los Ocarros Zoo (Colombia); *Adhin Muñoz, Corporación Autónoma Regional del Guavio*, Guavio Province (Colombia).

Southern Crab-Eating Fox

CERDOCYON THOUS ENTRERIANUS

BL: 59-73 cm. TL: 24.5-36.2 cm. H: 40 cm. W: 4.2-7.9 kg. DF: 42. CN: 74. A small to medium-sized Canid, with a short muzzle, and short and strong legs. Largest subspecies of Crab-Eating Fox. Coat is short and thick, coloration reddish brown, gray brown or dark gray, with a darker band along the back reaching the tail, and areas of red on the face, ears and paws. Considerable variation in pelage color can be observed, especially in terms of the amount of reddish coloration present on the head and shoulders and in ventral coloration. Front of the neck, breast, belly and inner side of the legs whitish or pale yellowish red. Lower legs are darker. Tail is long and bushy, darker dorsally, black tipped staying upright when excited. Ears are wide and round, lighter inside, and reddish brown outside. No sexual dimorphism.

Cerdocyon thous entrerianus

OTHER NAMES Crab-Eating Zorro, Savannah Fox, Common Zorro. *French*: Renard crabier, renard des savanes. *German*: Südlicher Maikong. *Spanish*: Zorro de monte, zorro de patas negras, zorro cangrejero, zorro perro. *Russian*: Южный майконг. *Portuguese*: Raposa, lobinho, cachorro-do-mato, guaraxaim. *Guaraní*: Aguärau. *Ayoreo*: Heapujague. *Chiquitano*: Quiara, nomantures.

TAXONOMY Considered a subspecies of Crab-Eating Fox (*C. thous*), but its validity has not been confirmed by genetic analysis. This subspecies belongs to the southern phylogenetic clade. Includes *riograndensis*, *mimax*, *fronto*, *tucumanus*, *jucundus*, *fulvogriseus* and *melampus*.

SIMILAR SPECIES Pampas Fox (*Lycalopex gymnocercus*) is similar in size, but has a thinner muzzle, longer ears, a bushier tail, and its coat is usually lighter in color, with lighter lower legs.

REPRODUCTION *Gestation*: 52-59 days. *Young per birth*: 3-6, 1 or 2 litters per year. *Weaning*: 90 days. *Sexual maturity*: 9 months. *Life span*: 15 years in captivity. *Breeding season*: Begins in November or December, and again in July. Births occur typically from January to March, and then in September to October. Pups open their eyes at 14 days. At 5 months the group breaks up.

BEHAVIOR *Social behavior*: Breeding pairs, with yearlings and pups. *Diet*: Opportunist, omnivore. During the wet season, the diet contains more crabs and other crustaceans, while during the dry season it contains more insects. Other foods consumed include turtle eggs, tortoises, fruit, eggs, lizards, rodents, birds and carrion. *Main predators*: Cougar. Mainly nocturnal, with peaks of activity after dusk and before dawn. Hideouts and dens are found in bushes and in thick grass, with multiple entrance holes per den. Despite being capable of tunneling, it uses dens made by other animals. It hunts individually or in pairs. It is easy to domesticate and farm. Territorial during the dry season; during rainy seasons, when there is more food, they pay less attention to territory. Home ranges from 0.6 to 0.9 km^2. Vocalizations include barking, whirring and howling, which occurs often when pairs lose contact with one another.

DISTRIBUTION *Native*: Argentina, Brazil, Bolivia, Paraguay, Uruguay. This species is relatively common throughout its range, from the provinces of Entre Ríos and adjacent N Buenos Aires (Argentina), and from the E Andean foothills (up to 2,000 m) in Bolivia and Argentina to the Atlantic forests of SE Brazil. In recent years, range extensions have been documented in Argentina.

HABITAT A variety of habitats, from savanna to woodland, and up to 2,000 m in NW Argentina. In Uruguay it prefers forest and edge areas, separating itself from Pampas Fox, which is found in more open country, but in NE Argentina it is found in all habitat types. More frequently recorded in the thicker habitats, the gallery forests and the shrubland without cattle, in the Iberá wetlands of NE Argentina.

CONSERVATION STATUS Least Concern. *CITES*: Appendix II. *Regional status*: Least Concern (Argentina), Priority for Conservation (Uruguay). It has no direct commercial value due to the unsuitability of the fur, which is coarse and short, but pelts have been traded as those of the Chilla and Pampas Fox in Argentina and Uruguay. Population is stable. Estimated population of 40,000 animals in Argentina.

PHOTO CREDITS *Juan Carlos Piola, Julian García,* El Palmar National Park (Argentina); *Pieter Verheij*, Pantanal (Brazil); *Joares May*, Caiman Ecological Refuge (Brazil).

Hoary Fox

LYCALOPEX VETULUS

BL: 49-71.5 cm (♂), 51-66 cm (♀). TL: 25-38 cm. H: 32.7-37.5 cm. W: 2.5-4.1 kg (♂), 3-3.6 kg (♀). SL: 11.4 cm. SW: 6.3 cm. DF: 42. CN: 74. A small-sized Canid, with a short muzzle, small teeth, and slender body and limbs. Smallest Brazilian Canid. Pelage contains a mixture of short, woolly, thin, rough fur and long, hard, erect fur. Coat color is grizzled gray, with upper parts of body pale gray, and yellow to fawn underparts. Near-melanistic forms may be found. Males may have a strip of black hair from nape to end of tail. Anterior part of neck is white and the chest and the remainder of the neck are yellow brown. Head is small. Lower jaw is black. Buff-yellow patch behind ear. Legs are tawny or reddish and thighs are crossed by a dark bar. Tip of the tail and superior base black. Females slightly smaller than males.

Lycalopex vetulus

OTHER NAMES Small-Toothed Dog, Field Fox, Hoary Zorro. *French*: Renard chenu, renard du Bresil. *German*: Brasilianischer Kampfuchs. *Spanish*: Zorro brasileño, zorro de campo común. *Russian*: Бразильская лисица. *Portuguese*: Raposa-do-campo, raposinha, cachorro-de-dentes-pequenos. *Tupy*: Jaguarapitanga. *Xavante*: Waptsà wa.

TAXONOMY Monotypic. Previously placed under *Pseudalopex* and *Dusicyon*. Includes *fulvicaudus*, *parvidens*, *sladeni* and *urostictus*. Despite its name, it is not a true Fox.

SIMILAR SPECIES It differs from the sympatric Crab-Eating Fox (*C. thous*) in having a shorter muzzle, a longer and thinner neck, thicker and woollier fur, rust-yellow ears and legs and a less robust body; pelage color alone is insufficient to differentiate the species.

REPRODUCTION *Gestation*: 50-60 days. *Young per birth*: 2-5. *Weaning*: 120 days. *Sexual maturity*: Unknown. *Life span*: 8 years in captivity. *Breeding season*: From late May to June, with births occurring from the end of July to September. They often use abandoned armadillo dens for rearing their pups. Because this species is monogamous, it is likely that the ♂ plays some role in caring for the young.

BEHAVIOR *Social behavior*: Breeding pairs. *Diet*: Omnivores, they appear to be termite specialists (*Syntermes* sp.), but may also eat rodents, fruit, grasshoppers and dung beetles. Termites and small mammals make up the majority of their diet during the dry season, and other insects and fruit make up the majority during the wet season. Its unique dental structure (reduced carnassials and broad molars) and small muzzle allow it to eat small insects. *Main predators*: Maned Wolf, Domestic Dog, parasitized, but not killed, by the vampire bat. Usually timid, but will aggressively defend their young. Diurnal, but often active at night and during twilight. Probably territorial. Parents often travel with their adult-sized offspring, and conflict over territory arises between parents and offspring during the dry season.

DISTRIBUTION *Native*: Brazil. Found only in Brazil, associated with the cerrado habitats (mosaic of grasslands and xerophytic vegetation) of the central Brazilian plateau, and peripheral transitional zones including dry open habitats of the Pantanal (Mato Grosso state). Confirmed in the states of Minas Gerais, São Paulo, Mato Grosso do Sul, Mato Grosso, Tocantins and Goiás, S and W Bahia, and W Piauí in Parque Nacional Serra da Capivara.

HABITAT Open cerrado habitats, but it adapts well to insect-rich livestock pastures and areas of agriculture (soybean, rice, corn, eucalyptus plantation). Rarely observed in densely wooded cerrado, floodplains, dry or gallery forests. Areas of high human population density are unlikely to be suitable.

CONSERVATION STATUS Least Concern. *CITES*: Not listed. *Regional status*: Vulnerable (Brazil). There are no population estimates. It is locally abundant in the central highland cerrado biome, but populations appear smaller than those of the sympatric Crab-Eating Fox. Its main threat is habitat destruction. It is not exploited for fur, but is persecuted by humans because it is thought to kill poultry.

PHOTO CREDITS *Stephen Davis* (Brazil); *Alexander Meyer* and *Nayer Youakim*, Municipal Zoological Park Quinzinho de Barros (Brazil).

Sechuran Fox

LYCALOPEX SECHURAE

BL: 50-78 cm. TL: 27-34 cm. H: 22-36 cm. W: 2.2-4.2 kg. SL: 11.2 cm. SW: 6.3 cm. DF: 42. CN: 74. A small-sized Canid. The smallest species of the genus *Lycalopex*. Pelage color is grayish, with pale underfur and agouti guard hairs. Underparts are white, fawn, or cream colored. Head is small, with a narrow and short muzzle. Face is gray with a narrow rufous-brown ring around the eyes, dark muzzle, and white upper lip and chin. Large ears, rufous on the back. Throat and chest are white with a gray band or collar across the chest. Upper parts of limbs are usually reddish. Feet are whitish. Tail is slender, relatively long, densely furred, ending in a dark tip. Females slightly smaller than males.

Lycalopex sechurae

OTHER NAMES Sechura Desert Fox, Peruvian Desert Fox. *French*: Renard de Sechura. *German*: Sechurafuchs. *Spanish*: Perro de monte de Sechura, zorra pampera, zorro de Sechura, juancito, zorro costeño, pacha zorro, pacter, pacterillo. *Italian*: Volpe di Sechura. *Russian*: Перунская (секуранская) лисица.

TAXONOMY Monotypic. Previously placed under *Pseudalopex* or *Dusicyon*. Despite their name, they are not true Foxes.

SIMILAR SPECIES Sympatric with Culpeo Fox (*L. culpaeus*) and probably, in the S limit of its distribution area, with the Chilla (*L. griseus*). Culpeo Fox is larger and has a reddish coloration, and Chilla has a rufescent head and a black spot on the chin.

REPRODUCTION *Gestation*: 55-60 days. *Young per birth*: Unknown. *Weaning*: Unknown. *Sexual maturity*: Unknown. *Life span*: Unknown. *Breeding season*: Probably around August. Births occur from October to January. Almost nothing is known about reproduction in this species.

BEHAVIOR *Social behavior*: Generally solitary, although occasionally seen traveling in pairs, or ♀ with pups; larger groups are usually only observed where food is concentrated. *Diet*: Opportunistic omnivore, capable of being strictly vegetarian when necessary. In deserts and dry forests, diets contain fruits, rodents, birds, reptiles, insects and scorpions. Along coastal beaches, crabs, carrion, and sea birds and their eggs are eaten. Lack of standing water in inland desert habitats suggests that it can survive without drinking. *Main predators*: Boa constrictor (pups), cougar, jaguar, but now uncommon in its range. Mainly nocturnal, spends the daylight hours in a den dug into the ground. Well adapted to desert life. Population density of 12.9 animals per km^2 in Bosque de Pomac (Peru).

DISTRIBUTION *Native*: Ecuador, Peru. Found in the coastal zones of NW Peru and extreme SW Ecuador. In Peru, it is distributed on the W slope of the Andes between the frontier with Ecuador and Lima. Animals found further S may be the Chilla (*L. griseus*). It is often observed in rural areas and disturbed environments from Piura Department to La Libertad Department in Peru. It may be seen in the following natural reserves of Peru: Tumbes National Reserve, Amotape Hills National Park, El Angolo, Sunchubamba, Pómac Forest Historical Sanctuary, Algarrobal el Moro, Laquipampa Natural Reservation, Calipuy National Reserve, Lachay National Reserve. It is uncommon in Ecuador, where it may be seen in Machalilla National Park, and Churute Mangroves Ecological Reserve.

HABITAT Various habitats, ranging from sandy deserts with low plant density, and adjacent beaches, to cultivated areas, dry forests, foothills, sea cliffs, and the W slopes of the Andes, to 1,000 m.

CONSERVATION STATUS Near Threatened. *CITES*: Not listed. *Regional status*: Near Threatened (Peru). Population is estimated to number fewer than 15,000 individuals. Main threats include the market for handicrafts and amulets, and persecution because of (unlikely) damage to livestock. It also faces some pressure in agricultural zones and from urbanization and habitat degradation, which is the main threat to this species in Ecuador.

PHOTO CREDITS *David Beadle, Fabrice Schmitt* and *Joan Egert*, Chaparri (Peru); *Christian Nunes*, Lomas de Lachey (Peru).

Darwin's Fox
LYCALOPEX FULVIPES

BL: 48.2-56.1 cm (♂), 48-59.1 cm (♀). TL: 17.5-25.5 cm. H: 17-26 cm. W: 1.9-3.9 kg (♂), 1.8-3.7 kg (♀). SL: 11.5 cm. SW: 6.7 cm. DF: 42. CN: Unknown. A small-sized Canid, with a stout frame, elongated and compact body and short legs. Coat is thick, dark grizzled gray to almost black in color, with a distinctive rusty-red color on the lower legs and around the ears. Underparts, chest, underside of the muzzle and the inside of the ears are a pale cream to white color. Tail is relatively short and bushy, dark gray. Muzzle is small and thin, extending into a rather rounded forehead. Females have a narrower muzzle than males, but otherwise they do not show external sexual dimorphism or differences in weight.

Lycalopex fulvipes

OTHER NAMES Darwin's Zorro. *French*: Renard de Darwin. *German*: Darwin-Fuchs. *Spanish*: Zorro chilote, zorro de Chiloé, zorro de Darwin, zorro azul. *Russian*: Чилоэсская (Дарвинская) лисица.

TAXONOMY Monotypic. Previously considered an insular subspecies of the Chilla Fox (*L. griseus*). Despite its name, it is not a true Fox.

SIMILAR SPECIES It can be distinguished from the sympatric Chilla Fox (*L. griseus*) by its smaller size, shorter tail and legs, dark brown pelage instead of gray, and rufescent areas on its head, ears and legs that are a deeper and richer shade.

REPRODUCTION *Gestation*: Probably 56 days. *Young per birth*: 2-3. *Weaning*: Probably 60 days. *Sexual maturity*: Probably 12 months. *Life span*: 7 years. *Breeding season*: Probably during July or August. During the few weeks after parturition, ♀ move little and apparently stay in the den. Biparental care is expected. After weaning ♀ spends less time with the pups, and a greater proportion of their interactions are agonistic, whereas ♂ spends more time playing with and grooming the pups.

BEHAVIOR *Social behavior*: Solitary, except during the breeding season when temporary pairs form; pairs appear to persist throughout the year on the mainland. *Diet*: Insects are the most abundant prey, followed by crustaceans, rodents, birds, amphibians, ungulates, reptiles and marsupials; it may also eat fruits and berries. It seldom eats carrion. Solitary hunters. Active throughout the day, but more so at night. Home ranges from 1 to 4.8 km², similar between ♂ and ♀, larger than expected for Foxes of that size; home ranges are elongated following the shoreline. Home ranges overlap extensively, with individuals of the same or different gender showing no apparent territorial behavior. They appear to be monogamous, allowing subordinates in their home ranges. Apparently unafraid of people or Dogs.

DISTRIBUTION *Native*: Chile. Endemic to Chile, with at least two subpopulations: on most of Chiloé Island, especially where forest remains, with the exception of the most populated areas in the E and NE; and in mainland Chile, in the coastal mountains in Nahuelbuta National Park, a small habitat island of highland forest surrounded by degraded farmlands and plantations of exotic trees. Intermediate populations have been found in Los Rios region (Alerce Costero Natural Monument, Oncol Park), and Los Lagos region (Puerto Octay, Chanchán) suggesting a wide distribution of Darwin's Fox throughout the Valdivian Coastal Range.

HABITAT Old-growth forest, secondary forest with shrubland, pastures and openings, dunes and sandy shores. Where sympatric, Chilla Fox (*L. griseus*) prefers open areas.

CONSERVATION STATUS Endangered. *CITES*: Appendix II. *Regional status*: Endangered (Chile). Total population is less than 700 individuals, most of them occurring on Chiloé Island. Protected in Nahuelbuta National Park, but substantial mortality sources exist when they move to unprotected areas. Its small population size, along with the rapid destruction due to cutting and burning of its putative habitat, the Valdivian rain forest, and its naiveness to potential diseases transmitted by the abundant and unleashed Dog populations put this species at high extinction risk.

PHOTO CREDITS *Yamil Hussein*, Región de la Araucanía (Chile); *Jorge Cárdenas*, *Richard Wof Miranda*, *Iñigo Bidegain* and *Kevin Schafer,* Chiloé Island (Chile).

Northern Pampas Fox

LYCALOPEX GYMNOCERCUS GYMNOCERCUS

BL: 59.7-74 cm (♂), 50.5-72 cm (♀). TL: 25-41 cm. H: 40 cm. W: 4-8 kg (♂), 3-5.7 kg (♀). SL: 14.3 cm. SW: 7.6 cm. DF: 42. CN: 74. A small to medium-sized Canid. The largest subspecies of Pampas Fox, more vividly colored than Southern subspecies (*antiquus*). Coat is brindled gray, with belly and inner surface of legs pale gray to whitish, and top and sides of the head reddish. Ventral surface of the head is pale gray to white. Lower mandible is black as far as the corners of the mouth (chin spot), a feature that distinguishes them from the Culpeo Fox. Ears are triangular, broad, large, reddish on the outer surface, white on the inner surface. Hind limbs are gray laterally with distal portions reddish, with a characteristic black spot on the lower rear side (thigh spot). Lateral surface of the front limbs is reddish. Paws are white to yellowish. Tail is long, bushy and gray, with a blackish line running along the center of the back, a black spot on the upper side and a black tip. Females slightly smaller than males.

*Lycalopex gymnocercus
gymnocercus*

OTHER NAMES Azara's Fox, Paraguayan Fox. *French*: Renard d'Azara. *German*: Nördlicher Pampasfuchs, Azarafuchs. *Spanish*: Zorro de la Pampa, zorro de Azara, zorro de campo, zorro de patas amarillas, zorro gris pampeano. *Russian*: Парагвайская пампасская лисица. *Portuguese*: Graxaim-do-campo, graxaim, sorro. *Guaraní*: Aguara.

TAXONOMY Previously classified under the genus *Pseudalopex*. Its taxonomic status is controversial, and some authors suggest that *L. gymnocercus* and *L. griseus* are conspecific, being clinal variations of one single species (*L. gymnocercus*). Despite their name, they are not true Foxes but are a unique genus more closely related to *Canis*. Three subspecies traditionally recognized: *L. g. gymnocercus*, *L. g. antiquus*, and *L. g. lordi*. The geographic limits of the ranges of subspecies are not precise. Includes *brasiliensis*, *protalopex*, *azarae*, *argenteus* and *attenuatus*.

SIMILAR SPECIES Crab-Eating fox (*Cerdocyon thous*) occurs in the N part of the range, is similar in size, but with shorter hair and rostrum, and shorter dark-colored legs.

REPRODUCTION *Gestation*: 55-60 days. *Young per birth*: 3-8. *Weaning*: 60 days. *Sexual maturity*: 12 months. *Life span*: 14 years in captivity. *Breeding season*: From July through October. Young are born between September and December. Pups will hunt with parents when they are 3 months old. ♂ bring food to their ♀ who stay at the den with pups. They den in any available cavity, including caves, hollow trees, and the burrows of viscachas or armadillos.

BEHAVIOR *Social behavior*: Solitary, forming monogamous pairs only during the breeding season; even when raising young together, adult Foxes generally hunt alone, marking their territory by defecating at specific latrine sites. *Diet*: Opportunistic omnivore, very broad, including mammals, birds, lizards, fish, crayfish, insects, carcasses of wild and domestic ungulates, and fruits. Although they are often blamed for killing sheep, they largely only scavenge carcasses, although there is evidence of predation on newborn lambs. *Main predators*: Cougar, Domestic Dogs. Nocturnal, becoming active at dusk, it may also be active during the day. It forages alone.

DISTRIBUTION *Native*: Argentina, Brazil, Paraguay, Uruguay. Found in the subtropical grasslands of NE Argentina, S Misiones, N Corrientes Province and E Formosa Province, Uruguay, Paraguay and E Brazil, from Parana state to Rio Grande do Sul state. Information on the limits of its distribution and the extent to which it overlaps with congeneric species is uncertain. The specific status of the Pampas Fox from E Bolivia remains unclear.

HABITAT Grasslands, open habitats and tallgrass plains and subhumid to dry habitats. It is also common on ridges, dry scrub lands and open woodlands. Tolerant of human disturbance, being common in rural areas. Where its range overlaps with that of the Crab-Eating Fox, the Pampas Fox selects more open areas.

CONSERVATION STATUS Least Concern. *CITES*: Appendix II. *Regional status*: Least Concern (Argentina). Population is unknown, but it seems abundant or common in most areas where the species has been studied. It is persecuted because it is believed to prey on livestock.

PHOTO CREDITS *Patrícia Retore*, Cambará do Sul (Brazil); *Ricardo Siqueira*, Campos de Cima da Serra (Brazil); *Bárbara Henriques* (Brazil); *Jose Irion Neto,* Serra do Faxinal (Brazil); Vinicios de Moura, Parque Nacional da Serra Geral (Brazil).

Mountain Pampas Fox

LYCALOPEX GYMNOCERCUS LORDI

BL: 64 cm. TL: 27-36 cm. H: 40 cm. W: 4.6 kg (♂), 4.2 kg (♀). SL: 14.3 cm. SW: 7.6 cm. DF: 42. CN: 74. A small to medium-sized Canid. The smallest subspecies of Pampas Fox, with pelage smoother and brighter, and more contrasting in color. Coat color is brindled gray, with paler gray underparts, and top and sides of the head reddish. There are characteristic dark spots in the pectoral and axillary regions of the body. Head, neck and large ears are reddish, as are the outsides of the legs. Ventral surface of the head is pale gray to white. Lower mandible is black as far as the corners of the mouth (chin spot). Hind limbs are gray laterally with distal portions reddish, with a characteristic black spot on the lower rear side (thigh spot). Tail is denser than in other subspecies, bushy and gray, with a blackish line running along the center of the back, and a black tip. Females are slightly smaller than males.

Lycalopex gymnocercus lordi

OTHER NAMES Azara's Fox, Azara's Zorro. *French*: Renard de la pampa. *German*: Berg-Pampasfuchs, Berg-Graufuchs. *Spanish*: Zorro gris serrano, zorro de la Pampa, zorro de campo, zorro del país, zorro de patas amarillas. *Russian*: Горная пампасская лисица.

TAXONOMY Considered a subspecies of Pampas Fox (*L. gymnocercus*). This subspecies is not recognized by some authors. The geographic limits of the ranges of subspecies are not precise.

SIMILAR SPECIES Culpeo Fox (*L. culpaeus*) is similar in size, but has more reddish coloration on the head, neck and ears, has a white lower mandible, and the black spot on the lower rear side of the hind limb is inconspicuous.

REPRODUCTION *Gestation*: 55-60 days. *Young per birth*: 2-5. *Weaning*: 60 days. *Sexual maturity*: 8-12 months. *Life span*: 14 years in captivity. There is no specific information for this subspecies, but probably similar to the other subspecies. Dens may be located in a variety of shelters (holes at the base of a tree trunk, in armadillo dens or among rocks). Cubs are frequently moved to a new location. Young stay at the den for the first 3 months. Both pair mates have been observed to guard the den and ♂ provide food to pups and ♀ at the den.

BEHAVIOR *Social behavior*: Solitary, forming monogamous pairs in the breeding season. *Diet*: Very broad, including mammals, birds, lizards, fish, crayfish, the larvae and adults of insects, carcasses of wild and domestic ungulates, and fruits. *Main predators*: Cougar, Domestic Dogs. There is no specific information for this subspecies, but probably similar to the other subspecies. Although they are often blamed for killing sheep, they largely only scavenge carcasses, although there is evidence of predation on newborn lambs. Mainly nocturnal, becoming active at dusk, although it may also be active during the day. They den in any available cavity, including caves, hollow trees and the burrows of viscachas or armadillos. Even when raising young together, adult Foxes generally hunt alone, marking their territory by defecating at specific latrine sites.

DISTRIBUTION *Native*: Argentina. Restricted to the Chaco-Yungas Mountain Tropical Forest ecotone in Salta Province (Güemes and Metán Departments) and Jujuy Province (San Pedro and Ledesma Departments) of Argentina. It is also found in Santiago del Estero Province.

HABITAT Open habitats and tallgrass plains and subhumid to dry habitats. It can be found in all habitats from the Puna to the Chaco and Yungas.

CONSERVATION STATUS Least Concern. *CITES*: Appendix II. *Regional status*: Least Concern (Argentina). The status of this subspecies is unknown. Hunting pressure has resulted in diminished populations in the province of Salta.

PHOTO CREDITS *Kevin Zaouali*, Jujuy (Argentina); *Luis César Tejo*, Salta (Argentina).

Southern Pampas Fox
LYCALOPEX GYMNOCERCUS ANTIQUUS

BL: 64 cm. TL: 22.6-39.8 cm. H: 40 cm. W: 3.7-8.2 kg (♂), 2.4-4.5 kg (♀). SL: 14.3 cm. SW: 7.6 cm. DF: 42. CN: 74. A small to medium-sized Canid. Coat color is brindled gray, with paler gray underparts, and top and sides of the head reddish. Head, neck and large ears are reddish, as are the outsides of the legs. Ventral surface of the head is pale gray to white. Lower mandible is black as far as the corners of the mouth (chin spot). Hind limbs are gray laterally with distal portions reddish, with a characteristic black spot on the lower rear side (thigh spot). Tail is long, bushy and gray, with a blackish line running along the center of the back, and a black tip. There is a generally a black spot on the upper side of the tail. Lateral surface of the front limbs is reddish. Females are slightly smaller than males.

Lycalopex gymnocercus antiquus

OTHER NAMES Azara's Fox. *French*: Renard d'Azara. *German*: Südlicher Pampasfuchs. *Spanish*: Zorro de la Pampa, zorro de Azara, zorro de campo, zorro del país, zorro de patas amarillas, zorro gris pampeano. *Russian*: Южная (аргентинская) пампасская лисица.

TAXONOMY Considered a subspecies of Pampas Fox (*L. gymnocercus*). Some authors suggest that *L. gymnocercus gracilis* and *L. griseus antiquus* are conspecific. The geographic limits of the ranges of subspecies are not precise. Includes *ensenadensis* (Buenos Aires Province, Argentina), and *fossilis*.

SIMILAR SPECIES Chilla (*L. griseus*) is similar in color and body proportions, but is smaller, with a more uniformly gray pelage and shorter legs. Culpeo Fox (*L. culpaeus*) is similar in size, but has more reddish coloration on the head, neck and ears, has a white lower mandible, and the black spot on the lower rear side of the hind limb is inconspicuous.

REPRODUCTION *Gestation*: 55-60 days. *Young per birth*: 3-8. *Weaning*: 60 days. *Sexual maturity*: 8-12 months. *Life span*: 14 years in captivity. *Breeding season*: From July to October. The young are born between October and December. Pups will hunt with parents when they are 3 months old. ♂ bring food to their ♀ who stay at the den with pups.

BEHAVIOR *Social behavior*: Solitary, forming monogamous pairs in the breeding season. *Diet*: Very broad, including mammals, birds, lizards, fish, crayfish, insects, carcasses and fruits. *Main predators*: Cougar, Domestic Dogs. Behavior probably similar to other subspecies of Pampas Fox. Active both during the day and night, although feeding activity becomes mainly nocturnal where heavily hunted. They den in any available cavity, including caves, hollow trees, and the burrows of viscachas or armadillos. Home range estimated at around 0.4-2.6 km². The long-distance calls, which show a peak in frequency during the breeding period, may serve to maintain contact between pair members, and are used in territorial behavior.

DISTRIBUTION *Native*: Argentina. Found in the Pampas grasslands, Monte shrublands and Espinal open woodlands of central Argentina, from Córdoba and San Luis Provinces to the Río Negro, and from the Atlantic coast to a poorly defined limit W of the Salado-Chadilevú River.

HABITAT Open habitats and tallgrass plains and subhumid to dry habitats, but is also common on ridges, dry scrub lands and open woodlands. In the driest habitats of its range, it is replaced by the Chilla. It has been able to adapt to the alterations caused by extensive cattle breeding and agricultural activities to its natural habitats.

CONSERVATION STATUS Least Concern. *CITES*: Appendix II. *Regional status*: Least Concern (Argentina). Most of its range has suffered massive habitat alteration, although it seems able to withstand the loss and degradation of its natural habitat, as well as hunting pressure. It continues to be hunted and demand for its fur exists. Hunting pressure has resulted in diminished populations in the province of Tucumán.

PHOTO CREDITS *Hernan Tolosa,* Parque Nacional Lihue Calel (Argentina); *Romina del Blanco*, Córdoba (Argentina); *Adwo*, Talampaya National Park (Argentina).

Patagonian Chilla

LYCALOPEX GRISEUS GRISEUS

BL: 52.1-59.7 cm (♂), 52-55.8 cm. TL: 29-34.4 cm. H: 32.8-36 cm. W: 2.4-3.2 kg (♂), 1.9-2.7 kg (♀). DF: 42. CN: 74. A small to medium-sized Canid. The largest subspecies of Chilla. Coat color is brindled gray, with agouti guard hairs and a short, dense pale undercoat. Underparts and inner surface of legs are pale gray. Head is reddish brown flecked with white. Lower mandible is black as far as the corners of the mouth (chin spot). Ears are large and triangular, white on the inner surface. Limbs are tawny to reddish and the thigh is crossed by a characteristic black spot (thigh spot). Paws are tawny. Tail is long, bushy and gray with a dark dorsal stripe and a dark tip with a paler, mottled underside. Females are slightly smaller than males.

Young

Lycalopex griseus griseus

OTHER NAMES South American Gray Fox, Patagonian Fox, Argentine Gray Fox, Gray Zorro. *French*: Renard gris de Patagonie. *German*: Patagonischer Kampfuchs, Südamerikanischer Graufuchs. *Spanish*: Zorro gris, zorro chilla, zorro chico, zorro gris chico. *Russian*: Патагонская серая лисица. *Araucano*: Nuru. *Puelche*: Yeshgai.

TAXONOMY Previously placed in the genus *Pseudalopex* and *Dusicyon*. Its taxonomic status is controversial, and some authors suggest that *L. griseus* and *L. gymnocercus* (Pampas Fox) are conspecific, being clinal variations of one single species (*L. gymnocercus*). Despite their name, they are not true Foxes, and are more closely related to the Wolves, Dogs, Jackals and Coyotes. Four subspecies traditionally recognized: *L. g. domeykoanus*, *P. g. gracilis*, *P. g. maullinicus*, and *P. g. griseus*. Includes *patagonicus*.

SIMILAR SPECIES Culpeo Fox (*L. culpaeus*) is generally larger, heavier, has a more reddish coloration on the sides, chin is white, and the black spot on the lower rear side of the hind limb is inconspicuous.

REPRODUCTION *Gestation*: 53-58 days. *Young per birth*: 4-6. *Weaning*: 4-5 months. *Sexual maturity*: Probably 12 months. *Life span*: Probably 14 years in captivity. *Breeding season*: August. Births occur in October.

BEHAVIOR *Social behavior*: Solitary, monogamous pairs during the breeding season, accompanied by occasional ♀ helpers. *Diet*: Small mammals, especially rodents, birds, arthropods, bird eggs, reptiles, fruit and carrion. *Main predators*: Domestic Dog. Crepuscular. Where their ranges overlap, it is in competition with the larger Culpeo Fox, which consumes larger prey, including the introduced European hare, and excludes the Chilla from the best prey territories. ♂ and ♀ of the pair maintain an exclusive home range year-round, which does not overlap with home ranges of neighboring pairs. Intraspecific interaction displays are few and usually aggressive.

DISTRIBUTION *Native*: Argentina, Chile. Found in the Pampas of W Argentina, Argentinean and Chilean Patagonia, S from Rio Negro Province to Strait of Magellan, Chile, E base of Andes of Chile. Introduced in Tierra del Fuego in 1951 to control European hare infestations. Other populations have been reported to exist in some of the S Atlantic islands, including the Falklands, but this requires confirmation.

HABITAT They generally inhabit plains and low mountains, but they have been reported to occur as high as 4,000 m. In S Chile (Nahuelbuta and Torres del Paine), they prefer shrubby open areas to those more dense patches where Darwin's Foxes occur. Culpeo Fox prefers mountains, rugged terrain and forested habitats. Burning and destruction of forests seems to have been advantageous for Chillas.

CONSERVATION STATUS Least Concern. *CITES*: Appendix II. *Regional status*: Least Concern (Argentina, Chile). Main threat in the past was commercial hunting. Illegal trapping still occurs. It is hunted for its pelt in Argentina and Chile. Estimated population in S Chile was 66,000 in 1982.

PHOTO CREDITS *Thomas Ricaud, Dukas Presseagentur, BiosPhoto*, Torres del Paine (Chile); *Sebastian Yima Flores* and *Carlos Ameglio*, Patagonia (Argentina).

Maullin's Chilla
LYCALOPEX GRISEUS MAULLINICUS

BL: 51.5-66 cm. TL: 11.5-33 cm. H: 33 cm. W: 2.5-5 kg. DF: 42. CN: 74. A small to medium-sized Canid. Coat color is brindled gray, with agouti guard hairs and a short, dense pale undercoat. Pelage is darker than in Northern Chilla (*domeykoanus*). Underparts are pale gray. Head is reddish brown flecked with white. Lower mandible is black as far as the corners of the mouth (chin spot). Ears are large and triangular, white on the inner surface. Limbs are tawny and the thigh is crossed by a characteristic black spot (thigh spot). Paws are tawny. Tail is long, bushy and gray with a dark dorsal stripe and dark tip with a paler, mottled underside. Females are slightly smaller than males.

Young

Lycalopex griseus maullinicus

OTHER NAMES South American Gray Fox, Gray Zorro. *French*: Renard gris. *German*: Grauer Kampfuchs. *Spanish*: Zorro gris, zorro chilla, zorro chico, zorro gris chico. *Russian*: Маульинская серая лисица. *Araucano*: Nuru.

TAXONOMY Considered a subspecies of Chilla (*L. griseus*), but its validity has not been confirmed by genetic analysis. Includes *trichodactylus* (Valdivia, Chile), and *torquatus* (Llanquihue, Chile).

SIMILAR SPECIES Darwin's Fox (*L. fulvipes*) is smaller; pelage darker brown, with deeper and richer-shaded rufescent areas on head, ears and legs, and the tail is not bushy. Culpeo Fox (*L. culpaeus*) is generally larger, heavier, has a more reddish coloration on the sides, chin is white, and the black spot on the lower rear side of the hind limb is inconspicuous.

REPRODUCTION *Gestation*: 53-58 days. *Young per birth*: 3-8. *Weaning*: 4-5 months. *Sexual maturity*: Probably 12 months. *Life span*: Unknown. *Breeding season*: August and September. Births occur in October. Dens are located in a variety of natural and man-made places, and may be changed to a new location during the nursing period. During the first 3-4 days, the mother rarely leaves the den, and the ♂ provisions her with food. Pups are cared for by both parents on an approximately equal time basis. Young Foxes start to emerge from the den when they are about 1 month old, and start to disperse (8-65 km) around 5-6 months later.

BEHAVIOR *Social behavior*: Solitary, monogamous pairs during the breeding season. *Diet*: Small mammals, especially rodents, birds, arthropods, bird eggs, reptiles, fruit and carrion. *Main predators*: Domestic Dog. Behavior probably similar to other subspecies of Chilla. Chillas and Culpeo Fox are allopatric in N Chile and central Argentina, whereas they are sympatric in the S regions of both countries. The similar size of both species in central Chile is due to the Chillas tending to use lower and more open habitats, while Culpeo Foxes usually occupy higher lands or more densely vegetated areas such as ravines. When in sympatry, Chillas are excluded from the richest patches by Culpeo Foxes, which are larger and more aggressive. Darwin's Fox may also be a potential competitor, since initial data on the ecology of sympatric populations of these Foxes suggest that they exhibit similar activity patterns, a high degree of overlap in home range and habitat use, and considerable overlap in their diets.

DISTRIBUTION *Native*: Argentina, Chile. Found in the S temperate forests of Argentina and Chile, Maullin, Valdivian forest region of S-central Chile, mainly in the provinces of Cautin, Valdivia (Araucania region), and Llanquihue.

HABITAT Plains and low mountains, shrubby open areas.

CONSERVATION STATUS Least Concern. *CITES*: Appendix II. *Regional status*: Least Concern (Chile). They are considered scarce in central Chile. They are hunted in the belief that they are voracious predators of small livestock, poultry and game, despite Foxes being protected by legal regulations.

PHOTO CREDITS *Marco Rojas Bertolone, Cristian Becker,* Araucania region (Chile); *Daniel Zuñiga*, Vicente Perez Rosales National Park (Chile); *Andy Urbina*, Corralco Mountain (Chile); *Cesar Santana*, Laguna Verde (Chile).

Northern Chilla

LYCALOPEX GRISEUS DOMEYKOANUS

BL: 51.5-66 cm. TL: 11.5-33 cm. H: 33 cm. W: 2.5-5 kg. SL: 11.1 cm. SW: 5.8 cm. DF: 42. CN: 74. A small to medium-sized Canid. The smallest subspecies of Chilla, with the largest ears. Coat color is brindled gray, with agouti guard hairs and a short, dense pale undercoat, paler than in Maullin's Chilla (*maullinicus*). Underparts are pale gray. Head is reddish brown flecked with white. Lower mandible is black as far as the corners of the mouth (chin spot). Ears are very large and triangular, white on the inner surface. Limbs are tawny and the thigh is crossed by a characteristic black spot (thigh spot). Paws are tawny. Tail is long, bushy, gray with a dark dorsal stripe and dark tip with a paler, mottled underside. Females are slightly smaller than males.

Lycalopex griseus domeykoanus

OTHER NAMES South American Gray Fox, Gray Zorro. *French*: Renard gris. *German*: Nördlicher Kampfuchs. *Spanish*: Zorro gris, zorro chilla, zorro chico, zorro gris chico. *Russian*: Северная серая южноамериканская лисица. *Quechua*: Atój.

TAXONOMY Considered a subspecies of Chilla (*L. griseus*), but its validity has not been confirmed by genetic analysis. Includes *rufipes* (Santiago Province, Chile).

SIMILAR SPECIES Sechuran Fox (*L. sechurae*) is probably sympatric in the S limit of its distribution area with the Chilla; the former is smaller, has a shorter snout, has little or no reddish coloring on the body and face and lacks the black spot on the chin. Culpeo Fox (*L. culpaeus*) is generally larger, heavier, has a more reddish coloration on the sides, chin is white, and the black spot on the lower rear side of the hind limb is inconspicuous.

REPRODUCTION *Gestation*: 55-60 days. *Young per birth*: 3-8. *Weaning*: 60 days. *Sexual maturity*: Probably 12 months. *Life span*: 14 years in captivity. *Breeding season*: August and September. Births occur in October. There is no specific information for this subspecies, but probably similar to other subspecies of Chilla.

BEHAVIOR *Social behavior*: Solitary, monogamous pairs during the breeding season. *Diet*: Composed primarily of rodents, secondarily of lizards and birds; tenebrionid beetles make up the bulk of the invertebrate prey eaten. In winter fewer rodents are eaten, and the relative importance of invertebrate prey increases. The importance of plant material, primarily berries, increases in the autumn. Domestic sheep are not a major diet component. Coastal animals may prey extensively on seabirds and crustaceans. *Main predators*: Domestic Dog. Behavior probably similar to other subspecies of Chilla. They are tolerant of very different climatic regimes in remarkably hot and dry areas. Crepuscular, they may be seen during both day and night.

DISTRIBUTION *Native*: Chile, Peru. *Introduced*: Falkland Islands (Malvinas). Found in central Chile, from Valparaiso, Valparaiso Province and Copiapo Province, northward to the S part of the province of Atacama, and southward to the vicinity of Concepcion, S Peru. Their presence has been confirmed recently for the coast of S Peru, from Lima to Tacna; it is suggested that the Gray Fox populations in Peru could be a new and distinct subspecies because of their disjunct distribution with respect to other subspecies from which they are separated by the Atacama Desert, a remarkable biogeographical barrier in N Chile. Other populations have been reported to exist on some of the S Atlantic islands, including the Falkland Islands.

HABITAT They inhabit plains and low mountains, but they have been reported to occur as high as 3,500-4,000 m. They generally prefer shrubby open areas. In central Chile, they hunt more commonly in flat, open patches of low scrub than in areas with dense vegetation or ravines. Chillas are tolerant of very different climatic regimes.

CONSERVATION STATUS Least Concern. *CITES*: Appendix II. *Regional status*: Least Concern (Chile), Data Deficient (Peru). In Chile, they are considered frequent in the northernmost and N regions.

PHOTO CREDITS *Basilio Caceres, Daniel Sziklai* and *José Luis Gutiérrez A.*, Pan de Azúcar National Park, Atacama (Chile).

Monte Desert Chilla

LYCALOPEX GRISEUS GRACILIS

BL: 50-54 cm. TL: 27-36 cm. H: 12.8 cm. W: 3 kg. SL: 14.1 cm. SW: 7.4 cm. DF: 42. CN: 74. A small to medium-sized Canid. Coat color is brindled gray, with agouti guard hairs and a short, dense pale undercoat. Pelage is darker than in Northern Chilla (*domeykoanus*). Underparts are pale gray. Head is reddish brown flecked with white. Lower mandible is black as far as the corners of the mouth (chin spot). Ears are large and triangular, white on the inner surface. Limbs are tawny and the thigh is crossed by a characteristic black spot (thigh spot). Tail is long, bushy, gray with a dark dorsal stripe and dark tip with a paler, mottled underside. Females are slightly smaller than males.

Young

Lycalopex griseus gracilis

OTHER NAMES South American Gray Fox, Patagonian Fox, Argentine Gray Fox, Gray Zorro. *French*: Renard gris d'Argentine, renard de Patagonie. *German*: Monte-Kampfuchs. *Spanish*: Zorro gris, zorro chilla, zorro chico, zorro gris chico. *Italian*: Volpe grigia sudamericana. *Russian*: Аргентинская серая лисица.

TAXONOMY Considered a subspecies of Chilla (*L. griseus*). Some authors have suggested it is conspecific with Pampas Fox (*L. gymnocercus*), on the basis of craniometric and pelage character analyses, and that both forms are clinal variations of one single species (*L. gymnocercus*). Includes *zorrula* (Catamarca, Argentina).

SIMILAR SPECIES Southern Pampas Fox (*L. gymnocercus antiquus*) is slightly more robust, with pelage more rufescent, but otherwise very similar (considered conspecific by some authors). Culpeo Fox (*L. culpaeus*) is generally larger, heavier, has a more reddish coloration on the sides, chin is white, and the black spot on the lower rear side of the hind limb is inconspicuous.

REPRODUCTION *Gestation*: 55-60 days. *Young per birth*: 3-8. *Weaning*: 60 days. *Sexual maturity*: Probably 12 months. *Life span*: 14 years in captivity. *Breeding season*: August and September. Births occur in October. There is no specific information for this subspecies, but probably similar to other subspecies of Chilla. Dens are created mostly in rock crevices, under shrubs, in burrows abandoned by other species, or at the foot of tree trunks.

BEHAVIOR *Social behavior*: Solitary, monogamous pairs during the breeding season. *Diet*: Very broad, including small mammals, especially rodents, birds, arthropods, bird eggs, reptiles, fruit and carrion. *Main predators*: Domestic Dog, Cougar. Behavior probably similar to other subspecies of Chilla. Most active at dusk and dawn. Chillas and Culpeo Fox are allopatric in central Argentina. When in sympatry, Chillas are excluded from the richest patches by Culpeo Foxes, which are larger and more aggressive. They den in any available cavity, including caves, hollow trees and the burrows of viscachas or armadillos.

DISTRIBUTION *Native*: Argentina. Found in W Argentina, from Santiago del Estero Province to W Rio Negro Province and Mendoza Province.

HABITAT Plains and low mountains, shrubby open areas.

CONSERVATION STATUS Least Concern. *CITES*: Appendix II. *Regional status*: Least Concern (Argentina).

PHOTO CREDITS *Javier Leonardo D'Uva, Eduardo Christello,* Merlo (Argentina); *Nayer Youakim*, Mendoza Zoo and Cafayate (Argentina).

Common Culpeo Fox

LYCALOPEX CULPAEUS CULPAEUS

BL: 63-88 cm. TL: 32-44 cm. H: 39.5-44 cm. W: 11.4 kg (♂), 8.4 kg (♀). SL: 16.4 cm. SW: 8.6 cm. DF: 42. CN: 74. A medium-sized Canid, the second largest canid in South America. Intermediate in size compared to other subspecies of Culpeo Fox. Coat is grizzled gray in color on the back, with agouti guard hairs, with ears, neck, legs, flanks and top of the head tawny to reddish brown. Fur is longer and denser in the winter months, particularly on the tail. Chin is light tawny. Belly is white to light tawny. Tail is very long, bushy, gray on the upper side, dull tawny on the underside, with a black tip and a darker spot on the upper side near the base. Inconspicuous brownish patch of pelage on back of the thighs. Bright tawny feet and legs. Females are smaller than males.

Young

Lycalopex culpaeus culpaeus

OTHER NAMES Culpeo, Andean Fox. *French*: Renard de Magellan. *German*: Gewöhnlicher Andenfuchs, Andenschakal. *Spanish*: Lobo andino, culpeo, zorro andino, zorro colorado común, zorro culpeo, tío juan. *Russian*: Обыкновенная андская лисица.

TAXONOMY Six subspecies traditionally recognized: *L. c. culpaeus*, *L. c. andinus*, *L. c. lycoides*, *L. c. magellanicus*, *L. c. reissii*, and *L. c. smithersi*. Subspecific status of *L. culpaeus* needs further revision. Includes *ferrugineus* (Andean Cordillera, Argentina, Rios Mendoza, Mendoza Province), *chilensis* (Chile), *amblyodon* (Chile, Valparaiso Province), *albigula* (Chile, central provinces).

REPRODUCTION *Gestation*: 55-60 days. *Young per birth*: 2-5. *Weaning*: 60 days. *Sexual maturity*: 12 months. *Life span*: 11 years. *Breeding season*: Between August and October, monoestrous. Births occur from October to December. Not much is known about parental care. ♀ nurse and care for the young extensively after gestation, but it has been reported that both parents might play a role in the care of offspring.

BEHAVIOR *Social behavior*: Generally solitary, mated pairs with their young during the breeding season. *Diet*: Opportunistic; it mainly feeds on rodents and lagomorphs, and occasionally on domestic livestock and young guanacos; it also feeds on insects, birds, lizards, carrion and fruit. More carnivorous and predatory than other South American Canids. *Main predators*: Cougars occasionally, but this is not an important cause of mortality. Activity patterns vary geographically, being diurnal or crepuscular in central Chile. They have been seen moving about 21 km in the deserts of N Chile. From summer to autumn they are at their highest activity level. They dominate potential competitors, including Chilla Fox (*L. griseus*), Geoffroy's cats, Pampas cats, grisons and various raptorial birds. In captivity, they make a mixed growl and scream noise. Home-range size of ♀ is three times that of ♂ and covers areas partially occupied by more than one ♂. Unafraid of humans.

DISTRIBUTION *Native*: Argentina, Chile. Found in central Chile from the province of Coquimbo southward mainly in the mountainous regions, meeting the range of *L. c. magellanicus* somewhere in S Chile, and W-central Argentina.

HABITAT Many habitat types, from rugged and mountain terrain up to the tree line, deep valleys and open deserts, scrubby pampas, sclerophyllous matorral, to broad-leaved temperate S beech forest in the S, reaching elevations up to 4,800 m.

CONSERVATION STATUS Least Concern. *CITES*: Appendix II. *Regional status*: Near Threatened (Argentina), Least Concern (Chile). Current population is the result of hunting pressure and food availability. It has been persecuted throughout its range for many decades, due to conflicts with humans and the commercial value of its fur. Populations that are harvested intensively may maintain viable levels through immigration from neighboring unexploited areas that act as refugia. When hunting pressure is reduced, Culpeo populations usually can recover quickly, as observed at the Chinchilla National Reserve and at Fray Jorge National Park, in Chile. In Chile, hunting has been banned since 1980, although law enforcement is not strict.

PHOTO CREDITS *Mariela Urra Schiaffino*, Zona Central (Chile); *Jorge Chacon* (Chile); *Andrés Sánchez G.*, Cajón del Maipo (Chile); *Juan Pablo Mejías, Jose Barrera Allendes*, Fray Jorge National Park (Chile).

Northern Culpeo Fox
LYCALOPEX CULPAEUS REISII

BL: 63-88 cm. TL: 32-44 cm. H: 40 cm. W: 6.7-8.1. SL: 15.5 cm. SW: 8.9 cm. DF: 42. CN: 74. A medium-sized Canid. The smallest subspecies of Culpeo Fox, lighter in color, with a shorter muzzle than southern subspecies. Coat is soft and woolly, light grizzled gray in color on the back, with agouti guard hairs, with ears, neck, legs, flanks and top of the head tawny to reddish brown. Fur is longer and denser in the winter months, particularly on the tail. Chin is light tawny. Belly is whitish gray. Tail is very long, bushy, gray on the upper side, dull tawny on the underside, with a black tip and a darker spot on the upper side near the base. Inconspicuous brownish patch of pelage on back of the thighs. Tawny feet and legs. Females are smaller than males.

Lycalopex culpaeus reisii

OTHER NAMES Ecuadorian Culpeo, Andean Fox, South American Fox, Andean Wolf. *French*: Renard de Magellan. *German*: Nördlicher Andenfuchs. *Spanish*: Lobo del páramo, lobo de la sierra, zorro culpeo ecuatoriano, zorro colorado ecuatoriano, lobo colorado. *Russian*: Северная андская лисица. *Quechua*: Atug.

TAXONOMY Considered a subspecies of *L. culpaeus* (Culpeo Fox), but its validity has not been confirmed by genetic analysis. Includes *riveti* (Pichincha Province in Ecuador).

SIMILAR SPECIES Sechuran Fox (*L. sechurae*) is much smaller, coat is much grayer, with little or no rufous coloring on the body. Crab-Eating Fox (*Cerdocyon thous*) is smaller, with a shorter, less bushy tail, and a darker gray color.

REPRODUCTION *Gestation*: 55-60 days. *Young per birth*: 3-8. *Weaning*: 60 days. *Sexual maturity*: 12 months. *Life span*: Probably 11 years in the wild. *Breeding season*: Probably from August to October. There is no specific information available for this subspecies, but probably similar to other subspecies of Culpeo Fox. ♂ assists in caring for pups. At 3 months, young hunt with their parents, and at 5 months they disperse. Dens are usually among rocks, under bases of trees or low shrubs, or in burrows made by other animals, such as viscachas and armadillos.

BEHAVIOR *Social behavior*: Generally solitary, mated pairs with their young during the breeding season. *Diet*: Throughout the year the composition of the diet varies, but consists primarily of mice, rabbits, birds, insects and plants; it may prey on introduced sheep and European hares. *Main predators*: Feral Dogs. There is no specific information for this subspecies, but probably similar to the Common Culpeo Fox. Nocturnal, especially in areas with human disturbance or in areas with Dogs. Home ranges average 4 km². Its abundance is negatively influenced by the presence of feral Dogs, which have been observed chasing Culpeo Foxes.

DISTRIBUTION *Native*: Colombia, Ecuador, Peru. Found along the Andes and hilly regions, from Putumayo and Nariño Provinces in SW Colombia, to Quito, Pichincha Province in Ecuador, to N Peru.

HABITAT Dry rough country and mountainous areas, from 1,800 to 4,000 m. They prefer grass páramo over other habitat types.

CONSERVATION STATUS Least Concern. *CITES*: Appendix II. *Regional status*: Vulnerable (Colombia and Ecuador). In Peru, it is not considered endangered and hunting may be legal if a management plan is approved by the government. It is intensely hunted for traditional witchcraft purposes. The presence of feral Dogs represents a more imminent threat than habitat loss and fragmentation. The status of this subspecies is unknown.

PHOTO CREDITS *Ammit*, *Nick Brown* and *Renata Dajczer*, Cotopaxi National Park (Ecuador).

Bolivian Culpeo Fox

LYCALOPEX CULPAEUS ANDINUS

BL: 63-88 cm. TL: 32-44 cm. H: 39.5-44 cm. W: 11.4 kg (♂), 8.4 kg (♀). SL: 15.5 cm. SW: 8.5 cm. DF: 42. CN: 74. A medium-sized Canid. Smaller and paler than southern subspecies, similar to *reissii*. Coloration is more suffused with buff above, especially anteriorly, the heavy black grizzling starting further back. Nape is strongly suffused with buff. Undersurface mostly whitish, suffused rufous buff. Throat almost white. Chin with an inconspicuous brownish patch. Ears, crown and limbs are rich ferruginous. Fur is longer and denser in the winter months, particularly on the tail. Tail is very long, bushy, dark gray on the upper side, dull tawny on the underside, with a black tip and a darker spot on the upper side near the base. Inconspicuous brownish patch of pelage on back of the thighs. Females are smaller than males.

Lycalopex culpaeus andinus

OTHER NAMES Culpeo, Andean Fox. *French*: Renard de Magellan. *German*: Bolivianischer Andenfuchs. *Spanish*: Lobo andino, culpeo, zorro andino, zorro colorado altiplánico, zorro culpeo, tio juan, zorro colorado puneño. *Russian*: Боливийская андская лисица. *Aymara*: Khamake. *Quechua*: Atoj.

TAXONOMY Considered a subspecies of *L. culpaeus* (Culpeo Fox), but its validity has not been confirmed by genetic analysis. Includes *culpaeolus*, and *inca* (Peru, from Sumbay, Arequipa, altitude 4,000 m, Chile, Argentina, La Pampa Province).

SIMILAR SPECIES Chilla Fox (*L. griseus*) is smaller and less stocky, has less reddish coloration on the sides, chin is black, and has a conspicuous black spot on the lower rear side of the hind limb. Pampas Fox (*L. gymnocercus*) is smaller, pelage coloration is relatively uniform, has a black chin, and a black patch of pelage on back of thighs.

REPRODUCTION *Gestation*: 55-60 days. *Young per birth*: 3-5. *Weaning*: 60 days. *Sexual maturity*: 12 months. *Life span*: Probably 11 years in the wild. *Breeding season*: Probably from June to October. ♂ assists in caring for pups. There is no specific information available for this subspecies, but probably similar to other subspecies of Culpeo Fox.

BEHAVIOR *Social behavior*: Generally solitary, mated pairs with their young during the breeding season. *Diet*: Throughout the year the composition of the diet varies, but consists primarily of mice, rabbits, birds, insects and plants; prey on introduced sheep and European hares less commonly than southern subspecies. In Altos de Chipana, it preys mainly on arthropods, secondarily on lizards, followed by micromammals, and birds. *Main predators*: Feral Dogs. Behavior is probably similar to other subspecies of Culpeo Fox. Mainly nocturnal, but may be less nocturnal when prey is low. Home ranges average 8.9 km², with home ranges of ♀ larger than those of ♂. As predators, they play a role in population control. They also eat fruit and are important in seed dispersal. Additionally, they assist in biodegradation, by eating the carrion of other species. They have been recorded moving linear distances of about 21 km in the deserts of N Chile. They adapt their movements and home ranges to prey availability.

DISTRIBUTION *Native*: Bolivia, Chile, Argentina, probably Ecuador. Found in the Andean range, Altiplano, N Chile from the province of Coquimbo eastward into W Argentina (Jujuy, Salta, Tucumán, Catamarca, and La Rioja Provinces, and southward to W San Juan Province, and probably NW Mendoza Province) and northward to W Bolivia (from Mount Sajama, Oruro Province), and S Peru, Pampa de Arrieros.

HABITAT Rugged, arid or semi-arid mountain ranges, either open or forested, associated with the Andean ranges up to 4,500 m elevation. In most areas, Culpeo Fox uses rugged and forested landscape, while Chilla Fox uses flatlands.

CONSERVATION STATUS Least Concern. *CITES*: Appendix II. *Regional status*: Endangered (Argentina), Vulnerable (Ecuador), Least Concern, hunting banned since 1980, although law enforcement is not strict. Not protected by law in Bolivia, although fur exports have been banned since 1986.

PHOTO CREDITS *Maria Luisa Lopez Estivill* and *Martin Schneiter*, Antofagasta region (Chile); *Elzbieta Sekowska* and *Vadim Ozz*, Potosi (Bolivia).

Achala Culpeo Fox

LYCALOPEX CULPAEUS SMITHERSI

BL: 63-88 cm. TL: 32-44 cm. H: 39.5-44 cm. W: 6.7-8.1 kg. SL: 16.0 cm. SW: 8.9 cm. DF: 42. CN: 74. A medium-sized Canid. The smallest and reddest subspecies of Culpeo Fox. Coat has an intense ferruginous coloration, less gray than in other subspecies. Fur is longer and denser in the winter months, particularly on the tail. Chin, throat and underparts are light tawny. Tail is very long, bushy, tawny, with a contrasting black tip and a black spot on the upper side near the base. Bright tawny feet and legs. Females are smaller than males.

Lycalopex culpaeus smithersi

OTHER NAMES Culpeo, Andean Fox. *French*: Renard de Magellan. *German*: Achala-Pampa-Andenfuchs. *Spanish*: Zorro colorado achaleño, zorro colorado de Achala. *Russian*: Центральноаргентинская (андская) лисица.

TAXONOMY Considered a subspecies of *L. culpaeus* (Culpeo Fox), but its validity has not been confirmed by genetic analysis. Considered a synonym of *L. c. andinus* by some authors.

REPRODUCTION *Gestation*: 55-60 days. *Young per birth*: 2-5. *Weaning*: 60 days. *Sexual maturity*: 12 months. *Life span*: Probably 11 years. *Breeding season*: Between August and October, monoestrous. Births occur from October to December. Reproduction probably as in other subspecies of Culpeo Fox. Not much is known about parental care. ♀ nurse and care for the young extensively after gestation, and ♂ probably assist in caring for pups.

BEHAVIOR *Social behavior*: Generally solitary, mated pairs with their young during the breeding season. *Diet*: They prey primarily on small and medium-sized native rodents (cavids and cricetines), but opportunistically consume other prey when these are abundant. They may also prey on hares, birds, lizards and carrion. Where livestock is abundant, they may consume carrion and young sheep; in these areas, the densities of native rodents are negatively associated with the abundance of livestock. Small livestock is more frequently consumed by the sympatric cougars. There is no difference in diet between seasons. *Main predators*: Feral Dogs, cougars occasionally, but this is not an important cause of mortality. Behavior is probably similar to other subspecies of Culpeo Fox. Mainly nocturnal.

DISTRIBUTION *Native*: Argentina. This subspecies is endemic to the Grandes and Comechingones Mountains, in the provinces of Córdoba and San Luis, in central Argentina. Its presence S of Santiago del Estero is not confirmed. This subspecies is isolated from the other subspecies, 400 km away from populations present in the Andes mountains, with the plains of La Rioja and San Juan Provinces in between.

HABITAT Mountain terrain in the Pampa de Achala, a rugged area with little vegetation, and rolling upland grasslands, at elevations between 1,900 and 2,300 m.

CONSERVATION STATUS Least Concern. *CITES*: Appendix II. *Regional status*: Endangered (province of Córdoba, Argentina). Often hunted because it is believed to prey on livestock. The main threat is persecution to reduce predation on livestock and poultry. Protected in the Quebrada del Condorito National Park.

PHOTO CREDITS *Julián García, José Fernando Cañas Aravena,* Quebrada del Condorito National Park (Argentina); *Federico J. Villegas*, Achala (Argentina).

Patagonian Culpeo Fox

LYCALOPEX CULPAEUS MAGELLANICUS

BL: 80.1 cm (♂), 78 cm (♀). TL: 44.5 cm. H: 42.7 cm. W: 8.4 kg (♂), 7.5 kg (♀). SL: 16.5 cm. SW: 8.9 cm. DF: 42. CN: 74. A medium-sized Canid, the second largest Canid in South America. Larger and grayer than northern subspecies of Culpeo Fox. Coat is long, grizzled gray in color on the back, with agouti guard hairs, heavy and richly colored, the tawny markings intense, and the body with considerable suffusion of tawny on ears, neck, legs, flanks and top of the head. More rufous than Tierra del Fuego Culpeo Fox, with white chest and throat. Fur is longer and denser in the winter months, particularly on the tail. Chin is light tawny. Belly is white to light tawny. Tail is very long, bushy, gray on the upper side, dull tawny on the underside, with a black tip and a darker spot on the upper side near the base. Inconspicuous brownish patch of pelage on back of the thighs. Bright tawny feet and legs. Females are smaller than males.

Young

Lycalopex culpaeus magellanicus

OTHER NAMES Culpeo, Andean Fox. *French*: Renard de Magellan. *German*: Patagonischer Andenfuchs, Magellanfuchs. *Spanish*: Lobo andino, culpeo, zorro andino, zorro colorado patagónico, zorro culpeo, tio juan. *Russian*: Патагонская андская лисица.

TAXONOMY Considered a subspecies of *L. culpaeus* (Culpeo Fox), but its validity has not been confirmed by genetic analysis. Includes *prichardi* (SE Patagonia, Argentina), *montanus* (Cordillera of Patagonia, S Chile and Argentina). Considered a synonym of *L. c. culpaeus* by some authors.

SIMILAR SPECIES Across Chile and W Argentina, Culpeo and Chilla Fox (*L. griseus*) are allopatric in the N and S of their range, and sympatric in central Chile. Culpeo is larger and stockier, and this size difference increases toward the S. Culpeo Fox has a more reddish coloration on the sides, chin is white, and the black spot on the lower rear side of the hind limb is inconspicuous. Darwin's Fox (*L. fulvipes*) is smaller and darker, and its tail is not as bushy.

REPRODUCTION *Gestation*: 58 days. *Young per birth*: 2-5. *Weaning*: 60 days. *Sexual maturity*: 12 months. *Life span*: Probably 11 years in the wild. *Breeding season*: From August to October. ♂ assists in caring for pups. There is no specific information available for this subspecies, but probably similar to the other subspecies.

BEHAVIOR *Social behavior*: Generally solitary, mated pairs with their young during the breeding season. *Diet*: In this region, they consume mainly exotic European hares, unlike in N Argentina and Chile, where they feed mainly on small native mammals. *Main predators*: Feral Dogs. Behavior probably similar to other subspecies of Culpeo Fox. Nocturnal in the absence of human persecution, probably due to the fact that main prey species in this area are nocturnal. Territorial. Home ranges average 4.5 km² in size, similar for ♂ and ♀. They have been recorded moving linear distances of about 7 km in NW Patagonia. They adapt their movements and home ranges to prey availability.

DISTRIBUTION *Native*: Argentina, Chile. Found in S Argentina, S Chile, Magallanes Province, Straits of Magellan and S Patagonia.

HABITAT Patagonian steppe, semi-arid shrublands, forests, up to 4,000 m elevation. In areas where it is sympatric with the smaller Chilla Fox (*L. griseus*) there is no overlap of local territories, and the latter species is able to survive in poorer habitat by supplementing its diet with beetles and plant material, especially from spring to autumn.

CONSERVATION STATUS Least Concern. *CITES*: Appendix II. *Regional status*: Endangered (Argentina), Least Concern (Chile), hunting banned since 1980, although law enforcement is not strict. The introduction of exotic prey species such as European hares and rabbits, as well as small-sized livestock has increased its distribution and abundance in Chile and Argentina. Its populations have also increased in many areas of Argentine Patagonia following the reduction of fur prices and hunting pressure. In the Patagonian provinces of Santa Cruz, Chubut and Río Negro, in extreme S Argentine, conflict exists between sheep stockbreeders and Culpeo Fox.

PHOTO CREDITS *Stuart-Lee*, Puerto Bories (Chile); *Alma Pilar Esteva, Joannis Stefan Duran*, Torres del Paine (Chile); *Michael Toussaint*, Milodon Cave, Puerto Natales (Chile).

Tierra del Fuego Culpeo Fox

LYCALOPEX CULPAEUS LYCOIDES

BL: 80.1-103 cm (♂), 78 cm (♀). TL: 44.5-53 cm. H: 42.7 cm. W: 8.4-14 kg (♂), 7.5 kg (♀). SL: 16.9 cm. SW: 9.1 cm. DF: 42. CN: 74. A medium-sized Canid, the second largest Canid in South America. Largest and heaviest subspecies of Culpeo Fox, with the most dense and luxuriant fur, and the longest muzzle. Overall grayish coloration with gray throat and chest. Ears, neck, legs, flanks and top of the head are tawny to reddish brown. Fur is longer and denser in the winter months, particularly on the tail. Chin is light tawny. Belly is white to light tawny. Tail is very long, bushy, gray on the upper side, dull tawny on the underside, with a black tip and a darker spot on the upper side near the base. Inconspicuous brownish patch of pelage on back of the thighs. Bright tawny feet and legs. Females are smaller than males.

Young

Lycalopex culpaeus lycoides

OTHER NAMES Culpeo, Fuegian Fox. *French*: Renard de Magellan. *German*: Feuerland-Andenfuchs. *Spanish*: Zorro fueguino, zorro culpeo fueguino, zorro colorado fueguino, lobo andino. *Russian*: Огненно-земельская андская лисица.

TAXONOMY   Considered a subspecies of *L. culpaeus* (Culpeo Fox), but its validity has not been confirmed by genetic analysis. Considered a synonym of *L. c. culpacus* by some authors.

SIMILAR SPECIES   Culpeo Fox is larger and stockier than the allopatric Chilla Fox (*L. griseus*), has a more reddish coloration on the sides, chin is white, and the black spot on the lower rear side of the hind limb is inconspicuous.

REPRODUCTION *Gestation*: 55-60 days. *Young per birth*: 3-4. *Weaning*: 60 days. *Sexual maturity*: 12 months. *Life span*: Probably 11 years in captivity. There is no specific information available for this subspecies, but probably similar to the other subspecies. ♂ assists in caring for pups. Young reach adult size in 7 months. Young are born with eyes closed, and at 2 days of age, they weigh about 166 g with a total length of 15.5 cm. Juveniles are still dependent while they begin to hunt with their parents until they are strong enough to fend for themselves.

BEHAVIOR *Social behavior*: Generally solitary, mated pairs with their young during the breeding season. *Diet*: In this region, they consume mainly exotic European hares, unlike in N Argentina and Chile, where they feed mainly on small native mammals. They may occasionally prey on guanacos up to 1 year of age. *Main predators*: Feral Dogs. Behavior is probably similar to other subspecies of Culpeo Fox. Communication in the wild has not been described. In captivity, they make a mixed growl and scream noise. Like other Canids, they are likely to use a broad suite of physical cues, scents, postures and sounds to communicate.

DISTRIBUTION *Native*: Chile. Confined to the island of Tierra del Fuego, and other small islands of Tierra del Fuego Province in Chile. It is not found on Navarrino and Cabo de Hornos Islands. This subspecies has always been considered rare in Argentina.

HABITAT Forest-grassland mosaic, meadows, sclerophyllous matorral, broad-leaved temperate southern beech forest in Tierra del Fuego, up to 1,000 m. Chilla Fox (*L. griseus*) prefers shrubby steppe while Culpeo Fox mainly lives inside the Magellanic forest; this may explain how forest destruction for sheep farming has been advantageous for Chillas and disadvantageous for Culpeos.

CONSERVATION STATUS Least Concern. *CITES*: Appendix II. *Regional status*: Endangered (Argentina), Vulnerable (Chile). Its fur is the most valuable. It has been heavily persecuted by sheep ranchers and pelt hunters over the last 150 years. Population is still declining despite several years of reduced hunting pressure. The main threat in this area is illegal hunting.

PHOTO CREDITS   *Allan Drewitt*, Tierra del Fuego National Park (Argentina); *Remco Douma* and *Pabo Omar Palmeiro*, Lapataia (Argentina); *Rob Sall,* Lapataia Bay, Tierra del Fuego (Argentina).

Wolf-like Canids

WOLVES, JACKALS, COYOTE, DHOLE, AFRICAN DOG AND DOMESTIC DOG

RECOGNITION Wolf-like Canids form a widely distributed group that includes species in the genus *Canis* (Wolves, Eurasian Jackal, Coyote, Dog), *Lycaon* (African Wild Dog), *Cuon* (Dhole), and *Lupulella* (Side-Striped and Black-Backed Jackals). All Wolf-like Canids have a similar basic form: a graceful body with relatively long legs, adapted for chasing prey. The tails are bushy and the length and quality of the pelage varies with the season. The muzzle portion of the skull is much more elongated than that of Felidae. With the exception of the four-toed African Wild Dog, there are five toes on the forefeet but the pollex (known as dewclaw) is reduced and does not reach the ground. On the hind feet, there are four toes, but in some Domestic Dogs, a fifth vestigial toe may be present. They exhibit the typical Canid dental formula, I 3/3, C 1/1, P 4/4, M 2/3 = 42, except Dholes, which have 40 teeth. Chromosome number of all Wolf-like Canids is 2n=78. *Canis* species can hybridize to produce fertile offspring.

PHYLOGENY The first recognized member of the Caninae subfamily, the Fox-sized *Leptocyon*, lived in North America in the early Oligocene (32-30 Ma). Later, in the medial Miocene (12-10 Ma), a Jackal-sized species of the Wolf-like clade began to appear in the form of the taxon *Eucyon*. It colonized Europe by the end of the Miocene (6-5 Ma), and was present in Asia in the early Pliocene (ca. 4 Ma). The genera *Canis* and *Lycaon* are first recorded around the boundary between the Miocene and the Pliocene (6-5 Ma) in the North American continent. While expanding their range into Eurasia and Africa, these Canids went through an extensive radiation, resulting in a series of closely related species with a predominant circumarctic distribution, enduring range expansions and contractions according to the warmer/colder climate cycles. The exact order of events then becomes very hard to follow because of the huge areas potentially covered by various species and the possibility of them crossing to and fro between Eurasia and America. The situation is made even more complex because significant climate changes often caused expansions, as well as reductions or extinctions, affecting a range of species. Coyote represents the only surviving endemic species in the New World, originating from the extinct *Canis lepophagus* 2.5-1 Ma. In contrast, *Canis* species diverged in the Old World during the late Plio-Pleistocene (2-1.5 Ma), colonizing Europe, Asia and Africa, and the radiation gave rise to Canid forms such as Wolves, Dholes and Wild Dogs. The Eurasian *Canis etruscus* and the further descendant form *C. mosbachensis* are regarded as the ancestors of Gray Wolves, Dholes and African Wild Dogs. This large radiation took place in Eurasia and Africa. Wolves emerged by 800,000 years ago and extended their habitat to North America by crossing the Bering Strait 100,000 years ago.

BEHAVIOR The sociality is variable between species, populations and individuals, but they all live in small families and display a range of feeding behaviors from scavenging and solitary hunting to organized attacks by a group of subadults and adults. Reproduction is generally monopolized by dominant females, and non-breeding individuals of both sexes may act as helpers. In contrast to Foxes, where young normally leave within 6-10 months after birth, Wolf-like Canids stay usually at least until the next breeding season or, more frequently, for the next 1-2 years.

DISTRIBUTION Wolf-like Canids occupy every continent except Antarctica, and most species are highly adaptive to a wide range of ecological conditions. They occupy almost every habitat except permanent ice and they are rare in tropical rain forests. Domestic Dogs have traveled with humans to every corner of the planet. Gray Wolves occur in Canada, Alaska and the northern USA, Europe and Asia. African Wolves occur in North and West Africa, while Ethiopian Wolves occur only in a few isolated pockets in Ethiopia. Coyotes, originally restricted to the open and arid plains of the western United States, are now one of the most widely distributed carnivores in North America. Side-Striped Jackals occur from northern South Africa to Ethiopia. Black-Backed Jackals are most typical in East Africa. Golden Jackals can be found in eastern and southern Europe, and parts of Asia. Dholes were historically found in East and South Asia, but their current range has been seriously reduced. African Wild Dogs remain in southern Africa and East Africa.

CONSERVATION The Ethiopian Wolf, with about 500 survivors, is the most vulnerable species; this animal lives only on rodents above 3,000 m on Ethiopian mountains, and its range is now reduced to seven small populations largely isolated from one another on the tops of different massifs. The Red Wolf was extinct in the wild by 1980, and now exists only in a reintroduced population in North Carolina (USA), with less than 150 survivors. The Gray Wolf, the most widely distributed mammal, has become extinct in much of western Europe, in Mexico and much of the USA, and its present distribution is more restricted. The African Wild Dog population may be as low as 6,000, and perversely it does not flourish in the rich game reserves as it is competitively inferior to lions and spotted hyenas. The fate of the Dhole is largely unknown but it has certainly suffered a huge contraction of its range.

Red Wolf
Canis rufus, 80

Eastern Wolf
Canis lycaon, 82

Arctic Wolf
Canis lupus arctos, 84

Mexican Wolf
Canis lupus baileyi, 86

Northwestern Wolf
Canis lupus occidentalis, 88

Plains Wolf
Canis lupus nubilus, 90

Coastal Wolf
Canis lupus ligoni, 92

Tundra Wolf
Canis lupus albus, 96

Eurasian Wolf
Canis lupus lupus, 94

Iberian Wolf
Canis lupus signatus, 98

Italian Wolf
Canis lupus italicus, 100

Tibetan and Himalayan Wolf
Canis lupus chanco, 102

Persian and Indian Wolf
Canis lupus pallipes, 104

Arabian Wolf
Canis lupus arabs, 106

Dingo
Canis lupus familiaris, 108

New Guinea Singing Dog
Canis lupus familiaris, 110

Domestic Dog
Canis lupus familiaris, 112

Ethiopian Wolf
Canis simensis, 116

Northern Coyote
Canis latrans, 118

Eastern Coyote
Canis latrans, 120

Western Coyote
Canis latrans, 122

Mexican and Central American Coyote
Canis latrans, 124

North African Golden Wolf
Canis lupaster lupaster, 126

West African Golden Wolf
Canis lupaster anthus, 128

East African Golden Wolf
Canis lupaster bea, 130

Eurasian Jackals
Canis aureus, 132

Northern Dhole
Cuon alpinus, 144

Southern Dhole
Cuon alpinus, 148

Cape Black-Backed Jackal
Lupulella mesomelas mesomelas, 156

East African Black-Backed Jackal
Lupulella mesomelas schmidti, 158

Sundevall Side-Striped Jackal
Lupulella adustus adustus, 160

Equatorial Africa Side-Striped Jackal
Lupulella adustus lateralis, 162

Kaffa Side-Striped Jackal
Lupulella adustus kaffensis, 164

South African Wild Dog
Lycaon pictus pictus, 166

East African Wild Dog
Lycaon pictus lupinus, 168

West, Central, North African Wild Dog
Lycaon pictus manguensis, 170

Red Wolf

CANIS RUFUS   (PROVISIONAL/SPECIES UNCERTAIN)

BL: 104-125 cm (♂), 90-120 cm (♀). TL: 33-46 cm. H: 61-66 cm. W: 22-41 kg (♂), 20-30 kg (♀). SL: 21.9 cm. SW: 11.7 cm. DF: 42. CN: 78. A large-sized Canid, intermediate between the Coyote and Gray Wolf, slender, long legged with proportionately large ears. Dorsal pelage is variable in coloration and generally is brownish or cinnamon, with gray and black shading on the back and tail. Melanism is uncommon. Tail is bushy and tipped with black. Belly, nose and throat are whitish buff. Muzzle, ears, nape and outer surfaces of the legs are tawny to cinnamon buff. Ears are proportionately larger than those of the Coyote and Gray Wolf. Females slightly smaller than males.

Young

Canis rufus

OTHER NAMES Florida Wolf, Mississippi Valley Wolf. *French*: Loup rouge. *German*: Rotwolf, Sumpfwolf. *Spanish*: Lobo rojo. *Italian*: Lupo rosso. *Russian*: Рыжий волк.

TAXONOMY Its validity as a distinct species is questioned, being considered an hybrid with Gray Wolf and Coyote, or a subspecies of the Gray Wolf. Three subspecies were recognized: *C. rufus floridanus* † (Florida Red Wolf), *C. rufus rufus* † (Texas Red Wolf) and *C. rufus gregoryi*, which is the only surviving subspecies, and the subspecies used for its reintroduction.

SIMILAR SPECIES Coyote is smaller with a more shallow profile and narrower head. Gray Wolf has a more prominent ruff and is larger overall.

REPRODUCTION *Gestation*: 61-63 days. *Young per birth*: 1-8. *Weaning*: Probably 50 days. *Sexual maturity*: 2-3 years. *Life span*: 5-14 years. *Breeding season*: February and March. Peak whelping dates occur from mid-April to mid-May. Monogamous, with both parents participating in the rearing of young. Pregnant ♀ may establish several dens; denning sites include hollow tree trunks, along stream banks and the abandoned earths of other animals. Dispersal typically occurs before individuals reach 2 years of age.

BEHAVIOR *Social behavior*: Extended family units from 1 to 12 individuals, including a dominant, breeding pair and offspring from previous years. *Diet:* Opportunistic predator and will take prey items that are available, mainly small mammals (white-tailed deer, raccoon, nutria and rabbits), but also birds, frogs and turtles. Primarily nocturnal, with crepuscular peaks of activity. More sociable than Coyote, but less so than the Gray Wolf. They may forage individually or hunt in groups of pack members. Territorial, they scent mark boundaries to exclude non-group members. Home ranges from 46 to 226 km². Well adapted to the hot, humid climate of SE United States, with relatively large ears for heat dissipation and molting once a year to replace their cold-season pelage. Vocalizations include the characteristic howl, along with a series of barks, growling and yaps.

DISTRIBUTION *Reintroduced*: United States (North Carolina). Historical range extended throughout E United States from the Atlantic Ocean to central Texas, and in the N from S Ontario (Canada) and N Pennsylvania, S to the Gulf of Mexico. Current range includes reintroduced populations in NE North Carolina, between the Albemarle and Pamlico Sounds. They have also been released on Bull's Island (South Carolina), St. Vincent Island (Florida), and Horn Island (Mississippi), and in Great Smoky Mountains National Park, but breeding and survival have been limited.

HABITAT These habitat generalists can thrive in most settings where prey populations are adequate and persecution by humans is slight. Extensive bottomland river forests and swamps, treeless agricultural lands, pocosins.

CONSERVATION STATUS Critically Endangered. *CITES*: Not listed. It was Extinct in the Wild by 1980, and reintroduced into North Carolina. Total population within the reintroduction area is 70. Abundance outside the reintroduction area is unknown. Approximately 200 are in captivity throughout the United States and Canada. Hybridization with Coyotes is the primary threat.

PHOTO CREDITS B. Bartel/USFWS, Bethany Weeks and Aimee Steeley, Point Defiance Zoo (USA).

Eastern Wolf
CANIS LYCAON   (PROVISIONAL/SPECIES UNCERTAIN)

BL: 105-125 cm. TL: 39-48 cm. H: 60-70 cm. W: 19.5-36.7 kg (♂), 17-32 kg (♀). SL: 24.9 cm. SW: 13.1 cm. DF: 42. CN: 78. A large-sized, lightly-built Canid, intermediate in size between Coyote and Gray Wolf. Coat from black to white, but typically consists of a grizzled grayish brown, mixed with cinnamon, rufous or creamy along the sides and beneath the chest, and salt-and-pepper black and gray guard hairs along the nape, shoulder and tail region. Black coats are relatively rare. Head is relatively large, with broad cheeks. Erect ears rounded at tip, relatively smaller, back of the ears is reddish. Light-colored slanted eyes. Elongated snout, with black nose and large inward-curved canine teeth. Straight bushy tail, relatively short, black tipped. Long legs with large front feet and smaller back feet.

Canis lycaon

OTHER NAMES Algonquin Wolf, Great Lakes Wolf, Eastern Timber Wolf. *French*: Loup de l'Est. *German*: Timberwolf. *Spanish*: Lobo rojo canadiense, lobo americano oriental. *Russian*: Восточный североамериканский лесной волк.

TAXONOMY Its validity as a distinct species has been questioned, being considered the result of hybridization among Gray Wolf and Coyote, or a Gray Wolf subspecies (*C. lupus lycaon*). There is general consensus that the historical and continued sympatric distributions of *C. lycaon*, *C. lupus* and *C. latrans* have led to widespread hybridization, backcrossing, advanced-generation hybridization, and introgression among these three taxa in E North America.

REPRODUCTION *Gestation*: 63 days. *Young per birth*: 3-7. *Weaning*: 42-56 days. *Sexual maturity*: 22 months. *Life span*: 4-15 years. *Breeding season*: February, with most births in April and early May. Only the dominant breeding pair mate; however, when prey in winter is abundant, a wolf pack may have multiple litters. Den sites typically found in conifer dominated forests close to a permanent water source. Suitable soil to construct a den, such as sand, is necessary for excavation. At 6-8 weeks pups are moved from the natal den to an initial rendezvous site within their territory. At 18 weeks, young are large enough to travel and hunt with the pack. They reach adult size by 6-8 months of age, and disperse up to 800 km.

BEHAVIOR *Social behavior*: Family groups of 3-6 animals, consisting of a pair of breeding adults and their young of 1-2 years old; packs usually smaller than in Gray Wolf. *Diet*: Primarily prey on white-tailed deer, but moose and beaver are very important secondary food sources. *Main predators*: Black bear on pups, other Wolves. Year-round residents of Algonquin Provincial Park, but they may travel long distances to find food. Summer home ranges are between 18 and 70 km^2, while winter territories are much larger, ranging from 104 to 311 km^2. The pack has a complex social hierarchy maintained through a variety of vocalizations, body postures and scent marking. They howl singly, to keep in contact with other members of the pack, or in groups, to defend a pack's territory from possible intruders.

DISTRIBUTION *Native*: Canada. Current range Is centered in E-central Ontario in the vicinity of Algonquin Provincial Park, extending W toward the vicinity of Georgian Bay in Lake Huron, and E into Quebec. To the N and NW they come in contact with Gray Wolves and admix with them, but rarely if ever breed with Coyotes. To the S and SE, they contact Coyotes and admix with these. They are considered extirpated throughout the NE United States, but they may disperse occasionally from Canada to NE New York, and Maine.

HABITAT Deciduous and mixed forest landscapes with low human density. It is most prevalent in areas with abundant prey, such as beaver, white-tailed deer and moose.

CONSERVATION STATUS Not evaluated by IUCN. *CITES*: Not listed. *Regional status*: Threatened (Canada). Population is considered stable or increasing, estimated at 1,000 to 4,400 wolves in the W Great Lakes (considered an admixture of Gray and Eastern Wolf), 590 in Quebec, and 500 in Ontario. Main threats include destruction of habitat and range, hybridization with Coyotes, and hunting and trapping, which do not distinguish between Gray and Eastern Wolves.

PHOTO CREDITS *Nancy Barrett*, *Scott Martin*, *Steve Dunford*, Algonquin Provincial Park (Canada).

Arctic Wolf
CANIS LUPUS ARCTOS

BL: 60-140 cm. TL: 30-50 cm. H: 63-79 cm. W: 35-50 kg (♂), 36-38 kg (♀). SL: 24 cm. SW: 14.5 cm. DF: 42. CN: 78. A large Wolf. Long, thick, thoroughly insulated fur. Coat is white year-round, but may be mottled with gray, brown and black. No black phase individuals. Slightly shorter muzzle, more rounded ears and shorter legs, as an adaptation to reduce heat loss. Hair between the pads of the feet. Nails are taupe color. Tail covered with a bushy white fur. Dark spot of fur covering the supracaudal scent gland, about 10 cm from the base of the tail. Slanted almond-shaped eyes, amber to brown or gold, with heavy dark black eye lining. Nose and lips are black. Females are smaller than males, with 5 pairs of mammae. Young are born with a brownish-gray coat and blue eyes.

Young

Canis lupus arctos

OTHER NAMES American Arctic Wolf, Melville Island Wolf, White Wolf, Polar Wolf. *French*: Loup arctique. *German*: Arktischer Wolf. *Spanish*: Lobo polar, lobo blanco. *Russian*: Арктический (полярный) островной волк.

TAXONOMY Considered a subspecies of Gray Wolf (*C. lupus*). Until recently, 24 subspecies of Gray Wolf were recognized for North America, but most authors now propose only 4 subspecies (Nowak and Federoff, 2002): *C. l. arctos* (Arctic Wolf), *C. l. nubilus* (Plains Wolf), *C. l. occidentalis* (Northwestern Wolf), and *C. l. baileyi* (Mexican Wolf). Wolf migration and extensive range obscure possible distinct subspecies through significant interbreeding. Variation within the same subspecies can be quite significant in terms of size and color. Includes *arctos* (found in Northwest Territories, Melville Peninsula and Nunavut, Sverdrup and Ellesmere Islands, and neighboring islands), *bernardi* (found at Banks and Victoria Islands of the Canadian Arctic), and *orion* (Greenland Wolf, found in N Greenland).

SIMILAR SPECIES Distinguished from *C. l. occidentalis* by its smaller size, whiter coloration, narrower braincase, and larger carnassials. Since 1930, there has been a progressive reduction in size in Arctic Wolf skulls, which may be the result of Wolf-Dog hybridization.

REPRODUCTION *Gestation*: 63 days. *Young per birth*: 2-3. *Weaning*: 42-56 days. *Sexual maturity*: 2 years. *Life span*: 7-9 years, 17 years in captivity. *Breeding season*: Once a year, in late March and early April. Births occur in late May to early June, about a month later than southern subspecies. Due to the permafrost they cannot dig dens so instead use rocky outcrops, caves or shallow depressions in the unyielding tundra soil. Young stay in the den for 2 weeks but remain near it for at least a month. Both parents care for and feed the litter, as do yearling and older sibling helpers. After 3 months the offspring officially join the pack.

BEHAVIOR *Social behavior*: Packs from 2 to 20 individuals, depending on food availability. *Diet*: Preys primarily on musk oxen, Arctic hare, caribou and seals; like other subspecies they opportunistically eat all other types of vertebrates available. In contrast to other subspecies, they will prey on anything and eat the entire carcass, including fur and bones. *Main predators*: Polar bear, rarely other Wolves. They can survive in subzero temperatures, in absolute darkness for 5 months per year, and without food for weeks. Like other wolves, they live and hunt in packs, have a social hierarchy and hold territories. They roam large areas due to the low density of prey, with territories of well over 2,500 km^2, much larger than their southern relatives. They mark their territory with urine and their own scent, as do other subspecies. They rarely come in contact with humans and have not suffered the same persecution and near extermination as other subspecies.

DISTRIBUTION *Native*: Canada, Greenland. Found above 67° N latitude. Still found in its original range.

HABITAT Taiga, tundra and barren grounds.

CONSERVATION STATUS Least Concern. *CITES*: Appendix II. Population status is stable. Hunted and trapped primarily by Inuit and other native people, but not threatened. A decline in Arctic prey can severely damage Arctic Wolf populations.

PHOTO CREDITS *Sergey Chichagov,* Klaipeda Zoo (Lithuania); *Josef Pittner*, Parc Omega (Canada).

Mexican Wolf

CANIS LUPUS BAILEYI

BL: 103-157 cm. TL: 35-42 cm. H: 60.9-81.2 cm. W: 30-41 kg (♂), 21-30 kg (♀). SL: 25.6 cm. SW: 14.7 cm. DF: 42. CN: 78. A small Wolf, the smallest subspecies of North America, with long legs and sleek body. Coat is dark yellowish-gray buff, gray or rust, heavily clouded with black over the back and tail, becoming pale buffy along flanks and outer sides of limbs. Solid black or white does not occur. Underparts pale, buffy whitish, varying to pale, grizzled grayish across throat. Feet dull white. Tail grizzled brownish gray above, and light buffy below, becoming black interspersed with a few gray hairs all around near tip. Nose and lips are black. Large head with a short thick muzzle. Top of head, ears and muzzle near ochraceous tawny. Slanted almond-shaped eyes, amber to brown or gold. Tail relatively large, covered with thin long fur. Nails are dark. Females are smaller than males, with 5 pairs of mammae.

Young

Canis lupus baileyi

OTHER NAMES *French*: Loup du Mexique, loup gris mexicain. *German*: Mexikanischer Wolf. *Spanish*: Lobo mexicano. *Italian*: Lupo messicano. *Russian*: Мексиканский волк. *Náhuatl*: Cuetlachtli, cuitlachcóyotl.

TAXONOMY Considered a subspecies of North American Gray Wolf (*C. lupus*). Includes *mogollonensis* (Mogollon Mountain Wolf †), and *monstrabilis* (Texas Gray Wolf †, found in central and S Texas).

SIMILAR SPECIES *C. l. nubilus* has a larger, wider skull, with a lighter pelt color. Coyotes weigh 2–3 times less, have smaller rounder heads, a smaller nose pad, more pointed ears, feet smaller in proportion to the body, and hold their tail downward whereas *baileyi* holds its tail straight out. It looks like a shaggy German Shepherd Dog but has predominantly longer forefeet and legs. Red Wolf (*C. rufus*) is smaller, with a comparatively delicate, narrow, flattened, Coyote-like skull, with relatively larger molars.

REPRODUCTION *Gestation*: 63 days. *Young per birth*: 4-7. *Weaning*: 42-56 days. *Sexual maturity*: 2 years. *Life span*: 15 years in captivity. *Breeding season*: Once a year from mid-February to mid-March. Dens are made under rock ledges, off the slopes of canyon walls or hills, with good visibility of the surrounding area. All members of the pack share in the care and feeding of pups.

BEHAVIOR *Social behavior*: Pack of 4-7 individuals, smaller than in northern subspecies, due to their preference for smaller prey. *Diet*: Prey primarily on elk, white-tailed deer and mule deer; they are also known to eat smaller mammals like javelinas, rabbits, ground squirrels and mice; they have been known to occasionally take cattle. In populated areas they are nocturnal, but otherwise diurnal. Like other subspecies, they are highly social, living in packs, led by a dominant pair. They are highly mobile predators and need room to roam as they have dispersal distances of several hundred km and recorded movements of around 1,000 km. They hunt along runways and hunting beats that follow stream beds, washes, old game trails, and old roads. Vocalizations include barks, howls, growls, whines and whimpers.

DISTRIBUTION *Native*: Mexico, USA. Once numbered in the thousands throughout SE Arizona, S New Mexico, W Texas and N Mexico. Reintroduced in Arizona, New Mexico and Mexico.

HABITAT Mountain forests, chaparral desert scrub, grassland valleys and wooded areas. They avoid desert scrub and semi-desert grasslands since they provide little cover or water. Between 900 and 3,660 m, or lower if they are in transit.

CONSERVATION STATUS Least Concern. *CITES*: Appendix II. *Regional status*: Endangered (USA); being the most endangered subspecies in North America, extirpated in the wild by the 1970s. In 1998, 11 Mexican Wolves were released back into the wild in Arizona (Apache National Forest) and New Mexico (Gila National Forest) in order to recolonize their former historical range. Recently, they have also begun to be reintroduced in Mexico. Estimated populations of 300 individuals in captivity and 100 in the wild in 2015. Major threats are habitat loss and degradation, and persecution for pest control.

PHOTO CREDITS *Glenn Nagel, Chad Horwedel* and *Craig Salvas*, Brookfield Zoo (USA); *Mark Dumont*, Columbus Zoo (USA); *Carol Urban*, Phoenix Zoo (USA).

Northwestern Wolf

CANIS LUPUS OCCIDENTALIS

BL: 112-170 cm. TL: 35-50 cm. H: 68-91 cm. W: 45-66 kg (♂), 36-59 kg (♀). SL: 23-30.5 cm. DF: 42. CN: 78. The largest Canid, and the largest subspecies of Wolf, more robust build than European subspecies, with a larger, rounder head, a thicker, more obtuse muzzle, shorter ears and bushier fur. Coat color ranges from black to nearly white, with every shade of gray and tan in between, with lighter fur on its legs and underparts. Gray or black wolves are most common. Short and thick neck, covered with a bushy fur. Slanted almond-shaped eyes, amber to brown or gold. Long, powerful legs, with broad feet and thick toes. Tail is long and bushy. Females are smaller than males, with 5 pairs of mammae.

black morph

winter coat

summer coat

Canis lupus occidentalis

OTHER NAMES British Columbia Wolf, Mackenzie Valley Wolf, Canadian Timber Wolf, Northern Timber Wolf, Alaskan Timber Wolf. *French*: Loup du Canada, loup de la vallée de Mackenzie. *German*: Mackenzie-Waldwolf. *Spanish*: Lobo del Mackenzie. *Russian*: Северозападный американский волк. *Nunamiut*: Amaguk.

TAXONOMY Considered a subspecies of North American Gray Wolf (*C. lupus*). Includes *alces* (Kenai Peninsula Wolf †), *columbianus* (British Columbia Wolf, found in British Columbia and SW Alberta), *griseoalbus* (Manitoba Wolf, found in N Manitoba and Saskatchewan, NE Alberta, and Northwest Territories), *mackenzii* (Mackenzie River Wolf, found in N Northwest Territories and Yukon), *pambasileus* (Yukon Wolf, found in interior Alaska), *sticte,* and *tundrarum* (Alaska Tundra or Barren-Ground Wolf, found in tundra region and Arctic coast of Alaska, Yukon and Northwest Territories).

REPRODUCTION *Gestation*: 63 days. *Young per birth*: 4-6. *Weaning*: 42-56 days. *Sexual maturity*: 2-3 years. *Life span*: 6-9 years, 17 years in captivity. *Breeding season*: Early January through late February. The alpha ♀ usually bears the only litter in a pack, and the proportion of ♀ breeding and the size of the litter strongly depend on nutrition. Births occur from April to May. Dens are located in a rock crevice or holes dug by the parents or even a tree stump. Pups are born deaf and blind, but can hear within 12 to 14 days, leave the den in 3 to 6 weeks, and by fall, they are large enough to travel and hunt with the pack. They become full-grown in 6 to 8 months.

BEHAVIOR *Social behavior*: Packs of 6-12 wolves, with some packs as large as 20-30. *Diet*: Bison, elk, caribou, musk ox, moose, Dall sheep, Sitka black-tailed deer, mountain goat, beaver, ground squirrel, vole, snowshoe hare, lemmings and salmon. Highly social, living and hunting in packs, with a strong dominance hierarchy. They carry their tails high and stand tall to communicate dominance. Packs often travel 15-50 or more km in a day during winter. They usually trot between 12 and 16 kmph, but they may run at speeds up to 70 kmph. Highly territorial, will defend their territories against intruders. Territory size from 900 km^2 in Yellowstone National Park to 1,500 km^2 in Alaska. Where prey are migratory, they generally track the migrations and can establish separate territories in the different seasonal ranges of their prey. They have keen senses of sight, hearing and smell.

DISTRIBUTION *Native*: Canada, USA. It inhabits parts of the W United States, W Canada, and Alaska, including Unimak Island of the Aleutians. Reintroduced into Yellowstone National Park and central Idaho in 1995; it has since spread into Washington, Oregon and Utah. Its distribution is known only in a general sense, and the boundaries between subspecies are not discrete.

HABITAT Nearly any habitat that supports sufficient prey, mountains, woodlands, and tundra (arid grassland).

CONSERVATION STATUS Least Concern. *CITES*: Appendix II. Estimated population between 7,000 and 10,000 in Alaska in 2006, and 1,200 in N Rocky Mountains (Greater Yellowstone Area, NW Montana, and Idaho).

PHOTO CREDITS *Dennis Matheson,* Grizzly & Wolf Discovery Center, MT (USA); *Ramiro Márquez*; *Graham Dickinson*, Cotswold Wildlife Park (UK); *Leo Keeler, Kim Reese* and *NK Sanford,* Denali National Park, AK (USA).

Plains Wolf
CANIS LUPUS NUBILUS

BL: 117-160 cm. TL: 47 cm. H: 65-80 cm. W: 45-68 kg (♂), 36-41 kg (♀). SL: 23.7 cm. SW: 14 cm. DF: 42. CN: 78. A large-sized subspecies. Long, thick, coarse fur, very variable in color, from gray to black, brown, buff or red, with most specimens being light colored. Lighter fur on its legs and underparts. Black individuals may occur. Short and thick neck, covered with a bushy fur. Slightly rounded ears. Slanted almond-shaped eyes, amber to brown or gold. Long, powerful legs, with broad feet and thick toes. Tail is long and bushy. Females are smaller than males, with 5 pairs of mammae.

summer coat   winter coat

Young

Canis lupus nubilus

OTHER NAMES Great Plains Wolf, Buffalo Wolf, Dusky Wolf. *French*: Loup des plaines, loup des bisons. *German*: Nebraska-Wolf. *Spanish*: Lobo de las grandes llanuras, lobo de Buffalo. *Russian*: Северовосточный равнинный волк.

TAXONOMY Considered a subspecies of North American Gray Wolf (*C. lupus*). Includes *hudsonicus* (Hudson Wolf), *labradorius* (Labrador Wolf), *manningi* (Baffin Island Wolf) and *variabilis* (North Dakota Wolf). This is the most difficult North American subspecies to evaluate, as it has a long history of being in contact and interbreeding with other Wolf populations (*C. l. baileyi* and *C. l. occidentalis*), Eastern Wolf, and Red Wolf and also hybridizing with Eastern/Red Wolf-Coyote hybrids.

SIMILAR SPECIES Coyote is much smaller, with narrower muzzle and black-tipped tail that is held down during running, in contrast to Wolf tail which is held more erect.

REPRODUCTION *Gestation*: 63 days. *Young per birth*: 4-6. *Weaning*: 42-56 days. *Sexual maturity*: 2-3 years. *Life span*: 13 years, 16 years in captivity. *Breeding season*: From early January through early March; however, the higher the latitude, the later the breeding. Usually only the dominant pair breeds. Births occur in late April or early May. Pups are moved from the den to rendezvous sites at 6-8 weeks of age. Various rendezvous sites may be used by a pack throughout the course of the summer. Pups remain at or near these sites while the adults hunt and bring back food. Young become fully grown in 6 to 8 months, and reach adult body weight and length toward the end of their second year.

BEHAVIOR *Social behavior*: Packs of 4-8 wolves. *Diet*: Caribou, white-tailed deer, moose, snowshoe hare, small birds, and rodents such as beaver. Highly social, living and hunting in packs, with a strong dominance hierarchy. Highly territorial, will defend their territories against intruders. Territories are separated on the landscape, and boundaries are marked with urine and feces. Territory size from 60 to 150 km² in W Great Lakes. They usually disperse 80 to 160 km from their natal pack. At any one time 5-20% of the Wolf population may be dispersing individuals. Usually a Wolf disperses to find an individual of the opposite sex, find a territory, and start a new pack. Some dispersers join packs that are already formed.

DISTRIBUTION *Native*: Canada, USA. Found in W Great Lakes region, Northwest Territories and Nunavut, N Manitoba, N Ontario, Quebec, N of Quebec city and St. Lawrence River, Labrador and Minnesota. It has been extirpated from Newfoundland. Its distribution is known only in a general sense, and the boundaries between subspecies are not discrete. The subspecific status of Wolves in S Alaska, the Pacific Northwest, and W and coastal regions of British Columbia is not well known.

HABITAT Nearly any habitat that supports sufficient prey, mountains, woodlands and tundra (arid grassland).

CONSERVATION STATUS Least Concern. *CITES*: Appendix II. Along with *C. l. occidentalis*, with which it shares a long and complex border, it is the most widespread North American Gray Wolf. Although relatively abundant, exact numbers are unknown.

PHOTO CREDITS *North Woods Photo*, International Wolf Center, MN (USA); *Tammy*, Artis Zoo (Netherlands); *Maxime Frechette*, Parc Omega (Canada).

Coastal Wolf
CANIS LUPUS LIGONI

BL: 110 cm. TL: Unknown. H: 61 cm. W: 22.7-51.7 kg (♂), 20.9-43.1 kg (♀). SL: Unknown. SW: Unknown. DF: 42. CN: 78. A dark and small subspecies of North American Gray Wolf, with coarser and shorter hair compared to continental Gray Wolves. Fur coloration varies considerably from pure white to uniform black, with most individuals having a brindled mix of gray or tan with brown, rust and ocher, black, or white. Black color morph is common, while pure white color morph is rare. Slightly rounded ears. Slanted almond-shaped eyes, amber to brown or gold. Long, powerful legs, with broad feet and thick toes. Front legs may show dark stripes. Tail is relatively short, with a black tip. Females are smaller than males, with 5 pairs of mammae.

black morph

Young

Canis lupus ligoni

OTHER NAMES Alexander Archipelago Wolf, Islands Wolf. *French*: Loup de l'Archipel Alexandre. *German*: Alexander-Archipel-Wolf. *Spanish*: Lobo del archipiélago Alexander. *Russian*: Волк Александровского Архипелага.

TAXONOMY Considered by some authors to be a synonym of *C. l. nubilus*. Genetic analyses suggest this subspecies has undergone a distinct evolutionary history, being isolated from continental Wolf populations, with two distinct genetic clusters: the Prince of Wales Island complex, which appears quite isolated, and Wolves in the rest of the Southeast. It has been proposed that all three coastal Wolves, *C. l. ligoni*, *C. l. columbianus* (British Columbia Wolf), and *C. l. crassodon* (Vancouver Island Wolf) should be recognized as a single subspecies, as they are phylogenetically related.

REPRODUCTION *Gestation*: 63 days. *Young per birth*: 1-8, averaging 4.1. *Weaning*: 42-56 days. *Sexual maturity*: 22-34 months. *Life span*: 6-8 years. *Breeding season*: February. They use dens from mid-April through early July with peak activity between early May and June. After early July, most dens are abandoned and pups are located to rendezvous sites typically less than 1 km from the natal den where they remain until October. Dens and rendezvous sites are generally located at lower elevations near fresh water. Dens are usually under the roots of trees and often associated with beaver activity. At this time, the pups typically are full size, although they weigh less than a yearling or adult, and begin traveling with the pack; most disperse the following spring as yearlings.

BEHAVIOR *Social behavior*: Packs of 2 to 12 Wolves, contain a pair of breeding adults plus other adults that may or may not breed. *Diet*: Opportunistic predators, eating a variety of prey species: Sitka black-tailed deer (which may comprise the majority of its diet in some areas), but also North American beaver, salmon, mountain goat, moose, elk, harbor seals and small mammals. Home range size is correlated with pack size, which is positively correlated with the area of winter deer habitat, ranging from 80 km^2 to 450 km^2 in size. They do not often disperse between islands.

DISTRIBUTION *Native*: Canada, USA. It occurs along the mainland of SE Alaska and coastal British Columbia, W of the Coast Mountains and on larger islands except Admiralty, Baranof, and Chichagof Islands and all of the Haida Gwaii, or Queen Charlotte Islands. The N, E and S boundaries of its range are not defined with certainty. A large portion reside within Alaska's Tongass National Forest.

HABITAT Closed-canopy and open-canopy old growth (particularly at low elevations and on S exposures) are the preferred habitats, generally at lower elevations (<100 m) throughout the year and seldom spend time above 400 m. They usually avoid clearcuts, second-growth forests, and roads (which they use most commonly at night).

CONSERVATION STATUS Least Concern. *CITES*: Appendix II. Estimated population of about 850–2,700 individuals, with approximately 62% of the rangewide population occurring in coastal British Columbia and 38% inhabiting SE Alaska. Prince of Wales Island and surrounding islands are estimated to support 50 to 159 wolves. There is growing concern that expanding road access, particularly on Prince of Wales Island, may increase mortality of Wolves there beyond sustainable levels. Not protected.

PHOTO CREDITS *Design Pics Inc.*, Tongass National Forest, AK (USA); *Max Waugh*, Vancouver Island, BC (Canada); *Jack Chapman*, Great Bear Rainforest, BC (Canada).

Eurasian Wolf
CANIS LUPUS LUPUS

BL: 105-160 cm. TL: 51-64 cm. H: 72-85 cm. W: 32-80 kg. SL: 25.6 cm. SW: 15.3 cm. DF: 42. CN: 78. The largest Eurasian subspecies, with animals in Russia and Scandinavia being larger and bulkier than those from western Europe. Fur is relatively short and coarse. Coat color is gray to fawn, occasionally showing a tint of red, with white on the throat that barely extends to the cheeks. Back and front paws may show dark stripes. Winter fur is dense and fluffy with short underfur and long, quite coarse guard hair. Black or white morphs are rare, and mostly the result of Wolf-Dog hybridization. Strong trunk with sloping back. Limbs are long and strong. Black claws. Head is large, heavy, with strong jaws, a long but not pointed muzzle, and broad forehead. Eyes yellow or greenish. Ears relatively small, triangular, with pointed tip, directed forward and widely separated. Tail fairly large, fluffy, hanging down to the tarsal joint. Females are slightly smaller than males, with 5 pairs of mammae.

winter coat

summer coat

Young

color variation

Canis lupus lupus

OTHER NAMES Common Gray Wolf, Middle Russian Forest Wolf. *French*: Loup gris, loup commun. *German*: Eurasischer Wolf, Europäischer Wolf, Gewöhnlicher Wolf. *Spanish*: Lobo euroasiático, lobo europeo. *Russian*: Евразийский волк.

TAXONOMY Considered a subspecies of Gray Wolf (*C. lupus*). Includes *cubanensis*, *campestris*, *arundinaceus*, *altaicus*, *canus*, *desertorum*, *communis*, *orientalis*, *kurjak*, and *variabilis*.

SIMILAR SPECIES North American subspecies have shorter ears, broader forehead, and thicker muzzle, with bushy hair behind the cheek, and its howl is louder, less melodious and protracted, with a stronger emphasis on the first syllable.

REPRODUCTION *Gestation*: 63 days. *Young per birth*: 5-6. *Weaning*: 56-70 days. *Sexual maturity*: 2-3 years. *Life span*: 6 years, 15 years in captivity. *Breeding season*: In January-February, and young are born in the end of April-May.

BEHAVIOR *Social behavior*: Large packs are non-existent in Europe as Wolf populations are significantly impacted by hunting. Packs consist of family members: parents, pups and 1- to 2-year-old animals. *Diet*: Opportunistic predator, preferring the most accessible and most abundant prey, depending on the season: red deer, roe deer, wild boar, elk, mouflon, chamois, saiga, livestock, hares, mice, voles, marmots, muskrats. Given the chance, they eat carcasses, fish, amphibians, reptiles, insects and berries and fruit. They have very quick digestion and under favorable conditions they can eat twice a day. Each pack inhabits its own territory which is marked and protected from neighbors. Home range size varies from 100 to 300 km². The home range is bigger in winter and in the N of the species distribution range. It can develop a speed of 40-50 kmph, and for shorter distances up to 65 kmph. Very cautious animal, therefore, direct observations are very unlikely. When persecuted intensively, Wolves are active mainly at night or at dawn and dusk.

DISTRIBUTION *Native*: Albania, Armenia, Austria, Azerbaijan, Belarus, Belgium, Bosnia and Herzegovina, Bulgaria, Croatia, Czech Republic, Denmark, Estonia, Finland, France, Georgia, Germany, Greece, Hungary, Ireland, Italy, Kazakhstan, Latvia, Lithuania, Luxembourg, Macedonia, Moldova, Montenegro, Netherlands, Norway, Poland, Romania, Russia, Serbia, Slovakia, Slovenia, Sweden, Switzerland, Ukraine, United Kingdom. In the 1980s, Wolf distribution range in Europe reached its minimum. However, in recent years there has been an increasing trend both for the range and population size.

HABITAT Forest, steppe zone, peat bogs. They also occur in farmlands provided that they are interspersed with forest patches and other suitable hideaways. In such places, synanthrope Wolf packs can form; they depend on humans for food and feed on livestock and their carcasses as well as at dump sites.

CONSERVATION STATUS Least Concern. *CITES*: Appendix II. *Regional status*: Endangered or Vulnerable (Sweden, Norway, Germany, France, Poland). Estimated total population in Europe is likely to exceed 10,000, and 40,000 in Russia. Protected by law in most European Union countries. Legally hunted in Russia, Belarus, Ukraine, Macedonia and Albania. Limited legal hunting is also carried out in Finland, Norway, Lithuania, Latvia, Estonia, Bulgaria, Romania and Slovakia.

PHOTO CREDITS *Kjetil Kolbjornsrud* (Norway); *Emmanuel Keller*, Steinerberg (Switzerland); *Vilmos Vincze*, Veresegyház (Hungary), *Erik Bundgaard*, *Thomas Krüger*, Altenfelden (Austria).

Tundra Wolf

CANIS LUPUS ALBUS

BL: 112-146 cm. TL: 41-52 cm. H: 75 cm. W: 40 kg (♂), 36.6 kg (♀). SL: 25.5 cm. SW: 14.6 cm. DF: 42. CN: 78. One of the largest subspecies of Wolf, slightly smaller than the Eurasian Wolf. Pelage is very long, dense, fluffy and soft. Coat color is very light, whitish to light gray with a reddish shade. Flanks, chest, paws and belly vividly white. Older animals are lighter in color, while juveniles have bluish-gray shades. Winter coat is darker, very luxuriant. Narrow belt of blackish hair along the back. Melanism is rare. A strong trunk with sloping back, with high shoulders and a lower, but strong and wide croup. Head large, heavy, with strong jaws, long but not pointed muzzle, and broad forehead. Eyes are yellow, widely separated and small. Ears relatively small, triangular in form with pointed tip, directed forward and widely separated. Limbs are long and strong, claws black. Tail fairly large, fluffy, hanging down to the tarsal joint. Females are slightly smaller than males.

Canis lupus albus

OTHER NAMES Eurasian Arctic Wolf, Turukhan Wolf. *French*: Loup de Sibérie. *German*: Polarwolf. *Spanish*: Lobo de tundra. *Italian*: Lupo della tundra. *Russian*: Тундровый волк.

SUBSPECIES Considered a subspecies of Gray Wolf (*C. lupus*). Includes *turuchanensis* (Turuchan Wolf), *kamtschaticus* (Kamchatka Wolf) and *dybowskii* (Southwest Kamchatka Wolf).

REPRODUCTION *Gestation*: 63 days. *Young per birth*: 2-6. *Weaning*: 45 days. *Sexual maturity*: 24 months. *Life span*: 16 years in captivity. *Breeding season*: Due to the high latitude of their environment, they breed much later in the year than most other Wolves, usually in late March through April. Heat lasts approximately 2 weeks. Parturition takes place in the warm months, when food stocks increase and become varied.

BEHAVIOR *Social behavior*: In summer, in the time of parturition and rearing the pups, adult Wolves live in pairs, while yearlings live singly or in small groups, not far from the parents. In winter, the yearlings join the adults with this year's young, forming a pack. Strange animals, born to other parents, are not admitted into the pack and are regarded as enemies. The average size of a pack is 5-10 individuals. *Diet*: They primarily prey on large mammals such as deer, wapiti, moose, caribou, bison, musk ox and mountain sheep. Their smallest prey taken consistently is beaver. They may also eat berries and fruits. Cannibalism is not rare; in times of hunger in winter, the pack often attacks weak or injured animals. Hungry Wolves fight fiercely for food, and frequently kill the weaker ones, which are afterward almost always consumed. They lead a nomadic way of life for most of the year, not adhering to stable hunting regions, and move great distances. Twice yearly they accomplish large meridional migrations connected with the driving of the deer herds. A small population of Wolves remains on the tundra in winter. They move out to the seacoast and near fishery stations, where only small herds of reindeer belonging to hunters engaged in the Arctic Fox harvest remain; the Wolves feed on fish and other animal waste. Places of diurnal rest, where dens are also located during the reproductive season, are usually especially well protected and are characteristically near watering places. The hunting territories of Wolves are various, and are restricted only by the possibilities of capturing food. Territories are distinguished by scent marks, where Wolves urinate.

DISTRIBUTION *Native*: Russia. Found in the tundra zone and the forest tundra of the European and Asian parts of Russia and in Kamchatka. Although they were eliminated from some of the Arctic islands N of Siberia, they have been recently seen on Wrangel Island. Outside the boundaries of Russia, they are perhaps in the extreme N of the Scandinavian peninsula, in Finland.

HABITAT Arctic and boreal regions of Russia roughly between 65 and 71° latitude. Wolves prefer to remain in the forest tundra and mossy bogs with less deep and more firm snow cover.

CONSERVATION STATUS Least Concern. *CITES*: Appendix II. *Regional status*: Not protected (Russia); its hunting is possible all year-round, being incentivized in some areas. They are especially vulnerable to the fur trade, as their pelages are more luxuriant than those of Eurasian Wolves.

PHOTO CREDITS *Pascale Delalandre,* Wolf Park, Gevaudan (France); *fStop Images GmbH*, Kurile Lake, Kamchatka Peninsula (Russia); *Alex Kantorovich*, Moscow Zoo (Russia); *Sergey Chichagov*, Yakutia (Russia).

Iberian Wolf

CANIS LUPUS SIGNATUS

BL: 100-130 cm. TL: 35-40 cm. H: 70-80 cm. W: 35-40 kg (♂), 25-30 kg (♀). SL: 23.2 cm. SW: 13.8 cm. DF: 42. CN: 78. A medium-sized Wolf, smaller, with a thinner build than European and North American subspecies, but bigger than North African subspecies. Coat color varies from a lighter gray or ocher in the summer to a darker reddish brown during the winter. Pelage variation is not as extreme as in their North American counterparts. Underbelly and legs are fawn. Distinctive dark vertical marks on the front legs. Dark mark along the saddle and tail. White marks on the upper lips, cheek (masseteric spot) and throat. Russet markings behind the ears. Eyes are generally pale yellow or amber. Dark marks on the tail and front legs. Females are slightly smaller than males, and have smaller heads. Young individuals have generally gray tones in winter, while in summer they present a characteristic dark brown color.

Young

Canis lupus signatus

OTHER NAMES *French*: Loup ibérique. *German*: Iberischer Wolf. *Spanish*: Lobo ibérico. *Portuguese*: Lobo. *Italian*: Lupo iberico. *Russian*: Иберийский волк.

TAXONOMY Considered a subspecies of Gray Wolf (*C. lupus*). Although this subspecies is not commonly recognized, morphometric analysis and molecular markers have shown a notable differentiation between Iberian Wolves and those found elsewhere in Eurasia. Includes *deitanus* (Murcia Wolf †, from SE Spain). Considered by some authors synonymous with *C. l. lupus*.

SIMILAR SPECIES This subspecies is distinguished by the black marks along its tail, back, jowls and front legs (*signatus* meaning marked).

REPRODUCTION *Gestation*: 63 days. *Young per birth*: 5-6. *Weaning*: 45-50 days. *Sexual maturity*: 22 months. *Life span*: 8 years, 16 years in captivity. *Breeding season*: At the end of winter (January to March). Only the dominant breeding pair mate. Births occur between May and June, normally in the early morning. The den is always very close to a reliable water source. Cubs are born blind and deaf, and they stay inside the den for 3 to 4 weeks. Once weaned, young rely on other members of the pack to feed them.

BEHAVIOR *Social behavior*: Small packs, up to 10, sometimes only a couple with a subadult. *Diet*: Roe deer, wild boar, sheep, rabbits and hares; in many regions of the Iberian Peninsula ungulates have disappeared and Wolves depend on garbage dumps and domestic livestock, most of which are taken as carrion; with the European Union's banning of leaving dead animals in the field, Wolves are killing more live sheep and cows. Galician Wolves feed off the remains of chickens, pig farms, and foals, Cantabrian Wolves take red deer, roe deer, and wild boar, and Castilian Wolves partly feed off rabbits. *Main predators*: Eagle owl, golden eagle (young).

DISTRIBUTION *Native*: Portugal, Spain. They were once present throughout the Iberian Peninsula, but are now confined to the NE of Spain (N Castilla y León, Galicia and Asturias), N of Portugal, and a few residual populations in the Sierra Morena (Jaén and Córdoba). Recently, they have managed to cross back over the river Duero and have begun to spread southward and eastward: two packs have been detected around Guadalajara and Madrid, and have started to move into Teruel in S Aragon. There is no confirmed presence of its existence in E Spain, although it is possible that some groups persist in the Pyrenees and in Basque Country (*C. l. italicus*).

HABITAT Habitats with low human population density (less than 10 inhabitants/km^2), up to 2,000 m, with protective cover against man, and a high density of prey species such as roe deer and boar.

CONSERVATION STATUS Near Threatened. *CITES*: Appendix II. *Regional status*: Vulnerable (Spain), but not protected N of the Duero River, and limited legal hunting is permitted. Protected in Portugal. Its population is slowly recovering from its 400-500 individuals in 1970 to as many as 2,000 in Spain, and 400 in Portugal in 2007. Population is expanding toward S and E. The small population of Sierra Morena is far from the main population in the N and is classified as Critically Endangered. The Extremaduran populations are believed to be extinct.

PHOTO CREDITS *Ulrike Joerres* and *Gea Strucks,* Gaia Park (Netherlands); *Andoni Canela*, Picos de Europa (Spain); *José R. Castelló*, Barcelona Zoo (Spain).

Italian Wolf

CANIS LUPUS ITALICUS

BL: 95-115 cm. TL: 31 cm. H: 65 cm. W: 25-45 kg (♂), 22-38 kg (♀). SL: 23.4 cm. SW: 13.6 cm. DF: 42. CN: 78. A medium-sized subspecies of Wolf, smaller than the Eurasian Wolf, similar in size to the Iberian Wolf. Coat is generally of a gray-fulvous color, shorter and dark reddish in summer. Black morphs have been reported. Underparts and cheeks are more lightly colored. Dark bands are present on the back, tail tip and occasionally along the forelimbs. Red shades on the head. Eyes are yellow and small. Ears relatively small, triangular in form with pointed tip, directed forward and widely separated. Tail is bushy, with a black tip. Females are slightly smaller than males.

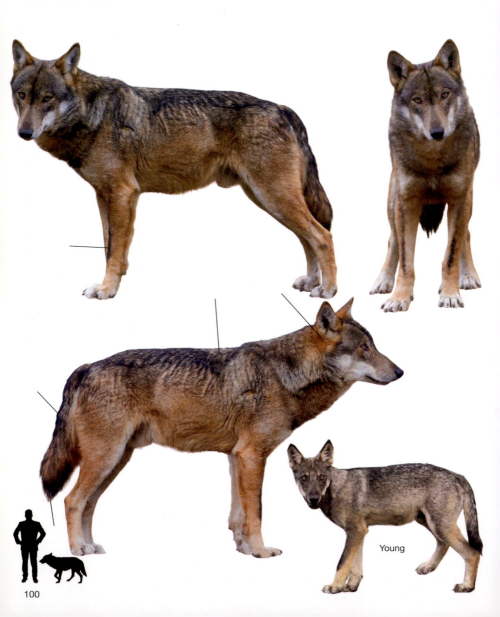

Young

Canis lupus italicus

OTHER NAMES Apennine Wolf. *French*: Loup d'Italie, loup des Abruzzes, loup des Apennins. *German*: Italienischer Wolf. *Spanish*: Lobo italiano, lobo de los Apeninos. *Italian*: Lupo appenninico. *Russian*: Апеннинский волк.

TAXONOMY Considered a subspecies of Gray Wolf (*C. lupus*). Although this subspecies is not commonly recognized, morphometric skull analysis and genetic analyses have shown differences between Italian Wolves and those found elsewhere in Eurasia. Considered by some authors to be synonymous with *C. l. lupus*.

SIMILAR SPECIES Its skull is rounder in form than that of the typical European Wolf, with a relatively narrow palate between the first premolars, a broad frontal shield and shallow jugal, and smaller teeth closely approaching those of Dogs and Golden Jackals in appearance.

REPRODUCTION *Gestation*: 63 days. *Young per birth*: 2-8. *Weaning*: 35-45 days. *Sexual maturity*: 1-5 years. *Life span*: 16 years. *Breeding season*: Mid-March. Pups weigh 250-350 g at birth and open their eyes at the age of 11-12 days.

BEHAVIOR *Social behavior*: Due to a scarcity of large prey in Italy, packs tend to be smaller than average, and usually limited to a nuclear family composed of a reproducing alpha pair and young subadults that remain with their birth family until they are old enough to disperse and produce pups. In areas where large herbivores such as deer have been reintroduced, such as the Abruzzo National Park, packs consisting of 6-7 individuals can be found. *Diet*: Medium-sized animals such as chamois, roe deer, red deer and wild boar. Its diet will also include small animals such as hares and rabbits. It will occasionally consume berries and herbs for roughage. In suburban areas, wolves will feed on garbage and livestock, especially sheep when they are not well protected by the farmer, and other domestic animals too. Nocturnal hunter. They can travel more than 30 km each night while feeding.

DISTRIBUTION *Native*: France, Italy, Switzerland. It was widespread on the Italian Peninsula, including Sicily, until the mid 1800s. It was largely extirpated in the Alps during the 1920s, and disappeared from Sicily in the 1940s. They occur now in the whole Apennines range from Liguria to Calabria and extend into N Lazio and central W Tuscany (provinces of Siena, Grosseto and Pisa). In recent years, they have also established in S France, particularly in the Parc National du Mercantour, in the Massif Central, the E Pyrenees, and the Jura and Vosges Mountains. It may also have expanded into Switzerland, in the S canton of Valais.

HABITAT Mountains and surrounding forested areas with lower human densities and less extensive agricultural utilization.

CONSERVATION STATUS Vulnerable. *CITES*: Appendix II. Population is estimated to be 500-800 individuals distributed along the Apennines. The population has limited exchanges with the population of the W Alps and recent genetic evidence indicates a flux of genes only in the direction toward the Alps. It is vulnerable to local extermination from human pressures. Hybridization with Dogs may also pose a problem. Protected in France, Italy and Switzerland.

PHOTO CREDITS *Arco Images* and *Saverio Gatto*, Civitella Alfedena, Abruzzo (Italy); *Antonio Iannibelli* (Italy).

Tibetan and Himalayan Wolf

CANIS LUPUS CHANCO

BL: 100-125 cm. TL: 30-40 cm. H: 58-85 cm. W: 22-45 kg. SL: 22.9 cm. SW: 12.6 cm. DF: 42. CN: 78. A long-furred subspecies of Wolf, slightly smaller than the Eurasian Wolf, with shorter legs, and longer thinner muzzle, larger than the Indian Wolf. Coat is long and woolly, which seasonally varies in color, usually buff brown, light brown or gray brown, with an admixture of darker black tones on the upper part of the body. Winter fur is soft, long, quite luxuriant, with a well-developed undercoat. Throat, chest, belly and inside of the legs are white to yellowish. Black and white saddle running from the shoulders to the loins. Head is wide, with a long rostrum, pale gray brown, and the forehead grizzled with short black and gray hairs. Muzzle is pale chestnut, or ochraceous, slightly mixed with gray. Ears are drabby gray or rich ochraceous. Occasionally, a dark stripe of varying intensity may be present on the forelegs. Tail is densely furred with long hairs, black tipped.

summer coat

Young

winter coat

Canis lupus chanco

OTHER NAMES Mongolian Wolf, Chinese Wolf, Korean Gray Wolf, Woolly Wolf. *French*: Loup de Mongolie, Loup de l'Himalaya. *German*: Tibetwolf, Tibet-Wollwolf. *Spanish*: Lobo tibetano, lobo del Himalaya. *Russian*: Тибетский волк, гималайский волк. *Tibetan*: Shanku, chanko. *Kashmiri*: Rame hoon.

TAXONOMY Considered a subspecies of Gray Wolf (*C. lupus*), but some authors suggest it to be a synonym of subspecies *C. l. lupus*. Includes *argunensis, coreanus, dorogostaiskii, niger, filchneri, karanorensis, laniger* and *tschilensis*. Tibetan Wolf and Himalayan Wolf are considered synonyms, but recent genetic studies suggest the Himalayan Wolf may be a distinct subspecies (*C. l. laniger*) or a full species (*C. himalayensis*), being one of the most basal lineages within *C. lupus*.

REPRODUCTION *Gestation*: 63 days. *Young per birth*: 4-6. *Weaning*: 35-45 days. *Sexual maturity*: 2-3 years. *Life span*: 6-10 years, 20 years in captivity. *Breeding season*: Between December and April; the higher the latitude, the later it occurs, with most births occurring in the spring or early summer. A pack usually produces a single litter unless the breeding ♂ mates with one or more subordinate ♀. The breeding pair prevents other Wolves from mating with one another. They prefer denning sites away from human habitation in afflicted regions. At 3 to 4 weeks, young leave the den. They are nurtured by their mother for 2 to 3 months, after which they begin to tag along with their parents hunting.

BEHAVIOR *Social behavior*: Solitary or small packs of 2-3 individuals, rarely more. *Diet*: Deer, blue sheep, saiga, horse, livestock (yak, dzo cow, goat and sheep); when food becomes scarce, it will feed on smaller animals like marmots, hares, ground squirrels, pikas and mice. The recent decline of wild ungulate populations in this area has increased conflicts between people and Wolves. They are diurnal, but rest during the heat of the day. They are well adapted to the cold environment. They are very shy and secretive and run away in human presence. Caves, crevices in rocks, and burrows in sand are used as shelter. They descend down to valleys in winter and ascend to the snowline in summer, migrating with the game. They are usually seen singly but are sometimes encountered in packs. They move over a large territory and the territory is marked by the pack by urine and feces at prominent spots. The whole pack feeds together on the prey.

DISTRIBUTION *Native*: Afghanistan, China, India, Kazakhstan, Kyrgyzstan, Mongolia, Nepal, Pakistan, Turkestan, Uzbekistan. Boundaries with the Indian Wolf to the S, and with other subspecies to the N and W are unclear.

HABITAT A wide range of habitats, including mountainous regions, tundra, forests, plains, deserts, alpine zone and agricultural areas. It prefers bare and open areas. It is abundant on the Tibetan Plateau and found at very high elevations. Not found in rain forests. They tend to wander around villages.

CONSERVATION STATUS Least Concern. *CITES*: Appendix I. *Regional status*: Near Threatened in Mongolia (estimated population over 10,000), Vulnerable in China (estimated population of 6,000), Critically Endangered in India (estimated population of 350 animals, captive breeding population of around 20), not protected in Tibet, and in Pakistan there are around 300-500. Trade of carcasses, pelts, bones, paws, teeth and trophies is important in China and Mongolia. Other threats include habitat loss, and persecution due to depredation on livestock.

PHOTO CREDITS *Emmanuel Keller, Puch Corinne*, Zürich Zoo (Switzerland); *Nayer Youakim*, Beijing Zoo (China).

Persian and Indian Wolf

CANIS LUPUS PALLIPES

BL: 76-120 cm. TL: 29-43 cm. H: 40-71 cm. W: 14-32 kg. SL: 21.5 cm. SW: 12.5 cm. DF: 42. CN: 78. A small to medium-sized subspecies of Wolf, smaller than the Eurasian Wolf, more slightly built, with dense and thin fur and little to no underfur, and whiter lower limbs. Coat varies greatly, from grayish brown to reddish white with gray tones, intermingled with black, especially on the dorsal crest, forehead and tip of the tail, with hair on the back longer. Coat is longer and thicker in winter, redder and shorter in summer, as the longer black and gray fur is shed. Melanism is rare, but almost white individuals have been recorded. Underparts are buff or creamish in color, almost white. Muzzle, cheek and upper throat are white, with ruff-like hair around the cheeks and neck. Pointed muzzle. Eyes yellowish brown. Ears narrow, light rufous on the back. Limbs are paler than the body. Ears are large and narrow. Tail is relatively short and thin, with a black tip. Young are born dark brown, with a white patch on the chest that fades with age. Females slightly smaller than males.

Subadult

Canis lupus pallipes

OTHER NAMES Iranian Wolf. *French*: Loup iranien, loup des Indes. *German*: Persischer Wolf, Indischer Wolf, Südwolf. *Spanish*: Lobo persa, lobo indio. *Russian*: Иранский (персидский) волк, Индийский волк. *Urdu*: Bhaghyar. *Hebrew*: Ze'ev. *Arabic*: Theeb. *Hindi*: Bheriya, nekra, bghana, hundar. *Tamil*: Onai. *Begali*: Hendol. *Marathi*: Landga. *Telugu*: Thodelu. *Kannada*: Tholla. *Gujarati*: Naar. *Kutchhi*: Bhagad.

TAXONOMY Considered a subspecies of Gray Wolf (*C. lupus*). Recent genetic research suggests that Wolves from India may represent a distinct species (*C. indica*).

SIMILAR SPECIES Arabian Wolf (*C. l. arabs*) has a lighter fur, is smaller in size and has a larger head. Tibetan Wolf (*C. l. chanco*) has much more underfur and is heavier set, has a longer muzzle, and a longer crest of black hair on its back.

REPRODUCTION *Gestation*: 63 days. *Young per birth*: 3-13. *Weaning*: 56-70 days. *Sexual maturity*: 22-46 months, occasionally 10 months. *Life span*: 13 years, 16 in captivity. *Breeding season*: In Pakistan from January to April; in India from mid-October to late November, after the rains, with most births in December. The dominant pair breeds, with subdominant ♀ under behaviorally induced reproductive suppression. ♂ help feeding the pups.

BEHAVIOR *Social behavior*: Small packs, rarely exceeding 5-12 individuals; long-term pairs are common; may be solitary in disturbed populated areas. *Diet*: Antelopes (blackbuck), livestock (sheep and goat), feral Dogs, rodents and hares. Almost nothing is known about the ecology, behavior and status of these Wolves. Mostly nocturnal. It usually hunts in pairs when targeting antelopes, with one Wolf acting as a decoy while the other attacks from behind. There have been some reported attacks on humans. Its territories range from 250 to 380 km². They dig deep burrows for daytime shelter, but where food is scarce they may become more nomadic, taking temporary shelter in disused porcupine burrows and natural caves, and they are known to follow prey species during certain seasons and are considered to be migrants. Usually silent, it rarely howls, but sometimes barks.

DISTRIBUTION *Native*: Afghanistan, India, Israel, Lebanon, Kuwait, Syria, Turkey, Pakistan.

HABITAT Shrublands, grasslands, semi-arid pastoral environments and open rocky hills, but not dense forests. Occasionally in open forests. There is also one confirmed record in the Sundarbans mangroves.

CONSERVATION STATUS Least Concern. *CITES*: Appendix II, Appendix I for populations in Pakistan and India. *Regional status*: Endangered (India), with an estimated population of 2,000-3,000. In Turkey they have no legal protection, with an estimated population of 7,000. Israel's conservation policies and effective law enforcement maintain a moderately sized Wolf population. In Afghanistan it is protected. In Pakistan, due to constant persecution it has become very rare, and may became extinct in the E of the country if hunting is not stopped and it is not protected. Threats include killing by local sheepherders, and habitat loss due to intensive agriculture, development and industry. In Iran, hybridization with Dogs is sporadic and can be a threat to Wolf populations if human perturbations increase.

PHOTO CREDITS *Mostafa Ghasemi Nejad* (Iran); *John T. L.* (India); *Viacheslav Belyaev* (India); *Indraneel Dani*, Nagpur (India); *Milind Raut*, Pune (India); *Devvratsinh Mori,* Wadhwan (India).

Arabian Wolf
CANIS LUPUS ARABS

BL: 70-80 cm. TL: 30-34 cm. H: 40-65 cm. W: 18-20 kg. SL: 19.2 cm. SW: 10.9 cm. DF: 42. CN: 78. One of the smallest subspecies of Wolf, with a very lean build and rather long legs. Coat is thin, short, wiry and light in color, varying from light brown through to a grayish yellow, with the underparts being paler or white, with a well developed spinal crest that runs from the start of the cervical region to the base of the tail. Cheeks are usually white. Hair on the back remains long, which is thought to be an adaptation against solar radiation. In winter, coat is thicker and longer, but not as long as in its northern subspecies. Ears are large compared to other subspecies, as an adaptation to dissipate heat. Their middle 2 toes are fused. Eyes are yellow, but may be brown, thought to be an indication of interbreeding with feral Dogs. Tail is long, with a black tip.

Young

Canis lupus arabs

OTHER NAMES Desert Wolf. *French*: Loup d'Arabie. *German*: Arabischer Wolf. *Spanish*: Lobo árabe. *Russian*: Аравийский волк. *Hebrew*: Ze'ev Aravi. *Arabic*: Theeb.

SUBSPECIES Considered a subspecies of Eurasian Gray Wolf (*C. lupus*). Its genetic diversity justifies the subspecific status, but it is not clear the degree to which genetic introgression from Domestic Dogs has influenced its composition and integrity.

SIMILAR SPECIES Persian Wolf (*C. l. pallipes*), which also occurs in the Middle East, N of the distribution of Arabian Wolf, is larger, with thicker, more luxuriant coats. It is not known if the two subspecies interbreed. Neither is information available to indicate whether the two populations share the same habitat, or whether they are spatially or temporally separated. Persian Golden Jackal (*C. aureus aureus*) is considerably smaller than Arabian Wolf, with shorter legs and less robust conformation.

REPRODUCTION *Gestation*: 63-65 days. *Young per birth*: 2-3. *Weaning*: 42-56 days. *Sexual maturity*: 24 months. *Life span*: Probably 10 years. *Breeding season*: Starts in October and runs through to December, unlike in N subspecies.

BEHAVIOR *Social behavior*: Small groups mainly due to lack of prey, tending to congregate together only during the mating season; they hunt alone, in pairs or occasionally in small groups of 3 to 4 Wolves; larger packs if food is less scarce. *Diet*: Small to medium animals including Cape hares, dorcas gazelles, Foxes, small birds, reptiles, rodents and insects, but also feed on carrion, and may eat fruit and plants. Opportunistic feeders, hunting alone, mainly at night, and may prey on domestic animals up to the size of a goat. Active mostly at sunset and night. During the day, they stay under cover, including bushes, boulders and shallow caves. This subspecies rarely howls, perhaps due to the fact that it is usually solitary. The only time it is known to be territorial is when its pups are born. They have large home ranges, from 11 to 33 km^2, which they patrol constantly. They escape the heat by digging deep dens and burrows, but as they cannot survive without water, they do not wander far into the great sand deserts.

DISTRIBUTION *Native*: Egypt, Israel, Kuwait, Jordan, Saudi Arabia, Oman, Yemen. *Extinct*: United Arab Emirates (UAE). It was once found living throughout the entire Arabian Peninsula, but now can only be found in small clusters in S Israel (Arava Valley and Negev Desert, where it may intergrade with *C. l. pallipes*), S Palestine, Oman, Yemen, S Jordan, Saudi Arabia and possibly in parts of the Sinai Peninsula in Egypt. It has not been seen in the wild in the UAE since the 1980s.

HABITAT Desert mountains and gravel plains, in arid and semi-arid open areas of the Middle East, not far from water.

CONSERVATION STATUS Critically Endangered. *CITES*: Appendix II. *Regional status*: Not protected, except in Oman and Israel, but rarely enforced. In Oman, its population has increased since hunting was banned. In Israel, there are between 100 and 150 in the Negev and the Ha'arava. In Syria, it has an estimated population of 200, 50 in Lebanon, 200 in Jordan, and between 300 and 600 in Saudi Arabia. Main threats include interbreeding with feral Dogs, systematic shooting, trapping and poisoning. In Oman they have also contracted rabies.

PHOTO CREDITS *Duha Alhadhimi*, Jeddah (Saudi Arabia); *Alex Kantorovich*, Abu Kabir University Zoo (Israel); *Zachi Evenor,* Tel Aviv Zoological Gardens (Israel); *Jonas Livet*, Sharjah Desert Park (UAE), The I. Meier Segals Garden (Israel).

Dingo
CANIS LUPUS FAMILIARIS

BL: 72-111 cm. TL: 21-36 cm. H: 54.6–60.5 cm. W: 8.6-21.5 kg (♂), 8.3-17.0 kg (♀). SL: 17.6 cm. SW: 10.2 cm. DF: 42. CN: 78. A large-sized Canid, strong to medium build, with long, thin legs. Coat is short, dense and soft, and varies in thickness depending on the climate, sandy to reddish brown, but may be white, sandy yellow, black, or tan and black. Melanism is uncommon. White markings on the chest, muzzle tag, legs and paws. Shoulders may have small, distinctive, dark stripes. Square and narrow muzzle. Ears are large and pointed and lack fur lining the insides. Eyes are almond shaped, amber brown in color. No dewclaws on their back feet. Tail is long and tapered, covered with slightly bushier hair than the rest of the body. Males are larger and heavier than females.

Young

Canis lupus familiaris (Dingo)

OTHER NAMES Australian Wolf. *French*: Dingo. *German*: Austalischer Dingo. *Spanish*: Dingo. *Russian*: Динго (вторично одичавшая домашняя собака). *Local names*: Joogong, mirigung, noggum, boolomo, papa-inura, wantibirri, maliki, kal, dwer-da, kurpany.

TAXONOMY There is currently debate about the correct taxonomy of Dingoes and other wild Dogs. Considered a feral Dog of ancient origins (Jackson et al., 2017), a subspecies of Gray Wolf (*C. lupus dingo*), or a full species (*C. dingo*) by some authors. Two recognized races, based on skull morphology, breeding pattern and pelage coloration: Australian Dingo and Thai Dingo. Includes *tenggerana*.

SIMILAR SPECIES Domestic Dogs and hybrids have smaller canines and carnassial teeth, differences in skull bones, curved foreheads and rounder jawlines. Domestic Dogs also show no seasonal pattern of breeding whereas Dingoes breed only once a year. Dingoes from N Australia are larger than S populations. Australian Dingoes are heavier than Asian ones.

REPRODUCTION *Gestation*: 63 days. *Young per birth*: 2-9. *Weaning*: 3-4 months. *Sexual maturity*: 2 years. *Life span*: 5-15 years. *Breeding season*: April to June, once a year. Pups are raised by the pack in a secluded den, such as a wombat burrow or cave. Subordinate animals may copulate and give birth, but their pups are killed and sometimes eaten by the dominant ♀ and other pack members.

BEHAVIOR *Social behavior*: Solitary, but occasionally form small hunting packs. *Diet:* Mainly mammals, but also birds, reptiles, insects, vegetation and other matter. In pastoral areas, they will attack and kill sheep and cattle. They do not bark, but can growl, howl and whimper. Often live in a stable pack with a communal territory and strict hierarchy enforced by a dominant alpha pair. Pack members frequently live alone, but come together to cooperatively hunt large prey or raise pups. Scent marking with urine, feces or gland extracts is ubiquitous, and may signal territory boundaries, use of shared resources such as water points or hunting areas, or reproductive status. Territory size is dependent upon prey availability and habitat, usually from 25 to 67 km².

DISTRIBUTION *Native*: Australia, China, Laos, Malaysia, Myanmar, Thailand. It is common in Australia in N, NW and central regions, rare in S and NE regions, and probably extinct in the SE and SW regions. It is not found in Tasmania. It is also common in Sulawesi, N and central regions of Thailand. Based on external phenotypic characters, they may also occur in Cambodia, China, Indonesia, Laos, Malaysia, Myanmar, Papua New Guinea, Philippines and Vietnam. Fossil evidence suggests that they arrived in Australia about 5,000 years ago; due to the origin of Dingoes in Southeast Asia, it is theorized that Dingoes were introduced to Australia by Asian seafarers.

HABITAT Habitats generalists, including tropical alpine moorlands, forested snow-clad peaks, arid hot deserts, and tropical wetlands and forests.

CONSERVATION STATUS Vulnerable. *CITES*: Not listed. Estimating its abundance is difficult because the external phenotypic characters of many hybrids are indistinguishable from pure individuals. Pure Dingoes are declining through hybridization with Domestic Dogs.

PHOTO CREDITS *Sylvie Lebchek* (Australia); *Craig Dingle* (Australia); *myself62,* Fraser Island (Australia).

New Guinea Singing Dog
CANIS LUPUS FAMILIARIS

BL: 78-91 cm (♂), 71-89 cm (♀). TL: 22-28 cm. H: 31.8-45.7 cm (♂), 32-42 cm (♀). W: 9.3-14.4 kg (♂), 8.6-12.5 kg (♀). SL: 16.3 cm. SW: 10.1 cm. DF: 42. CN: 78. A medium-sized Canid, relatively short legged and large headed. Coat is very variable, from pale brown, ginger, to black with tan, lighter on belly, inner surfaces of legs, and ventral brush of tail. Sides of neck golden. Black or very dark brown guard hairs on backs of ears and dorsal surface of tail above white tip. White on underside of chin, paws, chest and tail tip. May have white on muzzle, face and neck. Wide cheekbones, narrow muzzles, slightly forward leaning, triangular pricked ears, and triangular obliquely set eyes give their faces a distinctive appearance. Rear dewclaws not present. Tail creamy and bushy on underside. Young are dark chocolate showing gold flecks and reddish tinges.

Young

110

Canis lupus familiaris
(New Guinea Singing Dog)

OTHER NAMES New Guinea Dingo, Hallstrom Dog, Bush Dingo, New Guinea Highland Wild Dog. *French*: Chien chanteur de Nouvelle-Guinée, dingo de Nouvelle-Guinée. *German*: Neuguinea-Dingo, Urwalddingo. *Spanish*: Perro cantor de Nueva Guinea. *Russian*: Новогвинейский динго. *Indonesian*: Anging Penyani.

TAXONOMY Considered a feral derivative of ancient breeds of Domestic Dogs carried to New Guinea during prehistoric times by humans. Some authors suggest it is a Dingo, a distict subspecies (*C. l. hallstromi*), or even a full species (*C. hallstromi*), but there is no firm basis from which to assign a unique Linnaean name to these Dogs. All that is known has been gleaned from the captive population originating from individuals taken from the wild in the 1950s and 1970s. Virtually nothing is known about their natural history.

SIMILAR SPECIES Dingo is larger, with proportionately longer legs and narrower head.

REPRODUCTION *Gestation*: 63 days. *Young per birth*: 4-6. *Sexual maturity*: 2 years. *Life span*: 15-20 years. *Breeding season*: August in New Guinea, once a year. If a ♀ does not become pregnant, she will come into estrus again in 8-12 weeks, a pattern not recorded in other Canids. At the copulatory tie, the ♀ emits a distinctive repetitive sequence of loud, high-pitched yelping screams for several minutes, which has a strong arousal effect. About 3 minutes into the tie, ♀ begins a series of rhythmic abdominal contractions, in which the skin of the flanks and lumbar area is drawn forward. They have a strong tendency to target the genitals for both playful and aggressive bites; a cheek rub may be a marking behavior. Both parents participate in raising young.

BEHAVIOR *Social behavior*: Solitary and small groups of 3-5 individuals with ♂ and ♀. *Diet:* Small mammals, small reptiles, and birds. Little is known about Singing Dogs in the wild. Very shy and elusive. They probably hunt alone and do not live in packs, defending a territory in mated pairs. Although their group numbers may be small, there are social rules and a dominant Dog. Adapted to hunting in very steep, thickly vegetated terrain, with joints and spine extremely flexible for a Canid; they may climb and jump like a cat. They have several unique vocalizations: the howl is similar to a Wolf howl with overtones of whale song. When in a group, one animal starts and then others join on different pitches, each with its own unique voice. Some vocalizations resemble birdcalls. They also whine, yelp, bark and scream. They have a distinctive head toss in which the head sweeps to one side and the nose is rotated through a 90° arc to the midline, then rapidly returned to the starting position.

DISTRIBUTION *Native*: Indonesia (Papua Province), Papua New Guinea. Restricted to the upper mountains, at higher altitudes across the entire central mountain spine of the entire island of New Guinea.

HABITAT Mountains of New Guinea, from 2,500 to 4,700 m. Above the tree line, in the rocky barrens devoid of vegetation apart from lichens and mosses.

CONSERVATION STATUS Vulnerable. *CITES*: Not listed. A recent expedition has documented a healthy population above 4,500 m near Puncak Jaya (Papua Province). Estimated population in the wild is unknown.

PHOTO CREDITS *Matt Randle*, Exmoor Zoo (UK); *Keith Conover*, Los Angeles Zoo (USA); *Heather Paul*, Miller Park Zoo (USA).

Western Dog
CANIS LUPUS FAMILIARIS

BL: 9.5-200 cm. TL: 3-50 cm. H: 6.3-106.7 cm. W: 2.3-90 kg. SL: 12.2-21.1 cm. SW: 8-13.4 cm. DF: 42. CN: 78. A small to very large-sized Canid, with great variation in size, shape and appearance. Coat can be short or long, coarse-haired to wool-like, straight, curly or smooth, and is generally made up of a coarse guard hair and a soft undercoat. Color varies from white through grays to black, and browns from light to dark in a wide variation of patterns, and may display remnants of countershading, with dark coloring on the upper surfaces and light coloring below. Most breeds shed their coat. Head shape may be brachycephalic (broad-based skull and a short muzzle), mesaticephalic or dolichocephalic (narrow skull base with a long, narrow muzzle). Tail is variable in shape and length: straight, straight up, sickled, curled or corkscrewed, and may be absent in some breeds. Some breeds may have a fifth additional claw on the rear feet. Females have 5 pairs of mammary glands and are usually smaller than males.

Young

German Shepherd breed

Canis lupus familiaris

OTHER NAMES Domestic Dog. *French*: Chien. *German*: Haushund. *Spanish*: Perro doméstico. *Russian*: Домашняя собака.

TAXONOMY Considered a subspecies of Gray Wolf (*C. lupus familiaris*). Considered a full species (*C. familiaris*) by some authors, based on differences in morphology, physiology and behavior between Dog and Wolf, as well as data indicating that the split between the two taxa occurred prior to domestication. Two general races are recognized: Western Dogs (*familiaris*) and Pariah Dogs (*indica*). Western Dogs probably originated from domestication events in Europe and adjacent areas, and include most Domestic Dogs of the Holarctic, and most domestic breeds. Dogs in the N parts of Asia and North America are heavily influenced by hybridization with Gray Wolf, while in Asia there is a broad zone of introgression with Pariah Dogs. Feral Western Dogs do not reverse to Dingo-like appearance over time. While all Dogs are genetically similar, selective breeding has reinforced certain characteristics, giving rise to breeds. Modern Dog breeds are non-scientific classifications of Dogs kept by modern kennel clubs. Although breeds are genetically distinguishable, systematic analyses of the Dog genome have revealed only four major types of Dogs: Old World Dogs (Malamute, Shar Pei), Mastiff-type (English Mastiff), herding-type (Border Collie), and hunting-type.

REPRODUCTION *Gestation*: 58-68 days. *Young per birth*: 3-9. *Weaning*: 6-10 weeks. *Sexual maturity*: 6-12 months (later in large breeds). *Life span*: 12 years, to 24 years in captivity. *Breeding season*: Throughout the year, estrous twice a year, lasts 12 days. May be monogamous. Feral ♂ tend to compete for access to receptive ♀. Some feral populations may have a single ♂ and ♀ alpha pair, which dominate mating in a small family group, or pack. ♀ nurse and care for their young until they are weaned; ♂ seem to play no role in raising the young, which is unusual among Canids. In feral Domestic Dog packs, young are cared for by all members of the pack.

BEHAVIOR *Social behavior*: Groups of 2-6, or solitary. *Diet*: Omnivores, with a wide-ranging diet, including vegetables and grains, not being dependent on meat-specific protein; feral Dogs are primarily scavengers. *Main predators*: Wolf, Jackal, Coyote, leopard, spotted hyena, tiger. Feral Dogs are mainly nocturnal and crepuscular. It is the most vocal Canid, although barking appears to have little communication function; body and facial movements, odors, whines, yelps and growls are the main sources of communication. For long-range communication only barking and howling are employed.

DISTRIBUTION Worldwide. There are many commensal and feral populations, but the only ones known for sure to be secondarily wild are those on four islands in the Galapagos.

HABITAT In association with humans, in a wide variety of habitats.

CONSERVATION STATUS Domesticated. *CITES*: Not listed. Feral Dogs impact ecosystems primarily through predation on native wildlife, often resulting in severe population declines, especially of island endemic species. Many abandoned Dogs die from disease, starvation, and exposure, or become road casualties, but some join feral packs and run down the easiest prey available, which is often domestic livestock.

PHOTO CREDITS *Isselee* and *Pfluegler* (German Shepherd breed).

Pariah Dog
CANIS LUPUS FAMILIARIS

BL: 53-83 cm. TL: 20-32 cm. H: 40-63 cm. W: 9.5-20 kg. SL: 18.2 cm. SW: 11.3 cm. DF: 42. CN: 78. A medium-sized Dog of square to slightly rectangular build and short coat. Outer coat is dense, harsh, short to medium in length, usually dark brown to reddish brown, with or without white markings, in some cases pied. Shaded coats, brindles, solid white and dalmatian-type spotting are never seen. White facial markings along the sides of the cheeks and muzzle are not uncommon. Head is medium sized, wedge shaped. Muzzle is pointed, of equal or slightly greater length than the head. Forequarters are erect. Hindquarters are minimally angled. Eyes are almond shaped, dark brown. Ears are held erect, pointed or rounded at the tips, with a broad base, set low on the head. Tail is curled and held high when excited. Males usually larger than females.

Basenji Dog breed

Young

Canis lupus familiaris

OTHER NAMES Aborignal Dog, Feral Dog. *French*: Chien paria. *German*: Pariahund. *Spanish*: Perro paria. *Russian*: Аборигенные породы (домашних) собак.

TAXONOMY Considered a subspecies of of Gray Wolf (*C. lupus familiaris*). Pre-Columbian American breeds, Canaan breed of the Middle East, and some native African and East Asian breeds also belong to this type of Dog. It could conceivably represent a relict population of primarily wild *C. lupus familiaris*.

REPRODUCTION *Gestation*: 63 days. *Young per birth*: 3-9. *Weaning*: 8 weeks. *Sexual maturity*: 6-9 months. *Life span*: 12-15 years. *Breeding season*: In India, ♀ come into season around July to October, and most births occur in winter, from October to December. Unlike Western Dog breeds, Pariah Dogs breed only once a year. During the mating season the estrous ♀ may mate with several ♂.

BEHAVIOR *Social behavior*: Domesticated or feral. Pariah Dogs have a generalized typical appearance and share common characteristics not found in Western Dogs. They are extremely alert, very social and more active during mornings and evenings. They are very territorial and defensive and need good socializing. Breeds that are considered Pariah Dogs include: Indian Pariah, Canaan Dog, Basenji and Carolina Dog. Indian Pariah Dog is an ancient breed that is found all over the Indian subcontinent. They were hunting partners and companion animals and are still found with the aboriginal communities who live in forested areas in India. Canaan Dog is an ancient breed originated from the region encompassing Lebanon, Jordan and Israel. This breed was developed from redomesticated Pariah Dog stock captured from the Negev Desert and Zebulon Coastal Plain. Bedouins still use them for guarding their camps and sheep and for herding their flocks. Basenji Dog is an ancient African breed, first described by Europeans in 1895 in the Congo. They have lived with humans for thousands of years, originally kept for hunting small game by tracking and driving the game into nets. Both Dingoes and Basenji lack a distinctive odor, and are prone to howls, yodels and other vocalizations over the characteristic bark of modern Dog breeds. Carolina Dog comes out of the American Deep South and is thought to be a direct descendant of the ancient Pariah Dogs that accompanied Asians across the Bering Strait land bridge 8,000 years ago.

DISTRIBUTION Exists as commensal and feral populations over much of tropical Asia and on islands as far as New Guinea and historically Polynesia, including Hawaii and New Zealand. The only known secondarily wild population in the Americas, the Carolina Dog, might be extinct, although it was still present at Savannah River Site in South Carolina in 2007. Another wild (presumably secondarily) population, described from mountains of Java as *C. f.* var. *tenggerana*, also appears to be extinct. Other primarily wild populations might still exist in remote areas of Southeast Asia or adjacent islands, although no wild (primarily or secondarily) Dogs exist in Indochina.

HABITAT Domesticated.

CONSERVATION STATUS Domesticated and feral. *CITES*: Not cited. At risk of losing their genetic uniqueness by interbreeding with other Western Dog breeds.

PHOTO CREDITS *Sally Wallis, Jagodka, Onetouchspark and Vivienstock* (Basenji Dog breed).

Ethiopian Wolf

CANIS SIMENSIS

BL: 93-101 cm (♂), 84-96 cm (♀). TL: 29-40 cm (♂), 27-30 cm (♀). H: 53-62 cm. W: 14-19 kg (♂), 11-14 kg (♀). SL: 187 cm. SW: 101 cm. DF: 42 (lower third molar being absent occasionally). CN: 78. A medium-sized, slender Canid, with long legs and a long muzzle, resembling a Coyote both in shape and size. Distinctive reddish coat with a white throat, chest and underparts. Distinctive white band around the ventral part of the neck. Sharp boundary between the red coat and white marks. Broad pointed ears, directed forward. Thick bushy tail with a white base and a black tip. No dark patch marking the supracaudal gland. Front paws with 5 toes, including a dewclaw, hind paws with 4. Females are smaller than males, with a paler coat, and 4 pairs of mammae (only 3 pairs are functional). Young have a charcoal-gray coat with a buff patch on the chest and abdomen.

Young

Canis simensis simensis

Canis simensis citernii

OTHER NAMES Simien Jackal, Simien Fox, Abyssinian Wolf, Abyssinian Red Fox. *French*: Loup d´Abyssinie, kebero. *German*: Äthiopischer Wolf, Äthiopischer Schakal, Semien-Wolf. *Spanish*: Lobo etíope, caberú, chacal del Semién. *Russian*: Эфиопский шакал (волк). *Amharic*: Kai kebero, walgie. *Oromo*: Jeedala fardaa, arouayé.

TAXONOMY Two subspecies sometimes recognized based on skull morphology: *C. s. simensis* (NW of the Rift Valley), and *C. s. citernii* (SE of the Rift Valley; nasal bones longer).

SIMILAR SPECIES Jackals are smaller in size, with relatively shorter legs, and a different brownish to gray coat.

REPRODUCTION *Gestation*: 60-62 days. *Young per birth*: 2-6. *Weaning*: 10 weeks to 6 months. *Sexual maturity*: 2 years. *Life span*: 8-10 years. *Breeding season*: Between August and November, with ♀'s coat turning yellow and woollier, and the tail turning brownish, losing much of its hair. Births occur from October to December. Pups are toothless, with their eyes closed; they emerge from the den after 3 weeks. All members of the pack contribute to protecting and feeding the young, with subordinate ♀ sometimes assisting the dominant ♀ by suckling them.

BEHAVIOR *Social behavior*: Packs of 2 to 6 animals, up to 20, formed by dispersing ♂ and a few ♀ which, with the exception of the breeding ♀, are reproductively suppressed, with a well established hierarchy, with dominance and subordination displays being common. *Diet*: Rodents; occasionally mountain nyala calves, hares, hyraxes. *Main predators*: Spotted hyena, tawny eagle. It hunts alone. Territorial, with stable territories, averaging 6 km² in size, regularly scent marked. They interact aggressively and vocally with other packs. They rest together in the open at night, and congregate for greetings and border patrols at dawn, noon and evenings. They never sleep in dens, and only use them for nursing pups. They may shelter from rain under overhanging rocks and behind boulders. They have been observed forming temporary associations with troops of grazing gelada baboons.

DISTRIBUTION *Native*: Ethiopia. Endemic to the Ethiopian highlands, confined to seven isolated mountain ranges. NW of the Rift Valley there are populations in the Simien Mountains, Mount Guna, N Wollo and S Wollo highlands, and Menz. Extinct in Gosh Meda (N Shoa), Mount Choke and Gojjam. SE of the Rift Valley, in the Arsi Mountains (Mount Kaka, Chilalo and Galama range) and in the Bale Mountains, including the Somkaru-Korduro range.

HABITAT Isolated pockets of Afroalpine grasslands and heathlands, from above tree line at about 3,200 m up to 4,500 m (no recent records of the species at altitudes below 3,000 m). They prefer open areas with short herbs and grasses and low vegetation cover where rodents are most abundant, along flat or gently sloping areas with deep soils and poor drainage in parts.

CONSERVATION STATUS Endangered. *CITES*. Not listed. Estimated population of 300 to 400 individuals. The largest population occurs in the Bale Mountains in S Ethiopia. The population in N Ethiopia (Mount Guna) is functionally extinct. Main threats include loss of habitat due to high-altitude subsistence agriculture, overgrazing of highland pastures by domestic livestock, disease epizootics, road kills and shooting. Protected in Ethiopia.

PHOTO CREDITS *Christophe Cerisier, Arco Images, Robert Pickett, Luc Van der Biest, Will Burrard-Lucas*, Bale Mountains National Park (Ethiopia).

Northern Coyote

CANIS LATRANS

BL: 76.2-83.8 cm. TL: 30.5-39.4 cm. H: 50.8-66 cm. W: 10-18 kg. SL: 16.6-17.5 cm. SW: 9.7-10.4 cm. DF: 42. CN: 78. A medium-sized Canid with slender legs, small feet, prominent erect pointed ears, and a narrow pointed muzzle. A large-sized Coyote, with a pale coloration, lighter-colored upper parts, large ears and tail, with heavy and woolly pelage year-round. Upper parts coarsely mixed buffy gray and black above. Summer coat is predominantly gray, and winter coat is usually lighter in winter, although intensity and amount of coloring varies among individuals. Throat with long hairs sparingly tipped with blackish. Muzzle is dull ochraceous buff to pale fulvous, finely sprinkled with gray hairs above. Cheeks and upper lip are white. Back of ears is fulvous to buff. Eyes are yellowish. Underparts are whitish. Legs buffy ochraceous on outer side, whitish on inner side. Tail very bushy, ochraceous on distal two-thirds, black tipped, with a black patch at the base. Females are slightly smaller than males, with 4 pairs of mammae.

Canis latrans
(Northern Coyote)

OTHER NAMES *French*: Coyote du Nord. *German*: Nord-Kojote. *Spanish*: Coyote del norte. *Russian*: Северный койот.

TAXONOMY There are at least 19 subspecies traditionally recognized, but their validity has not been confirmed by genetic analysis, and due to their dispersion capacity and inbreeding, it is impractical to use this classification. Includes *incolatus, latrans* and *lestes*, which appear to intergrade imperceptibly.

SIMILAR SPECIES Distinguished from Dogs by their habit of carrying their tail low, almost between their hind legs, when running. Coyotes also have more elongate tracks, relatively longer canine teeth, and distinctive cranial features. They differ from Gray Wolves in being much smaller in size, and having smaller feet and skull. Foxes are much smaller.

REPRODUCTION *Gestation*: 58-65 days. *Young per birth*: 5-7. *Weaning*: 35-49 days. *Sexual maturity*: 10-12 months. *Life span*: 9 years, 18 years in captivity. *Breeding season*: From late January to March, with most births occurring from early April to late May. Dens are constructed in rangeland, in protected areas adjacent to farmland, on brushy hillsides, in thickets, and under rock ledges; they may also use abandoned badger, fox, rabbit or woodchuck dens. The young are principally cared for by the ♀, but the ♂ provides some care, and occasionally a nonbreeding sibling may assist. Pups emerge from the den in 2-3 weeks and begin to eat regurgitated food. Young disperse alone or sometimes in groups at 6-8 months of age. Family units may begin to break up as early as August, although they may remain together into November or even later.

BEHAVIOR *Social behavior*: Solitary; mated pairs during the breeding season; less social than Wolves. *Diet*: Opportunistic; diet consisting mainly of snowshoe hares, rodents and carrion, but may also eat marmots, muskrats, ground squirrels, fish, insects, ground-nesting birds, fruits, berries, seeds or grasses. When hunting in pairs or in packs, they may go after larger prey such as Dall sheep, caribou and reindeer, especially reindeer calves. *Main predators*: Wolf, cougar. Most active in the early evening and shortly before dawn; juveniles may be active during the daylight hours. They are highly vocal; the most common call is a long, mournful high-pitched howl that ends in a series of sharp yips and yaps; rarely heard except during the night. Home ranges from 8 to 100 km², home ranges of ♂ overlap considerably, but those of ♀ do not. Coyotes are absent or scarce where Wolves are abundant, and Foxes are similarly less abundant where Coyotes are numerous.

DISTRIBUTION *Native*: Canada, USA. They probably arrived in SE Alaska about 100 years ago.

HABITAT Almost any habitat, including urban areas, where prey is readily available. Prefers short- and mixed-grass prairies, open woodlands, brushy or boulder-strewn areas, and aspen parkland, but it has spread into the boreal forest. They may also be seen in urban areas.

CONSERVATION STATUS Least Concern. CITIES: Not listed. Hunting and trapping permitted. Not protected. The reduction of Wolves from many areas of North America, coupled with land-clearing activities, has contributed to expanding its range. A small number are trapped commercially each year in Alaska.

PHOTO CREDITS *Jessica Ellis/JEllisMedia*, Anchorage, AK (USA); *Moose Henderson*, Yellowstone National Park (USA); *Cathy Hart*, Denali National Park, AK (USA); *Gerry* and *Darren McKenzie*, Elk Island National Park (Canada).

Eastern Coyote
CANIS LATRANS

BL: 76-96 cm. TL: 30.4-38.1 cm. H: 53.3-66 cm. W: 11.3-20 kg (♂), 9.9-17.9 kg (♀). SL: 17.9-19.2 cm. SW: 10.2-10.8 cm. DF: 42. CN: 78. A medium-sized Canid with slender legs, small feet, prominent erect pointed ears, and a narrow pointed muzzle. A medium to large-sized Coyote, rather dark colored, with relatively short ears and a long muzzle. Coat coloration is variable, ranging from dark brown to blond or reddish blond, generally tawny gray brown with black tips. Black color phases have been reported. Upper parts mixed buffy gray and black above. Winter pelage somewhat more buffy. Throat whitish, with long hairs sparingly tipped with blackish, forming a ruff. Cheeks and upper lip are white, muzzle fulvous in color. Small ears, fulvous dorsally. Underparts are whitish. Legs whitish inside, dull fulvous outside. Tail is bushy and drooping, white basally, pale fulvous on distal half and tipped and edged in black. Females are slightly smaller than males, with 4 pairs of mammae.

Canis latrans
(Eastern Coyote)

OTHER NAMES Coywolf. *French*: Coyote oriental, Coyloup. *German*: Südost-USA-Kojote, Kojwolf. *Spanish*: Coyote oriental. *Russian*: Восточный койот.

TAXONOMY There are at least 19 subspecies traditionally recognized, but their validity has not been confirmed by genetic analysis, and due to their dispersion capacity and inbreeding, it is impractical to use this classification. Includes *frustror*, *thamnos* and possibly hybrids between Coyotes and Gray or Eastern Wolves (*C. latrans* var. or *C. latrans* x *C. lycaon*), with additional genetic input from Domestic Dogs. Subspecies appear to intergrade imperceptibly.

REPRODUCTION *Gestation*: 58-65 days. *Young per birth*: 5-12, usually 6 (litter size may be directly related to food availability). *Weaning*: 35-49 days. *Sexual maturity*: 12 months. *Life span*: 9 years. *Breeding season*: From late January to March. Births occur from late April through early May. They only use dens to give birth and nurse their young. They use several dens, with multiple entrances, not only to protect their pups from predators, but also to protect them from fleas and other parasites. Dens may form large underground chambers, up to 1.5-9 m, and usually have a mound of fresh dirt at the the entrance. Dens are hidden in the woods, dug into roots or under trees, occasionally in and around human structures (such as decks, sheds), or abandoned burrows of a badger, woodchuck, Fox or skunk. Both the ♂ and ♀ co-parent the puppies by feeding them regurgitated food. Helpers may also assist with pup rearing. Pups begin to crawl around the den after about 10 days when their eyes first open, and after 3 weeks of age they will venture outside the den to play. Young often disperse at 9-10 months of age.

BEHAVIOR *Social behavior*: Solitary, mated pairs, or in small packs consisting of one mated pair, their new young, and offspring from the previous season. *Diet*: Opportunistic, including small and medium-sized mammals (mice, voles, rabbits, woodchucks, fawns), but also larger mammals where available (adult deer); carcasses of deer are the mainstays of the diet; predation on livestock is minimal, and as long as there is wild prey available, livestock is generally avoided; they may feed on insects, persimmons, berries and other wild fruits during summer. *Main predators*: American black bear, Wolf. Mostly crepuscular and nocturnal, but may be seen during the day. They sometimes travel in large groups but usually hunt in mated pairs. Territorial, advertising their location with urine, feces and glandular markings, and sounds such as howling or yapping, especially during the denning season. They use a complex vocal system.

DISTRIBUTION *Native*: Canada, USA.

HABITAT Almost all available habitats including prairie, forest, desert, mountain and tropical ecosystems. They are most abundant along forest edges near pastures and crop lands and are often found around clearings where trees have been harvested. Its ability to exploit human resources allows it to occupy urban areas.

CONSERVATION STATUS Least Concern. CITIES: Not listed. They are viewed as a nuisance and often unjustly blamed for livestock losses caused by free-running Dogs. They play a beneficial role in consuming large numbers of rodents and rabbits, scavenging dead animals, and removing diseased and injured animals from deer populations. Not protected by law, may be hunted. Its pelt has been increasing in value.

PHOTO CREDITS *Maxime Frechette*, Parc Omega (Canada); *Lindell Dillon*, OK (USA); *John Pitcher,* MN (USA); *Jan Crites*, Batavia, IL (USA).

Western Coyote

CANIS LATRANS

BL: 73-81.5 cm (♂), 75.5-80.2 cm (♀). TL: 27.5-36.7 cm. H: 45-60.9 cm. W: 6.8-18 kg. SL: 15.9-17.4 cm. SW: 8.3-9.4 cm. DF: 42. CN: 78. A medium-sized Canid with slender legs, small feet, prominent erect pointed ears, and a narrow pointed muzzle. A small to medium-sized Coyote, darker and much more richly colored than Northern Coyotes, with larger ears. General color is buffy ochraceous to drab brown or dusky gray, mixed with black hairs. Summer coat is shorter. Throat is whitish, strongly grizzled with black-tipped hairs, forming a ruff. Underparts are whitish to pale fulvous. Long and slender muzzle, cinnamon rufous in color. Cheeks mixed gray and black. Upper lip and chin are grizzled grayish white. Medium to large-sized ears, fulvous dorsally, white inside. Legs are deep fulvous or rufous, paler inside, and may have black markings on the forelegs. Tail is pale fulvous ventrally, white basally, with a black tip, sometimes contains a tuft of white hairs. Females are slightly smaller than males, with 4 pairs of mammae. Pups are dark brown or gray black.

Young

Canis latrans
(Western Coyote)

OTHER NAMES *French*: Coyote de l'ouest. *German*: Westlicher Kojote. *Spanish*: Coyote occidental. Russian: Западный койот.

TAXONOMY There are at least 19 subspecies traditionally recognized, but due to their dispersion capacity and inbreeding, it is impractical to use this classification. Includes *clepticus*, *estor*, *mearnsi*, *ochropus*, *texensis* and *umpquensis*.

REPRODUCTION *Gestation*: 60-63 days. *Young per birth*: 5-7. *Weaning*: 35-49 days. *Sexual maturity*: 10-12 months, but most ♂ and ♀ breed first in second year. *Life span*: 10 years. *Breeding season*: From January or February in the low warm deserts, to March and April at higher altitudes. Most young are born from late April to early May. They are capable of digging their own burrows, but they often enlarge the burrows of woodchucks or badgers to use for their dens. Typically, even when denning in suburban areas, they choose sites where human activity is minimal. Territories frequently contain several den sites, and pups may be moved several times a week to lessen parasites that often infest dens and to avoid discovery by potential enemies. Pups are born blind and cannot open their eyes for about 10 days; they emerge from the den in 3 weeks. By late fall, juveniles may disperse to live independently, although if food resources are adequate, they can remain with their parents through the next year. While the ♀ cares for the new pups, other members of the pack may care for the mother, bringing her food, babysitting and even helping move pups to another den.

BEHAVIOR *Social behavior*: Solitary, mated pairs, or small family groups; pairs tend to remain together for years. *Diet*: Opportunist; primarily small mammals (eastern cottontail rabbit, thirteen-lined ground squirrels, white-footed mice, rats, ground squirrels, gophers, prairie dogs, lagomorphs), and carrion, but also takes some insects, reptiles, amphibians, fruits, and occasionally birds, their eggs, and deer fawns. Locally, some may take sheep and domestic fowl. Searches and pounces, stalks and chases, and may dig out prey. *Main predators*: Cougar. Mostly crepuscular and nocturnal, occasionally diurnal. Hunts either alone, in pairs, or in small family packs. Territorial, actively keeping non-family members outside their territory. Home range size varies depending on food availability. They are capable of running at speeds of up to 65 kmph and they can jump horizontal distances of up to 4 m. They have a good sense of smell, vision and hearing. They can be heard vocalizing (barking and howling) in the evening and night throughout most of the year, but they vocalize less when in the early stages of pup-rearing.

DISTRIBUTION *Native*: Mexico, USA.

HABITAT They inhabit all life zones of the Desert Southwest from low valley floors to the crest of the highest mountains, but especially open plains, grasslands and high mesas. Their natural habitat is open grassland, but they will move to wherever food is available. Found in agricultural lands, and at the edges, and sometimes well into developed areas including cities.

CONSERVATION STATUS Least Concern. CITIES: Not listed. Widespread. Hunting and trapping permitted. Not protected. They are the primary predator of endangered San Joaquin Kit Foxes and may limit the number and distribution of Gray Foxes in the Santa Monica Mountains.

PHOTO CREDITS *Bob Smith Images* and *Fred LaBounty*, Big Bend National Park, TX (USA); *Karen McCrorey*, Tucson, AZ (USA); *John A. Basanese*, Paicines, CA (USA); Don McCullough, Bodega Bay, CA (USA).

Mexican and Central American Coyote

CANIS LATRANS

BL: 73.3-82.6 cm. TL: 30.4-38 cm. H: 45.7-60.9 cm. W: 9-25 kg. SL: 16-19.3 cm. SW: 9.8-10.1 cm. DF: 42. CN: 78. A medium-sized Canid with slender legs, small feet, prominent erect pointed ears, and a narrow pointed muzzle. A small-sized Coyote, darker and redder in color, with larger ears and short muzzle. General color is buffy ochraceous to dark rusty rufous, profusely mixed with black hairs. Throat is whitish, strongly marked with black-tipped hairs. Top of the head grizzled grayish and ochraceous, mixed with black hairs between and above eyes. Muzzle is cinnamon rufous, with black hairs on sides of the face. Ears are relatively large, fulvous dorsally. Underparts whitish, strongly suffused with pale fulvous, with numerous black-tipped hairs. Legs are fulvous, whitish on inner side, and may have black markings on the forelegs. Tail overlaid with black and with larger black tip, pale buffy fulvous below, whitish at base. Females have 4 pairs of mammae.

Canis latrans
(Mexican and Central American
Coyote)

OTHER NAMES *French*: Coyote d'Amérique centrale, Coyote du Mexique. *German*: Zentralamerika-Kojote, Mexiko-Kojote. *Spanish*: Chacal rayado de América central y México. *Russian*: Центральноамериканский койот.

TAXONOMY There are at least 19 subspecies traditionally recognized, based mostly on size, cranial differences and location, but their validity has not been confirmed by genetic analysis, and due to their dispersion capacity and inbreeding, it is impractical to use this classification. Most subspecies appear to intergrade imperceptibly. Includes *cagotis, dickeyi, goldmani, hondurensis, impavidus, jamesi, microdon, peninsulae* and *vigilis*.

REPRODUCTION *Gestation*: 60-65 days. *Young per birth*: 3-12. *Weaning*: 35-49 days. *Sexual maturity*: 10-12 months. *Life span*: 6-8 years. *Breeding season*: From January to March in Mexico, and November to January in Central America. Several ♂ court one ♀ when she comes into estrus, which lasts from 4 to 15 days. ♀ choose one ♂ and normally stay with that ♂ through consecutive litters. Both parents take care of the pups, and the ♂ hunts and brings food to the ♀ during birthing and whelping. Often, older siblings help bring food to the ♀ and pups. Dens are dug or prepared on rocky ledges and brush-covered slopes with good visibility.

BEHAVIOR *Social behavior*: Solitary, mated pairs, or small family groups, from 2 to 4 animals. Monogamous. Bachelor ♂, nonreproductive ♀, and near-mature young may form loose, temporary associations for social contact or hunting. *Diet*: Small mammals, arthropods, fruits and carrion (road-killed mammals, birds, reptiles), but they also readily prey upon poultry, calves and small Dogs. In some arid areas lagomorphs are more important, especially during winter, but in grasslands, rodents and prairie dogs and kangaroo rats predominate. Close to human habitation garbage can be the main component of their diet. The endangered pronghorn antelope is rarely preyed on. Inland food scarcity promotes the displacement of Coyotes to coastal areas, where they have been observed in high densities. In the Vizcaino Desert, arthropods are the most frequent prey in the winter. *Main predators*: Cougar. Mostly crepuscular and nocturnal, occasionally diurnal, and may be seen during the day in the intertidal zone or close to shore. They rest in caves, under fallen trees, or in burrows. Differences in food availability may produce differences in home-range sizes. Adult pairs and groups occupy non-overlapping but contiguous home ranges. They deposit urine scent marks and scats more frequently on the edge than within the interior of their territories. It may compete only to a limited extent with other terrestrial or semi-arboreal carnivores, such as the Gray Fox, hog-nosed skunk, grison, coati, and raccoons, as well as wild cats, such as the jaguarundi and the ocelot. Coyotes vocalize most frequently during the breeding season.

DISTRIBUTION *Native*: Belize, Costa Rica, El Salvador, Guatemala, Honduras, Nicaragua, Panama, Mexico, USA, probably Colombia. It has recently expanded its distribution in Central America from Mexico.

HABITAT Semi-open second-growth forests, agricultural areas, semi-arid lowland plains and low mountains, desert plains coastal dunes.

CONSERVATION STATUS Least Concern. CITIES: Not listed.

PHOTO CREDITS *José Luis Ruiz*, Zoo San Juan de Aragon (Mexico); *Gerardo Marrón,* Guerrero Negro, Baja California (Mexico); *Lindell Dillon*, Rio Grande, TX (USA); *David Rodríguez Arias,* La Brisa, Alajuela (Costa Rica).

North African Golden Wolf
CANIS LUPASTER LUPASTER   (PROVISIONAL/SPECIES UNCERTAIN)

BL: 72.2-93 cm. TL: 29-34 cm. H: 38-40 cm. W: 10-15 kg. SL: 16.3 cm. SW: 8.9 cm. DF: 42. CN: 78. A medium-sized Canid, stoutly built, similar to a small Wolf. Coat is shaggy, grayish brown to yellowish gray in color, with a grizzled appearance, which tends to collect in streaks and spots, with a mane of longer hairs along the back. Underparts, inside of legs, throat, and margins of the mouth are whitish. Muzzle, backs of the ears and the outer surfaces of limbs are reddish yellow. Head is like that of a Domestic Dog with a distinct and rather slender muzzle. Ears are erect, relatively small, slightly pointed, covered in much shorter hair and are rufous behind. Legs long and slender, buffish with a black stripe along the back of the foreleg. Tail relatively short, bushy, black along the top, black tipped, not touching the ground, normally held below the line of the back.

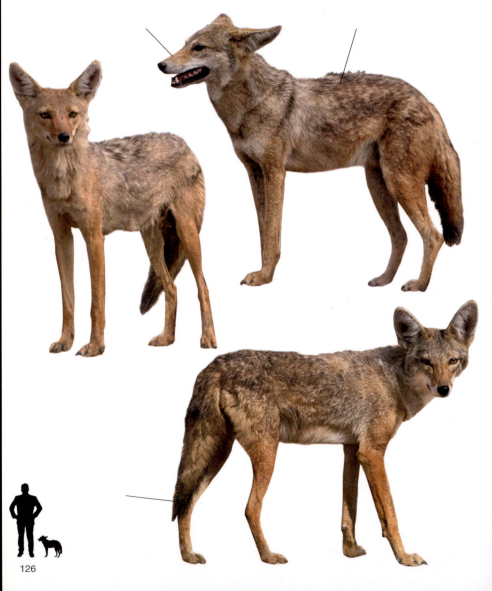

Canis lupaster lupaster

OTHER NAMES Egyptian Wolf, Sudan Golden Wolf, Variegated Wolf, Nubian Wolf, Dwarf Wolf, Algerian Golden Jackal, Morocco Wolf. *French*: Loup africain. *German*: Nordafrikanischer Goldwolf, Ägyptischer Goldwolf. *Spanish*: Lobo dorado egipcio, lobo dorado jaspeado. *Russian*: Североафриканский (золотистый) волк. *Arabic*: Ibn awi.

TAXONOMY At least three subspecies are traditionally recognized: *C. l. lupaster*, *C. l. anthus*, and *C. l. bea*, but recent genetic studies do not support distinctions between them. Formerly considered an African variant of the Eurasian Golden Jackal (*C. aureus lupaster*) or a subspecies of Gray Wolf (*C. lupus lupaster*), but molecular studies have demonstrated that it is distinct and more closely related to Gray Wolves and Coyotes. Considered a synonym of *C. anthus*.

SIMILAR SPECIES Syrian Golden Jackal (*C. aureus syriacus*) is smaller and more richly colored. Arabian Wolf (*C. lupus arabs*) is larger, with shorter coat and head less heavily furred, lighter in color, and with comparatively larger ears, longer limbed, and eyes wider set. Feral Domestic Dogs tend to have shorter coats, be stockier, much more rufous with white patches, though extremely variable, have larger ears, and the tail is not normally black tipped and is often carried high above the level of the back.

REPRODUCTION *Gestation*: 60 days. *Young per birth*: 4-5, up to 8. *Weaning*: 56-70 days. *Sexual maturity*: Probably 12 months. *Life span*: 14 years. *Breeding season*: Early spring, with most births occurring from March to May.

BEHAVIOR *Social behavior*: Sociable, in packs or more often pairs. *Diet*: Very varied; omnivorous and opportunistic, feeding on insects, snails, fish, chickens, young goats and sheep, as well as melons, watermelons, corn, small mammals (hares, rats, ground squirrels, cane rats), ground-nesting birds (francolins, bustards), lizards and snakes, and carrion; it has the habit of carrying off putrid or otherwise seemingly inedible items. *Main predators*: Spotted hyena. Largely nocturnal, especially where disturbed, but also reported active at dusk. Dens in natural caves, tombs or dense scrub. Hearing and scent excellent, sight good. Very vocal, with a characteristic howl often followed by a short yelp delivered just after sunset and before dawn. Barks when excited, growls when annoyed, and female reported to utter a "chak-chak" with closed mouth as warning to pups.

DISTRIBUTION *Native*: Algeria, Central African Republic, Djibouti, DR Congo, Egypt, Eritrea, Ethiopia, Libya, Mali, Mauritania, Morocco, Niger, Nigeria, Somalia, South Sudan, Sudan, Tunisia, Western Sahara. In Egypt, from the Western Desert, including Siwa, Dakhla, and Kharga E to North Sinai, the Delta, Cairo and environs, including Gebel Asfar and Dahsur, Wadi Natrum, Fayoum, the Nile Valley S to Lake Nasser.

HABITAT Agricultural areas, wasteland, and desert margins, rocky areas, and cliffs. Not a desert animal except for semi-arid northern coastal desert in Egypt. Up to 3,800 m in the Bale Mountains of Ethiopia.

CONSERVATION STATUS Not recognized by IUCN. *CITES*: Not listed. Widespread but probably declining in areas where it competes with feral Dogs, although some authors consider this subspecies to be Critically Endangered.

PHOTO CREDITS *Mark Piazzi*, Rift Valley (Ethiopia), *Ken Behrens* (Ethiopia); *Stuart Reeds*, Afar (Ethiopia).

West African Golden Wolf

CANIS LUPASTER ANTHUS   (PROVISIONAL/SPECIES UNCERTAIN)

BL: 72-94 cm. TL: 25.4 cm. H: 40-45 cm. W: 7-15 kg. DF: 42. CN: 78. A medium-sized Canid, stoutly built, similar to a small Wolf. The largest subspecies of African Golden Wolf, with longer ears, a shorter tail and a Dog-like head. Coat is deep gray in color, grizzled with yellow. Neck is grayish fawn, with gray predominating especially on the cheeks and below the ears. Underparts, inside of legs, throat, and margins of the mouth are whitish. Nose and forehead are grayish buff. Upper muzzle, limbs, back of the ears and tail are pure fawn in color. Head is Dog-like. Limbs are long and slender. Tail is relatively short, less hairy, with long hairs beneath and toward the tip buff, black tipped.

Wolf-like phenotype

Jackal-like phenotype

Jackal-like phenotype

Wolf-like phenotype

Canis lupaster anthus

OTHER NAMES Senegalese Golden Jackal. *French*: Loup africain, chacal du Sénégal. *German*: Senegal-Goldwolf. *Spanish*: Lobo dorado de Senegal. *Russian*: Западноафриканский (Сенегальский) золотистый волк.

TAXONOMY Considered a subspecies of African Golden Wolf (*C. lupaster*). Formerly considered an African variant of the Eurasian Golden Jackal (*C. aureus anthus*) or a subspecies of Gray Wolf (*C. lupus lupaster*). Molecular studies have demonstrated that African Wolves are more closely related to Gray Wolves and Coyotes, and appear to have separated from their Eurasian cousins over a million years ago, being sufficiently genetically distinct to be placed in a separate species. Includes *dorsalis*. Recent genetic studies do not support distinctions between subspecies of African Golden Wolves.

SIMILAR SPECIES Egyptian Wolf (*C. lupaster lupaster*) is slightly smaller, has shorter ears, has a black ring round the neck, and a stippled arrangement of black points on the back, smaller ears, a hairy and longer tail, and the head is less Dog-like. It is not known if both subspecies are present in Senegal, if hybridization occurs among them, or if they represent different species.

REPRODUCTION *Gestation*: 63 days. *Young per birth*: 1-9. *Weaning*: 56-70 days. *Sexual maturity*: Probably 12 months. *Life span*: 14 years. *Breeding season*: Unknown, but probably from October to December, with most births from December to March. Young are born in dens, which can take the form of existing earthen burrows of aardvark or warthogs, or rivulets, gullies, road embankments, drainage pipes and other man-made structures. Both parents and offspring from previous litters provision and guard the new pups.

BEHAVIOR *Social behavior*: Breeding pairs. *Diet*: Omnivorous and opportunistic foragers, feeding on invertebrates, fruits, reptiles, rodents (gerbils, mole rats), birds and small ungulates; human refuse is also consumed, and they also scavenge the carcasses of larger herbivores. They may prey on domestic livestock. *Main predators*: Spotted hyena. Active at all hours of the day, particularly during cloudy weather, mainly in the early morning and late afternoon. Nocturnal in areas of human habitation. Territorial. They frequently groom one another, particularly during courtship. Nibbling of the face and neck is observed during greeting ceremonies. When fighting, it slams its opponents with its hips, and bites and shakes the shoulder. Vocalizations include howls, barks, growls, whines and cackles. These howls are used to repel intruders and attract family members. On capturing large prey, it makes no attempt to kill it; instead it rips open the belly and eats the entrails. Small prey is typically killed by shaking, though snakes may be eaten alive from the tail end. It often caches food. It is fiercely intolerant of other scavengers, having been known to dominate vultures.

DISTRIBUTION *Native*: Senegal. There is no confirmed record from Gambia.

HABITAT A wide variety of habitats, but typically prefers semi-desert, short to medium grasslands and savannas.

CONSERVATION STATUS Not evaluated. *CITES*: Not listed. No reliable population estimates are available.

PHOTO CREDITS *Cécile Bloch* (Senegal).

East African Golden Wolf

CANIS LUPASTER BEA   (PROVISIONAL/SPECIES UNCERTAIN)

BL: 64-85 cm. TL: 20-27.5 cm. H: 40-42 cm. W: 6-10 kg. SL: 14 cm. SW: 7.7 cm. DF: 42. CN: 78. A medium-sized Canid, similar to a small Wolf. The smallest subspecies of African Golden Wolf. Coat is sandy or yellow brown in color. Back often has black, white and brown streaks of hair and may even have a dark saddle. Underparts and throat are whitish or pale buff. Relatively long muzzle. Backs of the ears are bright ochraceous. Legs are long and reddish in color, and forelegs have a black stripe in front. Tail is bushy, with the lower half being black. Females are slightly smaller than males, with 4 pairs of nipples. Young lack the black lining on the back and are lighter colored.

Young

Canis lupaster bea

OTHER NAMES Serengeti Golden Wolf. *French*: Chacal commun. *German*: Serengeti-Goldwolf. *Spanish*: Lobo dorado del Serengueti. *Russian*: Восточноафриканский (Кенийский) золотистый волк. *Swahili*: Bweha wa mbuga.

TAXONOMY Considered a subspecies of African Wolf (*C. lupaster*), but recent genetic studies do not support distinctions between them. Formerly considered an African variant of the Eurasian Golden Jackal (*C. aureus bea*) or a subspecies of Gray Wolf (*C. lupus lupaster*).

SIMILAR SPECIES Side-Striped Jackal (*Lupulella adustus*) has shorter ears, a pale side stripe and a white-tipped tail. Black-Backed Jackal (*Lupulella mesomelas*) has a distinct black line separating the back from the flanks. Some individuals in Serengeti National Park may have a black saddle, but it is more patchy and has more diffuse color separation between the back and flanks. Others may have black hair on the sides, which produces a side-striped effect similar to that of the Side-Striped Jackal. Egyptian Wolf (*C. l. lupaster*) is larger and has a darker coloration.

REPRODUCTION *Gestation*: 63 days. *Young per birth*: 1-9. *Weaning*: 56-70 days. *Sexual maturity*: Probably 12 months. *Life span*: 14 years. *Breeding season*: From October to December, with most births from December to March. Young are born in dens and both parents and offspring from previous litters provision and guard the new pups.

BEHAVIOR *Social behavior*: Long-term monogamous pairs and small groups averaging 3 individuals. *Diet*: Omnivorous and opportunistic foragers, feeding on invertebrates, fruits, reptiles, rodents (gerbils, mole rats), birds and small ungulates; human refuse and carrion are also consumed. They may prey on domestic livestock. *Main predators*: Spotted hyena. Active at all hours of the day, particularly during cloudy weather, mainly in the early morning and late afternoon. Nocturnal in areas of human habitation. Pairs defend year-round territories of 0.5-7 km² in size, but will go beyond these boundaries to gain access to fresh carcasses. They can trot for long distances in search of food, and are reported to have the ability to forgo water, obtaining much of their moisture requirements from their food. Densities range between 0.5 and 1 animal per km². Mated pairs will hunt cooperatively which permits them to harvest much larger prey (Thomson gazelles). In some areas, particularly where food resources are clumped, aggregations may occur. Single individuals typically hunt smaller prey such as rodents and birds, using their hearing to locate rodents in the grass and then pouncing on them by leaping through the air, or digging out gerbils from their burrows.

DISTRIBUTION *Native*: Kenya, Tanzania. Found throughout Kenya. In Tanzania, they are restricted to a small section of N Tanzania, between the central Serengeti and the W slopes of Mount Kilimanjaro. In Uganda and Rwanda they are presumably vagrants.

HABITAT Restricted to arid, open grasslands and open bushland. They are rare on the long-grass plains. Highly adaptable to human landscapes and frequently found around villages.

CONSERVATION STATUS Not evaluated. *CITES*: Not listed. No reliable population estimates are available. Population on the S plains in Serengeti National Park has declined by 60% since the early 1970s.

PHOTO CREDITS *Sandy Young, Munib Chaudry*, Ngorongoro Crater (Tanzania); *Chris Wallace, Alicia Wirz* and *Terje Kristoffersen*, Serengeti (Tanzania).

Persian Jackal
CANIS AUREUS AUREUS

BL: 71-81.5 cm (♂), 69.1-74.5 cm (♀). TL: 19.5-23 cm. H: 38-43 cm. W: 7-9 kg (♂), 6.3-9.9 kg (♀). SL: 15.6 cm. SW: 8.9 cm. DF: 42. CN: 78. A medium-sized Canid, with a relatively short body, long legs, coarse and harsh fur, furry tail, short and rounded ears. Muzzle is blunter and broader than in Fox, but more pointed than in Wolf. Winter coat is dull grayish straw with reddish-rusty shades, interspersed with black hairs on the back, and straw-ocher flanks. Summer coat is redder, shorter and coarser. Head, back of ears and sides of legs are reddish rust in color. Inside of ears is dirty strawish white. Underside, throat, inside of forelimbs and the area around eyes and lips are whitish. Flanks well differentiated from back by a more grayish-ocher shade. Lips and rhinarium are black. Medium-sized, bushy tail, dull gray, with a black tip. Round pupils. Females slightly smaller than males, with 4 pairs of mammae. Young are covered with dark sooty-brown hairs.

Canis aureus aureus

OTHER NAMES Asian Jackal, Middle Eastern Golden Jackal. *French*: Chacal doré. *German*: Persischer Goldschakal, Gewöhnlicher Goldschakal. *Spanish*: Chacal dorado persa. *Russian*: Персидский (обыкновенный) шакал. *Persian*: Shakhal, shoghál. *Arabic*: Ibn awa.

TAXONOMY Considered as a subspecies of *C. aureus* (Golden Jackal). As many as 13 subspecies are distinguished across the range (Wilson and Reeder, 2005). However, there is much variation and populations need to be re-evaluated using modern molecular techniques. The African subspecies have been reclassified as African Golden Wolves (*C. anthus*). Includes *hadramauticus* (Arabian Golden Jackal, from Saudi Arabia).

SIMILAR SPECIES Wolf is larger, with a longer and less bushy tail.

REPRODUCTION *Gestation*: 63 days. *Young per birth*: 1-6. *Weaning*: 50-90 days. *Sexual maturity*: 12 months. *Life span*: Unknown. *Breeding season*: Late winter or early spring in Pakistan. In Central Asia, they do not dig burrows, but construct lairs in dense tugai thickets, under tree roots or directly in dense thickets, in long grass plumes, shrubs and reed openings. Pups are born with shut eyelids and soft fur; at the age of 1 month, their fur is shed and replaced with a new reddish-colored pelt with black speckles. Their eyes typically open after 8–11 days, with the ears erecting after 10–13 days. The eruption of adult dentition is completed after 5 months.

BEHAVIOR *Social behavior*: Solitary or mated pairs. *Diet*: Small mammals, including gerbils, lizards, snakes, fish and muskrats, but also eat the fruits of wild stony olives, mulberries and dried apricots, as well as watermelons, muskmelons, tomatoes and grapes, and invertebrates, like mollusks and insects. Near the Vakhsh River, the spring diet consists almost exclusively of plant bulbs and the roots of wild sugarcane, while in winter it feeds on the fruit stones of wild stony olives. Relatively little information is available about its ecology. Mainly nocturnal and crepuscular, but occasionally seen during the day. Though solitary in hunting, they are social, and when first emerging to hunt at evening time they will give a chorus of shrill wails and yapping barks, quickly evoking a wailing chorus response by other individuals.

DISTRIBUTION *Native*: Afghanistan, Bahrain, India, Iran, Iraq, Kuwait, Oman, Pakistan, Qatar, Saudi Arabia, United Arab Emirates, Yemen. Widespread in Iran, Iraq, Pakistan, Afghanistan, and N Saudi Arabia. On the Arabian Peninsula it is restricted to a small part of E Saudi Arabia in the Hofuf area and around Al Asfah Lake, with one record from N Saudi Arabia. There have also been some records from N Kuwait, Qatar, Yemen and United Arab Emirates. Jackals from the Arabian Peninsula are sometimes assigned to *syriacus* subspecies, while those from Gujarat (India), Pakistan and Afghanistan are sometimes assigned to *indicus* subspecies.

HABITAT Lake sides, reeds, marshes and agricultural areas, up to 2,150 m. It can be found near human settlements. They avoid very steep mountain tracks, and higher elevations.

CONSERVATION STATUS Least Concern. *CITES*: Appendix III (India). There are no reliable estimates of population size. It conflicts with man in some areas, as it may eat some agricultural crops. However, its role in containing the rodent pest populations in agricultural crop areas cannot be ignored. It is also a useful scavenger, especially following the depletion of vulture populations in some areas.

PHOTO CREDITS *Fariborz Heidari*, Fars (Iran); *Manan Patel, Julian Thomas, Mustansir Lokhandwala,* Gir Forest (India).

European Jackal
CANIS AUREUS MOREOTICUS

BL: 74-84 cm. TL: 20-24 cm. H: 44.5-50 cm. W: 10-13 kg (♂), 6.5-7.8 kg (♀). SL: 15.3 cm. SW: 8.2 cm. DF: 42. CN: 78. A medium-sized Canid, with relatively long legs. The largest subspecies of Eurasian Jackal. Coat color variable seasonally, but usually reddish, golden brown and silverish. Individual variation in body color and especially in head and throat markings is quite common. Pelage on the back is often a mixture of black, brown, and white hairs. Underparts, throat, inside of forelimbs and the area around eyes and lips are lighter pale ginger to cream. Inside of ears is dirty strawish white. Tail is bushy with a tan to black tip. The naked lips and rhinarium are black. Round pupils. Females slightly smaller than males, with 4 pairs of mammae.

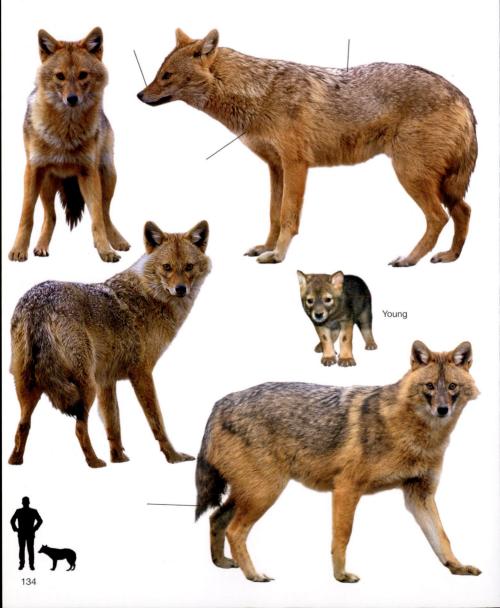

Young

Canis aureus moreoticus

OTHER NAMES Caucasian Jackal. *French*: Chacal doré. *German*: Europäischer Goldschakal, Schilfwolf. *Spanish*: Chacal europeo. *Russian*: Европейский шакал.

TAXONOMY Considered a subspecies of *C. aureus* (Golden Jackal).

REPRODUCTION *Gestation*: 63 days. *Young per birth*: 1-6. *Weaning*: 50-70 weeks. *Sexual maturity*: 11 months, but most likely to postpone reproduction and stay with the parental pair as helpers for at least a year. *Life span*: Unknown. *Breeding season*: Begins in early February, and occasionally late January during warm winters, to April. They usually give birth in burrows dug with the assistance of ♂, or they occupy derelict Fox or badger dens. The burrow is located either in thick shrubs, on the slopes of gullies or on flat surfaces. Burrows are simple structures with a single opening, 2 m long, while the nest chamber occurs at a depth of 1-1.4 m. Litters are sometimes located within the hollows of fallen trees, tree roots and under stones on river banks. Pups are usually born from late March to late April. Courtship rituals are remarkably long, lasting 26-28 days, during which the breeding pair remains almost constantly together. Pups begin to eat solid food at the age of 15-20 days.

BEHAVIOR *Social behavior*: Solitary or small groups of 5-7 individuals. *Diet*: Omnivorous, opportunistic forager, and not a persistent hunter; it primarily hunts hares and mouse-like rodents, as well as pheasants, francolins, ducks, coots, moorhens and passerines; it also eats fruits (fig, grape vine) and vegetables, insects, and birds and their eggs. *Main predators*: Wolf, Dog. It rarely hunts in groups, though packs of 8-12 Jackals consisting of more than one family have been observed in summer in Transcaucasia. Mated pairs hold territories. Mainly nocturnal, but may be seen during daylight hours in areas of low human disturbance. During the night they become very bold and approach human settlements. Its characteristic howling is a regular nighttime sound.

DISTRIBUTION *Native*: Albania, Armenia, Austria, Azerbaijan, Bosnia and Herzegovina, Bulgaria, Czech Republic, Croatia, Estonia, Georgia, Germany, Greece, Hungary, Italy, Moldova, Romania, Serbia, Slovakia, Slovenia, Turkey, Ukraine. Its current European range mostly encompasses the Balkans, where habitat loss and mass poisoning caused it to become extinct in many areas during the 1960s. It has recolonized its former territories in Bulgaria, and subsequently expanded its range into Romania and Serbia. They further expanded into Italy, Slovenia, Austria, Hungary and Slovakia during the 1980s. Recently, an isolated population was confirmed in W Estonia, much farther N than their common range. Whether they are an introduced population or a natural migration is yet unknown.

HABITAT Cultivated areas and wetlands in lower elevations, with adequate cover to be used for hiding and breeding, up to 1,050 m. They prefer to be close to human settlements where there are scavenging opportunities.

CONSERVATION STATUS Least Concern. *CITES*: Not listed. *Regional status*: Near Threatened (European Union), declared an alien, potentially invasive species in all Baltic States. Estimated population of 20,000-30,000, but there is a general lack of current information on density and population trends. The absence of its natural predator, the Wolf, is likely to influence expansion positively.

PHOTO CREDITS *Carlo Galliani* (Bulgaria); *Uros Poteko* (Slovenia); *Lajos Endredi*.

Syrian Jackal
CANIS AUREUS SYRIACUS

BL: 60-90 cm. TL: 20-30 cm. H: 44.5 cm. W: 8.8 kg (♂), 7.3 kg (♀). DF: 42. CN: 78. A medium-sized Canid, with relatively short body and long legs. A small subspecies of Eurasian Jackal. Fur is rather short and coarse, longer and grayer in winter. Coat color variable, usually reddish to golden brown, black yellowish to mottled gray dorsally, with a darker band running along the back from the nose to the tip of the tail, wider on the back, extending onto the lateral surfaces. Head and sides of legs are tawny red. Underside, throat and the area around eyes and lips are white to withish yellow. There are 2 dark bands across the lower throat and upper breast. Lips and rhinarium are black. Backs of ears are brown. Round pupils. Tail is relatively short, usually with a black tip. Females slightly smaller than males, with 4 pairs of mammae.

Young

Canis aureus syriacus

OTHER NAMES Palestine Golden Jackal. *French*: Chacal doré. *German*: Syrischer Goldschakal. *Spanish*: Chacal dorado sirio. *Russian*: Сирийский золотистый шакал. *Hebrew*: Tahn. *Arabic*: Wa wie.

TAXONOMY Considered a subspecies of *C. aureus* (Golden Jackal). Includes *palaestina*.

SIMILAR SPECIES It is larger than the Red Fox (*Vulpes vulpes palaestina* and *arabica*), with its relatively smaller, rufous ears and shorter, black-tipped tail. It is similar to a small Dog in appearance. Persian Wolf (*C. lupus pallipes*) is larger, with relatively larger legs and tail.

REPRODUCTION *Gestation*: 60-63 days. *Young per birth*: 1-6. *Weaning*: 50-90 days. *Sexual maturity*: 12 months. *Life span*: 14 years. Breeding season: February and March in Israel. Precopulatory behavior extends over a 4 months, and copulation takes place for about a week. Both parents take care of the young and regurgitate partially digested food; the ♂ will feed the ♀ during the first week or two after birth. The young, even after they are sexually mature, may stay with their parents and help to raise the next litter.

BEHAVIOR *Social behavior*: Solitary or small family groups, composed of mated pairs and their young adult offspring who are helping with the next litter; it is not clear yet whether the Jackals remain paired for many years. *Diet*: Omnivores and opportunistic, preying on small mammals and insects; they also feed on chicken carcasses, vegetables, fruit and garbage. In contrast with other subspecies, domestic ungulates (cattle and goats) are the main food of Jackals in this area. *Main predators*: Wolf. It remains in well-protected areas during the day and forages in more open areas at night. Occasionally, they may be active during the daytime, especially in the evenings or mornings. They scent mark their territory. Densities near human settlements may be greater. Jackals have been reported to carry a large proportion of the pathogens found in Domestic Dogs. Home ranges in Israel from 0.02 to 0.17 km^2, depending on food resources (smaller home ranges near villages). Its voice is a long howl followed by a series of yelping notes, usually emitted just after dark or at dawn.

DISTRIBUTION *Native*: Iraq, Israel, Jordan, Lebanon, Syria. Found in Syria (Al Bilaas, Tadmor, Bab Janné, and Iawit Mountains), Lebanon, Israel (N half to just S of Beersheba, but does not penetrate the desert), W Jordan, and extreme W and N Iraq (Rutba and Hussaiba). Boundaries with the Persian Jackal (*C. aureus aureus*) to the S and E are unclear.

HABITAT Adapted to a wide range of habitats: open areas with scattered trees and bushes, grass and copses, riparian areas, cultivated land, around orange groves, marshes, mountains and arid lands. It tends to invade rural and suburban areas, where it may come into contact with Domestic Dogs.

CONSERVATION STATUS Least Concern. *CITES*: Not listed. In the last few years, they have become overabundant in Israel, posing a possible threat to biodiversity in their native habitat. Its current status is difficult to ascertain, due to possible hybridization with Domestic Dogs and African Golden Wolves.

PHOTO CREDITS *Jan Rillich*, Yarkon Park (Israel), *Gabriel Enrique Levitzky*, Ashkelon (Israel).

Indian Jackal

CANIS AUREUS INDICUS

BL: 74.2-84 cm (♂), 74-80 cm (♀). TL: 22.3-26.4 cm. H: 38-43 cm. W: 7.6-10.8 kg (♂), 6.5-7.8 kg (♀). SL: 15.5 cm. SW: 9.1 cm. DF: 42. CN: 78. A medium-sized Canid, larger in size and with a darker and richer coat color than western subspecies (*aureus*). Scraggy, buff-gray coat, interspersed with black hair especially on the back. Coat color can vary seasonally from pale cream to tawny. Head and sides of legs are tawny red. Underside, throat and the area around eyes and lips are deep rich tan to buff. Lips and rhinarium are black. Medium-sized, bushy tail with a black tip. Backs of ears are brownish buff with an indistinct darker border and are upright pointed. Size similar in males and females, with females having 4 pairs of mammae.

winter coat

summer coat

Canis aureus indicus

OTHER NAMES Indian Golden Jackal, Himalayan Golden Jackal. *French*: Chacal de l'Inde. *German*: Indischer Goldschakal, Himalaya-Goldschakal. *Spanish*: Chacal indio. *Russian*: Индийский (североиндийский) золотистый шакал. *Hindi*: Gidad, siyar, srugal. *Kashmiri*: Gidah, shal.

TAXONOMY Considered a subspecies of *C. aureus* (Golden Jackal). Golden Jackal can breed with Domestic Dog in captivity, and anecdotal accounts exist of Indian feral Dogs that are strikingly similar to Jackals, but molecular studies have not detected evidence of hybridization in India.

SIMILAR SPECIES Wolf is similar in general appearance, but larger in size, with relatively larger legs, head and muzzle, and has a denser coat. Indian Fox is smaller.

REPRODUCTION *Gestation*: 63 days. *Young per birth*: 1-5. *Weaning*: 50-90 days. *Sexual maturity*: 12 months. *Life span*: 14 years. *Breeding season*: Throughout the year in India but in Pakistan during the spring and summer months. ♀ excavate a separate den before giving birth to young. Litters are born in the second week of April with up to 5 young per litter. The adult ♂ is an attentive mate and guards the entrance to the breeding burrow when the young are newly born and later on also assists in regurgitating food at the entrance of the den.

BEHAVIOR *Social behavior*: Solitary, in pairs, or in small groups of 3-5 comprising ♀ and their offspring of previous litter. *Diet*: Omnivorous and opportunistic forager and its diet varies according to season and habitat, and includes carcasses of domestic stock and ungulates (chital, buffalo, sambar), small mammals (rodents), poultry and wild birds. In agricultural landscapes, diet consists mainly of crops such as coarse grains (millets), fruits and sugarcane. *Main predators*: Tiger, leopard, Wolf. Normally hunt singly, but they are social in habit and invariably call to each other as they emerge in the early evening, each individual joining in an answering of yelping and barking. They emit a long, drawn-out wail followed by 3 to 5 rapidly repeated and high-pitched yelps which are taken up by other individuals within hearing. ♂ regularly scent mark their territory by depositing urine on conspicuous bushes and clumps of grass.

DISTRIBUTION *Native*: Bangladesh, Bhutan, India, Nepal, Pakistan. Found throughout India except the high Himalayas.

HABITAT Dry open country, forests, hillsides, scrub, grasslands, plains and deserts. It generally avoids extensive natural forest. It may be seen near cultivation (melon and sugarcane fields), and visit villages and small towns in search of food. Though they do not penetrate into higher mountain regions, they may be found in most of the broader Himalayan valleys, in central, E and W Nepal, in Nepal (Patukhali), Bhutan, and Pakistan (Khyber Pakhtunkhwa). The subspecific status of Jackals from Gujarat and Balochistan is unknown.

CONSERVATION STATUS Least Concern. *CITES*: Appendix III (in India). *Regional status*: Near Threatened (Pakistan). Locally common in Nepal and India. Perceived as an agricultural pest in Bangladesh. Estimated population of 80,000 for the Indian subcontinent. Considered an agricultural pest in certain parts due to its habit of eating sugarcane and chewing drip irrigation pipes. Dogs are considered a threat, both in terms of direct predation risk and pathogen spillover.

PHOTO CREDITS *Graham Ekins,* Ranthambhore Reserve (India), *M. S. Ranganathan*, *Bob Hawley*, *Suryanarayan Ganesh*, Pench Tiger Reserve (India); *Malay Nandy*, Kanha (India).

Sri Lankan Jackal
CANIS AUREUS NARIA

BL: 70.6-76.7 cm (♂), 61.5-72.1 cm (♀). TL: 20.8-23.5 cm. H: 38-43 cm. W: 5.4-8.6 kg. DF: 42. CN: 78. A medium-sized Canid, smaller than the northern Indian subspecies (*indicus*), with a shorter, smoother and not as shaggy coat, darker on the back, being black and speckled with white. Molting occurs earlier in the season than in northern Indian Jackals, and the pelt generally does not lighten in color. Underside is more pigmented on the chin, hind throat, chest and forebelly, while the limbs are rusty ochraceous or rich tan. Medium-sized, dark bushy tail, with a black tip. Females are slightly smaller than males, with 4 pairs of mammae.

Canis aureus naria

OTHER NAMES Southern Indian Jackal, Black-Backed Jackal. *French*: Chacal du Sri Lanka. *German*: Sri-Lanka-Goldschakal, Südindien-Goldschakal. *Spanish*: Chacal de Sri Lanka. *Russian*: Цейлонский (южноиндийский) золотистый шакал. *Hindi*: Gidad, siyar, srugal. *Tamil*: Narie. *Sinhalese*: Hiwala.

TAXONOMY Considered a subspecies of *C. aureus* (Golden Jackal). Includes *lanka* (Sri Lanka). Jackals in Sri Lanka have a rooted lobe on the inner side of the third upper premolar, and are slightly larger.

SIMILAR SPECIES Indian Jackal (*C. a. indicus*) is larger, with a longer coat, and a lighter-colored back.

REPRODUCTION *Gestation*: 60-63 days. *Young per birth*: 1-6. *Weaning*: 50-90 days. *Sexual maturity*: 12 months. *Life span*: Unknown. When ♀ comes into estrus, ♂-♀ pair engages in many dominance interactions, with tail raised and much growling and whimpering, and there may also be aggressive interactions with other members of the group.

BEHAVIOR *Social behavior*: Small groups of 8-12 animals, comprising a mated pair with young from different years. *Diet*: Omnivorous and opportunistic foragers, hunting small animals, and occasionally the young of larger mammals, and will take fruits to supplement their otherwise carnivorous diet. Their preference for small prey can bring them into conflict with poultry farmers. Scavenging provides only a relatively small part of their diet. Monogamous pairs, with a breeding pair establishing a territory and maintaining it through frequent scent marking and prominent dung middens. Pairs also howl together, often at night, to mark their territory. They hunt in pairs or small family groups. Upon capturing large pray, they make no attempt to kill it, but rip open its belly and eat the entrails. Small prey is typically killed by shaking, though snakes may be eaten alive from the tail end. They are in the habit of hiding food, building a store which helps them to eat when food is scarce. In areas with access to beach land, it is said that they also dig turtle nests looking for tasty eggs to feed on. Active during the day and at night, and it is not unusual to see them in the open during the hottest hours of the day in areas protected from hunting. They are able to regurgitate the meal, especially if they have pups or if a ♂ is feeding his mate shortly after birth.

DISTRIBUTION *Native*: Sri Lanka. Endemic to Sri Lanka (E, N-central, N and W provinces).

HABITAT Forests, grasslands, mangrove, urban and semi-urban areas. Tolerates human presence more readily than the Wolf and thus is often seen around human settlements.

CONSERVATION STATUS Least Concern. *CITES*: Appendix III (India). In Sri Lanka the population is stable, but conflict with humans and Dogs are on the increase. Jackals fall victim to snares intended for other wild animals, and are directly persecuted by farmers defending livestock. In addition, they also become the targeted victims of poisoned cattle carcasses meant for leopards.

PHOTO CREDITS *Charles Gibson*, Bundala (Sri Lanka); *Mystrg*, Yala National Park (Sri Lanka); *Gaurika Wijeratne* and *Priyantha de Alwis*, Kumana National Park (Sri Lanka).

Indochinese Jackal
CANIS AUREUS CRUESEMANNI

B: 79 cm. TL: 24 cm. H: 38-43 cm. W: 10.3 kg. DF: 42. CN: 78. A medium-sized Canid, smaller than the northern Indian subspecies (*indicus*). A small-sized subspecies of Eurasian Jackal. Coat is fulvous brown grizzled with blackish and whitish on the dorsum and flanks, with paler underparts. The dorsal grizzling is often patterned to give an evident saddle mark across the back. Plain rich sandy-rufous limbs, forehead and backs of the ears, all contrasting with the dorsum. Tail is relatively short, thick, plume shaped and usually held hanging down, rufous buff in color, darkening gradually to the rear.

Canis aureus cruesemanni

OTHER NAMES Siamese Jackal, Southeast Asian Golden Jackal. *French*: Chacal doré d'Asie du sud-est. *German*: Indochina-Goldschakal, Siam-Goldschakal. *Spanish*: Chacal dorado del sudeste asiático. *Russian*: Сиамский (индокитайский) шакал. *Thai*: Sòo-nák jîng-jòk.

TAXONOMY Considered a subspecies of *C. aureus* (Golden Jackal). Its status as a separate subspecies has been disputed as its classification is based mostly on observations of captive animals.

SIMILAR SPECIES Dholes have a rich red pelage, lacking any silvery grizzling, and have a different structure and size. Domestic Dogs may have a similar color, but usually lack the rich sandy-rufous color of limbs, forehead and backs of the ears, all contrasting with the dorsum, and the tail is usually thinner with sparser hair and often is held curved with the tip pointing upward.

REPRODUCTION *Gestation*: 60-63 days. *Young per birth*: 1-6. *Weaning*: Probably 50-90 days. *Sexual maturity*: 12 months. *Life span*: Unknown. *Breeding season*: Probably in February, with most births in April. Usually both parents share duties in caring for the young, and both regurgitate food for the pups. There is little specific information for this subspecies.

BEHAVIOR *Social behavior*: Mated pairs with family groups consistently of young from different years. *Diet*: Opportunistic omnivores and scavengers: small mammals, including small ungulates, birds, amphibians, reptiles, fruits, animal carcasses; during the dry season termites may become the main source of food. Main predators: Leopard, Dhole. Active by both day and night, but becomes more nocturnal in areas of human activity. Mainly solitary. A ♂ and ♀ will den and hunt together after mating and rearing their young. Another trait is to enter villages or camps to scavenge garbage, and to take chickens and ducks. They even raid crops such as sugarcane. Home ranges from 2 to 60 km², smaller near villages, and larger in natural areas where no anthropogenic food sources are available.

DISTRIBUTION *Native*: India, Laos, Myanmar, Thailand, and probably marginally in Cambodia and Vietnam. This subspecies is found from Laos, Thailand and Myanmar to E India. Widespread in Thailand N of the Isthmus of Kra, except possibly in the NE Khorat Plateau and the central valley of the Chao Phraya. It occurs in Khao Nang wildlife research center, Thung Yai and Huai Kha Khaeng wildlife sanctuary in W Thailand. In Laos it is found in Phou Xiangthong National Biodiversity Conservation Area, Dong Khanthung Protected Forest, and Pha Taem Protected Forest Complex. This species appears to be present but not common in N Myanmar; however, its status and distribution remain uncertain. Boundaries with the Indian Jackal (*C. a. indicus*) to the W (Assam, in E India) are unclear.

HABITAT Evergreen forests. Also in forested, mangrove, agricultural, rural and semi-urban habitats.

CONSERVATION STATUS Least Concern. *CITES*: Not included. Population estimates for this subspecies are not available. Indiscriminate killing by farmers and unrestrained shooting has caused their extirpation in many areas of N Thailand. Feral Dogs often kill Jackals in some areas of Thailand with high Dog densities. In reduced, fragmented Jackal populations, hybridization with Dogs and inbreeding among themselves may threaten the genetic integrity of this subspecies. The pelt is of little economic value.

PHOTO CREDITS *Jirawat Srikong, Gary Kinard,* Kaeng Krachan National Park (Thailand).

Northern Dhole

CUON ALPINUS ALPINUS, FUMOSUS AND HESPERIUS

BL: 88-135.5 cm. TL: 32-50 cm. H: 50 cm. W: 15-20 kg (♂), 10-13 kg (♀). SL: 17.4 cm. SW: 10.3 cm. DF: 40. CN: 78. A large-sized Canid. The largest subspecies of Dhole. Coat color is bright red to yellowish red. Winter coat is luxuriant and woolly, white underfur, and a larger mane. Summer coat is coarser and leaner. Back may be darker. Tail is bushy and darker, with a black tip. Undersides, chest and foreneck are whitish to pale ginger colored. Muzzle is brown, relatively short, relatively convex in profile. Ears triangular, with rounded tips. Eyes are amber. Toes are red, brown or white. The foretoe pads are joined at the base, near the main pad, unlike in most Domestic Dogs. Little sexual dimorphism. Females have 6 to 8 pairs of mammae. Young are blackish brown, gradually changing to red.

Young

Cuon alpinus alpinus

Cuon alpinus fumosus

Cuon alpinus hesperius

OTHER NAMES Siberian Dhole, East Asian Dhole, Ussuri Dhole, Alpine Wolf, Tien Shan Dhole (*hesperius*). *French*: Dhole de Sibérie, chien sauvage d'Asie. *German*: Alpenwolf, Nördlicher Rothund, Westlicher Rothund. *Spanish*: Cuón siberiano, dole, perro rojo, perro jaro, perro salvaje asiático. *Russian*: Северный красный волк: дальневосточный (*alpinus*), западнокитайский (*fumosus*), тяньшанский (*hesperius*). *Chinese*: Nyar.

TAXONOMY As many as 11 subspecies of this taxon have been described (Ginsberg and Macdonald, 1990), but their validity is doubtful. Based on genetic studies, two phylogeographic groups are recognized: a northern-Dhole group, historically occurring throughout East Asia to as far S as the Himalayan Mountains and the Yangtze River, which includes *C. a. alpinus*, *C. a. fumosus*, *C. a. hesperius*, *C. a. primaevus* and *C. a. laniger*; and a southern-Dhole group which includes *C. a. lepturus*, *C. a. dukhumensis*, *C. a. adjustus*, *C. a. infuscus*, *C. a. sumatrensis* and *C. a. javanicus*. Further research is needed to clarify the differences between N and S Dholes, especially because conservation efforts would need to employ different strategies for the two groups, as they occupy vastly different habitats and prey on different species. *C. a. alpinus* includes *antiquus*. *C. a. hesperius* includes *jason*.

REPRODUCTION *Gestation*: 60-63 days. *Young per birth*: 1-12. *Weaning*: 42-58 days. *Sexual maturity*: 12 months. *Life span*: 15 years in captivity. *Breeding season*: November to April. They do not engage in a copulatory tie when mating. Mating is not as restricted to certain individuals as it is in Wolf packs. ♀ are seasonally polyestrous, with a cycle of around 4-6 weeks. Other adults will help to feed the young of the dominant pair. At 10 days their body weight has doubled. By 8 weeks, young are less quarrelsome and aggressive, and more vigilant. At 3 months litters go on hunts, though the pack may not be fully mobile until 8 months. Young reach full adult size at 15 months.

BEHAVIOR *Social behavior*: Extended-family packs of 5-12 individuals. *Diet*: Hypercarnivory: small to medium-sized ungulates. Highly social. It is fond of water. It has some extraordinary vocal calls. Growl-barks and other noises alert pack-mates to danger. Calls also act as threats to scare off enemies. Its best-known sound is its strange whistle, which is used for contact within the pack.

DISTRIBUTION *Native*: China. *Regionally extinct*: Mongolia, North Korea, Russia, Singapore, South Korea. Historically, they occurred throughout South and East Asia, to as far N as the S parts of the Russian Federation, including the Amur region and upper Lena River N of Lake Baikal, and as far E as North Korea. They have disappeared from most of their historic range, and most remaining populations are fragmented and appear to be declining. In the 1980s they still occurred on Mount Pakdoo in NE North Korea, near the Chinese border, but they were likely extirpated at that time.

HABITAT Habitat generalist, from open country to dense forests and thick scrub jungles, avoiding desert regions.

CONSERVATION STATUS Endangered. *CITES*: Appendix II. Population for all subspecies is estimated at less than 2,500 animals. Habitat loss and the elimination of prey species pose the greatest threats to its survival. In recent years, sightings of Dholes have been exceedingly rare in China.

PHOTO CREDITS *Rickard Beldt*, Kolmården Wildlife Park (Sweden); *Paul Horvat* and *Frida Bredesen*, Parken Zoo (Sweden); *Klaus Rudloff*, Magdeburg Zoo (Germany).

Himalayan and Kashmir Dhole
CUON ALPINUS PRIMAEVUS AND LANIGER

BL: 91-98 cm (♂), 91.4-96 cm (♀). TL: 34.2-47 cm. H: 61 cm. W: 15.8 kg (♂), 10-13 kg (♀). SL: 18.8 cm. SW: 11 cm. DF: 40. CN: 78. A large-sized Canid. Similar to the Indian Dhole, but winter coat is longer and more luxuriant, with underwool, with the hair on the paws overlapping and largely concealing the pads, deeper red in color with a yellowish tinge, and darker at the neck. Kashmir Dhole is yellowish gray in color, paler than other subspecies. Sides of the neck whitish gray, ears and crown buff, muzzle and forelegs ochraceous buff, the hind legs paler, paws whitish buff, undersides whitish. Ears triangular, with rounded tips, whitish or buff inside. Short muzzle, convex, blackish. Eyes are amber. Legs are shorter in some alpine regions, paws with long white or reddish-brown fur. Tail same color as body, black distally.

summer coat

winter coat

Cuon alpinus primaevus

Cuon alpinus laniger

OTHER NAMES *French*: Dhole du Cachemire, dhole de l'Himalaya. *German*: Himalaya-Rothund, Kaschmir-Rothund. *Spanish*: Cuón del Himalaya. *Russian*: Гималайский красный волк (*primaevus*), кашмирский красный волк (*laniger*). *Nepali*: Bankukur, bwaso. *Kashmiri*: Jungli-kuta, ram-hun, ban-kuta, bhansa. *Tibetan*: Phara.

TAXONOMY Considered a subspecies of Dhole (*C. alpinus*). These subspecies are included in the northern-Dhole group.

SIMILAR SPECIES Gray Wolf (*Canis lupus chanco*) is notably larger and more stoutly built, with a distinctive grayish coat, ears pointed, penis more visible from side, and proportionally longer jaw relative to head length.

REPRODUCTION *Gestation*: 60-70 days. *Young per birth*: 2-6. *Weaning*: 42-58 days. *Sexual maturity*: 12 months. *Breeding season*: November to December, with most births occurring in January and February. Young are born in caves or under rocks.

BEHAVIOR *Social behavior*: Permanent communities, called clans, consisting of 2-11 members. *Diet*: Hypercarnivorous: blue sheep, serow, sambar, musk deer, tahr, wild pig, pikas, livestock, including cattle and Dogs; they may occasionally consume fruit, grass and other vegetation. They are not scavengers. They hunt during dawn or dusk in sites of minimum human disturbance. Rarely will they seek out domesticated animals as prey but due to increasing interaction with domesticated animals in pasture lands and these being easier to prey on than wild animals, their attacks on livestock have increased. They hunt in groups and locate prey by sight rather than by scent. They do not bark, but have a variety of calls including whistles, clucks, mewing and screaming. Dholes mark their path by dropping feces on regular spots.

DISTRIBUTION *Native*: Bhutan, China, India, Nepal. *C. a. primaevus* is found in the Himalayan region of Nepal, in the W (Rara and Khaptad National Parks, Dhorpatan Hunting Reserve) and extreme E parts of the country (Kanchenjunga Conservation Area). In S Nepal, they are found throughout much of the Terai Arc Landscape, including Chitwan and Bardia National Parks, and Parsa and Shuklaphanta Wildlife Reserves. It may occur in most protected areas in Bhutan, after being nearly extirpated in the 1980s. This subspecies has also been recently reported from Sikkim. *C. a. laniger* is found in NW India (Jammu and Kashmir), SW China and S Tibet.

HABITAT Forested areas, but can also be found on steppes and even on rocky slopes in the foothills of mountains, between 1,900 and 4,350 m. They may follow ridgelines of mountains along human and grazing trails. They avoid barren land, and habitat under anthropogenic pressure.

CONSERVATION STATUS Endangered. *CITES*: Appendix II. In Nepal, they are regarded as vermin due to their livestock killing behavior and were heavily persecuted in the past by poisoning and/or shooting, which led to a dramatic decline of the population. Habitat fragmentation due to slash/burn practice, forest products collection, and human-Dhole conflict are current threats. These subspecies are considered rare with a current population estimate of less than 500 individuals; however, this figure needs verification.

PHOTO CREDITS Based on camera traps from Kanchenjunga Conservation Area and Chitwan National Park (Nepal), and Khangchendzonga Biosphere Reserve, Sikkim (India); *Frida Bredesen; Julie Winkelman; Dr. Ajay Kumar Singh; Sergey Chichagov.*

Chinese Dhole

CUON ALPINUS LEPTURUS

BL: 91-98 cm (♂), 91.4 cm (♀). TL: 34.2-47 cm. H: 61 cm. W: 15.8 kg (♂), 10-13 kg (♀). SL: 17.9 cm. SW: 11.1 cm. DF: 40. CN: 78. A large-sized Canid, with a short rostrum. Coat is uniformly reddish in color, with thick underfur. Back sometimes darker to a varying extent by blackening of the tips of the hairs. Undersides, inside of limbs and neck from white to pale reddish, nearly matching the upper side. Summer coat is short, sleek and thin, with little or no underwool. Winter coat is longer and rougher, moderately thickened with underwool. Ears triangular, with rounded tips, about half the length of the face, whitish or buff inside. Short muzzle, convex, typically blackish, with black facial vibrissae. Eyes are amber. Outer side of the legs often with buff or white on the paws. Tail like the body, but black at least in its terminal half. Little sexual dimorphism. Females with 6 to 8 pairs of mammae.

summer coat

Young

winter coat

Cuon alpinus lepturus

OTHER NAMES Kiangsi Dhole. *French*: Dhole de Chine, cuon de Chine, chien sauvage de Chine. *German*: Kiangsi-Rothund. *Spanish*: Cuón chino, dole, perro rojo, perro jaro, perro salvaje chino. *Russian*: Среднекитайский красный волк. *Chinese*: Nyar.

TAXONOMY Considered a subspecies of Dhole (*C. alpinus*). This subspecies is included in the southern-Dhole group. Includes *clamitans*.

REPRODUCTION *Gestation*: 60-63 days. *Young per birth*: 1-12. *Weaning*: 42-58 days. *Sexual maturity*: 12 months. *Life span*: 15 years in captivity. *Breeding season*: November to April. They do not engage in a copulatory tie when mating. Mating is not as restricted to certain individuals as it is in Wolf packs. ♀ are seasonally polyestrous, with a cycle of around 4-6 weeks. Other adults will help to feed the young of the dominant pair.

BEHAVIOR *Social behavior*: Extended-family packs of 5-12 individuals, up to 25, with more ♂ than ♀, and usually just 1 breeding ♀. Large packs of over 40 may result from the temporary fusion of neighboring packs. Older Dholes sometimes vanish from the group. *Diet*: Hypercarnivory: wild boar, muntjac, sambar deer, wild sheep, wild goats, small deer, rodents and lagomorphs. Highly social and cooperative animal, with a strict social hierarchy. Dispersal is ♀-biased. Members over-mark each other's waste, creating individual latrines in the home range. These latrines serve intra-group communication. They are fond of water, and may be seen in shallow pools of water. Like Domestic Dogs, they wag their tail. They can also leap at least 2.3 m. It has some extraordinary vocal calls. It can make a high-pitched scream, mew, hiss, squeak, yelp, chatter, and can cluck like a chicken. Growl-barks and other noises alert pack-mates to danger; the large range of calls like these may have evolved to warn companions of different dangers—human, tiger, etc. Calls also act as threats to scare off enemies. Its best-known sound is its strange whistle, likened by early naturalists to the sound obtained when air is blown over an empty cartridge. These calls are used for contact within the pack. The repetitive whistles are so distinct that individual Dholes can be identified by them, and the source is easily located. Whistles travel well at ground level due to their frequency and structure.

DISTRIBUTION *Native*: China. Found in S China, S of the Yangtze River, although its current distribution is not well known (Fujian, Guangdong, Guangxi, Guizhou, Hubei and Jiangxi).

HABITAT Dry tropical deciduous forests, moist deciduous forests, evergreen forests, semi-evergreen forests, dry thorn forests, grassland, scrub forest mosaics and alpine steppe (2,100 m). They have not been reported from desert regions.

CONSERVATION STATUS Endangered. *CITES*: Appendix II. Protected in China. In the early 20th century the winter fur was prized by the Chinese, but currently their fur is not considered overly valuable. The most significant threat is habitat loss and degradation. They have been intentionally extirpated from some protected areas in SE China in an attempt to boost ungulate numbers. They are now very rare and have disappeared from most parts of S China. In view of their isolation, few, if any, remaining populations can be viable.

PHOTO CREDITS *Sergey Chichagov*, Riga Zoo (Latvia); *Corinne Puch*, Neunkirchen Zoo (Germany).

Indochinese Dhole

CUON ALPINUS INFUSCUS AND ADJUSTUS

BL: 91-98 cm (♂), 91.4 cm (♀). TL: 34.2-47 cm. H: 61 cm. W: 15.8 kg (♂), 10-13 kg (♀). SL: 17.1 cm. SW: 10.4 cm. DF: 40. CN: 78. A large-sized Canid. A medium-sized subspecies of Dhole, similar to the Indian Dhole, with a more rusty-red to uniformly brown color. Coat is short, with no underwool. Undersides are buffy grayish white. Winter coat is shorter and scantier than in northern subspecies. Back uniformly red or sometimes darker to a varying extent by blackening of the tips of the hairs. Undersides, inside of limbs, neck and front paws are lighter in color, buffy white to reddish, nearly matching the upper side. Ears triangular, with rounded tips, whitish or buff inside. Short muzzle, convex. Eyes are amber. Tail like the body, but black at least in its terminal half. Little sexual dimorphism. Females with 6 to 8 pairs of mammae.

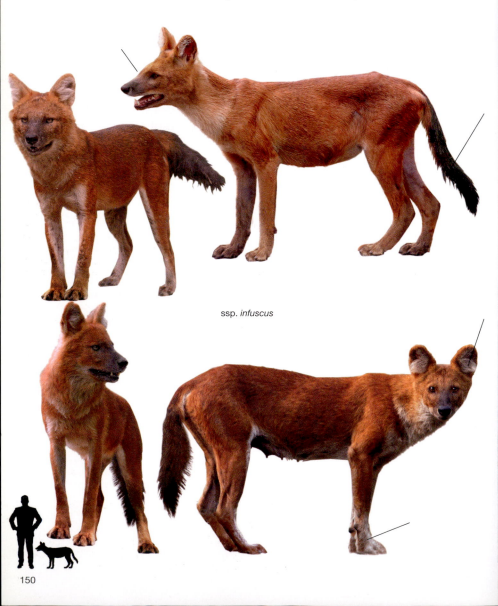

ssp. *infuscus*

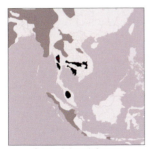

Cuon alpinus infuscus

Cuon alpinus adjustus

OTHER NAMES Nilgiri Dhole, Burma Dhole. *French*: Dhole du Tenasserim, dhole de Birmanie. *German*: Indochina-Rothund, Burma-Rothund. *Spanish*: Cuón de Indochina, perro rojo. *Russian*: Индокитайский красный волк (*infuscus*), бирманский красный волк (*adjustus*). *Malay*: Sirgala Aijing-kutar. *Thai*: Maa paa. *Burmese*: Tan-kwe.

TAXONOMY Considered a subspecies of Dhole (*C. alpinus*). These subspecies are included in the southern-Dhole group. *C. a. rutilans* is considered a synonym of *adjustus*.

SIMILAR SPECIES Dingo has a less bushy tail, which bends forward toward the head when held upright, the penis is more visible from side, ears are pointed, and jaw is proportionally longer relative to head length. Golden jackal is notably smaller, with proportionally shorter tail to body, coat yellowish brown and always grizzled, face thin and ears pointed, and a distinctive fast trotting gait. Gray Wolf is notably larger, with a distinctive grayish coat, ears pointed, penis more visible from side, and proportionally longer jaw relative to head length.

REPRODUCTION *Gestation*: 60-63 days. *Young per birth*: 1-12. *Weaning*: 42-58 days. *Sexual maturity*: 12 months. *Life span*: 15 years in captivity. Pups are born from November to March.

BEHAVIOR *Social behavior*: Extended-family packs of 5-12 individuals, up to 25, with more ♂ than ♀, and usually just 1 breeding ♀. *Diet*: An exclusively carnivorous diet (hypercarnivory); medium-sized to small ungulates (muntjac, sambar, wild pig, hog deer, serow). Crepuscular and diurnal. Highly social and co-operative animal. Home ranges from 12 to 49.5 km² in Thailand. Members over-mark each other's waste, creating individual latrines in the home range. These latrines serve intra-group communication. They are fond of water, and may be seen in shallow pools of water. Like Domestic Dogs, the Dhole wags its tail. They can also leap at least 2.3 m. They have some extraordinary vocal calls: high-pitched scream, mew, hiss, squeak, yelp, chatter and cluck. Its best-known sound is its strange whistle, likened by early naturalists to the sound obtained when air is blown over an empty cartridge. These calls are used for contact within the pack. The repetitive whistles are so distinct that individual Dholes can be identified by them, and the source is easily located. Whistles travel well at ground level due to their frequency and structure.

DISTRIBUTION *Native*: Bangladesh, Cambodia, China, India, Laos, Malaysia, Myanmar, Thailand. *Possibly extinct*: Vietnam. Found in E Bangladesh (Chittagong Hill Tracts and Sylhet districts), NE India (Arunachal Pradesh, Assam, Manipur, Meghalaya, Mizoram, Nagaland and Tripura), N and W-central Myanmar, Thailand, N and central Laos and S China (Yunnan).

HABITAT Primary, secondary and degraded forms of tropical dry and moist deciduous forests, although some individuals may be observed hunting in grasslands.

CONSERVATION STATUS Endangered. *CITES*: Appendix II. The size of subpopulations of Dholes has not been reported, but they occur at low densities.

PHOTO CREDITS *Arterra*, Huai Kha Khaeng Wildlife Sanctuary (Thailand); *Wildlife Alliance*, Phnom Tamao Wildlife Rescue Center (Thailand); *Rapeepong Puttakumwong* (Thailand).

Indian Dhole
CUON ALPINUS DUKHUNENSIS

BL: 91-97.8 cm (♂), 91.4 cm (♀). TL: 34.2-47 cm. H: 61 cm. W: 15-20 kg (♂), 10-13 kg (♀). SL: 17.9 cm. SW: 10.9 cm. DF: 40. CN: 78. A large-sized Canid, with a short muzzle. A small subspecies of Dhole, with a short coat. Coat is uniformly reddish in color, less intense and with a tawnier or yellower tinge than in northern and Indonesian subspecies. Undersides, inside of limbs and neck from white to pale reddish, nearly matching the upper side. Summer coat is short, sleek and thin, with little or no underwool. Winter coat is longer and rougher, moderately thickened with underwool. Ears triangular, with rounded tips, about half the length of the face, whitish or buff inside. Short muzzle, convex, typically blackish, with black facial vibrissae. Eyes are amber. Outer side of the legs often with buff or white on the paws. Tail like the body, but black at least in its terminal half. Little sexual dimorphism, with females slightly smaller than males, and 6 to 8 pairs of mammae.

Cuon alpinus dukhunensis

OTHER NAMES Tenasserim Dhole. *French*: Dhole de l'Inde, chien sauvage de l'Inde. *German*: Dekkan-Rothund. *Spanish*: Cuón indio. *Russian*: Индийский красный волк. *Hindi*: Son-Kutta, Jangli. *Tamil*: Vatai-Karau. *Ho*: Tani. *Kodava*: Kennai. *Marathi*: Kolasra. *Gujarati*: Earam-naiko. *Malayalam*: Hahmasai-kuta, kotsun, kolsa, kolarsi.

TAXONOMY Considered a subspecies of Dhole (*C. alpinus*). This subspecies is included in the southern-Dhole group, which is further divided into two distinct phylogeographical groupings, one extending from S, central and N India (S of the Ganges) into Myanmar, and the other extending from India N of the Ganges into NE India, Myanmar, Thailand and the Malaysian Peninsula.

REPRODUCTION *Gestation*: 63 days. *Young per birth*: 1-12. *Weaning*: 56 days. *Sexual maturity*: 12 months. *Life span*: 15 years in captivity. *Breeding season*: November to April, with most births in December in India. Dens are earthen burrows, or are constructed among rocks and boulder structures, in rocky caverns, or close to streambeds. Unlike some other Canids, it does not engage in a copulatory tie when mating. Also, mating is not as restricted to certain individuals as it is in Wolf packs, in which usually only the dominant pair can breed.

BEHAVIOR *Social behavior*: Permanent groups (clans), consisting of 8-15 members, often contain more ♂ than ♀, with usually just 1 breeding ♀. Occasionally, large groups of over 40 animals have been seen, possibly arising from the temporary fusion of neighboring packs. *Diet*: Hypercarnivorous with diet based primarily on small to medium-sized ungulates. Smaller species, such as civets, other small carnivores, and hares, are also consumed opportunistically. Bimodal or diurnal in habit, occasionally nocturnal. Highly social and cooperative. It regularly hunts in packs. Communal hunting is particularly important during the breeding season when pack members return to the den to regurgitate food for the mother and pups. Sometimes, they prefer to hunt individually or in pairs, focusing on smaller prey such as hares. They have an excellent sense of smell and sight allowing them to locate their prey easily. Home range sizes from 20 to 100 km². Territories are marked by latrines at trail and road intersections where all pack members defecate. Good swimmers, sometimes drive their prey into water. They possess a highly developed vocal communication system. Densities vary considerably, even between years in the same area, and are based upon food resources, disease outbreaks and poaching by humans.

DISTRIBUTION *Native*: India. Endemic to India, S of the Ganges. Found in Andhra Pradesh, Bihar, Chhattisgarh, Gujarat, Goa, Jharkhand, Karnataka, Kerala, Madhya Pradesh, Maharashtra, Orissa, Rajasthan, and Tamil Nadu. Very little is known about its distribution, but surveys indicate serious decline and fragmentation of the former range. The best remaining populations are probably to be found in central and S India, and the Western Ghats currently support a healthy metapopulation.

HABITAT Forest areas (reserve forests, degraded and multi-use forests) in India, up to at least 2,400 m. Not found in deserts, coasts, hilly terrain and mangroves. They avoid areas with human disturbance.

CONSERVATION STATUS Endangered. *CITES*: Appendix II. Protected in India. Treated as vermin and hunted across the India until they were protected in 1972. Threats include possible pathogen spillover such as canine distemper virus from Domestic Dogs.

PHOTO CREDITS *Hira Punjabi*, Nagarhole (India), *Daniel Goeleven*, Tadoba (India), *Anil Varma* and *Michael Francis*, Tadoba Andhari (India); *Aravind Venkatraman*, Bandipur (India).

Indonesian Dhole
CUON ALPINUS SUMATRENSIS AND JAVANICUS

BL: 80-91.4 cm (♂), 91.4 cm (♀). TL: 29.2-34.3 cm. H: 61 cm. W: 15.8 kg (♂), 10-13 kg (♀). SL: 15.7 cm. SW: 9.7 cm. DF: 40. CN: 78. A large-sized Canid. The smallest subspecies of Dhole, slender, with a short bright red coat and dark vibrissae. Coat is foxy ferruginous red to tawny brown, with lighter shades on the belly and inner sides of the legs. Back sometimes darker to a varying extent by blackening of the tips of the hairs. Undersides, inside of limbs and neck from white to pale reddish, nearly matching the upper side. Ears triangular, with rounded tips, about half the length of the face, whitish or buff inside. Short muzzle, convex, typically blackish, with black facial vibrissae. Eyes are amber. Outer side of the legs often with buff or white on the paws. Tail like the body, but black at least in its terminal half. Little sexual dimorphism. Females with 6-7 pairs of mammae.

Cuon alpinus sumatrensis

Cuon alpinus javanicus

OTHER NAMES Sumatran Dhole, Javan Dhole. *French*: Dhole de Sumatra, cuon de Sumatra. *German*: Sumatra-Rothund, Java-Rothund. *Spanish*: Cuón de Sumatra. *Russian*: Суматранский красный волк (*sumatrensis*), яванский красный волк (*javanicus*). *Indonesian*: Ajag, Anjing Hutan. *Malay*: Sirgala, Aijing-kutar.

TAXONOMY Considered a subspecies of Dhole (*C. alpinus*). Included in the southern-Dhole group. They could have originated from individuals introduced from India, although further studies are needed to confirm these findings. *C. a. javanicus* (Javan Dhole) is sometimes considered a synonym of *C. a. sumatrensis*, although the subspecific status of Dholes in Indonesia is unclear and requires further study.

REPRODUCTION *Gestation*: 60-63 days. *Young per birth*: 1-12. *Weaning*: 42-58 days. *Sexual maturity*: 12 months. *Life span*: 15 years in captivity. *Breeding season*: Mainly between January and May in E Java. Dens are constructed under rocks with one or multiple entrances, strategically placed to access water resources and prey; they may use porcupine dens.

BEHAVIOR *Social behavior*: Groups consisting of 5-12 animals. Occasionally it can live alone, as found in Gunung Leuser National Park. In tropical evergreen forests of Southeast Asia, they form smaller packs and presumably have smaller litters, probably due to the low prey biomass and small size of ungulate prey in these habitats. *Diet*: Almost exclusively carnivorous (hypercarnivory), ranging from small rodents and hares to large-sized ungulates (banteng, buffalo, rusa deer). Crepuscular and diurnal activity, but they may also hunt at night.

DISTRIBUTION *Native*: Indonesia (Sumatra and Java). Historically, they occurred throughout both Sumatra and Java; however, their current distribution on both islands is fragmented and greatly reduced. On Sumatra, they are found along the Barisan Mountain range, from the N to S parts of the island (Gunung Leuser, Kerinci Seblat and Bukit Barisan Selatan National Parks). Dholes are also found in several protected areas in lowland forests in the E-central part of the island (Tesso Nilo and Bukit Tigapuluh National Parks, Harapan Rainforest and Batang Hari Protection Forest). On Java, Dholes are found in national parks only in the extreme W (Gunung Gede Pangrango, Ujung Kulon and Gunung Halimum Salak National Parks) and E (Baluran National Park and Alas Purwo National Park) parts of the island. They are likely extirpated in other regions of the island.

HABITAT Habitat generalist, occurring in a wide variety of vegetation types, including primary, secondary and degraded forms of tropical dry and moist deciduous forests. They avoid human-disturbed habitats.

CONSERVATION STATUS Endangered. *CITES*: Appendix II. Status is unknown, but probably less than 250 individuals. It is the most threatened subspecies of Dhole.

PHOTO CREDITS *Yusuf Ijsseldijk*, Baluran National Park, E Java (Indonesia); *Vladimir Cech*, based on pictures from Baluran National Park, E Java (Indonesia).

Cape Black-Backed Jackal
LUPULELLA MESOMELAS MESOMELAS

BL: 69-81.2 cm (♂), 67.3-71.1 cm (♀). TL: 25-40 cm. H: 38-48 cm. W: 6.4-11.4 kg (♂), 5.4-10.0 kg (♀). SL: 14.5 cm. SW: 8.6 cm. DF: 42. CN: 78. A medium-sized, slender, long-legged Canid, with large ears. Pelage color is reddish brown to tan, redder on flanks and legs, with a distinctive well-defined black saddle, intermixed with silvery hair, extending from shoulders posteriorly to base of tail, narrowing toward lumbar region to a point at crown of tail. Lips and throat, chest, and inside of limbs are white. Winter coat of male adults may develop a reddish to an almost deep russet red color. Pointed, Fox-like muzzle. Erect and pointed ears. Tail is bushy and has a black tip, with black and white fur covering the basal third, and a distinctive black subcaudal marking. Females are slightly smaller and less richly colored than males, especially during the winter, with 3 to 4 pairs of mammae. Young are lead gray with an indistinct saddle.

Young

Lupulella mesomelas mesomelas

OTHER NAMES Red Jackal. *French*: Chacal à chabraque. *German*: Südafrokanischer Schabrackenschakal. *Spanish*: Chacal de lomo negro de sudáfrica. *Russian*: Южноафриканский (капский) чепрачный шакал. *Afrikaans*: Rooijakkals.

SUBSPECIES Two subspecies of *L. mesomelas* (Black-Backed Jackal) are recognized: *L. m mesomelas* (Cape Black-Backed Jackal), and *L. m. schmidti* (East African Black-Backed Jackal). Some genetic studies suggest that they may be two distinct species. Previously included in the genus *Canis*. Includes *achrotes*, *arenarum* and *variegatoides*.

REPRODUCTION *Gestation*: 60 days. *Young per birth*: 1-9. *Weaning*: 56-63 days. *Sexual maturity*: 11 months. *Life span*: 7 years, 14 years in captivity. *Mating season*: From late May to August. Most births occur from July to October. Pups are born in underground burrows dug by other species. Both ♂ and ♀ bring food to the young, often assisted by helpers. The young start to forage with their parents when they are about 14 weeks old; at this stage they no longer use the den.

BEHAVIOR *Social behavior*: Primarily monogamous, in small family groups with an alpha pair. Solitary individuals may be beta members of the pack, young dispersers, or older post-breeding Jackals. Large aggregations can occur at particularly rich food resources. *Diet*: Small mammals, reptiles, birds, carrion and fruit. Also young and adult ungulates ("hider" species that hide their young in thick vegetation). They also prey on livestock (young sheep and goats), although wild prey is preferred. *Main predators*: Leopards, spotted hyena, other large carnivores. Mainly nocturnal but seen regularly during the day. Territorial, using feces and urine to demarcate their territorial boundaries. Home-range size from 0.32 to 21.5 km². Ranges are generally defended and mutually exclusive for pairs, except in some areas such as Cape Cross Seal Reserve, where they are territorial only during the breeding season. Mated pairs will often cooperate in the capture of prey. Much more vocal than East African subspecies: a high-pitched, whining howl is used to communicate with group members, and may also function in territorial advertisement; an alarm call, consisting of an explosive yelp followed by a series of shorter high-pitched yelps, is used when disturbed.

DISTRIBUTION *Native*: Angola, Botswana, Lesotho, Mozambique, Namibia, South Africa, Swaziland, Zimbabwe. The Mozambique or Rhodesian Gap (from the Zambezi to Tanzania) separates the subspecies. The range of this subspecies extends from the Cape of Good Hope N to Angola, Zimbabwe and S Mozambique. It was absent from the highveld of Transvaal until 1950.

HABITAT A wide variety of habitats including arid coastal desert, montane grassland, open savanna, woodland savanna mosaics and farmland. They prefer open habitats and tend to avoid dense vegetation. In KwaZulu-Natal, in the Drakensberg, and in localities receiving more than 2,000 mm of rainfall, they are recorded from sea level to more than 3,000 m in altitude.

CONSERVATION STATUS Least Concern. *CITES*: Not listed. *Regional status*: Least Concern (South Africa). It has no legal protection except for protected areas. In Namibia and South Africa, they are common in protected areas where suitable habitat occurs. They occur in many livestock producing areas, where they are considered vermin, but despite strenuous control measures in many farming areas of S Africa remain they relatively abundant.

PHOTO CREDITS *Adrian Assalve* and *Joe McKenna*, Chobe (Botswana), *Anneska Van Der Spoel* (South Africa); *Smellme, Nicola Massier* and *Rob Sall*, Etosha (Namibia).

East African Black-Backed Jackal
LUPULELLA MESOMELAS SCHMIDTI

BL: 63-81 cm. TL: 20-24 cm. H: 45-50 cm. W: 6.8-13.6 kg. SL: 14.3 cm. SW 8.5 cm. DF: 42. CN: 78. A medium-sized, slender, long-legged Canid, with large ears. Slightly larger, less sexually dimorphic, and less rufous in color than South African subspecies. Pelage color is reddish brown to tan, redder on flanks and legs, with a distinctive well-defined black saddle, intermixed with silvery hair, extending from shoulders posteriorly to base of tail, narrowing toward lumbar region to a point at crown of tail. Lips and throat, chest, and inside of limbs are white. Head is light gray with reddish tinges. Pointed, Fox-like muzzle. Erect and pointed ears, tawny on the back. Tail is bushy and has a black tip, with black-and-white fur covering the basal third, and a distinctive black subcaudal marking. Females are slightly smaller and less richly colored than males, especially during the winter. Young are lead gray with an indistinct saddle.

Young

Lupulella mesomelas schmidti

OTHER NAMES Northern Black-Backed Jackal, Silver-Backed Jackal, Red Jackal. *French*: Chacal à chabraque d'Afrique Orientale. *German*: Ostafrikanischer Schabrackenschakal. *Spanish*: Chacal de lomo negro de África oriental. *Russian*: Восточноафриканский чепрачный шакал. *Somali*: Dauò dulmadù, dauà, dawa'o. *Swahili*: Bweha nyekundu.

SUBSPECIES Considered a subspecies of *L. mesomelas* (Black-Backed Jackal). Some genetic studies suggest that this may be a distinct species. Includes *elgonae* and *mcmillani*.

SIMILAR SPECIES Side-Striped Jackal has a white-tipped tail, gray on the back extends to the lower flanks, lacks the rich reddish color of the flanks and limbs, and has a more Dog-like face. Golden Jackal may have a less prominent black saddle, lacking the sharp contrast between the saddle and the flank, with a more patchy patterning, and body color is usually golden sand to fawn, not russet red.

REPRODUCTION *Gestation*: 60 days. *Young per birth*: 1-9. *Weaning*: 56-63 days. *Sexual maturity*: 11 months. *Life span*: 7 years, 14 years in captivity. *Mating season*: From late May to August. Most births occur from July to October. Pups are born in modified termitaria, disused burrows of aardvark or, less frequently, caves or other crevices, often with multiple entrances; they may dig their own dens. Parents and helpers feed pups by regurgitation. They are born blind, open their eyes at days 8–10, emerge from the den at 3 weeks, and are independent of the den at 14 weeks. They are able to hunt on their own at 6 months of age. Juveniles disperse at 1 year of age, although some may remain within their natal territory to act as helpers.

BEHAVIOR *Social behavior*: Life-long monogamous pairs, with 1-2 offspring from previous years. *Diet*: Opportunistic, generalist feeders. Diet varies according to food availability, including small to medium-sized mammals (murids, springhares, young ungulates), reptiles, birds and eggs, carrion and human refuse, invertebrates and plant matter. *Main predators*: Leopard, spotted hyena. Mostly nocturnal and crepuscular, although activity periods frequently extend into the day. Territorial, with home ranges from 0.7 to 3.5 km^2 in size. They are more aggressive and more common at large carnivore kills than other species of Jackal. Much less vocal than South African subspecies, probably to limit competition with the sympatric African Wolf; they do not howl, and instead vocalize with yaps interspersed with howls.

DISTRIBUTION *Native*: Djibouti, Eritrea, Ethiopia, Kenya, Somalia, South Sudan, Sudan, Tanzania, Uganda. It was once found as far N as Egypt, but the arrival of the African Wolf caused its range to shift southward. It is entirely absent from Zambia and it is absent through much of central and equatorial Africa.

HABITAT A wide variety of habitats including grassland, woodland savanna mosaics and farmland, although they avoid dense vegetation. They have also been recorded from the alpine zone of Mount Kenya at 3,660 m. When sympatric with African Wolf and Side-Striped Jackal, they use open grassland or wooded savanna.

CONSERVATION STATUS Least Concern. *CITES*: Not included. No legal protection except for protected areas. It is known to occur in many protected areas throughout its range, including Masai Mara (Kenya), Serengeti National Park, and Selous Game Reserve (Tanzania).

PHOTO CREDITS *MHGallery,* Ngorongoro (Tanzania), *Russell Pringle*, Masai Mara (Kenya); *Amrishwad*, Tarangire (Tanzania); *Michael Lane* and *Greg Christensen*, Mara (Tanzania).

Sundevall Side-Striped Jackal

LUPULELLA ADUSTUS ADUSTUS

BL: 66-77.5 cm (♂), 69-77 cm (♀). TL: 30.5-41 cm. H: 35-50 cm. W: 7.3-12.1 kg (♂), 7.2-10 kg (♀). SL: 15.3 cm. SW: 8.3 cm. DF: 42. CN: 78. A medium-sized, Dog-like Canid. The largest subspecies of Side-Striped Jackal, with a long, white-tipped tail. Pelage is tan to buff gray, with a darker back, and a more or less definite white or buff-colored side stripe, running from shoulder to hip with a black margin below. Undersides and throat are cream colored. Dog-like face, with a long and narrow muzzle. Ears are relatively small, gray to dark brown on the back. Legs are light gray brown, more buffy than the body. Tail is bushy, mostly black, with a distinctive white tip. Markings are less well defined in juveniles. Females are slightly smaller than males, and have 2 pairs of mammae.

Lupulella adustus adustus

OTHER NAMES Western Side-Striped Jackal. *French*: Chacal à flancs rayés. *German*: Gewöhnlicher Streifenschakal. *Spanish*: Chacal rayado. Russian: Западноафриканский полосатый шакал. *Afrikaans*: Witkwasjakkals. *Xhosa*: Udyakalashe. *Zulu*: Impungushe.

SUBSPECIES Three subspecies traditionally recognized (Kingdon, 1997): *L. a. adustus*, *L. a. kaffensis* and *L. a. lateralis*. Previously included in the genus *Canis*. It has been proposed to be included under *Schaeffia*, as it seems not to form a monophyletic group with the Black-Backed Jackal. Includes *hulubi* and *wunderlich*. Consensus is lacking regarding the number of subspecies, and differences may be a consequence of individual variation.

SIMILAR SPECIES Black-Backed Jackal is slightly smaller and lighter, with larger and pointed ears, a shorter more Fox-like tail, and it is more colorful, with a distinct dark saddle and a rich reddish color on the flanks and limbs.

REPRODUCTION *Gestation*: 57-64 days. *Young per birth*: 4-6. *Weaning*: 42-70 days. *Sexual maturity*: 9 months. *Life span*: 12 years in captivity. *Breeding season*: June to November in South Africa and Zimbabwe. Most births occur during August to January. Excavated termitaria and old aardvark burrows are commonly used as dens. ♀ with suckling young are sensitive to disturbance and they will carry the whole litter, one by one, to a new den if disturbed. Pups are blind at birth and open their eyes at 10 days. Both parents care for the pups and carry food in the mouth or regurgitate it. Young disperse at 11 months.

BEHAVIOR *Social behavior*: Monogamous pairs, although they are not always seen together, and usually forage alone; family groups with up to 7 individuals, comprising a breeding pair and their young, can occasionally be seen. *Diet*: Omnivorous, including fruits, seeds, small rodents, hares, gazelle fawns, invertebrates and carrion; it is less predatory than the Black-Backed Jackal and seldom targets large prey. Certain fruits may be taken almost exclusively when in season. *Main predators*: Leopard, spotted hyena, lion; young may be preyed on by eagles. Active at night, but also seen at dusk and in the early morning. They shelter in heavy undergrowth, in holes in the ground, or crevices among rocks. If alarmed, they generally flee to cover. When disturbed, they often adopt a nervous-looking zig-zagging, possibly in an attempt to identify the disturbance by smell. Probably highly territorial. Home range size of 0.2 km² in Zimbabwe. Vocalizations include barks, growls, yaps, crackles, whines, screams, a croaking distress call and a hooting howl.

DISTRIBUTION *Native*: Angola, Botswana, Congo, DR Congo, Gabon, Malawi, Mozambique, Namibia, South Africa, Swaziland, Zambia, Zimbabwe. NW KwaZulu-Natal marks its most southerly occurrence.

HABITAT Broad-leaved deciduous woodland, woodland savanna, and forest mosaics, all with a good water supply. They may occur near rural dwellings and farm buildings, and penetrate urban areas. They avoid very open grassland, thickly wooded areas and arid zones, and are not found in forest.

CONSERVATION STATUS Least Concern. *CITES*: Not listed. *Regional status*: Near Threatened (South Africa). Threats include Canid diseases, collisions with vehicles, and killings by poultry farmers. There is little evidence of extensive predation on stock. Population appears to be stable, but is rarely seen, due to its nocturnal and secretive habits.

PHOTO CREDITS *Leon Molenaar, Willie van Schalkwyk*, Kruger National Park (South Africa); *Chris Fourie* (South Africa); *David Schenfeld*, North-West (Botswana).

Equatorial Africa Side-Striped Jackal

LUPULELLA ADUSTUS LATERALIS

BL: 69-77 cm. TL: 30-41 cm. H: 45-50 cm. W: 7.3-12 kg (♂), 7.3-10 kg (♀). SL: 15.2 cm. SW: 8.0 cm. DF: 42. CN: 78. A medium-sized, Dog-like Canid. A small-sized subspecies of Side-Striped Jackal, with a long, white-tipped tail. Pelage is tan to dull gray in color, with a darker back, and a distinctive white or buff-colored side stripe, running from shoulder to hip, with a black margin below. Undersides, throat and chest are white, dark gray basally on the belly. Dog-like face, with a long and narrow muzzle. Ears are relatively small, dull light brown on the back. Legs are lighter than the body, ochraceous buff in color, and forelegs may have a black stripe from the shoulder to the knee. Tail is relatively long, mostly black with a distinctive white tip, although it may be mostly white with a black tip as in West Equatorial Africa. Markings are less well defined in juveniles. Females are slightly smaller than males, and have 2 pairs of mammae.

Lupulella adustus lateralis

OTHER NAMES East African Side-Striped Jackal, Elgon Side-Striped Jackal. *French*: Chacal à flancs rayés. *German*: Äquatorialafrika-Streifenschakal. *Spanish*: Chacal rayado. Russian: Восточноафриканский (центральноафриканский) полосатый шакал. *Swahili*: Bweha miraba. *Nde*: Ikhanka, igowa, ipungutjha enemida.

SUBSPECIES Considered a subspecies of *L. adustus* (Side-Striped Jackal). Includes *centralis* (from Cameroon and central Africa), *mcmillani* (Kenya) and *notatus* (Loita Side-Striped Jackal, from SW Kenya and Uganda, small race with white underparts, white-tipped tail and a conspicuous black side stripe). Consensus is lacking regarding the validity of subspecies of *L. adustus*, and differences may be a consequence of individual variation.

SIMILAR SPECIES Distinguished from the Black-Backed Jackal and the African Golden Wolf by its white-tipped tail, the Dog-like face, the smaller rounder ears, and its vocalizations (a series of yaps, rather than drawn-out howls).

REPRODUCTION *Gestation*: 57-64 days. *Young per birth*: 4-6. *Weaning*: 42-70 days. *Sexual maturity*: 9 months. *Life span*: 10 years in captivity. *Breeding season*: June to July, but some mating may take place throughout the year. Most births occur during August to November. Excavated termitaria and old aardvark burrows are commonly used as dens. Both parents care for the pups and carry food in the mouth or regurgitate it. Young disperse at 11 months.

BEHAVIOR *Social behavior*: Monogamous, territorial pairs, although individuals often forage alone. Family groups with up to 7 individuals, comprising a breeding pair and their young, can occasionally be seen. *Diet*: Omnivorous, including fruits, seeds, small rodents, hares, gazelle fawns, invertebrates and carrion. *Main predators*: Leopard, hyena, eagles. Typically more nocturnal and secretive than other Jackals, although diurnal sightings are not infrequent. It is more solitary and more nocturnal than the Black-Backed Jackal. Home range sizes of between 12 and 20 km². They mark their territories with scats and urine. Although it is larger than its Black-Backed relative, the Side-Striped Jackal is dominant and usually wins during disputes over food.

DISTRIBUTION *Native*: Benin, Burkina Faso, Burundi, Cameroon, Central African Republic, Chad, DR Congo, Côte d'Ivoire, Gambia, Ghana, Guinea, Guinea-Bissau, Kenya, Malawi, Mali, Mauritania, Mozambique, Niger, Nigeria, Rwanda, Senegal, Sierra Leone, Sudan, Tanzania, Togo, Uganda, Zambia. It apparently occupies the "tropical fox" niche in central Africa.

HABITAT A wide range of habitats, from bushland, wooded grassland, woodland, farmland and mountains up to 2,700 m. In areas of sympatry with Black-Backed Jackals and African Golden Wolves, they usually occupy areas of denser vegetation, whereas the other species tend to favor more open habitats.

CONSERVATION STATUS Least Concern. *CITES*: Not listed. No legal protection outside protected areas. Threats include Canid diseases, such as rabies and canine distemper virus, collisions with vehicles, and sometimes retribution killings by poultry farmers. Nothing is known about population trends.

PHOTO CREDITS *John Warburton-Lee*, Masai Mara (Kenya); *Malcolm Schuyl*, South Luangwa (Zambia); *Gerhard Borstlap*, Royal Zambezi (Zambia), *Geir Tore Gravdal*, Serengeti (Tanzania); *Ken Behrens*, Murchison Falls (Uganda).

Kaffa Side-Striped Jackal

LUPULELLA ADUSTUS KAFFENSIS

BL: 60-72 cm. TL: 27.6-32.5 cm. H: 35-50 cm. W: 9 kg (♂), 8.3 kg (♀). SL: 14.6 cm. SW: 7.9 cm. DF: 42. CN: 78. A medium-sized, Dog-like Canid. The smallest subspecies of Side-Striped Jackal, darker in color, with a smaller tail, lacking the distinctive white tip. Coat is grizzled grayish yellow to reddish brown in color, with a strong admixture of black on back. White stripe on side is usually inconspicuous or absent entirely. Undersides and throat are ochraceous rufous. Head is reddish brown. Dog-like face, with a long, narrow, dark gray muzzle, with black nose. Ears are relatively small, rounded, blackish gray behind. Legs are light gray brown to bright red brown, black lined on their upper parts, hindquarters being especially deep and rich in coloring. Tail is short, bushy, mostly black, without the distinctive white tip of other subspecies. Females are slightly smaller than males, and have 2 pairs of mammae.

Lupulella adustus kaffensis

OTHER NAMES Abyssinian Side-Striped Jackal. *French*: Chacal à flancs rayés. *German*: Kafue-Streifenschakal. *Spanish*: Chacal rayado. Russian: Абиссинский полосатый шакал. *Amharic*: Bula kebero.

SUBSPECIES Considered a subspecies of *L. adustus* (Side-Striped Jackal). Probably includes *bweha* (found W Kenya and South Sudan, a small reddish race, with a short black-tipped tail and darker legs and underparts), *elgonae* (Kenya, Uganda), and *namrui* (Sudan).

SIMILAR SPECIES Difficult to distinguish in the field from the African Golden Wolf (*C. anthus)*, as this subspecies lacks the white tail-tip and conspicuous pale lateral stripe that characterize South African forms. However, *L. adustus* ears are rounded and not pointed out as they are in *C. anthus*, being in addition of the same grizzled gray-brown color as the head, while in *C. anthus* ears are ginger or foxy red, strongly contrasting with the rest of the head color. The Ethiopian Wolf (*C. simensis*) is larger, with longer legs, has a distinctive reddish coat, white underparts, throat, chest and tail markings.

REPRODUCTION *Gestation*: 57-64 days. *Young per birth*: 4-6. *Weaning*: 42-70 days. *Sexual maturity*: 9 months. *Life span*: 10 years in captivity. *Breeding season*: Unknown. There is no specific information for this subspecies, but it is probably similar to other subspecies of Side Striped Jackal.

BEHAVIOR *Social behavior*: Monogamous pairs, although they are not always seen together, and usually forage alone; family groups with up to 7 individuals, comprising a breeding pair and their young, can occasionally be seen. *Diet*: Omnivorous, including fruits, seeds, small rodents, hares, gazelle fawns, invertebrates and carrion. *Main predators*: Leopard, hyena, eagles. Nocturnal at lowland locations, with some dawn and dusk activity. However, it may be diurnal as a local adaptive response to preying on the high-altitude rodent community (e.g. *Arvicanthis* species), which is, by and large, the most abundant food and has a marked diurnal activity. It is unknown if there is some competitive overlap between this Jackal and the Ethiopian Wolf were they are sympatric. It shows a remarkable adaptation and tolerance to human and cattle presence in the daytime.

DISTRIBUTION *Native*: Ethiopia, Somalia, probably Kenya, Uganda, and South Sudan. In Ethiopia it is a very rarely recorded subspecies, probably due to identification difficulties. It has been recorded in the Abune Yosef massif, in the Zigit area, between 3,550 and 3,900 m elevation, near Bilbala village (2,830 m), near Muja village (2,146 m), in Senkele Wildlife Sanctuary, in Nachisar National Park, and in Bale Mountains National Park. It has not been detected in the Simien Mountains. Subspecific status of Side-Striped Jackals from NE Uganda, South Sudan and W Kenya, which also lack the white-tipped tail, is not well known, but they may also belong to this subspecies.

HABITAT Open plain and moderately grazed mosaic of grass steppe, *Senecio* grasslands and giant lobelias, up to 3,900 m, well above level of the Afroalpine ecosystem. In Ethiopia, it is perhaps more commonly associated with forested habitats than *Canis aureus*.

CONSERVATION STATUS Least Concern. *CITES*: Not listed. Considered rare throughout its range.

PHOTO CREDITS *Ariadne Van Zandbergen* and *Jurriaan Persyn*, Kidepo National Park (Uganda); *Michael Kragh*, Kalabi (Uganda).

South African Wild Dog

LYCAON PICTUS PICTUS

BL: 95-120 cm. TL: 32-42 cm. H: 75-85 cm. W: 30 kg (♂), 24 kg (♀). SL: 21.1 cm. SW: 15 cm. DF: 42. CN: 78. A very large-sized but lightly built Canid, with long and slim legs, large rounded ears, and a heavy muzzle. The only Canid not having dewclaws on the forelimbs. Largest subspecies of African Wild Dog, more colorful than the East African subspecies. Coat is short on the legs and body and longer around the neck, giving a shaggy appearance. Coloration is distinctive but highly variable, with a combination of irregular black, yellow-brown, and white blotches on the back, sides and legs. Coloration is unique, and can be used to identify individual animals. Yellow-brown head with a black mask, black ears, and a black line following the vertical center line of the forehead, and a white tip to the tail. Females slightly smaller than males, with 6-7 pairs of mammae.

Young

Lycaon pictus pictus

OTHER NAMES Cape Hunting Dog, South African Painted Dog. *French*: Lycaon. *German*: Südafrikanischer Wildhund. *Spanish*: Licaón, perro salvaje sudafricano, perro cazador del Cabo. *Russian*: Капская (южноафриканская) гиеновая собака. *Afrikaans*: Wildehond.

TAXONOMY Five subspecies traditionally recognized (Wilson and Reeder, 2005): *L. p. pictus, L. p. lupinos, L. p. somalicus, L. p. sharicus,* and *L. p. manguensis*. Although S and E populations are genetically and morphologically distinct, there are probably no geographically distinct subspecies. Includes *cacondae, fuchsi, gobabis, krebsi, lalandei, tricolor, typicus, venatica, windhorni* and *zuluensis*.

SIMILAR SPECIES E African populations are duller in coloration. Specimens from the Cape have a large amount of orange-yellow fur overlapping the black, partially yellow backs of the ears, mostly yellow underparts, and a number of whitish hairs on the throat mane. In Mozambique are distinguished by the almost equal development of yellow and black, as well as having less white fur than the Cape form.

REPRODUCTION *Gestation*: 70 days. *Young per birth*: 8-12. *Weaning*: 35-91 days. *Sexual maturity*: 18-21 months. *Life span*: 6-11 years. *Breeding season*: March to September; pups are born from late May to early June. All pack members help to care for the pups. The denning period lasts about 12 weeks, and the mother is confined to the den, relying on other pack members to feed her by regurgitation at this time.

BEHAVIOR *Social behavior*: Packs averaging 8 adults and yearlings, but may be as small as a pair, or over 30. A typical pack consists of a dominant ♂ and ♀ that dominate breeding, their siblings and several related pairs of subordinate ♀ and ♂. *Diet*: The most carnivorous of the Canids: small to medium-sized antelopes in the area (steenbok, duiker); also species as small as hares, and as large as kudu and wildebeest. Packs will chase larger species but rarely kill them. Scavenging of carrion is rare. *Main predators*: Lion, spotted hyena; intraspecific conflicts between neighboring packs is also a large source of mortality. Highly social; hunting, breeding and dispersing in close cooperation with other pack members. Cursorial predators, chasing prey to exhaustion at speeds of up to 65 kmph. They can maintain 45 kmph for 5 km. Home range sizes from 560 to 3,000 km², with significant home range overlap between packs, excluding a core breeding area that each pack defends vigorously. They have a complex communication system incorporating olfactory, visual and auditory systems.

DISTRIBUTION *Native*: Angola, Botswana, Malawi, Namibia, South Africa, Zambia, Zimbabwe. *Probably extinct*: Mozambique, Swaziland. There are viable populations left in Kruger and Hwange National Parks (South Africa), Zambezi National Park (Zimbabwe) and Okavango region (Botswana).

HABITAT Short-grass plains, semi-desert, bushy savannas and upland forest. They prefer thicker bush. Most desert populations are now extirpated.

CONSERVATION STATUS Endangered. *CITES*: Not listed. Estimated population of 2,700 animals. Habitat fragmentation is the main threat, resulting in human-wildlife conflict and transmission of infectious disease. Nearly all individuals held in captivity have a S African origin.

PHOTO CREDITS *Régis Julié*, Motswari (South Africa); *Eric Isselee*; *Arno Meintjes*, Kruger (South Africa); *Frank Warwick* and *Ryan Kilpatrick*, Madikwe (South Africa).

East African Wild Dog

LYCAON PICTUS LUPINUS AND SOMALICUS

BL: 95 cm. TL: 23-30 cm. H: 65 cm. W: 18 kg (♂), 17 kg (♀). SL: 17.5 cm. SW: 12.5 cm. DF: 42. CN: 78. A very large-sized but lightly built Canid, with long, slim legs, large rounded ears, and a heavy muzzle. The only Canid not having dewclaws on the forelimbs. Smaller and less colorful than the South African subspecies. Coat is short on the legs and body and longer around the neck, giving a shaggy appearance. Extremely dark coloring, the yellow being reduced to a minimum, but highly variable. White spots rarely present on the upper surface. Underparts marbled black and white, without yellow, the 2 colors sharply defined from each other. Yellow-brown head with a black muzzle, black ears, and a black line following the vertical center line of the forehead, and a white tip to the tail. Tail yellow proximally, black mesially, and white terminally. Females slightly smaller than males, with 6-7 pairs of mammae.

ssp. *lupinus*

Lycaon pictus lupinus

Lycaon pictus somalicus

OTHER NAMES African Wild Dog, African Hunting Dog, African Painted Dog, Somali Wild Dog. *French*: Lycaon, chien sauvage d'Afrique, chien-hyène, cynhyène, loup peint, chien chasseur. *German*: Ostafrikanischer Wildhund, Hyänenhund, Picassohund. *Spanish*: Licaón, perro salvaje africano, lobo pintado, perro hiena. *Russian*: Восточноафриканская гиеновая собака. *Afrikaans*: Wildehond.

TAXONOMY Recent research shows an apparent gene flow between E and S Wild Dogs, so the existence of separate subspecies is no longer considered likely; however, it is possible that N, central, and W populations may be more distinct, but these populations are rare and difficult to study. *L. p. lupinus* includes *dieseneri*, *gansseri*, *hennigi*, *kondoae*, *lademanni*, *langheldi*, *prageri*, *richteri*, *ruwanae*, *ssongese*, *stierlingi*, *styxi*, *taborae* and *wintgensi*. *L. p. somalicus* includes *luchsingeri*, *ruppelli*, *takanus* and *zedlitzi*.

REPRODUCTION *Gestation*: 70 days. *Young per birth*: 6-16. *Weaning*: 91 days. *Sexual maturity*: 18-21 months. *Life span*: 6-11 years. *Breeding season*: Births occur any time of year, with a peak between March and June. Most packs hold a single breeding ♀, though subordinates of both sexes sometimes produce offspring that are raised, particularly in large packs. Cooperative breeding, in which adults of both sexes provide alloparental care by guarding and feeding pups. Juveniles are fully independent at 16-24 months but remain with their pack; ♀ are more likely to disperse, usually leaving in a subgroup with their sisters once they reach 2 years old.

BEHAVIOR *Social behavior*: Packs from 3 to 20 adults, up to 44 including yearlings and pups. *Diet*: Medium-sized ungulates, particularly gazelles and impala, but prey may range in size from hares and dik diks to kudu and even eland; they seldom kill livestock. *Main predators*: Lion, spotted hyena. Highly social, pack members seldom quarrel with one another, and serious fights are rare; they share food. It is a cooperative hunter, with several individuals literally tearing apart their prey on the run. Predominantly diurnal. Home ranges average 600-800 km². They are most reliably sought during denning season, in June and July, when pack members seldom range far from the denned pups.

DISTRIBUTION *Native*: Ethiopia, Kenya, South Sudan, Sudan, Tanzania. *Possibly extinct*: Uganda, Burundi, Eritrea, Rwanda. Once widespread through most of Africa, now extinct from many countries it was once present in.

HABITAT Habitat generalists, wooded savanna, short grasslands, montane forest and mangroves. They avoid areas of high prey density, apparently because larger carnivores prefer such areas.

CONSERVATION STATUS Endangered. *CITES*: Not listed. Tanzania holds critically important populations, harboring around 20% of the global population, including the world's second and third largest populations in the Selous and Ruaha ecosystems, thought to number 800 and 500 adults respectively. Persecution, habitat loss and disease are the main threats.

PHOTO CREDITS *Panoramic Images* and *Carl Jennings*, Selous (Tanzania); *LHildDVM*, Tsavo West (Kenya); *Hank Halsey*, Ol Pejeta (Kenya).

West, Central and North African Wild Dog

LYCAON PICTUS MANGUENSIS AND SHARICUS

BL: 71-80 cm. TL: 29-33.5 cm. H: 60 cm. W: 18 kg. SL: 17.5 cm. SW: 12.6 cm. DF: 42. CN: 78. A very large-sized but lightly built Canid, with long, slim legs, large rounded ears, and a heavy muzzle. The only Canid not having dewclaws on the forelimbs. There are few reported sightings of these subspecies. Coat is short on the legs and body and longer around the neck. Coloring is variable, from brownish black to yellow brown, with white and yellow blotches on the back, sides and legs. Underparts are black to yellowish brown, with indistinct yellowish and white blotches. Head is large, yellow brown in color, with a black short powerful muzzle, and a black line following the vertical center line of the forehead. Big rounded ears, black outside. Dark ring around the eyes. Lower limbs usually white, with dark spots. White-tipped tail. Females with 6-7 pairs of mammae.

Lycaon pictus manguensis

Lycaon pictus sharicus

OTHER NAMES Manga Hunting Dog, Mischlich's Hunting Dog, Chadian Wild Dog, Shari Hunting Dog, Central Hunting Dog, Ebermaier's Hunting Dog. *French*: Lycaon. *German*: Westafrikaner Wildhund, Zentralafrikanischen Wildhund, Hyänenhund, Picassohund. *Spanish*: Licaón de África occidental y central. *Russian*: Западноафриканская (*manguensis*), Центральноафриканская (*sharicus*) гиеновая собака.

TAXONOMY Considered a subspecies of African Wild Dog (*L. pictus*). These populations are very scarce and difficult to study, but they may be distinct from E and S Wild Dogs. Includes *mischlichi* and *ebermaieri*.

REPRODUCTION *Gestation*: 70 days. *Young per birth*: 8-12. *Weaning*: 91 days. *Sexual maturity*: 18-21 months. *Life span*: Unknown. *Breeding season*: At the beginning of the dry season, end of October, beginning of November, in Cameroon.

BEHAVIOR *Social behavior*: Solitary or small packs up to 15 in N Cameroon, including yearlings and pups. *Diet*: Medium to large-sized ungulates (kob, waterbuck, roan antelope, hartebeest, duiker, oribi), livestock. *Main predators*: Lion, spotted hyena. They are active mainly during the early morning or late evening, and hide in cooler holes during the hot midday. It has been reported that they sleep on the cold sand in the dry season and it seems that they make long daily movements after rains. They hunt in one area for some time before they move to other places, being forced to make large movements to make further kills. Lion distribution may have a strong influence on their migrating behavior. If they are found in large packs, they do not show fear toward human presence, but solitary animals avoid humans.

DISTRIBUTION *Native*: Benin, Burkina Faso, Cameroon, Central African Republic, Niger, Senegal. *Possibly extinct*: Chad, Côte d'Ivoire, DR Congo, Guinea-Bissau, Mali, Nigeria. *Regionally extinct*: Egypt, Gabon, Gambia, Ghana, Libya, Mauritania, Sierra Leone, Sudan, Togo. Formerly distributed throughout sub-Saharan Africa, they have now disappeared from much of their former range. Only two small subpopulations of West African Wild Dog (*manguensis*) survive in the Niokolo-Koba National Park (Senegal) and in the W Transfontier Park and in Pendjari Biosphere Reserve (Benin, Burkina Faso and Niger), although it is unlikely that a viable population still exists in these areas. The only country in N Africa in which they may still persist is Algeria, but there is no information on their current status, and this subpopulation does not exceed 50 individuals. Small subpopulations of Central African Wild Dog (*sharicus*) occur in Bamingui-Bangoran, Chinko, Zemongo Faunal Reserve, and Manovo-Gounda-St. Floris National Park (Central African Republic), Faro and Benoue National Parks (N Cameroon), and probably also in Bahr Salamat, Siniaka-Minia Faunal Reserves (Chad), and in Sudan.

HABITAT Wooded savanna, short grasslands, montane forest and mangroves.

CONSERVATION STATUS Critically Endangered. *CITES*: Not listed. West African population is currently estimated at just 70 individuals, and continues to decline as a result of ongoing habitat fragmentation, conflict with human activities, and infectious disease. Its social organization renders it susceptible to inbreeding depression at low population densities and this also may have contributed to the extinction of populations isolated in protected parks and reserves. Central African population was estimated at just 291 individuals in 2012.

PHOTO CREDITS Based on photos from Chinko Nature Reserve (CAR); *Arnoud Quanjer, Andrew Allport* and *Stuart G. Porter.*

Red Fox-Like Canids
TRUE FOXES, BAT-EARED FOX AND RACCOON DOG

RECOGNITION Red Fox-like Canids, also called Vulpine Foxes, are a group of very small to small-sized Canids, characterized by a long, low body, with relatively short legs, a long pointed muzzle, large triangular ears, and a bushy tail that is at least half as long as the head and body. They have black, triangular face marks between eyes and nose, long black vibrissae, oval-shaped eyes with elliptical pupils, and the tip of the tail is often a different color from the rest of the coat. Color is usually reddish, sandy yellow or brown, with adults exhibiting more than one color, but in some species it may be completely white or black. Supracaudal gland is well developed. There is no marked sexual dimorphism, with males being slightly larger. Females usually have four pairs of nipples. Seasonal dimorphism may be sharp in some northern forms, but is revealed almost solely in degree of fur density and length. The skull is flattened in comparison with *Canis*, with an elongated rostrum. They exhibit the typical Canid dental formula, I 3/3, C 1/1, P 4/4, M 2/3 = 42, except Bat-Eared Foxes, which have six extra molars. Some species have a pungent odor, arising mainly from a gland located on the dorsal surface of the tail. Most species in this group belong to the monophyletic genus *Vulpes* (true Foxes). *Vulpes* was once considered a subgenus of *Canis*, but is now considered genetically distinct. *Fennecus* (Fennec Fox) and *Alopex* (Arctic Fox) are genetically so similar to the genus *Vulpes* that they are now included in this genus. The phylogenetic position of *Otocyon* (Bat-Eared Fox) and *Nyctereutes* (Raccoon Dog) is highly uncertain, but recent sequencing data suggests placement of both of these genera in the *Vulpes*-like clade.

PHYLOGENY During the late Miocene (ca. 10 Ma), the true Fox clade emerged and underwent modest diversification to initiate primitive species of both *Vulpes* and *Urocyon*. *Vulpes* spread out from North America, independent from the *Canis* clade, presumably via the Bering land bridge, and colonized Asia, and later, Africa and Europe. *Vulpes* species were widespread and diverse in Eurasia during the Pliocene. Red Fox and Arctic Fox appeared in North America only in the late Pleistocene, evidently as a result of immigration back to the New World. Up to 13 species of *Vulpes* have survived to the present time throughout Africa, Eurasia and North America, making it the most diverse living Canid genus. The Bat-Eared Fox may represent a late Pliocene immigration event to the Old World, independent of other Foxes (ca. 3 Ma), probably from India. The Raccoon Dog was an early immigrant to the Old World, with a useful fossil record in Asia and Europe dating from the late Miocene to the middle Pliocene (5.5 to 3 Ma); however, it is still far from clear what its original stock in North America was, with some studies suggesting that it is either more basal to the Vulpines or within the Fox lineage.

BEHAVIOR Foxes are generally solitary, forming monogamous mated pairs during the breeding season, and living in small family groups. They can dig their own dens but will often enlarge burrows of other species. Foxes are omnivores and generalist predators, with a diet largely made up of small vertebrates such as rodents, reptiles and birds, and small invertebrates such as insects, and can include eggs, plants and fruits. Foxes may cache excess food, burying it for later consumption, usually under leaves, snow or soil. Bat-Eared Fox is the only member of the Canid family that is truly insectivorous, lacks a carnassial shear, and has up to four pairs of extra molars. The Raccoon Dog is the only member of this group able to climb trees.

DISTRIBUTION Found on every continent except Antarctica. By far the most common and distributed species is the Red Fox, spread across the entire Northern Hemisphere from the Arctic Circle to North Africa, Central America and Asia, and introduced to Australasia in the 19th century. The Arctic Fox is found in the cold regions of the Arctic, while there are species that prefer the arid environment of lower latitudes. The Blanford's Fox inhabits the semi-arid regions of the Middle East, while the Corsac Fox inhabits the arid regions of Central Asia. The Cape Fox, Pale Fox and Fennec Fox inhabit the arid and semi-arid regions of southern Africa, central Africa, and northern Africa respectively. The Rüppell's Fox is found in both Asia and Africa. The Kit and Swift Fox are found in the arid regions of North America. The Indian Fox is endemic to the Indian subcontinent, and the Tibetan Fox is found in the plateau regions of Tibet and Ladakh.

CONSERVATION Like many carnivores, Foxes have at times been both persecuted and valued by humans. They have been pursued by trappers for the value of their fur, by hunters as a game animal, and by those who perceive them as livestock predators. Today management approaches and public attitudes toward Foxes have changed in some regions. They play an important role in regulating abundant species of small mammals, and Foxes have adapted to living in close proximity to people. Most species are not under threat, but current statistics on some populations are not well known and these populations may be threatened.

summer
(blue morph)

summer
(white morph)

Arctic Fox
Vulpes lagopus, 176

winter

Swift Fox
Vulpes velox, 184

Kit Fox
Vulpes macrotis macrotis, 186

San Joaquin Kit Fox
Vulpes macrotis mutica, 188

summer

winter

Corsac Fox
Vulpes corsac, 190

Pale Fox
Vulpes palida, 194

Indian Fox
Vulpes bengalensis, 196

Cape Fox
Vulpes chama, 208

black-tipped tail

white-tipped tail

Blanford's Fox
Vulpes cana, 206

Tibetan Fox
Vulpes ferrilata, 192

Fennec Fox
Vulpes zerda, 204

Rüppell's Fox
Vulpes rueppellii, 198

silver-black color morph

cross color morph

summer

winter

North American Red Fox
Vulpes fulva, 210

Indian form

desert form

Eurasian Red Fox
Vulpes vulpes, 226

Mainland Raccoon Dog
Nyctereutes procyonoides, 260

Japanese Raccoon Dog
Nyctereutes viverrinus, 266

South African Bat-Eared Fox
Otocyon megalotis megalotis, 270

East African Bat-Eared Fox
Otocyon megalotis virgatus, 272

Common Arctic Fox

VULPES LAGOPUS LAGOPUS

BL: 49-57 cm (♂), 47-55 cm (♀). TL: 23-32 cm. H: 25-30 cm. W: 2.8-4.9 kg (♂), 2.5-3.6 kg (♀). SL: 11.7 cm. SW: 6.9 cm. DF: 42. CN: 48-50. A small Fox, with a relatively compact body, short legs, round ears and a short snout. A small-sized subspecies of Arctic Fox, with southern forms being larger than northern forms. Coat is thick and dense in winter, with a majority of this fur being fine underfur. Summer coat is thinner. Molting is from May to early July, and from September to December. Two color morphs: white morph is pure white in winter, changing to brown dorsally, and light gray to white on its underside in summer; blue morph is brown tinged with a blue sheen in winter, changing to brownish dusky in summer, usually darkest on top of head and rump, with face and legs mixed with white hairs, and ears strongly edged with white. White morph predominates in this subspecies. Yellow eyes, with elongated pupils. Thickly haired feet. Tail is long and bushy. Females smaller than males, with 6 to 7 pairs of mammae.

winter coat
(white morph)

winter coat
(blue morph)

summer coat
(white morph)

176

Vulpes lagopus lagopus

OTHER NAMES Polar Fox, White Fox, Snow Fox. *French*: Renard polaire, isatis. *German*: Gewöhnlicher Polarfuchs. *Spanish*: Zorro ártico, zorro polar. *Russian*: Материковый (обыкновенный) песец.

TAXONOMY Four subspecies traditionally recognized: *V. l. lagopus* (most of the range), *V. l. beringensis* (Commander Islands, Russia), *V. l. fuliginosus* (Iceland, Greenland, Svalbard) and *V. l. pribilofensis* (Pribilof Islands, Alaska). Two ecotypes recognized: Lemming Foxes (continental Eurasia, North America, the Canadian archipelago and E Greenland), and coastal Foxes (Iceland, Svalbard, S, W and NW Greenland). Previously included in the genus *Alopex*. Closely related to the North American Kit and Swift Fox. This subspecies includes *argenteus*, *caerulea*, *ungava*, *hallensis*, *innuitus* and *sibiricus*.

SIMILAR SPECIES Red Fox is larger, with a white-tipped tail, longer legs and reddish color.

REPRODUCTION *Gestation*: 52 days. *Young per birth*: 6-12, exceptionally up to 25. *Weaning*: 28-42 days. *Sexual maturity*: 10-12 months. *Life span*: 10 years. *Breeding season*: April and May. Newborns of both color phases are covered with short velvety dark brown fur, which becomes lighter and longer after the pups reach 2 weeks of age. Blue-phase pups acquire their characteristic dark color by the time they are 2 months old. They prefer to den in light, sandy soil along riverbanks, on small hillocks, and occasionally in talus. On the open tundra, dens are usually a mound 1-4 m high.

BEHAVIOR *Social behavior*: Monogamous pairs in the breeding season. *Diet*: Lemming Foxes, typical of inland locations, have mostly white coats, migrate further and feed on lemmings and other small rodents; coastal Foxes live along the coasts of the Arctic, have mostly blue coats and feed on migratory birds, eggs, fish, seal carcasses and marine invertebrates. *Main predators*: Red Fox, wolverine, golden eagle, brown bear, Wolf. Mainly nocturnal, but their activity patterns are flexible depending on their prey. They may travel great distances during winter and traverse extensive pack ice fields. They may follow polar bears to scavenge kill remains. Territories are defended directly by chasing and mobbing and indirectly via scent marking and vocalizations, especially during the denning season. They scent mark by defecating on visually conspicuous or elevated landmarks such as rocks and eskers. Good swimmers. Common vocalizations include growls, barks and coughs, but also employ visual signs for communication.

DISTRIBUTION *Native*: Canada, Finland, Norway, Russia, Sweden, United States. Circumpolar distribution, including the Arctic and tundra zones of North America and Eurasia, parts of the alpine zones of Fennoscandia, and islands of the Arctic, North Atlantic and North Pacific Oceans. In North America, Arctic Foxes also occur on several Aleutian Islands in Alaska, where they were introduced for fur farming.

HABITAT Arctic and alpine tundra, often near coasts.

CONSERVATION STATUS Least Concern. *CITES*: Not listed. *Regional status*: Critically Endangered (Norway), protected by law in Finland, Sweden and Norway. It is fairly abundant in North America. The release of many Arctic Foxes to over 450 islands in Alaska had catastrophic effects on island avifauna populations.

PHOTO CREDITS *Jim Fowler*, Hudson Bay (Canada); *Prof. Dirk HR Spennemann*, Shemya Island, AK (USA); *Dan Mongrain,* Toronto Zoo (Canada); *Graphic Jackson*, Churchill, MB (Canada); *Jim Cumming* (Canada).

Bering Arctic Fox

VULPES LAGOPUS BERINGENSIS

BL: 49-57 cm (♂), 47-55 cm (♀). TL: 23-36 cm. H: 25-30 cm. W: 4-8.8 kg (♂), 3.2-7.2 kg (♀). SL: 13.2 cm. SW: 7.5 cm. DF: 42. CN: 48-50. A small Fox, with a relatively compact body, short legs, round ears and a short snout. A large subspecies of Arctic Fox, similar to Pribilof Arctic Fox (*pribilofensis*), with more luxuriant fur than mainland subspecies. Individuals from Mednyi Island are larger than those from Bering Island. Coat is thick and dense in winter, with a majority of this fur being fine underfur. Summer coat is thinner. Blue morph predominates, and white individuals are extremely rare. Coat is a uniformly diffuse brownish gray tinged with a blue sheen in winter, changing to brownish dusky in summer, usually darkest on top of head and rump, with face and legs mixed with white hairs, and ears strongly edged with white. Yellow eyes, with elongated pupils. Thickly haired feet. Tail is long and bushy. Females slightly smaller than males, with 6 to 7 pairs of mammae.

summer coat
(blue morph)

winter coat
(blue morph)

Vulpes lagopus beringensis

OTHER NAMES Bering Island Fox, Commander Polar Fox. *French*: Renard polaire de l'Île Béring. *German*: Bering-Polarfuchs. *Spanish*: Zorro polar de las islas del Comandante. *Russian*: Командорский голубой песец.

TAXONOMY Considered a subspecies of Arctic Fox (*V. lagopus*). Includes *beringensis* (Bering Island), and *semenovi* (Mednyi Island).

REPRODUCTION *Gestation*: 52-54 days. *Young per birth*: 1-13, usually smaller litter than mainland subspecies. *Weaning*: 28-35 days. *Sexual maturity*: 12 months. *Life span*: Probably 10 years. *Breeding season*: Early September to early May. Dens are located under stones, in scree, and in crevices, mainly on elevated points, attached to the coastline and less frequently situated deep in the tundra. Dens are used for many years and have many entrance holes, and numerous paths connect breeding burrows with dens and shelters, and stretch to rich feeding areas within each home range. Conspicuous mounds, resulting from the accumulated scent posts, concentrate in the tundra around breeding burrows. Young disperse over shorter distances than mainland subspecies, with ♂ dispersing farther than ♀.

BEHAVIOR *Social behavior*: Families comprised of 1 ♂ and up to 4 ♀; a single ♂ may have a home range encompassing 2 breeding dens, each with a ♀ group including 1 or 2 lactating ♀ and 1 ♀ helper. In most families, there is 1 helper, a non-reproductive ♀. Polygyny is more common than in mainland subspecies. *Diet*: On both islands, in summer, they feed on colonies of sea birds the most intensively; they also turn to abundant and easily accessible sources of food, such as corpses of whales and other sea mammals beached by the sea or food dumps near human settlements. *Main predators*: None. They show a system of territorial defense, which is seen also in other subspecies, characterized by display, mobbing and direct aggression against an intruder, combined with territorial barks, expressive postures and urine and feces markings, performed many times a day during the breeding season and if provoked by meetings with Foxes or human intruders. Home ranges along the seashore average 2.0 km^2, much smaller than in mainland subspecies. Owing to the small home ranges, neighboring families are at short distances and barking is used frequently as communication within and between family groups. They display little fear of people.

DISTRIBUTION *Native*: Russia. Restricted to the Commander Islands (Bering and Mednyi Islands) in the Bering Sea. On Mednyi Island, they are largely restricted to a narrow strip along the coastline where food sources are concentrated.

HABITAT The habitat conditions of this island subspecies differ sharply from the continental ones: there are no other native land predators on the islands, the climatic conditions are quite mild, and food resources are stable and highly productive.

CONSERVATION STATUS Least Concern. *CITES*: Not listed. Until the mid-20th century, the population on Mednyi Island remained stable at about 1,000 Foxes but crashed in the late 1970s due to epizootic mange. Currently the population consists of less than 100 individuals. In contrast, the Bering Island population has not suffered serious declines, and population remains stable, at about 600 adult animals.

PHOTO CREDITS *Alexander Gos'kov, Dmytro Pylypenko, tryton2011* and *Maximilian Buzun,* Commander Islands (Russia).

Iceland Arctic Fox

VULPES LAGOPUS FULIGINOSUS

BL: 45-67 cm. TL: 25-42 cm. H: 28 cm. W: 2.5-5 kg. SL: 11.9 cm. SW: 6.9 cm. DF: 42. CN: 48-50. A small Fox, with a relatively compact body, short legs, round ears and a short snout. A small-sized subspecies of Arctic Fox, with white and blue morphs being common along the W coast of Greenland, and Iceland, and white morphs being in a great majority in NE Greenland and Svalbard. Winter coat is very dense and thick. Summer coat is thinner. Molting is from May to early July, and from September to December. White morph is pure white in winter, changing to mottled gray brown dorsally, and light gray to white on its underside in summer. Blue morph is gray brown, with a bluish tinge in winter, changing to dark gray brown in summer. Yellow eyes, with elongated pupils. Thickly haired feet. Tail is long and bushy. Females slightly smaller than males, with 6 to 7 pairs of mammae.

winter coat
(white morph)

summer coat
(white morph)

winter coat
(blue morph)

summer coat
(blue morph)

Vulpes lagopus fuliginosus

OTHER NAMES Sooty Arctic Fox. *French*: Renard polaire d'Islande. *German*: Island-Polarfuchs. *Spanish*: Zorro polar de Islandia. *Russian*: Исландский (Гренландский) песец. *Icelandic*: Refur, tófa.

TAXONOMY Considered a subspecies of Arctic Fox (*V. lagopus*). Includes *groenlandicus* and *spitzbergenensis*.

REPRODUCTION *Gestation*: 52-54 days. *Young per birth*: 5-10, smaller litter than mainland subspecies. *Weaning*: 28-35 days. *Sexual maturity*: 12 months. *Life span*: 10 years. *Breeding season*: March. Births occur in late May or early June. The ♂ has a full role in bringing up the pups, but nonbreeding yearling ♀ may assist mated pairs for the first 6-8 weeks. Dens are often located under large rocks.

BEHAVIOR *Social behavior*: Mated pairs; monogamous. *Diet*: The coast is very important and a stable resource of edible things, such as birds and eggs, seal carcasses, and invertebrates. In inland habitats main foods include ptarmigan in winter, and migrant birds, particularly waders and geese, in summer. Sheep are a relatively unimportant constituent of the diet. There are no lemmings in Iceland, Svalbard and W Greenland. Since the food abundance is highly seasonal, they cache food for the winter. *Main predators*: None. During the mating season, they have a territory, the size of which depends on food availability, ranging from 35 to 50 km^2. They have a number of adaptations that allow them to survive the harsh Arctic winter: a lower metabolic rate and lower body temperature in winter, which allows them to conserve energy, a superbly insulated winter coat, with a thick layer of fat as a food reserve; the short snout and small rounded ears also help to conserve heat.

DISTRIBUTION *Native*: Iceland, Greenland, Norway (Svalbard). Found throughout Iceland, with a higher density in the W fjords. In Svalbard, they are found on all the islands.

HABITAT Arctic tundra, along rocky beaches, and far out and widely dispersed on the frozen pack ice. They prefer the tundra in the vicinity of bird cliffs during the summer.

CONSERVATION STATUS Least Concern. *CITES*: Not listed. Population in Iceland had been growing quite steadily up until 2010, but has shrunk by one-third over the past four years, at about 6,000-7,000 animals. Main threats include climate change, lack of prey, and hunting at all seasons; they are regarded as vermin for supposed sheep-killing and damage to eider colonies. Its fur is not used anymore since it lost value. The Hornstrandir Nature Reserve is one of the few regions where it is protected in Iceland. Arctic Foxes were bred on farms in Iceland from the 1930s until the late 1940s, and again after 1980; the farm-bred blue Foxes are larger and more fertile than the native animals and their color is much lighter. Some have escaped and bred with Icelandic Foxes in the wild, especially in the SW, so gene swamping may represent a threat to the Icelandic Arctic Fox. Population on Svalbard is stable, estimated at 2,500 animals, despite centuries of intense hunting; outside the protected areas, locals are still allowed to hunt during a certain period in the winter. The Arctic Fox was eradicated on Jan Mayen in the 1930s as a result of trapping. Population in Greenland is also currently stable and is estimated at more than 10,000 animals.

PHOTO CREDITS *Elma Ben*, Hornstrandir Nature Reserve (Iceland); *Pétur Bjarni Gíslason*, Vestgronland (Greenland); *Aleviga, Spitsbergen* and *Arterra Picture Library*, Svalbard Islands (Norway); *Scott Lamont*, Kulusuk (Greenland); *Kaity Barrett*, Reykjavik (Iceland).

Pribilof Arctic Fox

VULPES LAGOPUS PRIBILOFENSIS

BL: 45-67 cm. TL: 25-42 cm. H: 28 cm. W: 1.4-9 kg. SL: 12.7 cm. SW: 7.2 cm. DF: 42. CN: 48-50. A small Fox, with a relatively compact body, short legs, round ears and a short snout. The largest subspecies of Arctic Fox, with a longer rostrum. Blue color phase predominates in this subspecies. Coat is thick and dense in winter, with a majority of this fur being fine underfur. Blue morph is brown tinged with a blue sheen in winter, changing to brownish dusky in summer, usually darkest on top of head and rump, with face and legs mixed with white hairs, and ears strongly edged with white. White morph is pure white in winter, the only marking being the small black nose pad, while in summer it is brown dorsally and light gray to white on its underside. Yellow eyes, with elongated pupils. Thickly haired feet. Tail is long and bushy. Females are slightly smaller than males, with 6 to 7 pairs of mammae.

winter coat
(white morph)

Young

summer coat
(blue morph)

Vulpes lagopus pribilofensis

OTHER NAMES Blue Fox. *French*: Renard polaire des Îles Pribilof. *German*: Pribilof-Polarfuchs. *Spanish*: Zorro polar de las islas Pribilof. *Italian*: Volpe artica. *Russian*: Песец островов Прибылова.

TAXONOMY Considered a subspecies of Arctic Fox (*V. lagopus*).

REPRODUCTION *Gestation*: 51-54 days. *Young per birth*: 7, up to 15. *Weaning*: 28-35 days. *Sexual maturity*: 9-10 months. *Life span*: Unknown. *Breeding season*: Between February and May. Births take place from April to July. They den in sandy, well drained soils in low mounds and river cutbanks, and in coastal areas near food resources, such as seal rookeries. Social organization of this subspecies appears complex, and only a small percentage of adult and yearling ♀ bred. A high degree of conspecific tolerance exists between certain individuals. Most nonbreeding Foxes attend the litters of breeding pairs. Attendant Foxes protect, play with, and probably feed pups. Old and sick individuals interact with pups at den sites and rendezvous areas. Yearlings of both sexes are widely tolerated near pups and breeding adults. Some yearlings attend multiple dens.

BEHAVIOR *Social behavior*: Family units of Arctic Foxes aggregate during mating and pup rearing, then break up and are solitary during the fall and winter. *Diet*: Opportunistic feeders, eating small mammals, birds, bird eggs, carrion and garbage when available. *Main predators*: None. Exceptionally adapted for the extreme cold conditions of the Arctic region, with a highly insulating fur, compact body, foot thermoregulation and reduced metabolism during cold weather or food shortage. Mean home range size for both sexes is small relative to that reported for Arctic Foxes in other areas. Yearling home ranges show a large degree of overlap, while core areas are virtually discrete. Most yearlings engage in sporadic and unpredictable forays outside their normal home ranges, increasing in distance and duration over the summer.

DISTRIBUTION *Native*: United States (Alaska). Restricted to the Pribilof Islands, on both St. George and St. Paul Islands.

HABITAT Associated with treeless coastal areas and sea ice.

CONSERVATION STATUS Least Concern. *CITES*: Not listed. *Regional status*: low status and high biological vulnerability; action needed (USA). Populations of this subspecies are at critically low levels and appear to be declining further. The estimated population on St. Paul Island was 230 animals in 1991. Threats include significant reduction in food resources, increased exposure to diseases and toxins, and unsustainable levels of direct human persecution. Additionally, the decline in sea ice has likely led to increased genetic isolation. Misinformation as to the origin of Arctic Foxes on the Pribilofs continues to foster negative attitudes, and the long-term persistence of this endemic subspecies is in jeopardy.

PHOTO CREDITS *Monte M. Taylor, Scot Loehrer, Design Pics Inc.,* and *Steven Metildi*, St. Paul Island, Pribilofs (Alaska); *Doug Sonerholm*, St. George Island, Pribilofs (Alaska).

Swift Fox
VULPES VELOX

BL: 50-54.5 cm (♂), 47.5-54 cm (♀). TL: 22.5-28 cm. H: 30-32 cm. W: 2-2.5 kg (♂), 1.6-2.3 kg (♀). SL: 11.2 cm. SW: 6.4 cm. DF: 42. CN: 50. A small Fox. Winter coat is a dark buffy gray across the back extending into a yellow-tan to ochraceous-buff coloration on the sides, legs and ventral surface of the tail. Back appears to be grizzled due to the presence of conspicuous black and white guard hairs. Underfur is thick. Throat, chest and belly are pale yellow to white. Summer coat is shorter and may be rufous in coloration. Black patches on either side of the muzzle. Ears are large, pointed and erect, cream to white inside. Feet covered by coarse fur. Tail is long, bushy, with a slight black patch over the tail gland, and a black tip. Females are slightly smaller than males.

summer coat

winter coat

summer coat

winter coat

Vulpes velox

OTHER NAMES *French*: Renard véloce. *German*: Swiftfuchs. *Spanish*: Zorro veloz, zorro cometa. *Italian*: Volpe americana, volpe veloce. *Russian*: Американский корсак.

TAXONOMY Monotypic. It was split into two subspecies: *V. v. velox* (Southern Swift Fox) and *V. v. hebes* (Northern Swift Fox, Canada, slightly larger and paler), but this distinction is not generally recognized. Some authors consider Swift Fox and Kit Fox a single species.

SIMILAR SPECIES Distinguished from all other North American foxes, except the Kit Fox, by its small size and black-tipped tail. Distinguished from the Kit Fox by its shorter and more widely spaced ears, its shorter tail, and its more rounded and Dog-like head (compared with the broader head and narrower snout of the Kit Fox).

REPRODUCTION *Gestation*: 50-53 days. *Young per birth*: 1-6. *Weaning*: 6-7 weeks. *Sexual maturity*: 1-2 years. *Life span*: 3-6 years, 14 years in captivity. *Breeding season*: late December to February, with populations in N regions breeding later. Births occur from February to early May. Parental care is overseen by both parents.

BEHAVIOR *Social behavior*: Lasting mated pairs. Diet: Opportunistic: mice, cottontail rabbits, carrion, but occasionally other small mammals, birds, insects, reptiles and amphibians, varying seasonally. *Main predators*: Coyote, badger, golden eagle, bobcat. Mainly nocturnal, although they may rest in the sun outside their dens during the day. They generally hunt at sunrise and sunset. They do not appear to be territorial and home ranges may overlap in high-quality habitat. ♀ maintain territories and family structure, whereas ♂ tend to emigrate. Home range size from 7.6 km² to 32 km². They are den dependent, relying on dens for shelter, escape from predators, and rearing of young. Unlike other Canids, they use multiple den sites year-round. They may run faster than 60 kmph. Vulnerable to trapping, due to their curious nature. Vocalizations include purrs, growls, whines and shrill yaps.

DISTRIBUTION *Native*: United States. *Regionally extinct*: Canada. Found in W South Dakota, S and E Wyoming, W Kansas, W Oklahoma, E and N Colorado, NW Texas, and E New Mexico. Reintroduction programs in Canada (S Alberta and S Saskatchewan) and Montana have established wild populations. There is a zone of hybridization with Kit Fox in E New Mexico and W Texas.

HABITAT Short-grass and mixed-grass prairies in gently rolling or level terrain. They sometimes inhabit plains and prairie areas that are intermixed with winter wheat fields. They avoid these densely vegetated habitats.

CONSERVATION STATUS Least Concern. *CITES*: Not listed. *Regional status*: Endangered (USA, Canada). Population is stable in Kansas, Colorado, Oklahoma and New Mexico. In Texas and Wyoming, populations are fragmented and vulnerable. It is rare in Nebraska, South Dakota and Montana, and extirpated from North Dakota. Reintroduced population in Canada is estimated at 300 individuals, isolated from the contiguous range in the United States. Main threats include conversion of grassland to cropland, road developments, Red Fox expansion and competition, poisoning to kill Coyotes and predation by Coyotes.

PHOTO CREDITS *Sam Houston*, Houston Zoo (USA); *Debi Dalio,* Fort Worth Zoo (USA); *Nano Maus*, Henry Doorly Zoo (USA); *Gerard W. Beyersbergen*, Onefour (Canada); *Rob Palmer*, Pawnee National Grassland, CO (USA).

Kit Fox

VULPES MACROTIS MACROTIS

BL: 47-52 cm (♂), 45.5-53.5 cm (♀). TL: 26-32.3 cm. H: 30-32 cm. W: 1.5-2.5 kg (♂), 1.6-2.2 kg (♀). SL: 10.5 cm. SW: 5.7 cm. DF: 42. CN: 54. A small-sized Fox, with a small, slim body, long slender legs and large ears. Coat coloration is yellowish gray to dusty grizzled, becoming paler on the sides, and pale yellow to white on the underparts. Shoulders, lower sides, flanks and a strip across the chest are buffy to orange. Underfur is heavy. Sides of the muzzle, lower lip and posterior upper lip are blackish or brownish. Relatively large ears, tan to gray on the back, changing to buff or orange at the base, with a thick border of white hairs on the forward inner edge and inner base. Narrow muzzle. The soles of the feet are protected by stiff tufts of hair. Tail is long and bushy, tapering slightly toward the tip, with a pronounced black spot over the caudal gland, and a black tip. Females are slightly lighter than males, but there is no other obvious sexual dimorphism.

Young

Vulpes macrotis macrotis

OTHER NAMES Desert Kit Fox, Swift-Footed Fox. *French*: Renard nain. *German*: Gewöhnlicher Kitfuchs. *Spanish*: Zorro kit, zorra norteña. *Russian*: Американская лисица.

TAXONOMY As many as eight subspecies have been traditionally recognized, although probably only Kit Foxes in San Joaquin Valley warrant subspecific designation (Hall, 1981). Includes *neomexicana* (NW Chihuahua, Colorado, New Mexico, W Texas), *arsipus* (N Sonora, SE California, S Arizona), *devia* (S Baja California), *nevadensis* (Great Basin), *tenuirostris* (N Baja California) and *zinseri* (N-central Mexico). Kit Foxes hybridize with Swift Foxes, and some authors have suggested that they are conspecific.

SIMILAR SPECIES Distinguished externally from other North American Foxes, except the Swift Fox and Gray Fox, by their small size and black-tipped tail. Swift Fox has smaller ears, shorter tail, and less angular appearance. Gray Fox is slightly larger, has proportionally smaller ears and legs, and has a black ridge on the tail and lower back.

REPRODUCTION *Gestation*: 49-55 days. *Young per birth*: 1-6. *Weaning*: 90 days. *Sexual maturity*: 12 months. *Life span*: 4 years, 12 years in captivity. *Breeding season*: December through February, with births from late January to March. ♂ provision ♀ for the first few weeks of pup rearing. At weaning, both parents bring food to the den. Pups emerge when they are 4-5 weeks old and begin to forage with the parents at 3-4 months of age. Young generally disperse in October. They can dig their own dens but will often enlarge burrows of badgers and other species. Dens are used as rest sites, shelter against harsh weather, to bear and rear young, and to escape predators, and are used primarily by the members of the resident family and may be used repeatedly over multiple generations. Frequent den switching is common.

BEHAVIOR *Social behavior*: Mated pairs with pair bonds that last several years; monogamous with occasional polygyny. *Diet*: Lagomorphs, prairie dogs, and kangaroo rats, but also will feed on ground-nesting birds, reptiles and insects; cactus fruits may be eaten if available. They also will consume human foods and will cache food for use at a later time. They do not need access to water. *Main predators*: Coyote, Red Fox, Domestic Dog, bobcat. Primarily nocturnal, with peaks in activity occurring during crepuscular periods. Daytime hours are usually spent resting in or near the den. Home range estimates vary from 2.5 to 11.6 km². Mated pairs are territorial with home ranges that overlap little with neighboring pairs. Territories are maintained primarily by scent marking. Vocalizations include growls, barks, whimpers and purrs.

DISTRIBUTION *Native*: Mexico, United States. It occurs from N Mexico and Baja California N through W Texas, W of the Rocky Mountains to SW Idaho and SE Oregon, and in portions of California, Arizona, Nevada, Utah, New Mexico and W Colorado.

HABITAT Mixed-grass shrublands, shrublands, grasslands, and margins of pinyon-juniper woodlands, deserts with xeric shrubland and sandy soils.

CONSERVATION STATUS Least Concern. *CITES*: Not listed. *Regional status*: Vulnerable (Mexico), Threatened (Oregon), Endangered (Colorado), protected non-game species (Idaho), protected furbearer species (Utah, Arizona, Nevada, New Mexico and Texas). Populations appear to be declining in parts of their range. Its pelt has little market value. The main threat is habitat conversion and degradation.

PHOTO CREDITS *Robert Shantz*, Arizona (USA); *Welcomia* (USA); *Jorn Vangoidtsenhoven*, Death Valley National Park, CA (USA).

San Joaquin Kit Fox

VULPES MACROTIS MUTICA

BL: 50 cm (♂), 48.5 cm (♀). TL: 28.4-29.5 cm. H: 30 cm. W: 2.3 kg (♂), 2.1 kg (♀). DF: 42. CN: 54. A small-sized Fox, with small, slim body and long slender legs, and large ears. The largest subspecies of Kit Fox. Coat coloration is generally tan in the summer and silver gray in the winter. Guard hairs on the back are black tipped, which accounts for the grizzled appearance. Underparts are light buff to white, with the shoulders, lower sides, flanks and chest buff to a rust color. Relatively large ears, set close together, dark on the back side, with a thick border of white hairs on the forward-inner edge and inner base. Narrow muzzle. Tail is long and bushy, tapering slightly toward the tip, typically carried low and straight, black tipped. Females are slightly smaller than males.

Young

Vulpes macrotis mutica

OTHER NAMES Curtailed Fox. *French*: Renard nain de San Joaquin. *German*: San-Joaquin-Kitfuchs. *Spanish*: Zorro kit de San Joaquín, zorrita de San Joaquín. *Russian*: Сан-Хоакинская лисица.

TAXONOMY Considered a subspecies of Kit Fox (*V. macrotis*).

SIMILAR SPECIES Red Fox is heavier, has a white-tipped tail, and a different coat color. Gray Fox also has a black-tipped tail, but is larger and more robust, has smaller ears, and a distinctive black stripe running along the top of the tail. Young Coyotes may be misidentified as Kit Foxes.

REPRODUCTION *Gestation*: 48-52 days. *Young per birth*: 2-6. *Weaning*: Probably 90 days. *Sexual maturity*: 12 months. *Life span*: 8 years, 10 years in captivity. *Breeding season*: Between late December and March. Litters are born in February and March. During this period the ♂ provides most of the food for the ♀ and the pups. Pups emerge above ground at 1 month of age. After 4 to 5 months the family bonds begin to dissolve and the young begin dispersing. Offspring of both sexes sometimes remain with their parents through the following year and help raise a subsequent litter. They use dens for shelter, reproduction and escape from predators; numerous dens may be used throughout the year. They either construct dens by digging or use existing dens and structures created by other animals, such as ground squirrels, badgers, and Coyotes, or human-made structures. Entrances are usually from 20 to 25 cm in diameter, normally higher than wide.

BEHAVIOR *Social behavior*: Mated pairs year-round; monogamous. *Diet*: Varies regionally and seasonally, according to the availability of prey, and includes kangaroo rats, pocket mice, white-footed mice, other nocturnal rodents, California ground squirrels, black-tailed hares, San Joaquin antelope squirrels, desert cottontails, ground-nesting birds, chukars and insects. *Main predators*: Coyote, Red Fox, Domestic Dog, bobcat, large raptors. Nocturnal, typically hunting at night, although may hunt during daylight hours when necessary, as illustrated by their consumption of the diurnal ground squirrel. Home ranges from 2.6 to 31 km^2.

DISTRIBUTION *Native*: United States. It currently inhabits certain regions of the San Joaquin Valley floor and the surrounding foothills, from S Kern County N to Contra Costa, in California. Three core Kit Fox populations are found in the Carrizo Plain, W Kern County, and the Ciervo Panoche Natural Area.

HABITAT Grasslands and shrublands, many of which have been extensively modified. They may also inhabit oak woodland, alkali sink shrubland, and vernal pool and alkali meadow communities.

CONSERVATION STATUS Least Concern. *CITES*: Not listed. *Regional status*: Endangered (USA), Threatened (California). Historically abundant in the San Joaquin Valley and surrounding areas, but their populations have been reduced as a result of urban and agricultural development, oil and gas development, as well as predator and rodent control programs. Carrizo Plain has the largest population, with an estimated 250 to 600 individuals. Habitat destruction is the greatest threat. Expansion of Red Foxes may be a factor in the apparent decline in the NW segment of their range.

PHOTO CREDITS *Don Quintana*, *Mark A. Chappell*, *Purestock* and *Rick Derevan*, San Joaquin Valley, CA (USA); *Kevin Schafer*, Carrizo Plain National Monument, CA (USA).

Corsac Fox
VULPES CORSAC

BL: 45-60 cm (♂), 45-50 cm (♀). TL: 19-35 cm. H: 30-35 cm. W: 1.6-3.2 kg (♂), 1.9-2.4 kg (♀). SL: 9.6-11.8 cm. SW: 5.7-7.1 cm. DF: 42. CN: 36. A small-sized Canid, with relatively broad ears, a short pointy face, and a short tail. Coat is short, buff to straw gray in summer, shading to rufous, while in winter it is long and grayish white. Forehead is darker with pale markings around mouth, chin, throat and groin. A patch of dark fur extends from the inner corner of each eye down the sides of the muzzle to the nose. Ears are large and broad. Legs are light yellow anteriorly and rusty yellow laterally. Winter coat is thick, silky and soft, straw gray in color, with a darker line running down the back. Teeth are small. Tail is dark ocher to gray brown, with a dark spot about 6-7 cm from the base in the supracaudal gland, and a black tip. Females are similar to males. Newborns are light brown, with a monocolored tail.

summer coat

Young

winter coat

Vulpes corsac corsac

Vulpes corsac kalmykorum

Vulpes corsac turkmenicus

OTHER NAMES   Corsac, Steppe Fox. *French*: Renard corsac. *German*: Steppenfuchs, Korsak. *Spanish*: Zorro estepario, zorro corsac. *Russian*: Корсак. *Chinese*: Sha Hu. *Farsi*: Roubaah-e Torkamani. *Mongol*: Khiars. *Pashto*: Lumbara. *Urdu*: Loomari.

TAXONOMY   *V. c. corsac* (Kazakhstan Corsac Fox, includes *scorodumovi* and *nigra*, N Kazakhstan, S Siberia, Transbaikalia, NE China, Mongolia): largest subspecies, with fluffy and dense winter fur, without admixture of reddish tones in winter fur; *V. c. kalmykorum* (Caucasus Corsac Fox, N Uzbekistan, Caucasus); *V. c. turkmenicus* (Turkmen Fox, S Uzbekistan, S Kazakhstan, Turkmenistan, N Iran, N Afghanistan, NW Kyrgyzstan, W Tajikistan): smallest subspecies, with shorter, coarser winter fur of dirty-grayish color and reddish tones. There are wide zones of transition between subspecies.

SIMILAR SPECIES   Red Fox is slightly larger, with a white-tipped tail and dark brown or black forelegs. Tibetan Fox is slightly larger, with a white tail tip.

REPRODUCTION   *Gestation*: 52-60 days. *Young per birth*: 2-6. *Weaning*: 28 days. *Sexual maturity*: 9 months. *Life span*: 9 years. *Breeding season*: January to March. Several ♂ run behind a ♀ in estrus and fights often occur between the ♂. Monogamy is established when the ♀ chooses a ♂. Earliest births are in mid-March, but most occur in April. ♂ participate in raising and feeding young but stay in another den or just outside the natal den. They will often take burrows of other animals to raise their young in. Young are born blind and with closed auditory meatuses. Juveniles emerge from dens in mid-May. Young grow rapidly, reach adult size in 4 months.

BEHAVIOR   *Social behavior*: Family groups. *Diet*: Opportunistic forager and hunter; small to medium-sized vertebrates (vole, gerbil, jerboa, hamster, squirrel, pika, bustard), insects, and fruits. They may scavenge carcasses. Can go without water for extensive periods of time. *Main predators*: Wolf, Red Fox, Dog, eagles, owls. Mainly nocturnal, but may be seen during twilight and daytime hours. Very social, living in large groups with several burrows interconnected. It hunts alone or in small packs. Territory sizes are variable, from 1.9 to 11.4 km². They are nomadic and do not keep a fixed home range, and will migrate when food is sparse, ranging from 50 to 600 km. They scent mark with urine and feces near natal dens to maintain territories and as a way of intraspecific communication. Corsac Fox lacks the musky odor of other Vulpine foxes. Excellent climbers, but slow runners. The most common vocalization is barking.

DISTRIBUTION   *Native*: Afghanistan, China, Iran, Kazakhstan, Kyrgyzstan, Mongolia, Russia, Tajikistan, Turkmenistan, Uzbekistan.

HABITAT   Grassland steppes, semi-deserts and deserts, avoiding mountains, forested areas, dense vegetation and cultivated lands.

CONSERVATION STATUS   Least Concern. *CITES*: Not listed. *Regional status*: Endangered (Iran), Vulnerable (China), Near Threatened (Mongolia). There are no estimates of population size and few details are known about the characteristics of regional populations, but it is considered widespread and common. Main threat is poaching; they are rather slow runners and are easily caught by hunters, and their population has been reduced in areas where they have been heavily hunted for their fur.

PHOTO CREDITS   *Ulli Joerres,* Dierenrijk (Netherlands); *FLPA, Werner Layer, Ronan Kennedy*, Tayto Park (Ireland); *Thomas Langenberg,* Öndorkhan (Mongolia).

Tibetan Fox

VULPES FERRILATA

BL: 51.5-71.7 cm (♂), 49-66.2 cm (♀). TL: 21-47 cm. H: 26.7-35.4 cm. W: 4.4-5.7 kg (♂), 3.6-4.1 kg (♀). SL: 13.9 cm. SW: 7.5 cm. DF: 42. CN: 36. A small-sized Canid, with a conspicuously narrow and long muzzle and a rather square head. Pelage is soft and thick, pale gray agouti or sandy, with a tan to rufous band along the dorsum. Muzzle, crown and neck are reddish. Underparts are white. Vertical gray to black bands between the forelegs and chest. Ears are small, white inside, tan outside. A distinctive elongated muzzle. Forelegs are russet. Tail is bushy, mostly gray, with a dark streak near the base in the supracaudal gland, and a white tip.

Vulpes ferrilata

OTHER NAMES Tibetan Sand Fox. *French*: Renard du Tibet. *German*: Tibetfuchs. *Spanish*: Zorro tibetano. *Italian*: Volpe delle sabbie tibetana. *Russian*: Тибетская лисица. *Chinese*: Zang Hu. *Tibetan*: Wa, wamo.

TAXONOMY Monotypic. Includes *ekloni*. Closely related to Corsac Fox.

SIMILAR SPECIES Corsac Fox, which is sympatric in N parts of its range, has a black-tipped tail, with russet-gray pelage, and a white chin. Red Fox is similar in size, but longer legged, slenderer, has longer, sharply pointed ears, lacks the distinct line along the midflank that separates gray from russet color, and the gray to black bands running vertically between the russet forelegs and white chest.

REPRODUCTION *Gestation*: 50-55 days. *Young per birth*: 2-5. *Weaning*: Unknown. *Sexual maturity*: Unknown. *Life span*: Probably 8-10 years. *Breeding season*: December to March, with births occurring in February to May. Monogamous. Dens are usually found in grasslands with moderate slopes. Young do not emerge from the dens until they are several weeks old. ♂ participate in pup rearing.

BEHAVIOR *Social behavior*: Solitary, although they can be seen in family groups of a mated pair with young. *Diet*: A foraging specialist, preying predominantly on pikas, but also rodents, other small mammals, lizards, insects, berries and carrion. *Main predators*: Feral Dogs, Gray Wolf, raptors. Crepuscular, most active at dawn and dusk, although can be seen at any time of the day. They spend considerable time resting in small burrows, hollows and rock crevices; there may be 1 to 4 entrances to a den. They may form commensal relationships with brown bears during hunts for pikas, in which they capture pikas excavated but not captured by bears. Also reported to scavenge on Wolf kills. Not territorial, and many pairs have been found living in close quarters and sharing hunting grounds. They often deposit their droppings in conspicuous places. Vocalizations consist of short yips to communicate over short distances; no long-distance communication is known.

DISTRIBUTION *Native*: China, India, Nepal. Found in the steppes and semi-deserts of the Tibetan Plateau from the Ladakh area of India, E across China including parts of Xinjiang, Gansu, Qinghai and Sichuan Provinces and all of Tibet, and into Yunnan, in the Mustang area in Nepal N of the Himalaya. There are no confirmed records for Bhutan. There is a confirmed record from Sikkim.

HABITAT Upland plains and hills, sparse grasslands devoid of trees and shrubs, up to 5,200 m, most typically above 3,500 m. Rarely encountered where pikas are absent.

CONSERVATION STATUS Least Concern. *CITES*: Not listed. *Regional status*: Endangered (China), Data Deficient (Nepal). Estimated population of 10,000. There are no major threats, although habitat loss and poisoning of pikas across much of the Tibetan Plateau may damage Tibetan Fox populations. They are hunted for pelts, which are manufactured into hats in Tibet. Legally protected in several large Chinese reserves: Arjin Shan, Xianza, Chang Tang, Kekexili, and Sanjiangyuan.

PHOTO CREDITS *Jan Reurink*, Burang, Tibet (China); *Shanghai Wu*, *Biosphoto* and *Andy D*, Qinghai–Tibetan Plateau (China); *Kenneth Sims-Korba*, Tibet (China).

Pale Fox
VULPES PALLIDA

BL: 41.2-46.8 cm (♂), 41.5-46.6 cm (♀). TL: 18-22.4 cm. H: 25 cm. W: 1.2 kg (♂), 1.2 kg (♀). DF: 42. CN: 70. A small-sized Canid. Coat is thin and short, pale sandy fawn to creamy white in color, finely speckled, but there is some variation in the intensity of the color. Darker mid-dorsal line in some individuals. Flanks paler than dorsal pelage. Underparts are buffy white. Face is pale, with a narrow elongated muzzle. Eyes are large, surrounded by a dark brown or black ring. Ears are large, rounded at the tip, white inside, rufous brown outside. Relatively long legs, rufous in color. Tail is bushy and long, reddish brown, with a dark patch over the caudal gland, and a black tip. No sexual dimorphism.

ssp. *oertzeni*

194

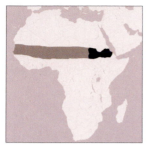

Vulpes pallida pallida

Vulpes pallida oertzeni

Vulpes pallida harterti

Vulpes pallida edwardsi

OTHER NAMES Pallid Fox, African Sand Fox. *French*: Renard pâle. *German*: Blassfuchs. *Spanish*: Zorro pálido. *Russian*: Африканская лисица: Кордофанская (Суданская) бледная (*pallida*), Южносахельская бледная (*oertzeni*), Нигерийская бледная (*harterti*), бледная лисица Эдвардса (*edwardsi*).

TAXONOMY Four subspecies are traditionally recognized: *V. p. pallida* (Kordofan Pale Fox, includes *sabbar*, found in Kordofan in Sudan, South Sudan, Eritrea and Ethiopia); *V. p. oertzeni* (South Sahel Pale Fox, found in N Cameroon, Chad, NE Nigeria, and Darfur in Sudan); *V. p. harterti* (Nigerian Pale Fox, found in Burkina Faso, Benin, Niger and N Nigeria); *V. p. edwardsi* (Edward's Pale Fox, found in Mali, S Mauritania, Senegal and Gambia). There is insufficient data available to assess the validity of these subspecies, and variation may be clinal.

SIMILAR SPECIES North African Red Fox (*V. vulpes*), sympatric only in N Sudan, is larger, with shorter legs and ears dark backed and more pointed. Fennec Fox (*V. zerda*), sympatric in N part of the range, is smaller, with proportionately longer ears. Rüppell's Fox (*V. rueppellii*) has larger ears, and its tail is usually white tipped.

REPRODUCTION *Gestation*: 51-53 days. *Young per birth*: 3-6. *Weaning*: 42-56 days. *Sexual maturity*: Unknown. *Life span*: 4-16 years in captivity. *Breeding season*: From April to June, before the rainy season. Young are born in self-dug burrows.

BEHAVIOR *Social behavior*: Pairs or small groups with 3 adults (1 ♀ and 2 ♂). *Diet*: Insects and fruits, but may also prey on small mammals (rodents), reptiles, ground-nesting birds and their eggs; they may also prey on domestic fowl. They are unable to tolerate totally waterless conditions, although they can survive dry seasons, presumably on the residual moisture in their prey. *Main predators*: Eagles, owls. One of the least known Canids, and little is known about its movements and home ranges. Predominantly nocturnal, it is active from dusk until dawn, resting during the day in self-dug burrows. The burrows are large, with tunnels extending 10-15 m and opening into small chambers lined with dry vegetable material. Fecal latrines are located just outside these burrows. Mated pairs are territorial, with home ranges of between 3 and 10 km² in Niger.

DISTRIBUTION *Native*: Benin, Burkina Faso, Cameroon, Chad, Eritrea, Ethiopia, Gambia, Mali, Mauritania, Niger, Nigeria, Senegal, South Sudan, Sudan. Found in the semi-arid Sahel of Africa, bordering the Sahara to the N. The S limit of its range extends into N Guinean savanna zones. It ranges from Mauritania, Senegal and Gambia through Nigeria, Cameroon and Chad to the Red Sea.

HABITAT Dry, sandy and stony marginal sub-Saharan desert and semi-desert areas, but it may also inhabit moister savanna areas, and areas near human habitation and cultivated fields.

CONSERVATION STATUS Least Concern. *CITES*: Not listed. Estimated population of 100,000, being one of the least known African Canids, but it seems relatively widespread in the ecological band between the true desert of the Sahara and the sub-Saharan savannas. No major threats are known, although they may be persecuted locally since they are known to kill domestic fowl.

PHOTO CREDITS *Markus Lilje*, Waza National Park (Cameroon).

Indian Fox

VULPES BENGALENSIS

BL: 39-57.5 cm (♂), 46-48 cm (♀). TL: 24.5-35 cm. H: 26-28 cm. W: 1.8-3.6 kg (♀). SL: 11.1 cm. SW: 6.4 cm. DF: 42. CN: 60. A small-sized Fox. Coat is short and smooth, variable in color, from silver gray to grayish rufous, minutely speckled with white, pale rufous yellowish or creamy white ventrally, varying with the season and locality. Chin and throat are white. Long, pointed ears, dark brown on the back, with black margin, white inside. Rhinarium is naked and lips are black. Elongated muzzle. Black spot on each side of the muzzle in front of the eye. Limbs are brownish to bright rufous. Tail is long and bushy, with a dark patch over the caudal gland, and a sharply defined black tip. Females have 3 pairs of mammae.

Young

Vulpes bengalensis

OTHER NAMES Bengal Fox. *French*: Renard du Bengale. *German*: Bengalfuchs. *Spanish*: Zorro bengalí, zorro indio. *Italian*: Volpe del Bengala. *Russian*: Бенгальская лисица. *Hindi*: Lomri, Lokri. *Bengali*: Khek sial. *Bihari*: Khekar, khikir. *Nepali*: Phusro Phyauro.

TAXONOMY Monotypic.

SIMILAR SPECIES The smallest fox in India. Distinguished from Red Fox by the black-tipped tail, grayish body pelage that lacks mixing of red hairs, brownish or rufous legs, ears that are the same color as nape or darker (but never with a black patch as in the Red Fox), and smudges of black hairs around upper part of muzzle in front of eyes.

REPRODUCTION *Gestation*: 53 days. *Young per birth*: 3-6. *Weaning*: 30 days. *Sexual maturity*: 1-2 months. *Life span*: 6-8 years. *Breeding season*: November to January. Births from February to April. They use more than 1 breeding den during the reproductive period, possibly to avoid predators. Dens are situated in the open plains, and typically have various entrances; in alluvial plains, dens take advantage of any small rise in the ground, to prevent being flooded. In human-dominated landscapes, they may use human-made structures (tailings, irrigation bunds, pipes). During pup-rearing season, most of the time is spent in resting, followed by searching for food. One parent always watches the activity of pups outside the den.

BEHAVIOR *Social behavior*: Breeding pairs that may last a lifetime. *Diet*: Omnivorous: insects, small mammals (rodents), reptiles, birds and fruit. *Main predators*: Wolf, feral Dog. Crepuscular and nocturnal, but may also hunt at mid-day in absence of large predators and abundance of food. They seem to hunt alone. Not strictly territorial, but exhibit this behavior sometimes. It is a den-dependent species, and breeding pairs use dens primarily for reproduction and pup-rearing, but also for resting during the dry season. Dens are large and complex with multiple chambers and escape routes. Wide range of vocalizations: a chattering cry is the most common call, but also growl, whine, whimper and bark. It does not appear to practice site-specific defecation.

DISTRIBUTION *Native*: Bangladesh, India, Nepal, Pakistan. Endemic to the Indian subcontinent, ranging from the foothills of the Himalayas in Nepal to the S tip of the Indian peninsula. In the N part of the Indian subcontinent, it extends from Sindh Province of Pakistan to N Bengal in India. It is not found in Afghanistan, Iran and W and E Ghats of India.

HABITAT Semi-arid, flat to undulating terrain, scrub and grassland. It avoids dense forests, steep terrain, tall grasslands and true deserts. They may compete with the desert race of the Red Fox. They do not penetrate into the mountainous tracts of Balochistan or the Himalayas. Tolerant of human presence, they can be found in agricultural fields and the vicinity of rural habitation.

CONSERVATION STATUS Least Concern. *CITES*: Appendix III. *Regional status*: Vulnerable (Bangladesh, Nepal), Near Threatened (Pakistan). Protected in India and Bangladesh, but it has not been the focus of targeted conservation efforts. Widespread in the Indian subcontinent, but occurring at low densities throughout its range, with population on the decline due to loss of short grassland-scrub habitat to intensive agriculture, industry and development projects. There is also a limited localized trade for skin, tail, fur, and teeth and claws. There is no quantitative data available on its population size.

PHOTO CREDITS *Narasimha Kumar*, Jaisalmer, Rajasthan (India); *Ganesh H. Shankar* (India); *Tinamous*, Gujarat (India).

Nubian Rüppell's Fox

VULPES RUEPPELLII RUEPPELLII AND CYRENAICA

BL: 41.9-51.9 cm (♂), 41.1-55.9 cm (♀). TL: 27-39 cm. H: 25 cm. W: 1.4-2.3 kg (♂), 1.4-1.8 kg (♀). SL: 11 cm. SW: 5.8 cm. DF: 42. CN: 40. A very small-sized and slender Canid, with relatively short legs, large and broad ears and a short muzzle. Coat is fine and soft, thicker and darker in winter and lighter colored in summer, pale sandy to beige in color, but may be grayish in rockier areas, with black speckling. Grayish buff on the sides, with a sandy-yellow or brown flush on the dorsal midline, elbows and heel. Underparts are beige to fawn, almost white. Face very pale, with contrasting black whisker patches running up to the eye. Large ears, white inside, pale to cinnamon rufous outside. Limbs are rufous with some black hairs, with lower parts whitish. Soles of feet covered by soft, long hairs. Tail is long, rich, and bushy, with a dark marking at the caudal gland, and a white tip. Females slightly smaller than males, with 3 pairs of mammae. Juveniles with a light reddish coat.

ssp. *rueppellii*

Vulpes rueppellii rueppellii

Vulpes rueppellii cyrenaica

OTHER NAMES Sand Fox. *French*: Renard famélique, renard de Rüppell. *German*: Nubischer Sandfuchs, Nubischer Rüppellfuchs. *Spanish*: Zorro de Rüppell. *Russian*: Песчаная лисица нубийская (*rueppellii*), ливийская (*cyrenaica*). *Arabic*: Tha'leb al-ramli, tha'leb sahrawi.

TAXONOMY *V. r. caesia*, *V. r. cyrenaica* (includes *cufrana*), *V. r. rueppellii* (includes *famelicus* and *somaliae*), *V. r. sabaea* and *V. r. zarudnyi*. The validity of these subspecies has not been confirmed by genetic analysis. Considered monotypic by some authors.

SIMILAR SPECIES Fennec Fox is much smaller and paler, with shorter legs, larger ears with darker markings on the back of the ears, shorter and black-tipped tail, and fur is paler and finer; confusion is common with juvenile Rüppell's Fox. Pale Fox, found in N Sudan, is slightly smaller in size, and the tip of the tail is black. Red Fox is larger and more robust, reddish in color, with a dark belly, longer limbs and tail, shorter ears, and back of the ears dark; tail tip is also white.

REPRODUCTION *Gestation*: 51-53 days. *Young per birth*: 3-5. *Weaning*: 42-56 days. *Sexual maturity*: 9-10 months. *Life span*: 12 years in captivity. *Breeding season*: December to February, with births from March to July.

BEHAVIOR *Social behavior*: Monogamous pairs during the breeding season. *Diet*: Omnivorous and opportunistic; small mammals and birds, but also lizards, insects, fruits (dates) and grass; may survive in areas with little available water. *Main predators*: Eagle, owl. Crepuscular and nocturnal, but it is sometimes seen during the day. It appears to have little fear of humans and will come close to campsites to scavenge for food scraps. They utilize breeding and resting dens either dug themselves at the base of trees and bushes or under slabs of rocks, or enlarged burrows of lizards or badgers. They are agile and climb trees, fences and rocks. When threatened by a predator, it will hump its back, raise its tail, and spray its potential enemy with a special secretion from the anal gland. Territorial, and both sexes scent mark the territory. ♂ spray urine on borders, but do not leave feces. ♀ have a well-developed violet gland that is used to scent mark the den site. Very vocal, including a bark, angry yelps and also chattering. They have excellent vision and hearing, as well as a well-developed sense of smell. Soles of feet are covered in long and soft hairs that conceal the pads completely.

DISTRIBUTION *V. r. rueppellii*: Djibouti, Egypt, Eritrea, Ethiopia, Somalia, Sudan. In Egypt it is the most widespread Fox and the most likely to be seen in a true desert environment; they are found throughout the Western and Eastern Deserts, in the Sinai, and also around Lake Nasser, including Wadi Allaqi. Mostly absent from the Nile Valley and its margins, where the Red Fox is found, although they have also been recorded at Wadi Natrun and in the Fayoum.

HABITAT Arid steppe, sand and stone deserts, semi-deserts and rocky wadis, with a clear preference for open stony habitats with sparse vegetation cover. At oases, it can be found in more vegetated areas, such as palm groves, and around wells. It may also be seen in farmland and lake margins. It usually avoids large sand dune areas, where the Fennec Fox is present.

CONSERVATION STATUS Least Concern. *CITES*: Not listed. There is no estimate of total population size.

PHOTO CREDITS *Stijn Aelbers, Stefan Cruysberghs* and *Gabriel Rif*, White Desert, Farafra (Egypt).

Northwest African Rüppell's Fox

VULPES RUEPPELLII CAESIA

BL: 45 cm. TL: 35 cm. H: 30 cm. W: 1.1-2.3 kg (♂), 1.1-1.8 kg (♀). SL: 11 cm. SW: 5.8 cm. DF: 42. CN: 40. A very small-sized and slender Canid, with relatively short legs, large and broad ears, and a short muzzle. A dark-colored subspecies of Rüppell's Fox. Coat is fine and soft, thicker and darker in winter and lighter colored in summer, dull ochraceous in color, with black speckling, with a silvery grayish to brown flush on the dorsal midline, elbows and heels. Head and neck are buff, with contrasting black whisker patches running up to the eye. Ears are white inside and pale to cinnamon rufous outside. Underside is beige to fawn. Limbs are rufous with some black hairs, with lower parts whitish. Soles of feet almost completely covered by hairs. Long, rich, bushy tail, with a dark marking at the caudal gland, and a white tip.

Vulpes rueppellii caesia

OTHER NAMES Sand Fox. *French*: Renard famélique, renard de Rüppell. *German*: Nordwestafrikanischer Sandfuchs, Nordwestafrikanischer Rüppellfuchs. *Spanish*: Zorro de Rüppell. *Russian*: Западноафриканская песчаная лисица.

TAXONOMY Considered a subspecies of Rüppell's Fox (*V. rueppellii*). The validity of this subspecies has not been confirmed by genetic analysis. Rüppell's Fox is considered monotypic by some authors.

SIMILAR SPECIES Fennec Fox is much smaller, with shorter legs, larger ears with darker markings on the back of the ears, shorter and black-tipped tail, and fur is paler and finer; confusion is common between juvenile *V. rueppellii* and adult *V. zerda*. Pale Fox is slightly smaller in size, and the tip of the tail is black. Red Fox is larger and more robust, reddish in color, with longer limbs and tail, with shorter ears, and back of ears dark; tail tip is also white.

REPRODUCTION *Gestation*: 51-53 days. *Young per birth*: 2-3. *Weaning*: 42-56 days. *Sexual maturity*: 9-10 months. *Life span*: 7 years, 14 years in captivity. *Breeding season*: Probably from November to January, with births in March. Pups are blind, and remain dependent on their parents for 4 months before leaving the den, and disperse at 6-7 months.

BEHAVIOR *Social behavior*: Monogamous pairs during the breeding season. *Diet*: Omnivorous and opportunistic; invertebrates, rodents, birds, lizards, snakes, and plant material, fruits, and roots, which likely provide much of their moisture requirements. *Main predators*: Golden eagle, owl. Behavior probably similar to other subspecies of Rüppell's Fox, but its ecology outside of the Arabian Peninsula remains largely unknown. Crepuscular and nocturnal, but some may be active during the daytime in Western Sahara. In this area, they may use very exposed dens, often in the middle of plains, and they will flight if disturbed. They are solitary foragers, and may visit human settlements at night. Adapted to survive in extremely arid environments.

DISTRIBUTION *Native*: Algeria, Chad, Mali, Mauritania, Morocco, Niger, Western Sahara.

HABITAT Sand and stone deserts, on the fringes of the Sahara, in mountain massifs and near oases. It usually avoids extreme arid regions in the middle of the Sahara. In Niger and Morocco it is found in areas with sparse vegetation cover, dominated by small bushes mostly concentrated in wadis, and in coastal areas with extremely sparse vegetation and without any trees, but it avoids large sand dune areas, where the Fennec Fox is present. In Algeria, it occurs in large ergs.

CONSERVATION STATUS Least Concern. *CITES*: Not listed. Its status remains largely unknown, but densities are generally low, higher in areas where food is more freely available and where other carnivores, such as the Red Fox, Jackal, Fennec Fox, sand cat, or striped hyena, are absent. Locally extirpated in areas of the northern fringe of the Sahara due to competitive exclusion by Red Fox, usually near human settlements. In Morocco they may be hunted, as they are considered pests. They are occasionally killed for food, but rarely hunted for sale of furs. Threats include indiscriminate use of poisons.

PHOTO CREDITS *Gérard Schmitt*, Parc National du Banc d'Arguin (Mauritania).

Arabian Rüppell's Fox

VULPES RUEPPELLII SABAEA AND ZARUDNYI

BL: 40-51 cm (♂), 34-56 cm (♀). TL: 26-35.5 cm. H: 30 cm. W: 1.1-2.3 kg (♂), 1.1-1.8 kg (♀). SL: 10.8 cm. DF: 42. CN: 40. A very small-sized and slender Canid, with relatively short legs, large and broad ears, and a short muzzle. A small-sized subspecies of Rüppell's Fox, generally paler than other subspecies, more uniformly sandy color, almost white in older individuals. Coat is fine and soft, pale creamy white to pale rufous in color, with very little black speckling, and a sandy-yellow or brown flush on the dorsal midline, elbows and heel. Underparts are white. Face very pale, with very little buffy orange around the eyes, and a weak blackish patch on the sides of the muzzle. Ears are white inside and pale to cinnamon rufous outside, without black. Limbs are beige with lower parts whitish. Soles of feet almost completely covered by hairs. Tail is long and bushy, with a dark marking at the caudal gland, and a white tip. Females slightly smaller than males, with 3 pairs of mammae. Newborns are grayish brown.

ssp. *sabaea*

Vulpes rueppellii sabaea

Vulpes rueppellii zarudnyi

OTHER NAMES Rüppell's Desert Fox, Sand Fox. *French*: Renard famélique, renard de Rüppell. *German*: Arabischer Sandfuchs, Arabischer Rüppellfuchs, Persischer Sandfuchs. *Spanish*: Zorro de Rüppell de Arabia. *Russian*: Песчаная лисица аравийская (*sabaea*), переднеазиатская (*zarudnyi*). *Arabic*: Tha'leb al-ramli, tha'leb sahrawi, husseine, abul hussein. *Persian*: Rubâh-e sheni. *Hebrew*: Shual HaNegev, Shual Holot.

TAXONOMY Considered a subspecies of Rüppell's Fox (*V. rueppellii*).

SIMILAR SPECIES Blanford's Fox has a longer and bushier tail, is slightly larger, has bare foot pads, and prefers rocky mountain slopes, avoiding the foothills and plains. Arabian Red Fox is larger and more robust, with coarser fur, reddish in color, with longer limbs and tail, with shorter ears, backs of the ears are dark; tail tip is also white.

REPRODUCTION *Gestation*: 51-56 days. *Young per birth*: 1-4. *Weaning*: 42-56 days. *Sexual maturity*: 9-10 months. *Life span*: 12 years in captivity. *Breeding season*: Mid-November to February, with births from March to July. The Foxes living in the Al Dhafra region in Abu Dhabi are known to have their dens located in eolianite stratum in gravel plains or between sand dunes.

BEHAVIOR *Social behavior*: Solitary or small family groups; monogamous pairs during the breeding season. *Diet*: Omnivorous and opportunistic; small mammals and birds, but also lizards, insects and grass; may survive in areas with little available water. *Main predators*: Eagle, owl. Crepuscular and nocturnal. They utilize breeding and resting dens either dug themselves at the base of trees and bushes or under slabs of rocks, or enlarged burrows of lizards or badgers. They are agile and climb trees, fences and rocks. When threatened by a predator, it will hump its back, raise its tail, and spray its potential enemy with a special secretion from the anal gland. Territorial, and both sexes scent mark the territory. ♂ spray urine on borders, but do not leave feces. ♀ have a well-developed violet gland that is used to scent mark the den site. Soles of feet are covered in long and soft hairs that conceal the pads completely.

DISTRIBUTION *V. r. sabaea* is found in Iraq, Iran, Israel (western side of the Dead Sea and Wadi Araba), Jordan, Oman, Saudi Arabia, Syria, United Arab Emirates and Yemen. *V. r. zarudnyi* is found in Afghanistan (Baluchistan), Iran (Sistan, Baluchestan, Fars, Khuzestan, and the island of Qeshm), Pakistan, Saudi Arabia.

HABITAT Arid steppe and desert regions of the Arabian Peninsula, in low stony hills and wadis.

CONSERVATION STATUS *Least Concern. CITES*: Not listed. *Regional status*: Vulnerable (Pakistan), Endangered (Oman, United Arab Emirates). It is probably declining throughout its range. Its status in Saudi Arabia and Yemen is unknown, but it may be widespread. In Israel it is almost extinct due to competitive exclusion by Red Foxes. Threats include droughts and overgrazing with associated habitat loss, fragmentation and degradation, competition with Red Foxes (*V. vulpes arabica*), which are perceived to be increasing in numbers due to their commensalism with humans, competition with Domestic Dogs and cats, canine diseases and associated parasites, collateral damage while targeting other carnivores by poisoning and trapping and occasionally for food.

PHOTO CREDITS *Jonas Livet*, Sharjah Desert Park (United Arab Emirates) and Oman Mammal Breeding Centre (Oman).

Fennec Fox

VULPES ZERDA

BL: 24-41 cm (♂), 34-39.5 cm (♀). TL: 12.5-31 cm. H: 15-20.3 cm. W: 0.7-1.9 kg. SL: 8.3 cm. SW: 4.8 cm. DF: 42. CN: 64. A very small-sized Fox, the smallest Canid, with large ears, short legs and a small muzzle. Coat is long, woolly and dense, reddish cream, light fawn or almost white in color. Flanks and underparts are almost white. Head is whitish, with a dark brown streak extending from the inner eye down and outward to either side of the muzzle. Large black eyes. Distinctive large ears, darker dorsally and whitish inside. Limbs are reddish sandy in color to nearly white. Dense fur on the feet extends to cover the pads. Tail is short and bushy, rufous in color, with a black patch near the dorsal base, and a black tip. Females have 3 pairs of nipples.

Young

Vulpes zerda

OTHER NAMES *French*: Fennec. *German*: Fennek, Wüstenfuchs. *Spanish*: Fenec, zorro del desierto. *Russian*: Фенек. *Arabic*: Fanak.

TAXONOMY Monotypic. Previously included in the genus *Canis* and *Fennecus*. Molecular data suggest it is within *Vulpes*, although it has some differences with other *Vulpes*: lacks musk glands, has only 32 chromosome pairs and displays behaviors uncharacteristic of Foxes. Includes *arabicus*, *aurita*, *brucei*, *cerda* and *zaarensis*.

SIMILAR SPECIES Rüppell's Fox is larger in size, has a darker, longer, and denser fur, a longer white-tipped tail, longer legs and smaller ears.

REPRODUCTION *Gestation*: 50-52 days. *Young per birth*: 1-4. *Weaning*: 61-70 days. *Sexual maturity*: 9 months. *Life span*: 10 years, 12-14 years in captivity. *Breeding season*: January-February, but can produce a second litter if the first is lost. Following mating, ♂ becomes very aggressive and protective of ♀, providing her with food during her pregnancy and lactation periods. ♂ play a role in pup rearing. Births occur between March and April. When pups are born, the ears are folded over and the eyes are closed, opening at around 10 days and the ears lifting soon afterward.

BEHAVIOR *Social behavior*: Mated pairs and their offspring. Diet: Omnivorous: jerboa, gerbil, and other small rodents; occasionally birds, eggs, lizards, insects, and also some plant material, including melons, dates collected on the ground, tubers and roots, and human garbage. May subsist without water, and tolerate extremely high concentrations of urea in urine. *Main predators*: Eagle owl. Nocturnal. Highly social, typically resting while in contact with each other, and may share burrows with up to 12 other individuals, but they hunt singly. Playing behavior is common, including among adults of the species. Burrows are extensive, usually at the base of low hills or dunes where moisture concentrates, keeping their dens cool even in the hottest weather. They have a variety of calls, including barking, a purring sound similar to that of a domestic cat, and a snarl if threatened. Their ears are used to radiate heat from the body. They have hairy soles to protect them from the hot sand. ♂ mark territory with urine.

DISTRIBUTION *Native*: Algeria, Chad, Egypt, Libya, Mali, Mauritania, Morocco, Niger, Sudan, Tunisia, Western Sahara, and probably in Israel, Jordan, Kuwait, Oman, Saudi Arabia, Yemen. Widespread in N Africa, ranging from Western Sahara and Mauritania to N Sinai. Its occurrence on the Arabian Peninsula is unclear because of confusion with the young of the Arabian subspecies of Rüppell's Fox.

HABITAT Arid desert environments. Stable sand dunes are the ideal habitat, although they also live in very sparsely vegetated sand dunes near the Atlantic coast. Ability to burrow in sandier substrates than other Canids provides them with a competitive advantage in dune systems.

CONSERVATION STATUS Least Concern. *CITES*: Appendix II. *Regional status*: Legally protected in Morocco, Algeria, Tunisia and Egypt. Common throughout the Sahara. Construction of roads and new human settlements is increasing the disturbance and risk to some populations. It is commonly trapped and sold commercially in N Africa for exhibition or sale to tourists.

PHOTO CREDITS *Juniors Bildarchiv, marksdl* and *Tomoko Ichishima*, Inokashira Park (Japan); *Svetlana Valuiskaya, Helen Haden*, Drusillas Zoo Park (UK).

Blanford's Fox

VULPES CANA

BL: 38.5-47 cm (♂), 38.5-45 cm (♀). TL: 26-41 cm. H: 26-28 cm. W: 0.8-1.4 kg (♂), 0.8-1.6 kg (♀). SL: 8.4 cm. SW: 5.1 cm. DF: 42. CN: Unknown. A very small-sized Fox, with a long and bushy tail, and large ears. Coat is brownish gray, with a dark mid-dorsal band along the back and tail and white-tipped hairs. Underparts are white to pale yellow. Winter coat is soft and woolly, with a dense, black overwool. Summer is paler and less dense. Head is orange buff in color, especially in the winter coat. Narrow face, with a pointed muzzle, and a dark band extending from the upper lip to the eye. Ears are large, pale brown on both sides, with long white hairs along the anteromedial border. Eyes are dark. Limbs are pale yellowish white, dark gray posteriorly, sometimes with a dark stifle. Small feet with naked foot pads. Tail is very long and bushy, brownish gray, with a dorsal black spot at the base, and a black tip (white in some individuals). Females slightly smaller than males, with 3 pairs of nipples. Juveniles have a darker coat.

white-tipped tail

black-tipped tail

Vulpes cana

OTHER NAMES Afghan Fox, Royal Fox, Black Fox, King Fox, Cliff Fox, Baluchistan Fox. *French*: Renard de Blanford, Schardel. *German*: Afghanfuchs, Canafuchs. *Spanish*: Zorro de Blanford, zorro afgano, zorro persa. *Russian*: Афганская лисица. *Pashto*: Splem Geedar. *Persian*: Sha rubah. Hebrew: Shual Tsukim.

TAXONOMY Monotypic. Closely related to Fennec Fox.

SIMILAR SPECIES Pelage color in Iran and further E is predominantly gray, whereas in animals from the Arabian Peninsula, Israel and Egypt it is beige. Animals from SW Arabia frequently have a white tail tip. Rüppell's Fox is slightly larger, with a relatively shorter and less bushy tail, and larger ears. Fennec Fox is smaller, lighter in color, has larger ears, and has hairy foot pads. Red Fox is much larger, with a relatively shorter tail, back of the ears are black, and tail is white tipped.

REPRODUCTION *Gestation*: 50-60 days. *Young per birth*: 1-3. *Weaning*: 30-45 days. *Sexual maturity*: 8-12 months. *Life span*: 5 years, 10 years in captivity. *Breeding season*: December to February. Births occur in March or April. Monogamous. Young are entirely dependent for food upon their mother's milk until they begin to forage for themselves, as adults do not carry food to the young. ♂ have been observed grooming juveniles, but there is no indication that the ♂ provides food either to the ♀ or to the pups. Dens are located in small clefts in the rock, and they never dig burrows. Dens are used both for rearing young during spring and for daytime harborage throughout the year. Young remain in their natal range until October or November in the year of their birth.

BEHAVIOR *Social behavior*: Solitary, mated pairs during the breeding season. *Diet*: Insects and fruits, but may also prey on small mammals, lizards and birds; they rarely drink water. *Main predators*: Red Fox, eagles, owls. Nocturnal, though it may be seen during the day. They generally become active soon after dusk and are active throughout the night. Solitary hunters; even mated pairs tend to forage independently. Monogamous pairs occupy territories of 1.6 km², with little overlap between territories. During winter and spring, both members of a pair frequently occupy the same den, or adjacent dens at the same site, while during summer and autumn they often den in separate locations. They are excellent jumpers and tree-climbers, having sharp, curved claws and hairless pads for traction; their long, bushy tails serve as a counterbalance. Very sensitive to sound and very shy, running away with a fast ground-hugging run.

DISTRIBUTION *Native*: Afghanistan, Egypt, Iran, Israel, Jordan, Oman, Pakistan, Saudi Arabia, Turkmenistan, United Arab Emirates, Yemen.

HABITAT Dry foothills and mountainous regions, steep, rocky slopes, canyons and cliffs, creek bed patches, below an altitude of 2,000 m. They avoid higher mountain ranges.

CONSERVATION STATUS Least Concern. *CITES*: Appendix II. *Regional status*: Near Threatened (Pakistan). Estimated population of 5,000, being fairly common in some parts of its range. Habitat destruction and human persecution are the major possible threats. In Pakistan and Afghanistan, its pelt is valued and the species has been hunted extensively. Protected by law in Israel. Hunting banned in Oman, Jordan and Yemen. There is no legal protection in Egypt, Saudi Arabia, United Arab Emirates, Iran, Afghanistan or Pakistan.

PHOTO CREDITS *Alex Kantorovich*, Beersheba Zoo (Israel); *Mr. Blueberry,* Negev Desert (Israel); *Jonas Livet*, Sharjah Desert Park (United Arab Emirates).

Cape Fox

VULPES CHAMA

BL: 45-61 cm (♂), 51-62 cm (♀). TL: 25-40 cm. H: 30-43 cm. W: 2-4.2 kg (♂), 2-4 kg (♀). SL: 10.1 cm. SW: 5.1 cm. DF: 42. CN: 54. A small-sized, lightly built Canid, with slender legs. Coat is soft, silver gray on the back and reddish brown to pale tawny brown on the flanks and underside. Molting period from October to December. Neck, legs and chest are lighter, from a pale reddish brown to almost white. Dark coloring around the mouth. Large pointed ears, reddish brown on the back, with an inner white fringe. Pointed muzzle, light in color. Hind limbs have a dark brown patch on the back of the thighs. Paws are pale fawn to reddish. Tail is long and bushy, darker than the rest of the body, with a dark patch over the caudal gland, and a black tip. Females are slightly smaller than males, with 3 pairs of mammae.

Young

Vulpes chama

OTHER NAMES Silver Fox, Silver-Backed Fox, Cama Fox. *French*: Renard du Cap. *German*: Kap-Fuchs, Kamafuchs. *Spanish*: Zorro del Cabo. *Russian*: Южноафриканская лисица. *Afrikaans*: Silwervos, draajakkals. *Sesotho*: Mophèmè. *Setswana*: Lesiê.

TAXONOMY Monotypic. Includes *hodgsoni* and *variegatoides*.

SIMILAR SPECIES The only true Fox in S Africa. Bat-Eared Fox is similar in size, but its coat is more bushy and silvery gray, with larger dark-backed ears, and black legs.

REPRODUCTION *Gestation*: 50-53 days. *Young per birth*: 1-6, usually 3. *Weaning*: 112 days. *Sexual maturity*: 9 months. *Life span*: 6-10 years. *Breeding season*: Year-round, with most births between August and October. **The adult** ♀ remains with newborn young in an excavated or adapted burrow, and is provisioned by the adult ♂. Pups begin to forage with the ♀ at about 16 weeks, become independent of her at about 21 weeks, and disperse after 9 months of age.

BEHAVIOR *Social behavior*: Monogamous pairs, but each one forages separately. *Diet*: Primarily small rodents, but also insects, birds, reptiles, hares, springhares, and fruit (bluebush berries); they also eat carrion when available, and may sometimes prey on newborn lambs. *Main predators*: Black-Backed Jackal, caracal, leopard. Mainly nocturnal, although youngsters are known to play outside the den during the day. It can be spotted during the early mornings and early evenings. Territorial, based on high site fidelity and low overlap of home ranges between neighboring Foxes. ♀-based social organization, with ♀-biased dispersal. Territories are maintained by frequent marking. Home ranges are 1 to 30 km², with differences in size based on food resources and Black-Backed Jackal density. Densities inversely related to Black-Backed Jackal densities, due to the high predation and spatial displacement of Cape Foxes by Jackals. It can dig its own hole, but prefers to use existing dens that were dug by another species like the springhare. When attacked, it will growl and spit at its opponent; it will raise its tail whenever excited. It is normally silent, but communicates with chirps, calls, or by whining. A high-pitched howl, answered by the mate with a bark, is probably a long-range contact call, or an advertisement that an area is occupied. A bark is also used as an alarm call. Facial expressions, but not tail positions, play a prominent role in communication.

DISTRIBUTION *Native*: Angola, Botswana, Namibia, South Africa. Widespread in the central and W regions of S Africa, reaching to SW Angola. It has recently expanded its range to the SW where it reaches the Atlantic and Indian Ocean coastlines. Status in Swaziland is uncertain, but they may occur in the SW. Not confirmed from Lesotho.

HABITAT Open arid country, grassland with scattered thickets, and lightly wooded areas, particularly in the dry Karoo regions, the Kalahari and the fringes of the Namib Desert. Also penetrate moderately dense vegetation in lowland fynbos in the W Cape, as well as extensive agricultural lands. Not found in forested areas.

CONSERVATION STATUS Least Concern. *CITES*: Not listed. *Regional status*: Least Concern (South Africa). Common across much of its range. Estimated population of 50,000-100,000. Illegal use of agricultural poisons on commercial farms poses the main threat. Treated as a vermin across most of its range, but partially protected in several South African provinces.

PHOTO CREDITS *Thomas Kalcher* and *Nico Smit,* Kalahari Desert (South Africa); *Bildagentur Zoonar GmbH* (South Africa).

Eastern American Red Fox
VULPES FULVA FULVA

BL: 60-71.8 cm. TL: 31-39.4 cm. H: 40 cm. W: 3.5-5.4 kg (♂), 4-4.5 kg (♀). SL: 13.4 cm. SW: 6.9 cm. DF: 42. CN: 34. A small-sized Canid, with long and slender legs and pointed muzzle, and long brush-like tail. A small-sized subspecies of North American Red Fox, with a relatively short tail and muzzle. Pelage is bright golden fulvous, varying to fulvous, darkest along middle of back, slightly grizzled with white in the rump. Chin, throat and band down belly white. Face rusty fulvous, profusely grizzled with white. Muzzle slender and pointed, white on upper lip. Ears relatively large, pointed, erect, black backed, and usually white inside. Black on feet reaching the thighs. Tail is fulvous, profusely mixed with black hairs on the undersurface, with a black spot near the base, and a white tip. Females smaller than males. North American Foxes are comparatively lightweight, rather long for their mass, and have considerable sexual dimorphism, compared with Eurasian Foxes.

winter coat

Young

summer coat

Vulpes fulva fulva

OTHER NAMES North American Red Fox. *French*: Renard roux-fauve, renard oriental. *German*: Ostamerikanischer Rotfuchs. *Spanish*: Zorro común de América del Norte. *Russian*: Восточная американская рыжая лисица.

TAXONOMY Until recently Red Foxes in North America were considered both native and nonnative, but recent phylogenetic studies argue against any major substantial contribution of European ancestry to North American populations and are consistent with the previous classification of North American Red Fox as a distinct species (*V. fulva*). However, at least some Red Foxes in the E United States may be hybrids between North American and European Red Foxes introduced from the British Isles in the late 1700s. At least 9 subspecies are generally recognized in North America (Aubry, 1983 and 2009, Kamler and Ballard, 2002; Sacks: 2010): *V. f. fulva* (E United States), *V. f. rubricosa* (central and E Canada), *V. f. regalis, V. f. alascensis, V. f. abietorum* (boreal Alaska and Canada), *V. f. macroura* (Rocky Mountains), *V. f. cascadensis* (Cascade Range), *V. f. necator* (Sierra Nevada) and *V. f. patwin* (Sacramento Valley).

REPRODUCTION *Gestation*: 51-53 days. *Young per birth*: 4-7. *Weaning*: 60 days. *Sexual maturity*: 12 months. *Life span*: 5 years, 9 years in captivity. *Breeding season*: From December to February, with a peak in late January. Births occur in late March or early April. Dens are constructed during late winter in loose, well-drained soils.

BEHAVIOR *Social behavior*: Mated pairs. *Diet*: Rabbits and mice, but may also eat smaller amounts, poultry, squirrels, muskrats, quail, small nongame birds, insects, nuts and fruits. Poultry loss to this species is largely due to improper husbandry practices. It does not exert real pressure on game bird populations. *Main predators*: Coyote, lynx. Generally nocturnal, although they can also be observed during the day, especially in open areas. During midday they return to their denning area. They increase their daylight activity during autumn and winter. Non-migratory, and usually use the same area for life, and their size varies with the habitat, food abundance, and time of year, averaging 8-10 km². During late winter home ranges are larger, due to a decrease in available food. Population densities average 2-3 per km², but in suitable habitat may range up to 32 per km².

DISTRIBUTION *Native*: Canada, United States. Found in E United States: Florida, Georgia, Alabama, Mississippi, Louisiana, E Texas, Oklahoma, Arkansas, Tennessee, South Carolina, North Carolina, Virginia, Kentucky, Illinois, Indiana, Ohio, West Virginia, Maryland, Delaware, New Jersey, Pennsylvania, Wisconsin, Michigan, Connecticut, Rhode Island, Massachusetts, Vermont, New Hampshire, Maine; and SE Canada: S Quebec, and S Ontario.

HABITAT Mixed vegetation communities that occur on edge habitats with a high level of diversity. In developed areas they will inhabit areas that offer a combination of woodland and agricultural land. They can also be found in suburban and, less commonly, urban areas where food is readily available.

CONSERVATION STATUS Least Concern. *CITES*: Not listed. Populations are largely controlled by sarcoptic mange and associated secondary infections. Habitat competition from Coyotes also depresses Red Fox numbers, especially in SE states.

PHOTO CREDITS *William V. Schmitz* and *Robert Peal*, Bombay Hook, NJ (USA); *Peter Kefali*, Ocean, NJ (USA); *Susan Liddle*, Island Beach State Park, NJ (USA).

Nova Scotia, Newfoundland and Labrador Red Fox
VULPES FULVA RUBRICOSA

BL: 66.5-74.5 cm (♂), 57.9-62.6 cm (♀). TL: 33.6-44.5 cm. H: 35-45 cm. W: 4.1-7.3 kg (♂), 3.6-5.7 kg (♀). DF: 42. CN: 34. A small to medium-sized Canid, with long and slender legs and pointed muzzle, and long brush-like tail. One of the largest subspecies of North American Red Fox, smaller than Eurasian Red Foxes, darker in color, with a large, very broad and bushy tail. Black, silver and cross color phases are common. Pelage is variable, pale golden fulvous to deep rich and very dark fulvous. Throat and chest are white. Muzzle slender and pointed, white on upper lip. Ears relatively large, pointed, erect, black backed and usually white inside. Black legs usually up to the thighs. Tail is very long, thick, and bushy, pale buffy yellowish to rich dark fulvous, mixed with black hairs, most abundant below, and white tipped. Females are slightly smaller than males.

Young

Vulpes fulva rubricosa

OTHER NAMES Reddish Fox, Bang's Red Fox. *French*: Renard roux. *German*: Rotfuchs. *Spanish*: Zorro común. *Russian*: Восточноканадская (Лабрадорская) рыжая лисица.

TAXONOMY Considered a subspecies of North American Red Fox (*V. fulva*). Includes *bangsi* (N Quebec, Newfoundland and coast of Labrador) and *deletrix* (Newfoundland).

REPRODUCTION *Gestation*: 51-53 days. *Young per birth*: 4-8. *Weaning*: 56-70 days. *Sexual maturity*: 12 months. *Life span*: 6 years. *Breeding season*: From December through March, with peak activity in late January. Young are born during March and early April. Both parents take part in raising the pups. Family groups stay intact until mid-September, when pups begin to disperse. Most of the dispersal takes place during mid-September to early October with greatest dispersal distances occurring from October through December. ♂ generally disperse twice the distance of ♀, commonly moving 30-65 km before settling in new territories. Quite often ♀ offspring will remain close to, or share their mother's territories. Related ♀ tolerate each other's presence, but territories of unrelated ♀ are clearly defined and adhered to.

BEHAVIOR *Social behavior*: Mated pairs during the breeding season. Monogamous; the pair may separate during the year, but will reunite for mating. *Diet*: Small rodents and other small to mid-sized mammals (voles, snowshoe hares, lemmings, squirrels, rabbits and mice); additional spring foods include grasses and forbs, birds and bird eggs, and carrion; they rely heavily on berries, plants and insects during the summer; apples are utilized when they become available. *Main predators*: Coyote, Wolf, lynx. Most active from dusk to dawn, moving away from secure den sites primarily during the hours of darkness. They hunt mostly toward sunset, during night and early morning. Home range sizes vary considerably, depending on food abundance, degree of interspecific and intraspecific competition, type and diversity of habitat, and presence of natural and physical barriers (0.7-2.3 km² on Prince Edward Island, 32 km² in Maine). Home ranges of ♂ clearly overlap those of at least 1 or more ♀. They oftentimes travel much of their home range each night. They use smelly droppings and urine as scent markings to define territories. Red Foxes have a sharp bark, used when startled and to warn other Foxes.

DISTRIBUTION *Native*: Canada. Found in Nova Scotia, including Cape Breton Island, New Brunswick, Prince Edward Island, Newfoundland and Labrador, central Quebec to S end of James Bay, and NE Ontario west to Lake Superior.

HABITAT A variety of habitats, closely associated with areas where crop land and fields are intermixed with adjacent wooded tracts. Logging and farming activities open the forest canopy and improve conditions for Red Fox. On Prince Edward Island they prefer dunes, shrubs, agricultural fields, and human-use habitats, while forest and water habitats are used less. They avoid burned and open conifer forest.

CONSERVATION STATUS Least Concern. *CITES*: Not listed. Leading causes of mortality include trapping, hunting, and road kills. Rabies and sarcoptic mange are natural mortality factors which can substantially decrease local populations. The recent increase in Coyote numbers and distribution in this area may have adverse affects on its population.

PHOTO CREDITS *Scott Martin* and *Jim Cumming*, Algonquin Provincial Park, ON (Canada); *Mircea Costina*, QC (Canada); *Eric Bégin*, Melocheville, QC (Canada).

Northern Plains Red Fox

VULPES FULVA REGALIS

BL: 65.8-69.7 cm. TL: 39.2-42 cm. H: 38-45 cm. W: 3.2-11.3 kg. DF: 42. CN: 34. A small to medium-sized Canid, with long and slender legs and pointed muzzle, and long brush-like tail. A large-sized subspecies of North American Red Fox, with very large and broad ears, and very long tail. Pelage is golden yellow or pale yellowish fulvous, becoming almost buffy white on face and posterior part of back. Throat and chest are white. Face, top of head and base of ears pale straw yellow becoming pale fulvous around eyes, with a darker area on each side of nose. Muzzle slender and pointed, white on upper lip. Ears large, pointed, erect, black backed and usually white inside. Legs abruptly red or rusty fulvous, in striking contrast with yellow of body. Black of feet very pure but restricted in area. Tail is long, golden yellow at the base, without black hairs, with the rest of tail to white tip buffy, strongly intermixed with long black hairs, especially on underside. Females smaller than males.

cross
color phase

Young

Vulpes fulva regalis

OTHER NAMES Royal Fox. *French*: Renard roux des plaines du Nord, renard royal. *German*: Northern-Plains-Rotfuchs, Königs-Rotfuchs. *Spanish*: Zorro común de las Grandes Llanuras. *Russian*: Рыжая лисица Великих равнин.

TAXONOMY Considered a subspecies of North American Red Fox (*V. fulva*).

SIMILAR SPECIES Gray Fox is s slightly smaller, grayer in color on the back, with reddish legs and a black-tipped tail, and is found in areas fairly heavily covered with wood or brush. Arctic Fox is considerably smaller, has a shorter, less tapered head with shorter, rounded ears, and its winter and summer pelage is different in color. Coyote is larger in size, has a shorter tail, and has round pupils.

REPRODUCTION *Gestation*: 51-53 days. *Young per birth*: 1-9. *Weaning*: 56-90 days. *Sexual maturity*: 12 months. *Life span*: 5 years. *Breeding season*: January or February. Young are born in March or April. Dens may be burrows dug by themselves, abandoned ones previously used by other Foxes or other species, various natural cavities such as caves, hollow trees and logs, openings in very thick brush or piles of wood debris, or in structures such as barns and other outbuildings, grain elevators, haystacks and culverts. Some dens may be reused year after year. At birth, pups weigh about 100 grams and are blind, and will remain in the den for 3-4 weeks. During this period, both parents work to bring food to the den. Foxes often have more than one den and if a den is disturbed, they will move their young to another den. All juveniles disperse when they are 6-8 months old. The longest dispersal distances are made by ♂. Dispersal by adults also occurs, usually in response to reduced availability of food on the home range.

BEHAVIOR *Social behavior*: Mated pairs during the breeding season; monogamous. *Diet*: Rabbits, mice, ground squirrels, small mammals, birds, carrion, poultry, insects, fruits, and small amounts of plant material are eaten by Foxes; when rabbits and mice are abundant, they make up the bulk of the food supply, but if they are scarce, they will turn to other less easily caught species such as muskrats and game birds. They also eat fruit, insects and carrion. *Main predators*: Coyote, Wolf, cougar, lynx. Most active at night, though It may be seen hunting or traveling at any time of day. Solitary hunters and do not hunt in packs. Except for the period when the young are small, they do not use dens extensively. During the day they rest in some secluded spot or on some open ridge where they can see any approaching danger. Even in the coldest weather they do not usually seek the shelter or den. They are territorial and home ranges of family groups rarely overlap.

DISTRIBUTION *Native*: Canada, United States. Found in central Canada, from W side of Great Lakes and SW side of Hudson Bay throughout NW Ontario, Manitoba, Saskatchewan and E Alberta; and in N-central United States, Northern Plains, including Minnesota, North Dakota, South Dakota, Iowa, Nebraska, Kansas and Missouri. Subspecific status of Foxes in Nunavut is unclear.

HABITAT A wide variety of habitats including prairies, forests, small patches of timber interspersed with pastures, agricultural fields and urban areas. Their distribution and density may be limited by competition with and avoidance of Coyotes.

CONSERVATION STATUS Least Concern. *CITES*: Not listed.

PHOTO CREDITS *Christy Hader* and *outdoorsman*, MN (USA); *John Woodnutt,* Churchill, MB (Canada).

Alaska Red Fox
VULPES FULVA ALASCENSIS

BL: 56-82 cm. TL: 35-45 cm. H: 35-50 cm. W: 2.7-6.8 kg. SL: 14.5 cm. SW: 8.2 cm. DF: 42. CN: 34. A small to medium-sized Canid, with long and slender legs and pointed muzzle, and long brush-like tail. A large-sized subspecies of North American Red Fox, with large and long tail, long fur and small ears, very similar to *abietorum*. Pelage is golden fulvous, long and full on neck and anterior part of back, almost forming a ruff, shorter and coarser on posterior part of back and rump, where it is more grizzled in color. Throat and chest are white. Face and head grizzled fulvous and buffy, strongly rusty on top of nose and around eyes, paler on cheeks and forehead. Muzzle slender and pointed, white on upper lip. Ears relatively large, pointed, erect, black backed, and usually white inside. Tail is very long, thick and bushy, fulvous like back, with the usual admixture of black hairs, and a white tip. Black, silver and cross color phases are common. Females smaller than males.

cross
color phase

Young

silver
color phase

red
color phase

Vulpes fulva alascensis

OTHER NAMES *French*: Renard roux d'Alaska. *German*: Alaska-Rotfuchs. *Spanish*: Zorro común de Alaska. *Russian*: Аляскинская рыжая лисица.

TAXONOMY Considered a subspecies of North American Red Fox (*V. fulva*). Its geographic range has not been well defined, and its taxonomic validity has not been tested. Includes *harrimani* (Kodiak, Geese, Ugak and Marmot Islands), and *kenaiensis* (Kenai Peninsula).

REPRODUCTION *Gestation*: 52 days. *Young per birth*: 3-7. *Weaning*: 90 days. *Sexual maturity*: 12 months. *Life span*: 3 years. *Breeding season*: February and March. Breeding dens are usually dug in sandy knolls with sunny south-facing exposures; at each den there are a series of about half a dozen large burrows, from 20 to 25 cm in diameter, connected with each other underground. The ♀ is confined to the den during the pups' first few days of life, depending on her mate to supply food, but soon begins to leave the den for short periods to forage on her own. By their third month, the pups begin learning to hunt. In early winter the young disperse to seek out a new home range.

BEHAVIOR *Social behavior*: Mated pairs; ♂ and ♀ may remain as breeding pairs for several years and work cooperatively to rear offspring. *Diet*: Small mammals (mice, voles, shrews, snowshoe hare, common muskrats), and birds (ptarmigan) in winter. In summer it also eats eggs of ground-nesting ducks, marsh birds, grasses and sedges, and berries. On the Arctic tundra, it feeds mainly on collared lemming, tundra voles and Arctic ground squirrels. *Main predators*: Lynx, Wolf, Coyote, wolverine, eagles and perhaps bears. Solitary and territorial. Territories average 2.9 km^2 in size, often bounded by rivers or other natural barriers. Related Foxes do not share home range resources, and ♀ occupy smaller ranges.

DISTRIBUTION *Native*: Canada, United States. Found in most of Alaska, N and central Yukon Territory, and Northwest Territories. It occurs throughout most of mainland Alaska and on several far E Aleutian Islands. They are uncommon along the mainland of SE Alaska N of the Taku River, and rare along the S mainland. Commercial Fox farming resulted in the introduction of Red Foxes to many N Pacific islands. It occurs throughout the Yukon.

HABITAT A wide variety of habitats, ranging from tundra to boreal forests, steppe and temperate deserts. In Alaska they prefer riparian drainages in the mountains and foothills, coastal plains and river valleys. In the Yukon they inhabit white spruce forests, subalpine areas of willow and soapberry, and alpine tundra. Small numbers have begun to inhabit the Arctic tundra of the far north over the last century, where they compete with the Arctic Fox; in these areas, they have been observed digging Arctic Foxes from their dens and killing them. The expansion of the Coyote's range has affected its distribution.

CONSERVATION STATUS Least Concern. *CITES*: Not listed. Populations in Alaska and the Yukon are considered large and abundant. It was the first furbearer to be raised in captivity for pelt production.

PHOTO CREDITS *Richard Fitzer*, Haines, AK (USA); *Sarkophoto*, *Cecoffman*, Denali, AK (USA); *Drew Hamilton*, Kenai Peninsula Borough, AK (USA); *Risha Isom*, Kodiak, AK (USA).

British Columbia Red Fox
VULPES FULVA ABIETORUM

BL: 56-80 cm. TL: 33-40 cm. H: 35-40 cm. W: 5-6.5 kg (♂), 4-5 kg (♀). SL: 14.5 cm. SW: 7.8 cm. DF: 42. CN: 34. A small to medium-sized Canid, with long and slender legs and pointed muzzle, and long brush-like tail. A large-sized subspecies of North American Red Fox, with larger and longer tail, longer and fuller fur, and smaller ears, very similar to *alascensis*, with a longer, thinner face. Pelage is golden fulvous, long and full on neck and anterior part of back, almost forming a ruff, shorter and coarser on posterior part of back and rump, where it is more grizzled in color. Throat and chest are white. Face and head grizzled fulvous and buffy, strongly rusty on top of nose and around eyes, paler on cheeks and forehead. Muzzle slender and pointed, white on upper lip. Ears relatively large, pointed, erect, black backed, and usually white inside. Black on feet may be greatly restricted. Tail is very long, thick and bushy, fulvous like back, with the usual admixture of black hairs, and a white tip. Females smaller than males.

Young

Vulpes fulva abietorum

OTHER NAMES Fir Fox, Fir Wood Fox. *French*: Renard roux du Canada. *German*: Britisch-Kolumbien-Rotfuchs. *Spanish*: Zorro común de Columbia Británica. *Russian*: Рыжая лисица Британской Колумбии.

TAXONOMY Considered a subspecies of North American Red Fox (*V. fulva*). The geographic range of most North American subspecies has not been well defined, and their taxonomic validity has not been tested.

REPRODUCTION *Gestation*: 51-53 days. *Young per birth*: 4-5, up to 12. *Weaning*: 35 days. *Sexual maturity*: 10 months. *Life span*: 10 years. *Breeding season*: February and March. Dens usually have 1 or more openings, and the tunnels are an average of 1 to 1.5 m below ground. The ♂ may bring food to the den until the ♀ can leave the pups a short time, then they both hunt. They remain with the pups until dispersal. Dens are usually located on hillsides in or near heavy brush or woodlands. Dens may be built by the foxes themselves, or may be enlarged versions of dens previously constructed by other small mammals.

BEHAVIOR *Social behavior*: Mated pairs and their pups. *Diet*: Small rodents (vole, mouse), but also larger mammals, birds (including the eggs and young of game birds and many ground-nesting passerines), amphibians, reptiles, insects, plant matter, especially berries and other fruits in season, and carrion. When prey is abundant, they will cache excess food items at dens or bury them at selected locations. *Main predators*: Coyote, bobcat, lynx, golden eagle. Most active from dusk to dawn. They are usually solitary hunters as adults and are highly mobile, foraging in an extensive area. They have non-overlapping territories among family groups, with territorial boundaries defined by scent marking with urine or feces on a regular basis. In subalpine habitat in NW British Columbia, summer ranges range from 3 to 34 km².

DISTRIBUTION *Native*: Canada, United States (Alaska). Occurs throughout W Canada, in S Yukon and Northwest Territories, interior British Columbia and adjacent coastal SE Alaska, and N Alberta. In British Columbia, it is found over most of the mainland, but is most common in the central and N parts; it does not regularly occur in the wet coastal forests W of the Coast Range, or naturally on any of the coastal islands, although it does appear in agricultural and suburban habitats in the lower mainland.

HABITAT Relatively open habitats, often with patches of cover interspersed with small openings, although large expanses of alpine tundra and subalpine parkland are also commonly used. Because of its relatively low foot-loading, it is able to stay on the surface in snow and is better adapted than the Coyote for occupation of high-elevation areas. Closer to civilization, it will live in agricultural areas where farmlands alternate with woodlots, cut-over shrublands, and meadows. In large cities, it uses ravines, parks, and golf courses, as well as large, well-vegetated lots among low-density housing.

CONSERVATION STATUS Least Concern. *CITES*: Not listed. Harvests of Foxes were highest in the 1930s and early 1940s, but then declined sharply as pelt prices dropped. Predator control programs aimed at Coyotes and Wolves had a significant impact on populations in the 1950s and 1960s.

PHOTO CREDITS *Jean-Guy Dallaire* and *James Tupper*, AB (Canada); *Alan D. Wilson*, Horsefly Peninsula, BC (Canada); *Keith Williams*, Yukon Territory (Canada); *Cats99*, Fairview, AB (Canada).

Rocky Mountain Red Fox

VULPES FULVA MACROURA

BL: 55.8-68.5 cm (♂). TL: 35-40 cm. H: 38.1-40.6 cm. W: 3.2-6.8 kg (♂). DF: 42. CN: 34. A small-sized Canid, with long and slender legs and pointed muzzle, and long brush-like tail. A montane, small-sized subspecies of North American Red Fox, with a very large tail, paler coloration and less pronounced black on feet and legs. Pelage is yellowish fulvous, darkest on median line, palest on sides of neck and flanks. Throat and chest are whitish, darkened by underfur showing through. Face is buffy fulvous and whitish, nose dull brownish fulvous, grizzled with buffy. Ears relatively large, pointed, erect, black backed, white inside. Outer sides of legs dark reddish fulvous. Black of forefeet reaching to elbow, black of hind feet narrow and hardly reaching ankle. Tail is very long, thick and bushy, grizzled grayish buff mixed with black hairs, the black hairs on upper side of base forming a broad blackish patch, white tipped. Females smaller than males.

Young

cross
color phase

Vulpes fulva macroura

OTHER NAMES Long-Tailed Red Fox, Wasatch Mountain Fox. *French*: Renard roux des Rocheuses. *German*: Felsengebirgs-Rotfuchs. *Spanish*: Zorro común de las Montañas Rocosas. *Russian*: Длиннохвостая американская рыжая лисица.

TAXONOMY Considered a subspecies of North American Red Fox (*V. fulva*). It is one of three mountain North American Red Foxes that also include the Sierra Nevada Red Fox (*V. f. necator*) and the Cascade Red Fox (*V. f. cascadensis*).

REPRODUCTION *Gestation*: 51-53 days. *Young per birth*: 2-3, reproductive output is generally low in montane Foxes. *Weaning*: 56-70 days. *Sexual maturity*: 12 months. *Life span*: 5.5 years. *Breeding season*: Between December and March. Similar to lowland-dwelling North American Red Fox subspecies. Births occur from March through May in sheltered dens. Dens may be burrows dug by themselves, abandoned ones previously used by other Foxes or other species, various natural cavities such as caves, hollow trees and logs, openings in very thick brush or piles of wood debris, or in structures such as barns and other outbuildings, grain elevators, haystacks and culverts. Both parents aid in providing the pups with food and protection. Juveniles disperse when they are 6-8 months old. The longest dispersal distances are made by ♂. Dispersal by adults also occurs, usually in response to reduced availability of food on the home range due to climatic factors, or to a more general cyclic crash of an important prey species.

BEHAVIOR *Social behavior*: Mated pairs. *Diet*: Small mammals; as winter progresses, when it is difficult to break through the layers of snow to gain access to small mammals, they turn more to scavenging from carcasses left by larger predators or excavate and consume cached food. *Main predators*: Coyote. Adapted to survive in harsh winter conditions at high elevations. They exploit higher elevations more than Coyotes, which may be a spatial competition avoidance mechanism since there are few if any Coyote territories above 2,100 m. They are better adapted to hunt in deep snow, as their relatively large feet and long track length allow Foxes to stay on top of the snow.

DISTRIBUTION *Native*: Canada, United States. Found in NW United States and SW Canada; Rocky Mountains, Wasatch Range, near Great Salt Lake, Utah, mountains of Colorado and Wyoming. Also described from E Oregon, mountainous parts of Idaho, Montana, Black Hills of South Dakota, and S in Rocky Mountains to N New Mexico and N Arizona. In Canada it occurs in extreme SE British Columbia, S Alberta and probably SW Saskatchewan. The subspecific status of the Red Fox inhabiting lowlands in those areas is unclear, and may be *V. f. macroura* that could have descended from the montane habitats back to the plains, or *V. f. fulva* that could have migrated from the surrounding region. In addition, it is unknown where the dividing line is between these two subspecies or if an integradation zone exists. Red Foxes at Yellowstone National Park belong to the *macroura* subspecies.

HABITAT Forested habitats at high elevations in the Rocky Mountains, from 1,350 to 3,000 m. They prefer habitats close to the edge of a major structural change in vegetation. To avoid Coyotes, they may have to survive in between, on the periphery, or at higher elevations than Coyotes.

CONSERVATION STATUS Least Concern. *CITES*: Not listed.

PHOTO CREDITS *Rinus Baak* and *Michelle Holihan,* Yellowstone National Park, WY (USA); *JD Hascup*, Jasper National Park, AB (Canada).

Cascade Red Fox

VULPES FULVA CASCADENSIS

BL: 60-71 cm (♂), 56-58 cm (♀). TL: 32-41.2 cm. H: 38-44 cm. W: 4-4.5 kg (♂), 3.5-3.7 kg (♀). DF: 42. CN: 34. A small-sized Canid, with long and slender legs and pointed muzzle, and long brush-like tail. This is a montane, small-sized subspecies of North American Red Fox, with a relatively short tail, deep rusty to yellow in color. Pelage is straw yellow to deep rusty dorsally grading to rusty grizzled with white posteriorly and lighter rust along sides. Underfur is light gray. Throat and chest are white with gray underfur. Belly is all white. Muzzle slender and pointed, white on upper lip. Ears relatively large, pointed, erect, black backed, white inside. Black of ears and feet greatly restricted. Tail very pale, sparsely overlain with black-tipped hairs, tipped with white. Silver phase is common, being entirely black except for an area on the posterior dorsum grizzled with white and sometimes an area grizzled with white on the shoulders, and the white tip on the tail. Females slightly smaller than males.

Young

cross
color phase

Vulpes fulva cascadensis

OTHER NAMES Cascade Mountains Red Fox. *French*: Renard roux des Cascades. *German*: Kaskadengebirgs-Rotfuchs. *Spanish*: Zorro común de la cordillera de las Cascadas. *Russian*: Рыжая лисица каскадных гор.

TAXONOMY Considered a subspecies of North American Red Fox (*V. fulva*). It is one of three mountain North American Red Foxes that also include the Sierra Nevada Red Fox (*V. f. necator*) and the Rocky Mountain Red Fox (*V. f. macroura*).

REPRODUCTION *Gestation*: 51-53 days. *Young per birth*: 4-8. *Weaning*: 60 days. *Sexual maturity*: Unknown. *Life span*: Unknown. *Breeding season*: Late January to early February. Births occur from mid-March to mid-May. Dens are located in stands of trees, and their placement, the number of entrances, and their size are not different from those of other subspecies in North America.

BEHAVIOR *Social behavior*: Mated pairs. *Diet*: Pocket gophers, voles, lagomorphs, insects, and fruit and berries, but also birds and their eggs, opossums, insectivores, a variety of other rodents, and occasionally other carnivores; in local situations it consumes garbage and carrion. In the winter, mammals are the principal food items; in the spring, birds become a minor component of the diet and continue as such through the summer and fall; in the early summer, fruits and insects are important food items. *Main predators*: Coyote. This montane subspecies appears to be specialized for occupying subalpine and alpine habitats, and may possess physiological adaptations that other populations lack. Home ranges are small in subalpine meadows, larger in poorer habitat on the E slope of the Cascades. They do not migrate to lower elevations in winter, although they increase their home range size during the months when snow is on the ground.

DISTRIBUTION *Native*: Canada, United States. This subspecies occurs on the NW coast of the United States and Canada: S British Columbia, Cascade Range in Oregon and Washington, and N Sierra Nevada in California, but the limits of its range are not well defined. It occurs at low abundance throughout Mount Rainier National Park, at sites on the Gifford Pinchot National Forest, and as sparse detections in the North Cascades ecosystem. Some authors state that Oregon animals are *V. f. necator*.

HABITAT Restricted to upper montane forest, subalpine parkland, and alpine zone of Cascade Range. This subspecies appears able to move through areas of timber, but dense timber may partially obstruct movement and colonization. Lowland populations probably correspond to other introduced subspecies.

CONSERVATION STATUS Least Concern. *CITES*: Not listed. *Regional status*: Critically Imperiled (Oregon, Washington). It is one of the most threatened subspecies, as its range is small and apparently much reduced from historical times, facing numerous threats. The population size at Mount Rainier and Mount Adams is unknown, and its status elsewhere in its range is unknown. Significant threats to all populations include growing Coyote populations, which increase risk of predation and competition, habitat loss and fragmentation due to recreational development, and habitat loss due to encroachment of woody vegetation. There is a potential for genetic erosion, due to small population sizes.

PHOTO CREDITS *Robert McRae, David Pickles, Paul Thomson, Gary Fua, Dani Tinker* and *Dave Biddle*, Mount Rainier National Park, WA (USA).

Sierra Nevada Red Fox
VULPES FULVA NECATOR

BL: 67.5 cm (♂), 61.3 cm (♀). TL: 34.5-38.1 cm. H: 35-40 cm. W: 4-4.2 kg (♂), 3.3-3.5 kg (♀). SL: 14.5 cm. SW: 7.6 cm. DF: 42. CN: 34. A small-sized Canid, with long and slender legs and pointed muzzle, and long brush-like tail. A montane, small-sized subspecies of North American Red Fox, with a relatively short tail. Pelage is dark dull rusty fulvous, resembling that of *fulvus*, becoming much paler on sides, where the whitish underfur shows through. Throat and chest are white. Face dull fulvous, strongly grizzled with whitish. Sides of nose dusky, darker than in *fulvus*, grizzled with buffy. Cross and silver color phases are very common in this subspecies. Black of legs much restricted. Tail is relatively small, differing widely from the big tail of *macrourus*, fulvous in color at base, becoming buffy whitish and profusely mixed with long black hairs, base with a black spot, and white tip. White-tipped tails are common to all color phases.

Vulpes fulva necator

OTHER NAMES High Sierra Fox, Murdering Fox. *French*: Renard roux de Sierra Nevada. *German*: Sierra-Nevada-Rotfuchs. *Spanish*: Zorro común de Sierra Nevada. *Russian*: Рыжая лисица заснеженных гор.

TAXONOMY Considered a subspecies of North American Red Fox (*V. fulva*). It is one of the mountain North American Red Foxes. Lowland California Red Foxes living in the San Joaquin Valley, the San Francisco Bay area, and S California may be descended from a mix of subspecies from several areas, and are considered to be non-native in California; those are larger and more richly colored.

REPRODUCTION *Gestation*: 51-53 days. *Young per birth*: 2-3, reproductive output is generally low in montane Foxes. *Weaning*: 56-70 days. *Sexual maturity*: 12 months. *Life span*: 5.5 years. *Breeding season*: Between December and March. Similar to lowland-dwelling North American Red Fox subspecies. Births occur from March through May in sheltered dens.

BEHAVIOR *Social behavior*: Mated pairs, predominantly monogamous. *Diet*: Opportunistic predators and foragers, with a diet primarily composed of small rodents, but also including deer carrion, particularly in winter and spring, and manzanita berries, particularly in fall. *Main predators*: Golden eagle. Most active at dusk and at night when many rodents are most active. This montane subspecies is characterized by specialized adaptations to cold areas, including a particularly thick and deep winter coat, small toe pads that are completely covered in winter by dense fur to facilitate movement over snow, a smaller size that may also facilitate movement over snow by lowering weight supported per square centimeter of foot pad. Its smaller size may also be due to reduced abundance of prey at higher elevations. In Lassen, home ranges range from 0.03 to 6.9 km² in summer, larger in winter. At Sonora Pass home ranges average 9.1 km².

DISTRIBUTION *Native*: United States. Only two populations persist today; one near Lassen Volcanic National Park, and a second near Yosemite National Park and Sonora Pass. Some authors include Red Foxes of the Oregon Cascades in this subspecies. Subspecific status of Foxes in Nevada is unknown.

HABITAT Multiple habitat types in the alpine and subalpine zones (near and above tree line), meadows and rocky areas.

CONSERVATION STATUS Least Concern. *CITES*: Not listed. *Regional status*: Critically endangered, and possibly declining, with an estimated population likely less than 50. Main threats include small population size and isolation, hybridization with non-native Red Fox, climate change, and competition and predation from Coyotes. It is protected from hunting and trapping by California fish and game laws. It does not enjoy any elevated conservation status in the states of Oregon or Nevada.

Sacramento Valley Red Fox

VULPES FULVA PATWIN

BL: 67.2 cm (♂), 65.2 cm (♀). TL: 41.6 cm. H: 35-45 cm. W: 4.7 kg (♂), 4.0 kg (♀). DF: 42. CN: 34. A small to medium-sized Canid, with long and slender legs and pointed muzzle, and long brush-like tail. A large-sized and lankier subspecies of North American Red Fox. Pelage is dark dull rusty fulvous, becoming paler on sides. Throat and chest are white. Face dull fulvous, grizzled with whitish. Sides of nose dusky, grizzled with buffy. Muzzle slender and pointed, white on upper lip. Ears relatively large, pointed, erect, black backed, white inside. Black legs. Tail is relatively small, fulvous in color at base, becoming buffy whitish and profusely mixed with long black hairs, base with a black spot, and white tip. Females are smaller than males.

Vulpes fulva patwin

OTHER NAMES Central Valley Red Fox. *French*: Renard roux. *German*: Sacramento-Rotfuchs. *Spanish*: Zorro común del Valle de Sacramento. *Russian*: Рыжая лисица калифорнийской долины.

TAXONOMY Considered a subspecies of North American Red Fox (*V. fulva*). It was previously considered an introduced species, but it is indigenous to California and phylogenetically most closely related to Sierra Nevada Red Fox (*V. f. necator*).

REPRODUCTION *Gestation*: 61-63 days. *Young per birth*: 1-10. *Weaning*: 56-70 days. *Sexual maturity*: 12 months. *Life span*: 6 years. *Breeding season*: December to January. Most births occur in late February and early March. Den sites are closely associated with grasslands and occur away from flooded agriculture, wetlands and heavily urbanized areas. Den sites may be excavated ground squirrel burrows, or located under sheds or woodpiles, in culverts, road cuts, and between buildings.

BEHAVIOR *Social behavior*: Mated pairs; monogamous. *Diet*: Mainly small mammals, berries, plants. *Main predators*: Coyote, Dog. Gray Foxes affect the distribution and abundance of Sacramento Valley Red Foxes, probably through exploitative competition, resulting in exclusion from riparian areas or patches of dense vegetation capable of providing refuge from Coyotes. However, direct interference from Coyotes is probably far more significant than exploitative competition with Gray Foxes.

DISTRIBUTION *Native*: United States. It is endemic to the Sacramento Valley, California, occurring from Cottonwood to the Delta, W of the Sacramento River, and from Chico to Sacramento, E of the Sacramento River. Hybridization with introduced Red Foxes is found on the S and SE margins of the range, possibly facilitated by low densities of native Foxes in these areas. All Red Foxes S of the American River and Delta and W of the Sacramento Valley (Sonoma County), in lowland areas, are probably introduced Red Foxes, which derive largely from fur farm stock exhibiting ancestry from an admixture of diverse and phylogenetically distant sources.

HABITAT Arid grasslands. They usually avoid flooded agriculture and wetlands, and heavily urbanized areas, which marks an important difference from non-native Red Foxes. They may use areas close to human structures if heavy cover is nearby.

CONSERVATION STATUS Least Concern. *CITES*: Not listed. *Regional status*: It may qualify for threatened or endangered status (California). Anecdotal and genetic evidence suggest that this subspecies has declined considerably in abundance and range. While introgression occurs and could pose a greater threat in the future, some type of reproductive barrier with non-native Foxes appears to be in place.

Scandinavian Red Fox
VULPES VULPES VULPES

BL: 73.3 cm (♂), 70.5 cm (♀). TL: 31-55 cm. H: 35-40 cm. W: 5.8 kg (♂), 4.9 kg (♀). SL: 15 cm. SW: 8.3 cm. DF: 42. CN: 34. A small to medium-sized Canid, with long and slender legs and pointed muzzle, and long brush-like tail. A large-sized subspecies of Red Fox, with teeth larger and more robust than in the central and southern subspecies. Pelage is yellowish brown and brighter, more inclined toward reddish along median dorsal region and on face, duller and more yellowish or grayish on sides of body to shoulder and on sides of neck to base of ear, the flanks and usually the sides sprinkled with white hairs. Underparts very variable, ranging from whitish to slaty black. Ears relatively large, pointed, erect, tawny or buff at base and on inner surface, black or very dark brown on the terminal half of outer side, in strong contrast with surrounding parts. Muzzle slender and pointed, dull white on upper lip. Tail is long, thick and bushy, with abundant underfur, white tipped. Feet dusky or blackish. Females are smaller than males.

Young

Vulpes vulpes vulpes

OTHER NAMES Common Red Fox. *French*: Renard roux d'Europe. *German*: Skandinavischer Rotfuchs. *Spanish*: Zorro común escandinavo. *Russian*: Скандинавская рыжая лисица. *Norwegian*: Rødrev.

TAXONOMY Considered a subspecies of Red Fox (*V. vulpes*). Includes *lineatus* (Skane, Sweden), *nigro-argenteus* (Lofoten Islands, Norway), *nigrocaudatus* (Uppland, Sweden), *septentrionalis* (Norway) and *variegatus* (Uppland, Sweden).

SIMILAR SPECIES North American Red Foxes (*V. fulva*) are comparatively lightweight, rather long for their mass, and with considerable sexual dimorphism. Arctic Fox (*V. lagopus*) is visibly smaller, has a shorter, less tapered head with shorter, rounded ears, and its winter and summer pelage is different in color.

REPRODUCTION *Gestation*: 51-53 days. *Young per birth*: 3-10. *Weaning*: 56-70 days. *Sexual maturity*: 10-12 months. *Life span*: 9 years. *Breeding season*: From December to January. Reproduction varies in relation to food abundance, with a lower rate of reproducing ♀ with scarcity of rodents. Migration in juveniles occurs between 6 and 12 months of age. They can migrate over large distances in a short period of time, especially young ♂.

BEHAVIOR *Social behavior*: Solitary, monogamous pairs. *Diet*: The presence of lynx feeding on roe deer creates an important, stable food supply for Foxes, as scavenging on roe deer may replace feeding on presumably less profitable food such as fish and reptiles, invertebrates and vegetables. In addition to carrion it eats mostly rodents and small to medium-sized mammals, but also insects and berries. In the N part of its range the prey is mostly voles, whereas in the S rabbits and hares are the majority. *Main predators*: Wolf, lynx. Mainly nocturnal. Its density varies from 0.2 to 0.4 per km² in forest landscape, to 0.8 in pasture landscape. As one of its main food sources is voles, population can fluctuate due to a changing population of voles. Arctic and Red Foxes have similar food niches, which suggests they compete for territories, and Arctic Foxes rarely breed close to dens occupied by reproducing Red Foxes. This can explain observed changes in Arctic Fox distribution over the last century.

DISTRIBUTION *Native*: Denmark, Norway, Sweden. Found in W, central and N Europe.

HABITAT It lives in a range of different habitats, but prefers rich biotopes, such as open farmland, arable fields and pasture areas, as there is often more food available in these habitats, such as voles, than in the forest. They may venture onto the tundra.

CONSERVATION STATUS Least Concern. *CITES*: Not listed. Considered one of the largest threats to the endangered Arctic Fox. Population in Scandinavia has increased after an intensive outbreak of sarcoptic mange in the 1980s and 1990s. Regional warming, increased supplies of anthropogenic food items, and the increase and expansion of ungulate populations have also positively affected populations. Fox farming is no longer economically viable in Sweden and since 2001, Fox farming is no longer carried out there. In Denmark, a ban on Fox farming was introduced in 2009. Norway remains one of the world's foremost Fox fur producing countries. Hunting is permitted.

PHOTO CREDITS *Kjejoh,* Tåsjö (Sweden); *Lext* and *Päivi Paddler* (Norway); *lumofisk,* Henningsvaer (Norway); *Trond Hynne,* Hallem (Norway).

European Red Fox

VULPES VULPES CRUCIGERA

BL: 62-72 cm (♂), 61 cm (♀). TL: 34-41 cm. H: 35-40 cm. W: 6.7 kg (♂), 5.4 kg (♀). SL: 15 cm. SW: 8.2 cm. DF: 42. CN: 34. A small to medium-sized Canid, with long and slender legs and pointed muzzle, and long brush-like tail. A large-sized subspecies, smaller than the Scandinavian Fox, with teeth distinctly smaller. Pelage is variable in color, usually reddish brown, but can be orange or bright yellowish with a dark stripe down the back. Sides of neck and region immediately behind shoulder lighter than median dorsal area. Posterior half of back with evident white frosting in some specimens, scarcely any in others. Throat and chest are white. Muzzle slender and pointed, white on upper lip. Ears relatively large, pointed, erect, black backed, and usually white inside. Underparts are dull slaty overlaid with white. Limbs are commonly black. Tail is long and bushy, with a white tip. Females are slightly smaller than males.

Young

Vulpes vulpes crucigera

OTHER NAMES Crucigera Fox, British Red Fox. *French*: Renard roux d'Europe. *German*: Europäischer Rotfuchs. *Spanish*: Zorro común europeo. *Russian*: Европейская рыжая лисица.

TAXONOMY Considered a subspecies of Red Fox (*V. vulpes*). Includes *alba, cinerea, crymensis, diluta, europaeus, hellenica, hypomelas, krimeamontana, lutea, melanogaster, meridionalis, nigra, stepensis, tobolica* and *toschii*.

REPRODUCTION *Gestation*: 51-53 days. *Young per birth*: 4-10. *Weaning*: 56-70 days. *Sexual maturity*: 10 months. *Life span*: 14 years in captivity. *Breeding season*: From December to February. They breed once a year with pups born in spring, generally in dens but also in hollow trees, rock crevices, under houses or in log piles.

BEHAVIOR *Social behavior*: Solitary, monogamous. *Diet*: Field voles, birds, rabbits, insects, earthworms, grasshoppers, beetles, blackberries, plums and carrion. Surplus food is buried. In some circumstances they may kill lambs and goat kids, but they do not have the size and strength to hold and immobilize large prey like adult sheep or goats, or to crush large bones. *Main predators*: Birds of prey, Dogs. Solitary hunters, but evidence suggests that family groups occupy well-defined home ranges. Family groups usually consist of a ♂ and ♀ Fox with pups, but non-breeding, subordinate ♀ may also be present. Rural home ranges in Australia are about 5 km², but this can vary widely and depends on resource availability. Most active from dusk until dawn and usually rest during the day in an earth den. They may also hunt and scavenge during the day. Feces and urine are used to define territories by scent marking conspicuous landmarks like tussocks of grass and rabbit warrens. These scent marks are distributed throughout its range, especially in places that are visited often. They communicate by sound as well as by scent marking and body language. Young Foxes use aggressive yapping and a resonant howl during the winter mating season. Vixens and pups will bark and whimper softly. Adult Foxes also make vocalizations that can sound like screaming.

DISTRIBUTION *Native*: Albania, Austria, Belarus, Belgium, Bosnia and Herzegovina, Bulgaria, Croatia, Czech Republic, Estonia, Finland, France, Germany, Greece, Hungary, Ireland, Italy, Latvia, Lithuania, Luxembourg, Macedonia, Moldova, Monaco, Montenegro, Netherlands, Poland, Russia, Serbia, Slovakia, Slovenia, Switzerland, Ukraine, United Kingdom. Introduced in Australia and Virginia (United States) for hunting purposes.

HABITAT Almost every habitat: sea cliffs, sand dunes, salt marshes, peat bogs, high mountains, woodland and particularly abundant in urban areas.

CONSERVATION STATUS Least Concern. *CITES*: Not listed. Populations have increased in most areas, with a concurrent increase in range, although numbers have fluctuated with the availability of the food supply. They are considered a major predator of ground-nesting birds, including game species and those of conservation concern. It is also a potential vector for the rabies virus. In Australia, they are a major pest species that threatens agricultural and native species alike.

PHOTO CREDITS *Linda Stanley*, Poole (UK); *Peter Trimming*, Felcourt (UK); *Alex Witt*, Stoke Newington (UK); *Colin Price*, Brocton (UK); *Stu232*, Staffordshire (UK).

East Russian Red Fox

VULPES VULPES BERINGIANA AND RELATED SUBSPECIES

BL: 63.8-72 cm. TL: 36.2-43 cm. H: 35 cm. W: 3.3-6 kg. SL: 15.4 cm. SW: 8.0 cm. DF: 42. CN: 34. A small to medium-sized Canid, with long and slender legs and pointed muzzle, and long brush-like tail. A large subspecies of Red Fox, brightly colored. Pelage is variable in color, usually intense orange red, forming a distinct cross on back and shoulders. Some individuals may be much yellower and lighter. Flanks are yellower and more vivid. Neck and throat are white. Underparts are orange-red-yellow to white. Head is orange above, somewhat lighter than back. Backs of ears are black. Lips are white. Tail is long and bushy, reddish yellow to dark orange buff, having long hair with black tips, with a whitish tip. Limbs are orange, with a variable black pattern in front of carpal joints sometimes faintly marked. Little sexual dimorphism.

Young

Vulpes vulpes beringiana

Vulpes vulpes jakutensis

Vulpes vulpes dolichocrania

Vulpes vulpes daurica

OTHER NAMES Kamchatka Red Fox, Anadyr Fox, Tundra Fox (*beringiana*), Yakutsk Red Fox (*jakutensis*), Trans-Baikal Red Fox (*daurica*). *French*: Renard roux. *German*: Kamtschatka-Rotfuchs, Jakutischer Rotfuchs, Fernöstlicher Rotfuchs, Daurischer Rotfuchs. *Spanish*: Zorro de Kamchatka. *Russian*: Анадырская рыжая лисица (*beringiana*), Якутская рыжая лисица (*jakutensis*), Уссурийская рыжая лисица (*dolichocrania*), Забайкальская рыжая лисица (*daurica*).

TAXONOMY Considered a subspecies of Red Fox (*V. vulpes*). Includes *schantaricus* (Great Shantar Island), *sibiricus*, *ognevi* (Zeya-Bureya Plains) and *ussuriensis* (Ussuri Region). The validity of this and other subspecies has not been confirmed by genetic analysis.

SIMILAR SPECIES Arctic Fox is smaller in size, with shorter legs, muzzle and rounded ears, and pelage color is different.

REPRODUCTION *Gestation*: 51-53 days. *Young per birth*: 3-9, up to 13. *Weaning*: Unknown. *Sexual maturity*: Unknown. *Life span*: Unknown. *Breeding season*: Late December to late March. There is no specific information for these subspecies, but probably similar to other Red Foxes. The young are born from March to May. Dens are located under big rocks, roots of big trees, or in cracks and caves of cliffs. ♂ help with parental care. Dispersal occurs in the fall, with the ♂ generally dispersing farther than ♀.

BEHAVIOR *Social behavior*: Solitary, monogamous. *Diet*: Small ground-dwelling mammals, including lagomorphs and sciurids, but may also take galliformes, frogs, snakes, insects, berries and vegetables. Carrion may be seasonally important. Surplus food is buried. *Main predators*: Birds of prey, Dogs. There is no specific information for these subspecies, but probably similar to other Red Foxes. Predominantly nocturnal, with a tendency toward crepuscularity and, although diurnal activity is common in some areas, they typically spend the day resting in cover. Very mobile, often covering several km per day, with non-overlapping territories. Territories are larger in winter than in summer. Arctic and Red Foxes may coexist without antagonistic interactions when there is enough food, but in some cases Arctic Foxes may be chased or even killed by Red Foxes.

DISTRIBUTION *Native*: Russia, Mongolia. These subspecies are found in Asian Russia and N Mongolia: *V. v. beringiana* is found in NE Siberia, shores of Bering Strait, including Kamchatka and Anadyr region in Chukotka; *V. v. jakutensis* occurs in Sakha Republic and E Siberia; *V. v. dolichocrania* occurs in SW Primorsky Krai, Amur Oblast, and SE Siberia; *V. v. daurica* occurs in Republic of Buryatia, Kyakhta, S Transbaikalia, S Siberia and N Mongolia. Boundaries with other subspecies of Red Fox are unclear.

HABITAT Mixed landscapes consisting of scrub, woodland and farmland, but also found in dense woodland, tundra, coastal dunes, and above the tree line in mountain ranges, from sea level up to 3,000 m. During the last century, they have expanded its distribution into the Arctic.

CONSERVATION STATUS Least Concern. *CITES*: Not listed. Regarded as a pest in most areas, and unprotected. Hunting is regulated.

PHOTO CREDITS *Ivan Vdovin*, Okhotsk, Kamchatka Peninsula (Russia); *Budkov Denis*, Kamchatka Peninsula (Russia).

Iberian Red Fox

VULPES VULPES SILACEA

BL: 60-80 cm. TL: 25-50 cm. H: 35-50 cm. W: 4.6-8.6 kg (♂), 3.1-7.8 kg (♀). SL: 15.3 cm. SW: 8.3 cm. DF: 42. CN: 34. A small to medium-sized Canid, with long and slender legs, pointed muzzle, and long brush-like tail. A medium-sized subspecies of Red Fox, with reddish tints mostly replaced by buffy and grayish. Pelage is light ochraceous buff dorsally grading to black, creamy white and russet, the black predominating along midline of neck and between shoulders. Throat, chest, shoulders, base of forelegs and underparts are dull white, everywhere clouded with slaty black. Head and face tawny ochraceous. Muzzle slender and pointed, white on upper lip. Ears relatively large, pointed, erect, black backed, pale cream buff inside. Tail light buffy gray, sparsely overlain with black-tipped hairs, most noticeable on lower surface, tipped with white. Legs tawny ochraceous buff, with black-tipped hairs on outer surface, and feet strongly washed with black. Females smaller than males.

winter coat

Vulpes vulpes silacea

OTHER NAMES *French*: Renard roux ibérique. *German*: Iberischer Rotfuchs. *Spanish*: Zorro común ibérico. *Russian*: Иберийская рыжая лисица. *Portuguese*: Raposa-vermelha.

TAXONOMY Considered a subspecies of Red Fox (*V. vulpes*). The validity of this and other subspecies has not been confirmed by genetic analysis. Various Spanish populations show great variability in size.

REPRODUCTION *Gestation*: 52 days. *Young per birth*: 1-7. *Weaning*: 35-63 days. *Sexual maturity*: 12 months. *Life span*: 14 years. *Breeding season*: From January to February. Most births occur from March to April. Cubs are born blind and with grayish color. They open their eyes at the age of 11-14 days. Both parents take care of the pups. The pups stay with their parents until autumn and then gradually leave the area and become independent.

BEHAVIOR *Social behavior*: Solitary, but also mated pairs, or small groups composed of 1 ♂ and 2-3 related ♀. *Diet*: A generalist and opportunistic predator; small mammals are the most important prey consumed (rodents, insectivores, lagomorphs); arthropods, fruits, birds, reptiles and carrion are good supplementary food resources. The intake of lagomorphs and small mammals is greatest in Mediterranean scrub and forest, respectively. Reptiles and invertebrates are consumed mostly during summer; fruits and seeds in autumn. *Main predators*: Wolf, Iberian lynx, Dogs, golden eagle and Eurasian eagle-owl. Mainly nocturnal and crepuscular. Diurnal activity decreases in areas with higher levels of human disturbance and increases in dense habitats. Home ranges on the Iberian Peninsula from 0.7 to more than 30 km².

DISTRIBUTION *Native*: Portugal, Spain. Found on the Iberian Peninsula S of the Pyrenees. It is not found in Baleares and Canarias islands. The subspecies in the Pyrenees is *V. v. crucigera*, but it is unknown if there may be an area of intergradation.

HABITAT It prefers large forested habitats with autochthonous oaks and holm oaks. It commonly uses irrigation channels with close proximity of cover. It is often associated with human population nuclei, as it finds abundant and easily available food supplies in rubbish dumps and livestock carrion. Up to 3,000 m in altitude.

CONSERVATION STATUS Least Concern. *CITES*: Not listed. It is fairly common and widespread throughout the Iberian Peninsula, with densities from 0.8 animals per km² in rain-fed areas to 2.5 per km² in irrigated areas. Main threats include habitat fragmentation and road kills. In Spain, it is a game species than can be legally culled outside the hunting season with a special permit.

PHOTO CREDITS *Luis Jiménez Delgado*, Sierra de Cazorla (Spain); *Aitor Ivàñez Monerris*, Sierra de Cazorla (Spain); *Pablo Barrena*, Villarreal de San Carlos (Spain); *Cláudia Matos*, Serrejón (Spain); *Chiaroscuro Fotografia*, Abantos (Spain).

Sardinian Red Fox

VULPES VULPES ICHNUSAE

BL: 59-64 cm. TL: 28-34 cm. H: 35-50 cm. W: 5-7 kg (♂), 4.5-6.5 kg (♀). SL: 12.9 cm. SW: 7.8 cm. DF: 42. CN: 34. A small to medium-sized Canid, with long and slender legs, pointed muzzle, and long brush-like tail. Smaller than continental subspecies, with a darker color, and relatively smaller ears. Pelage is ochraceous rufous, grading dorsally to drab-gray to tawny-clay color, and ventrally to dull tawny. Sides of neck, upper foreleg and axilla tawny buff. Head, sides and back much speckled by the presence of a buffy white subterminal area on each hair. Throat, chest and underparts in front of forelegs buffy white tinged with brown. Face and head dark rufous, lighter on base of ears and neck. Muzzle slender and pointed, white on upper lip. Ears relatively large, pointed, erect, black backed, pale dull tawny inside. Tail ochraceous rufous, sparsely overlain with black-tipped hairs, fading through a buffy gray to the whitish-buff tip. Legs ochraceous rufous, slightly clouded with blackish.

234

Vulpes vulpes ichnusae

OTHER NAMES *French*: Renard roux de Sardaigne. *German*: Sardischer Rotfuchs. *Spanish*: Zorro común de Cerdeña. *Italian*: Volpe sarda. *Russian*: Сардинийская рыжая лисица.

TAXONOMY Considered a subspecies of Red Fox (*V. vulpes*). The validity of this and other subspecies has not been confirmed by genetic analysis. Red Foxes from Sardinia seem to be more closely related to Bulgarian Foxes than to Iberian Foxes. It might be the only autochthonous living mammal of Sardinia and Corsica or it may have been introduced by humans in the Early Neolithic, about 7,000 years ago.

REPRODUCTION *Gestation*: 50-60 days. *Young per birth*: 3-8, up to 12. *Weaning*: 63 days. *Sexual maturity*: 10 months. *Life span*: 7 years, 12 years in captivity. *Breeding season*: From January to March. Most births occur from April to May. There is no specific information for this subspecies, but probably similar to continental Red Foxes. Pups are born blind and with grayish color. They open their eyes at the age of 11-14 days. Both parents take care of the pups. The pups stay with their parents until autumn and then gradually leave the area and become independent.

BEHAVIOR *Social behavior*: Solitary, but also mated pairs. *Diet*: A generalist and opportunistic predator; small mammals are the most important prey consumed (rodents, insectivores, lagomorphs), followed by fruits (strawberrys, dates, pears); arthropods, birds, reptiles and carrion are good supplementary food resources. In the Natural Reserve at Mount Arcosu, insects are the most frequent source of nutrition, with a significant contribution of mammals such as deer, which may be attributed to the finding of carcasses rather than to predatory behavior. *Main predators*: Golden eagle. There is no specific information for this subspecies, but probably similar to continental Red Foxes.

DISTRIBUTION *Native*: France, Italy. Endemic to Sardinia and Corsica islands. Some authors believe that both *ichnusae* and continental *crucigera* subspecies may be present on these islands.

HABITAT They prefer high maquis and riparian vegetation, and avoid the low maquis and the garrigue. In summer, high temperatures and drought force them to move over wide areas in search of food.

CONSERVATION STATUS Least Concern. *CITES*: Not listed. It is common on both islands. It is not protected by law.

PHOTO CREDITS *Enrico Puddu*, Sardinia (Italy); *Federico Ecca, Ales*, Sardinia (Italy); *Silvio Figus*, Sardinia (Italy); *Fabio Murru*, Sardinia (Italy).

Cyprus Red Fox

VULPES VULPES INDUTUS

BL: 59-64 cm. TL: 28-34 cm. H: 35-50 cm. W: 5-7 kg (♂), 4.5-6.5 kg (♀). SL: 12.9 cm. SW: 7.8 cm. DF: 42. CN: 34. A small to medium-sized Canid, with long and slender legs, pointed muzzle, and long brush-like tail. A small-sized subspecies, similar to the Sardinian Red Fox, but usually paler in color with legs blackish in strong contrast with color of sides. Pelage is variable in color, dull yellowish buff, grading dorsally to slaty gray to nearly russet. Throat, chest and underparts in front of forelegs buffy white, clouded by the dark underfur. Face and head ochraceous buff, lighter on base of ears and neck. Muzzle slender and pointed, white on upper lip. Ears relatively large, pointed, erect, black backed, pale dull tawny inside. Tail buffy clay color, white tipped. Legs are grizzled blackish with inner surfaces washed with dull ochraceous. Feet are blackish.

dark morph

Young

236

Vulpes vulpes indutus

OTHER NAMES Cypriot Fox. *French*: Renard roux de Chypre. *German*: Zypern-Rotfuchs. *Spanish*: Zorro común de Chipre. *Russian*: Кипрская рыжая лисица.

TAXONOMY Considered a subspecies of Red Fox (*V. vulpes*). The validity of this and other subspecies has not been confirmed by genetic analysis, and some authors have found evidence that this subspecies was imported at least twice from different source populations.

REPRODUCTION *Gestation*: 50-55 days. *Young per birth*: 3-8. *Weaning*: 42-84 days. *Sexual maturity*: 9 months. *Life span*: 7 years, 12 years in captivity. *Breeding season*: From January to February. Most births occur from April to May. Pups are born blind and with grayish color. They open their eyes at the age of 11-14 days. Both parents take care of the pups. The pups stay with their parents until autumn and then gradually leave the area and become independent.

BEHAVIOR *Social behavior*: Solitary, but also mated pairs. *Diet*: A generalist and opportunistic predator; fruits, various kinds of plants, rodents, hares, rabbits, birds and their eggs, insects, reptiles and turtle eggs. *Main predators*: Golden eagle. Usually nocturnal. On cold nights their movements decrease while hot and humid nights are ideal for exploring and hunting. Usually it lives in caves, dense shrubs or holes in the ground that it opens by itself. Its dens are characterized by the number of entrances and exits that they have. Home range averages 10 to 20 km^2.

DISTRIBUTION *Native*: Cyprus. Endemic to Cyprus, where it is the only wild carnivore present. It is absent from Crete and other smaller Aegean Islands.

HABITAT Due to its high capability to adapt to any type of habitat, it is found throughout the island: upland, lowland and coastal areas, dense forests, areas with shrubs, and parks, even close to populated areas depending on the availability of food.

CONSERVATION STATUS Least Concern. *CITES*: Not listed. It can be found in many areas even though its population has been constantly declining over the last two decades. Because it has been considered harmful for livestock, it has been hunted mercilessly. It is now protected by law in Cyprus, although there have been recent attempts to include it as a game species. They are also killed on roads and poisoned on farms.

PHOTO CREDITS *Marios Perikli Theodorou*, Paphos (Cyprus); *Zeki Gursel*, Mia Milia (Cyprus); *itchenbirds*, Koprulu (Cyprus); *Ertac Cuneyt* (Cyprus); *George Konstantinou*, Nicosia (Cyprus).

Arabian Red Fox

VULPES VULPES ARABICA

BL: 52-63 cm (♂), 42-58.5 cm (♀). TL: 25.8-38.3 cm. H: 32.5-37.5 cm. W: 2.4-3.2 kg (♂), 2-3 kg (♀). SL: 12.0 cm. SW: 6.6 cm. DF: 42. CN: 34. A small-sized Canid, with long and slender legs and pointed muzzle, and long tail. The smallest subspecies of Red Fox, with a pale and short coat, and very large ears. Pelage is short, pale reddish brown in color. Throat, chest and belly vary from black to off-white. Underparts vary from whitish to slaty black. Muzzle slender and pointed, white on upper lip. Ears very large, with black tips and a white anterior margin. Tail is very long, dull fulvous to buffy white, with black hairs, usually without a black basal spot, white tipped. Legs same color as the body, fading to white distally on the paws, with a darker patch on front of the forelegs. Feet with fur between the toes. Females 15% smaller than males.

winter coat

summer coat

Young

Vulpes vulpes arabica

OTHER NAMES *French*: Renard roux d'Arabie. *German*: Arabischer Rotfuchs. *Spanish*: Zorro común de Arabia. *Russian*: Аравийская рыжая лисица. *Arabic*: Tha'leb ahmar, hosseini.

TAXONOMY Considered a subspecies of Red Fox (*V. vulpes*). The validity of this and other subspecies has not been confirmed by genetic analysis.

SIMILAR SPECIES Rüppell's Fox is superficially similar, but considerably smaller, has proportionately larger ears, and is a uniform creamy-white to pale rufous color. Blanford's Fox is smaller, has a larger tail, which can be almost the same length as the body, has very large and prominent ears, a dark mid-dorsal band extending from the neck to the extremely bushy tail, which can have either a black or white tip, and its feet are smaller than those of *V. vulpes* or *V. rueppellii* and, unlike these species, the pads are bare, providing sure footing in rocky terrain. Eurasian subspecies are considerably larger, with a darker-colored pelage.

REPRODUCTION *Gestation*: 52 days. *Young per birth*: 5 (on average). *Weaning*: 49-56 days. *Sexual maturity*: Unknown. *Life span*: 5 years. *Breeding season*: December to February. Births occur usually in early spring in a den situated between boulders, in natural crevices or a burrow the Fox digs for itself. Pups open their eyes after 10 days. At 7 or 8 weeks of age the pups begin foraging with the vixen, before dispersing to seek out new territories.

BEHAVIOR *Social behavior*: Solitary. *Diet*: Opportunistic and omnivorous, they will eat almost anything they can catch or find, including a variety of small mammals, birds, insects, carrion, plants and fruits. *Main predators*: Dogs. They are most active at night. They are not territorial, and individuals do not avoid each other at territory boundaries. It is suggested that their extremely harsh environment, with spatially and temporally variable food supplies, leads to the formation of loosely knit social groups. Aggregations of up to 4 Foxes are regularly seen in these areas. They may live a nomadic life and only temporarily occupy particular home ranges. They have fur between their toes, to prevent burning of the feet, larger ears to maintain their body temperature, and a lighter-colored pelage, as an adaptation to the arid habitat. Highly adaptable, the species has benefited from the expansion of human habitation, particularly from the associated rat and mice populations.

DISTRIBUTION *Native*: Jordan, Kuwait, Oman, Qatar, Saudi Arabia, United Arab Emirates, Yemen. Found on the Arabian Peninsula and probably in Iraq and Israel.

HABITAT Occupies a wide range of habitats, including mountains, coasts, deserts, cities, and even small offshore islands, though not recorded from the interior of extensive dune areas such as Rub Al Khali. In rocky mountainous areas it is probably less common than Blanford's Fox. Less well adapted than Rüppell's Fox to the most arid areas. It may use food-rich sites associated with human activity.

CONSERVATION STATUS Least Concern. *CITES*: Not listed. No estimate of population size is available, but it is believed to be increasing, aided in part by spread of human settlements. Occurs in many protected areas. Numbers fluctuate apparently in connection with outbreaks of rabies and/or other diseases. Rarely occurs in trade in this region. Subject to persecution and poisoning by livestock herders.

PHOTO CREDITS *Jem Babbington*, Dhahran Hills (Saudi Arabia).

Palestinian Red Fox

VULPES VULPES PALAESTINA

BL: 55-62.5 cm (♂), 45.5-61.5 cm (♀). TL: 30.5-41.2 cm. H: 35 cm. W: 2-4 kg. SL: 12.7 cm. SW: 7.0 cm. DF: 42. CN: 34. A small-sized subspecies of Red Fox. Pelage color is slate gray with some reddish and brownish tinges, with a near suppression of rufous, except on the face. Head is reddish brown, shading into buffy gray on the muzzle. Ears are black on the back. White or light gray stripe on either side of the neck separating the rufous dorsal surface from the slate-gray ventral fur of the neck and chest. Pelage is thicker and fuller in winter. Summer pelage is much thinner and lighter. Legs are grayish rufous or fulvous, with a darker patch on front of the forelegs. Tail is large, bushy, reddish brown, grayish brown laterally and ventrally, and usually white tipped. Feet with fur between the toes. Females slightly smaller than males, lacking the slate-gray ventral pigmentation.

summer coat

winter coat

Young

240

Vulpes vulpes palaestina

OTHER NAMES Reddish-Gray Palestine Fox. *French*: Renard roux de Palestine. *German*: Palästina-Rotfuchs. *Spanish*: Zorro común de Palestina. *Russian*: Палестинская рыжая лисица.

TAXONOMY Considered a subspecies of Red Fox (*V. vulpes*). Some authors regard this subspecies as part of a cline involving both the Egyptian Red Fox (*V. v. aegyptiacus*) and the Arabian Red Fox (*V. v. arabica*). The validity of this and other subspecies has not been confirmed by genetic analysis.

SIMILAR SPECIES Fennec Fox is much smaller, easily distinguished by its light color and large ears. Rüppell's Fox is smaller, with short legs and broad ears, pale sandy color, back of ears pale brown, black patches on face, tail tip white. Blanford's Fox is smaller, with a relatively longer tail.

REPRODUCTION *Gestation*: 50-53 days. *Young per birth*: 2-5. *Weaning*: Unknown. *Sexual maturity*: Unknown. *Life span*: 4.5 years. *Breeding season*: Probably from December to February. Births occur in March or April in Lebanon. Dens are usually dug on the sides of hills in protected areas between boulders, among rocks, or in thick plant cover, although burrows in the sides of tels and streams banks are not uncommon.

BEHAVIOR *Social behavior*: Solitary; mated pairs during the breeding season. *Diet*: Opportunistic and omnivorous; they feed on small mammals (jerboas, small rodents), fruits (figs, grapes), ground-roosting birds, insects, fish, reptiles and other food items. *Main predators*: Coyote. Although mostly nocturnal, they are active during many daylight and nighttime hours. During the spring and summer they spend the daylight hours in the burrow and feed only at night, while in the winter, it is not uncommon to find them lying in some protected place at some distance from the burrows during the day, and it is probable that feeding takes place during the day as well.

DISTRIBUTION *Native*: Israel, Lebanon, Palestine, Syria. It has been reported from near Haifa, Mount Carmel, Jerusalem, Beersheba, Jerusalem and Bethlehem areas, Sinai, the Dead Sea Basin, Haluza Sands, and Negev. In Lebanon it occurs at all elevations from the coast and Bekaa Valley to the tops of the mountains, but occurs most frequently in proximity to cultivation. Boundaries with *V. v. arabica*, *aegyptiacus*, *flavescens* and *pusilla* are unclear. *V. v. palaestina* is the prevailing form on the Mediterranean sections from Ramleh and Jerusalem up to Lebanon. *V. v. aegyptiacus* is frequently found in the S and E deserts and steppes, S of the Arabah, in the S Philistine plain and in the mountains of S Judea. *V. v. flavescens* is an Irano-Turanian intruder in Galilee, and the largest of the three forms.

HABITAT Coastal plains, but it also occurs in most habitats except the extreme arid regions. It is less common in areas where Rüppell's Fox (*V. rueppellii*) and Fennec Fox (*V. zerda*) occur, perhaps due to interspecific competition.

CONSERVATION STATUS Least Concern. *CITES*: Not listed.

PHOTO CREDITS *Liora Levin* (Israel); *Roni Alush* (Israel); *Gabriel Enrique Levitzky,* Ashkelon (Israel).

Persian Red Fox

VULPES VULPES FLAVESCENS AND ANATOLICA

BL: 46.5-65 cm. TL: 33.5-46 cm. H: 35 cm. W: 2.2-3.2 kg. SL: 12.6 cm. SW: 7.4 cm. DF: 42. CN: 34. A small-sized Canid, with long and slender legs and pointed muzzle, and long brush-like tail. Medium to small-sized subspecies, less reddish than European subspecies, closely related to *karagan*, but smaller. Pelage is pale yellow or light gray, sometimes reddish brown, with a gray admixture on the sides of the body and a yellowish brown crosswise pattern on the back and shoulders. It usually lacks the reddish color tones of other subspecies. Winter fur is long and soft, much shorter and sparser in summer. Undersides are dark gray to oehraceous rufous. Throat and chest are grayish white. Muzzle is yellowish creamy to reddish brown, with a dark gray or blackish-brown band. Ears relatively large, much longer than in northern subspecies, black on the back. Paws are thickly covered with hair. Sides of forelegs are fulvous. Tail is very long, thick and bushy, slightly reddish black to brown dorsally and pale buff or gray ventrally, with a white tip.

Vulpes vulpes anatolica

Vulpes vulpes flavescens

OTHER NAMES Anatolian Red Fox, Kurdistan Red Fox, Trans-Caucasian Montane Red Fox, Turkmenian Red Fox. *French*: Renard roux de Perse. *German*: Persischer Rotfuchs. *Spanish*: Zorro común de Persia. *Russian*: Малоазиатская рыжая лисица, Персидская (Туркменская) лисица. *Turkish*: Kızıl Tilki. *Persian*: Rubâh-e ma'muli.

TAXONOMY Considered a subspecies of Red Fox (*V. vulpes*). Includes *alticola, cinerascens* and *splendens*. Considered a synonym of *V. v. aegyptiacus* by some authors. There is still a lack of information about the genetic diversity and phylogeographic structure of the Red Fox from Turkey and the Middle East, except in Israel. Studies indicate high genetic diversity and no genetic isolation of these Fox populations.

REPRODUCTION *Gestation*: 50-55 days. *Young per birth*: 3-12. *Weaning*: 42-56 days. *Sexual maturity*: 9-10 months. *Life span*: 12 years in captivity. *Breeding season*: More prolonged than that of northern subspecies; pairs form in November, and begin mating throughout December and January. Pups are born in February-March. It may build temporary burrows in its desert environment, dug with an entrance facing south in order to shield itself from northerly winds. Burrows have 3-5 entrances, but those located in appropriated gerbil colonies may have up to 15. Communal denning as well as the presence of helpers at the den has been recorded.

BEHAVIOR *Social behavior*: Solitary; mated pairs during the breeding season. *Diet*: Opportunistic and omnivorous; diet depends on its habitat and prey availability, and is composed of Guenther's voles, grapes, Tristram's jird, birds, cockchafers, apricots and blackberries; in Dalyan (Turkey) they raid eggs of loggerhead turtles (*Caretta caretta*), carry eggs inland, and cache them on topographically distinct features such as spurs of rocks; adult Foxes may store turtle eggs specifically to feed their offspring. In Akyatan they feed on eggs of green turtles (*Chelonia mydas*). They also scavenge on the leftovers of other species and usually follow brown bears in NE Turkey to find food. Population density varies from 4 individuals per km² in S Anatolia to 0.15-0.22 per km² in central Anatolia. Unlike other Red Fox subspecies, they often hunt during the day, thus coinciding with the activity patterns of great gerbils.

DISTRIBUTION *Native*: Armenia, Iran, Iraq, Turkey. *V. v. anatolica* is found W Asia Minor. *V. v. flavescens* occurs in N Iran and probably in contiguous parts of Afghanistan, Turkmenistan, Pakistan, Uzbekistan, Iraq and Kurdistan. It is found in all regions of Iran with the exception of the N forests and the drier parts of the central deserts, where it is replaced by Rüppell's Fox.

HABITAT Found in all habitats: sea coasts, steppe, maquis, forest, alpine habitats, areas with shrubs, and parks, even close to populated areas depending on the availability of food. Black pine habitat is used relatively more frequently than other habitat types. Often seen in farmland in search of rodents.

CONSERVATION STATUS Least Concern. *CITES*: Not listed. It is widespread and common, but population trends are not well known. Main threats include habitat loss, hunting and poisoning. It is a vector of rabies in Turkey, and studies have shown a transmission of the virus between Dogs and Red Foxes and an increase in the number of rabies cases for wild Red Foxes in Turkey since 2000.

PHOTO CREDITS *Fariborz Heidari,* Tondro, Khorasan Province (Iran); *Alex Kantorovich*, Tashkent Zoo (Uzbekistan); *A. Omer Karamollaoglu*, Golbasi, Ankara (Turkey).

Punjab Red Fox
VULPES VULPES PUSILLA

BL: 51.8-57.9 cm (♂), 48.2-55.8 cm (♀). TL: 31-44.7 cm. H: 35 cm. W: 3-5 kg (♂), 2-2.4 kg (♀). SL: 12.3 cm. SW: 6.9 cm. DF: 42. CN: 34. A small-sized Canid, with long and slender legs and pointed muzzle, and long brush-like tail. A small-sized subspecies of Red Fox, smaller than *montana* and *griffithii*. Pelage is short, uniform in color, light fulvous to rusty brown, spangled with whitish above, and gray flanks. Cheeks, sides of neck and body are white. Shoulder and haunch are mixed black and white. Summer coat is noticeably lighter in color. Underparts are ashy gray to white. Face is light fulvous. Muzzle slender and pointed, with white chin. Ears relatively large, pointed, erect, black posteriorly. Legs fulvous externally, white on the inner side, with a blackish border on the forelegs, and white on front of the hind legs below hock. All feet white. Tail is very long, ochraceous above with black-tipped hairs, largely tipped with white.

Young

Vulpes vulpes pusilla

OTHER NAMES White-Footed Fox, Desert Red Fox. *French*: Renard roux de l'Inde, renard du Penjab. *German*: Punjab-Rotfuchs. *Spanish*: Zorro común de la India. *Russian*: Пустынная (белоногая) лисица. *Hindi*: Lúmri, Lokri. *Baluchi*: Lombar. *Persian*: Rubâh-e ma'muli.

TAXONOMY Considered a subspecies of Red Fox (*V. vulpes*). Includes *persicus* (E Iran and Pakistan) and *leucopus*.

SIMILAR SPECIES One of the three subspecies of Red Fox found in India, the other two being the Kashmir Red Fox (*griffithii*) and the Tibetan Red Fox (*montana*). Indian Fox (*V. bengalensis*) is smaller, has a black tail tip, and is usually lighter and more rufous in color.

REPRODUCTION *Gestation*: 50-53 days. *Young per birth*: 6-7. *Weaning*: 42-56 days. *Sexual maturity*: 10 months. *Breeding season*: From November to February. Both parents care for the pups until late summer, when they are able to fend for themselves. Pups are born with their eyes closed and will not emerge from their dens for around 10 to 15 days. After this, they may venture out under the watchful eye of their parents.

BEHAVIOR *Social behavior*: Solitary, mated pairs during the breeding season. *Diet*: Small mammals (including rodents), spiny tailed lizards, birds, including waterfowl, leaves of halophytic plants, as well as melons and berries. During rains, when grasshoppers are attracted to vehicle lights, they pounce upon them. It may also opportunistically scavenge for food. During the breeding season, it mainly preys on gerbils or other desert rodents. These rodents are either dug out of their burrows or caught by stalking them like a cat. *Main predators*: Dog, Jackal, large raptors. Perfectly adapted to harsh climatic conditions where temperatures reach 50°C and average annual rainfall is less than 60 mm. The sandy-yellow coat of the desert Fox provides excellent camouflage in the desert habitat. It is an agile hunter with long legs that allow it quick, short bursts of speed. Sand dunes and sandy river beds are used to fashion their dens and feeding and denning behavior is influenced by changing seasons. In the non-breeding season Foxes use a simple den with a single entrance. While breeding, more complex dens with multiple openings are used to offer escape routes in the event of any threat. Such complex dens are sophisticated structures that include an elaborately maintained nursing chamber. The den plays an important role in the control of pest species and helps in the dispersal of seeds.

DISTRIBUTION *Native*: Iraq, Iran, India, Pakistan. Found in Sindh, S Balochistan, and Punjab Provinces in Pakistan, and NW India, in the desert regions of Rajasthan, N Gujarat (Banni grasslands), Punjab and Madhya Pradesh (in the ravines of the Chambal River), in S Iran and in Iraq.

HABITAT Desert and semi-desert habitats. It avoids dense forests.

CONSERVATION STATUS Least Concern. *CITES*: Appendix II (India). *Regional status*: Near Threatened (Pakistan), protected in India. However, in winter months when it has a rich coat, the animal is poached by desert nomads for trading and meat. This data-deficient subspecies needs research on its ecology and distribution, since not much is known about it. It is considered rare in Gujarat, where it is restricted to arid saline desert. In the Rajasthan desert, it is also considered rare.

PHOTO CREDITS *Stuart Reeds, Sumeet Moghe, Hemis, Nirav Bhatt* and *Rupal Vaidya*, Little Rann of Kutch (India).

Caucasian Red Fox

VULPES VULPES ALPHERAKYI, CAUCASICA AND KURDISTANICA

BL: 50-80 cm. TL: 25-45 cm. H: 35.5 cm. W: 4 kg. SL: 13.3-15 cm. SW: 7.3-7.8 cm. DF: 42. CN: 34. A small to medium-sized Canid, with long and slender legs and pointed muzzle, and long brush-like tail. A large (*caucasica*), medium (*kurdistanica*) to small-sized (*alpherakyi*) subspecies. Eastern forms (*alpherakyi*) have a short and sparse coat, dirty brownish to red grayish in color, strongly streaked with black and white, with a reddish stripe on the back. Underparts are dirty dusky gray. Muzzle with a blackish band from eye to lip. Black pattern on the legs and paws well developed. Northern forms (*caucasica*) have a longer coat, gray to brownish rusty red in color, with a whitish-gray tint on the back and a crosswise pattern on the shoulders, darker on the neck, throat, breast and belly. Black pattern on the legs is present. Mountain forms (*kurdistanica*) have the thickest and longest coat, light gray, pale yellow to reddish brown in color, with a light reddish stripe on the back, speckled with white. Throat and anterior part of neck are grayish. Underparts are grayish white. Backs of ears are pure black.

ssp. *caucasica*

ssp. *alpherakyi*

Vulpes vulpes alpherakyi

Vulpes vulpes caucasica

Vulpes vulpes kurdistanica

OTHER NAMES Eastern Trans-Caucasian Fox, Trans-Caucasian Valley Fox (*alpherakyi*), North Caucasian Fox (*caucasica*), Kurdistan Fox, Trans-Caucasian Mountain Fox (*kurdistanica*). *French*: Renard roux du Caucase. *German*: Ost-Transkaukasus-Rotfuchs, Kaukasus-Rotfuchs, Kurdistan-Rotfuchs. *Spanish*: Zorro común del Caúcaso. *Russian*: Восточнокавказская (азербайджанская) лисица (*alpherakyi*), Северокавказская лисица (*caucasica*), Закавказская горная (курдистанская) лисица (*kurdistanica*). *Turkish*: Kızıl Tilki.

TAXONOMY Considered a subspecies of Red Fox (*V. vulpes*). The validity of this and other subspecies has not been confirmed by genetic analysis. Includes *alticola* (Lake Sevan in Armenia).

SIMILAR SPECIES *V. v. caucasica* is the largest of the three subspecies. *V. v. kurdistanica* is intermediate in size, and its coat is longer and lighter in color.

REPRODUCTION *Gestation*: 50-55 days. *Young per birth*: 3-12. *Weaning*: 42-56 days. *Sexual maturity*: 9-10 months. *Life span*: Unknown. *Breeding season*: Probably December to February. They dig their own burrows, especially in places with sandy soils, or may use badger's burrows. Dens are usually located in an elevated place, in ravine slopes. In summer they live in the burrows until the pups grow and have learned to procure food themselves, while in winter they do not use burrows. Depending on weather conditions the animals rest in the daytime under stones, crowns of trees, and in rock caves.

BEHAVIOR *Social behavior*: Solitary or in monogamous pairs. *Diet*: Generalist and opportunistic omnivore, feeding mainly on small rodents; they may eat shrews if they are very hungry. In spring and summer carabid beetles constitute an important part of the diet. On the seashore, they may also eat dead birds, fish and crayfish. *Main predators*: Unknown. Active early in the morning and late in the evening. In summer, they are active both day and night.

DISTRIBUTION *Native*: Armenia, Georgia, Iran, Kazakhstan, Russia, Turkey, Turkmenistan, Ukraine. *V. v. alpherakyi* occurs on the plains of E Transcaucasia in the Kura and Arax, in Azerbaijan, W to Tbilisi, on the Caspian coast, in W Kazakhstan, and W Turkmenistan. *V. v. caucasica* is found in the mountains and foothills of the N Caucasus Mountains, Transcaucasia, and Ciscaucasia in SW European Russia, North Ossetia-Alania. It is rare in W Transcaucasia, which is rich in forests and mountains. *V. v. kurdistanica* is found in W Kurdistan, NE Turkey, Gelsk Valley, Kars district in W Transcaucasia, and Armenia. This subspecies is widespread in the Armenian highlands, in the mountainous areas of the Lesser Caucasus. Boundaries with other subspecies are unclear.

HABITAT Almost every habitat, with higher densities in the zones of semidesert, steppe, foremontane forest steppe and highland steppe. They are rare in the mountainous beech forests of the S slopes of the Greater Caucasus. Often seen in farmland in search of rodents. *V. v. kurdistanica* is found in subalpine and alpine zones, excluding subnival and nival belts, and in secondary steppes.

CONSERVATION STATUS Least Concern. During historical time the range and population of Foxes in the Caucasus have apparently thrived under the favorable influence of agriculture, and even concentrated human presence has failed to reduce their numbers.

PHOTO CREDITS *Andrey Kotkin*, Baku Zoo (Azerbaijan), *Alex Kantorovich*, Rostov Zoo (Russia).

Tibetan and Kashmir Red Fox

VULPES VULPES MONTANA AND GRIFFITHII

BL: 59.9-75.2 cm (♂), 56.9-66 cm (♀). TL: 34-50 cm. H: 35 cm. W: 4.6-5.1 kg (♂), 3.6-4 kg (♀). SL: 13.6 cm. SW: 7.3 cm. DF: 42. CN: 34. A small to medium-sized Canid, with long and slender legs and pointed muzzle, and long brush-like tail. A medium-sized subspecies of Red Fox, smaller than continental European subspecies, with a thick, long and luxuriant winter fur. Pelage is very variable from bright reddish bay to bright yellowish fulvous, with variable amounts of black or gray brown in the pelage. Winter coat with paler and yellow thick luxuriant underfur. Throat and chest are white to dark gray. There may be some black on the nape and shoulders. Underparts are white to dark gray. Face and head are tan to fulvous with a blackish patch on the muzzle. Ears relatively large and pointed, black posteriorly, fringed with white hair inside. Legs darkish tawny with some black and white hairs on their front surfaces. Tail is very long, thick and bushy, white tipped.

Vulpes vulpes montana

Vulpes vulpes griffithii

OTHER NAMES Montane Red Fox, Hill Fox. *French*: Renard roux de montagne. *German*: Tibet-Rotfuchs. *Spanish*: Zorro común del Tibet. *Russian*: Ладакская (Тибетская) рыжая лисица, Кашмирская горная лисица. *Hindi*: Lomri. *Nepali*: Phauro, wamu. *Kashmiri*: Luh, laash, potsolov. *Tibetan*: Whatse. *Urdu*: Loomari.

TAXONOMY Considered a subspecies of Red Fox (*V. vulpes*). Includes *himalaicus*, *ladacensis*, *nepalensis* and *waddelli*. The validity of these subspecies has not been confirmed by genetic analysis.

SIMILAR SPECIES Jackals are larger in size, and have a relatively shorter and less bushy tail, shorter ears, and rounder muzzle. Compared to *V. v. griffithii*, *V. v. montana* is slightly larger, has more prominent white patches from cheeks to throat, tail is relatively thicker and more bushy, and its winter coat is darker.

REPRODUCTION *Gestation*: 50-55 days. *Young per birth*: 3-12. *Weaning*: 42-56 days. *Sexual maturity*: 10-12 months. *Life span*: Unknown. *Breeding season*: End of winter, with births occurring in the spring. Pups are cared for by both parents, and remain in or near the den for the first 3 months of their lives. Communal denning, with more than 1 litter having been reported, but a single pair with pups is the most common breeding unit. The breeding pair is often associated with non-breeding family members. These are usually ♀ and may act as helpers. Almost all ♂ and a variable proportion of ♀ disperse at 6 to 10 months.

BEHAVIOR *Social behavior*: Solitary; monogamous pairs during the breeding season. *Diet*: Small mammals (pikas, marmots, voles, mouse-hares, serow, musk deer), ground birds and their eggs, as well as fallen fruit and berries, and insects. They occasionally prey on young lambs, poultry and pheasant. They may eat anthropogenic food near human areas. *Main predators*: Unknown. The animal is active by night. However, it can also be seen during dusk and dawn. It rests in crevices and burrows during the daytime.

DISTRIBUTION *Native*: Afghanistan, Bhutan, China, India, Nepal, Pakistan. *V. v. montana* is found in the Himalayas, in W China (Yunnan and Tibet), Nepal, N India (Sikkim, Kumaon in Uttarakhand, Punjab) and Pakistan (Punjab Province to Gilgit). *V. v. griffithii also* occurs in the Himalayas, in N and W areas of Pakistan, including the mountains and valleys of Balochistan and NW Frontier Province, in Jammu and Kashmir in India, and in Afghanistan in Badakhshan, Balkh, Faryab, Kabul, Kandahar, Jowzjan Provinces.

HABITAT Thorn bushes, willows, scrub along dry rivers and cultivated land of subalpine zones between 300 and 5,500 m above sea level. It also inhabits sandy wastes, riverbeds and sand dunes in semi-arid regions. It often occurs in close association with humans and avoids dense forests.

CONSERVATION STATUS Least Concern. *CITES*: Not listed. *Regional status*: Data Deficient (Pakistan). It seems to be common in the Himalayas. In Pakistan, it seems to be common throughout most of the country, although it was considered Near Threatened in 2003. It is hunted throughout its range for its luxurious coat, and subject to severe persecution in Afghanistan and Pakistan, because it is considered destructive to poultry.

PHOTO CREDITS *Jan Reurink,* Lunggar, Tibet (China); *Saurabh Sawant*, Ladakh (India); *Aditya "Dicky" Singh*, Hemis National Park, Ladakh (India).

Karagan Red Fox

VULPES VULPES KARAGAN AND OCHROXANTA

BL: 52.5-68.5 cm (♂), 52-62.8 cm (♀). TL: 30.5-48.0 cm. H: 35 cm. W: 3.3-5.8 kg (♂), 3.2-5.8 kg (♀). SL: 13.8 cm. SW: 7.6 cm. DF: 42. CN: 34. A small to medium-sized Canid, with long and slender legs and pointed muzzle, and long brush-like tail. A medium to large-sized subspecies. Pelage is variable in color, usually dusky gray to light ochraceous buff or orange, without the red tints of the European subspecies. Winter fur is pale, straw yellowish with a rusty admixture on the back, neck and shoulders. Fur is coarser, not so thick and downy as that of the central Russian subspecies. Underparts are dirty yellowish gray whitish. Muzzle slender and pointed, narrower than in European subspecies, rusty yellow, with no definite blackish stripes, white on upper lip. Legs are straw yellowish, with a slightly expressed black pattern on their anterior parts (sometimes this pattern is absent). Tail is proportionately longer, light straw whitish in color, with a tint of blackish hair, and a white tip. No sexual dimorphism.

Vulpes vulpes karagan

Vulpes vulpes ochroxanta

OTHER NAMES Karagan Red Fox, Fergana Fox (*karagan*), Kazakhstan Red Fox, Tian-Shan Red Fox (*ochroxanta*). *French*: Renard roux du Fergana. *German*: Karagan-Rotfuchs, Kirgistan-Rotfuchs. *Spanish*: Zorro común de Fergana. *Russian*: Караганка (*karagan*), Тяньшанская рыжая лисица (*ochroxantha*).

TAXONOMY Considered a subspecies of Red Fox (*V. vulpes*). Includes *ferganensis*, *melanotus*, *pamiriensis* and *tarimensis*.

SIMILAR SPECIES Heavier than subspecies from S parts of Asia, but lighter than those in more N parts of Russia. The sympatric Corsac Fox (*V. corsac*) is smaller, with a shorter tail, a smaller muzzle, and ears spaced at base.

REPRODUCTION *Gestation*: 50-55 days. *Young per birth*: 3-12. *Weaning*: 42-56 days. *Sexual maturity*: 10 months. *Breeding season*: More prolonged than that of northern subspecies; from December to April. It may build temporary burrows in its desert environment, dug with an entrance facing south in order to shield itself from northerly winds. Burrows have 3-5 entrances, but those located in appropriated gerbil colonies may have up to 15.

BEHAVIOR *Social behavior*: Solitary or monogamous pairs, especially in areas with low food availability. *Diet*: Small mammals (voles), insects, reptiles, birds, carrion and plant material (pistachios, capers, watermelon, various grasses and seeds), which represents an important component during periods of low prey availability. *Main predators*: Wolf, Domestic Dog, probably large raptors. Primarily active at night, but they often hunt during the day, thus coinciding with the activity patterns of great gerbils. They occupy relatively large home ranges, with mean home range sizes in Mongolia of 15.4 km², with ♀ and adults occupying larger ranges than yearlings. They may kill Corsac Foxes and represent one of their principal competitors in some regions; however, most accounts of interference competition have been based largely on incidental sightings and observations and the evidence has been little more than circumstantial inference.

DISTRIBUTION *Native*: Kazakhstan, Kyrgyzstan, Mongolia, Russia. In Mongolia it is found at low densities, and it is most abundant in mountainous habitats in Hentii and Hövsgöl mountain ranges, but also occurs in Orhon and Selenge River basins in NE and SW Khangai Mountains. Also occurs in steppe habitats in E Mongolia, Mongol Altai Mountains and Gobi Altai Mountains. *V. v. ochroxanta* occurs in the Tian Shan and Dzungarian Alatau mountains.

HABITAT Found across steppe, semi-desert and desert environments. The sympatric Corsac Fox appears to occupy primarily open grassland, shrubland steppe and semi-deserts, while Red Foxes occupy all major vegetation zones from lowland desert regions to high alpine environments.

CONSERVATION STATUS Least Concern. *CITES*: Not listed. *Regional status*: Near Threatened (Mongolia), but hunting is permitted. Exploitation occurs throughout its range, although no population data are available at present. Main threats include hunting for skins, for international trade, and poisoning campaigns to control Brandt's vole (*Lasiopodomys brandtii*). Also susceptible to rabies and sarcoptic mange.

PHOTO CREDITS *Khumbaa Tumendelger*, Gobi (Mongolia); *Magnet Soronzonbold*, Övörkhangai (Mongolia); *Purevsuren Tsolmonjav*, Ömnögovi (Mongolia); Darren Shemya (Kazakhstan).

Hokkaido Red Fox

VULPES VULPES SCHRENCKI AND SPLENDIDISSIMA

BL: 78 cm. TL: 32.2-44 cm. H: 31.9-38.7 cm. W: 4.8-6.2 kg (♂), 4-5 kg (♀). SL: 13.8 cm. SW: 7.5 cm. DF: 42. CN: 36-40. A small to medium-sized Canid, with long and slender legs and pointed muzzle, and long brush-like tail. Pelage is variable in color, usually orange red, with a distinct cross on back and shoulders. Flanks are yellower. Neck and throat are white. Underparts are white with a reddish-brown wash. Head is orange above, with the crown not paler than back and shoulders. Backs of ears are black. Lips are white. Tail is long and bushy, reddish yellow to dark orange buff, with a whitish tip. Legs are orange, with a variable black pattern on front of carpal joints.

winter coat

summer coat

Vulpes vulpes schrencki

Vulpes vulpes splendidissima

OTHER NAMES Schrenck's Red Fox, Sakhalin Red Fox, Kuril Island Fox. *French*: Renard roux de Sakhaline, renard roux d'Hokkaido. *German*: Hokkaido-Rotfuchs, Sachalin-Rotfuchs. *Spanish*: Zorro común de Hokkaido. *Russian*: Russian: Лисица острова Хоккайдо (*schrencki*), Курильская рыжая лисица (*splendidissima*). *Japanese*: Kita-kitsune.

TAXONOMY Considered a subspecies of Red Fox (*V. vulpes*). Two subspecies occur on the Japanese islands: *V. v. schrencki* on Hokkaido Island, *V. v. japonica* on Honshu, Shikoku and Kyushu Islands, geographically separated by Tsugaru Strait between Hokkaido and Honshu Islands, a biogeographical boundary known as Blakiston's Line. Additionally, population in S Hokkaido seems genetically well differentiated from other groups on the island.

SIMILAR SPECIES *V. v. japonica* has a smaller body size, but a wider skull, with smaller molars and premolars.

REPRODUCTION *Gestation*: 53 days. *Young per birth*: 3-4 (mean litter size). *Weaning*: 42-56 days. *Sexual maturity*: 12 months. *Life span*: 4 years. *Breeding season*: Late January to February, usually behind other areas in Japan. Most births occur in late March to late April. Survival rate of adult Foxes is much higher than in other areas of Japan. Dens are usually associated with relatively steep slopes near streams and open spaces in woodlands, and mainly used during the mating, parturition and rearing season, although they utilize dens throughout the year, except in August and September.

BEHAVIOR *Social behavior*: Solitary, monogamous. *Diet*: Omnivorous; in Hokkaido, the main food in winter is voles (*Clethrionomys rufocanus*), fish, livestock (carrion), wild birds, hares and poultry; coastal Foxes feed mainly on fish, livestock and wild birds, while inland Foxes take mainly voles, hares and poultry. They prefer some specific food species, such as the gray red-backed vole and the tara vine fruit, over similar food species. Solitary hunters. While on Honshu, they tend to be completely nocturnal, on Hokkaido they are also diurnal in winter and not particularly shy. Home ranges from 1.5 to 8.1 km² in size on Hokkaido, varying with habitat condition. In rural farmland and unmanipulated environments, they usually are strictly territorial, with exclusive family ranges, whereas in urban environments ranges may overlap, even in high-density areas.

DISTRIBUTION *Native*: Japan, Russia. Found on Sakhalin, Southern Kuril Islands (Kunashiri, Etorofu) in E Asian Russia, and Hokkaido in N Japan. Introduced in Saitama and Chiba Prefectures in Japan, where it competes and hybridizes with native *V. v. japonica*.

HABITAT Various habitat. Tundra, deserts, forests, grasslands, city areas in coastal to alpine zones.

CONSERVATION STATUS Least Concern. Widely distributed on Hokkaido, although sarcoptic mange has participated in the reduction of populations. They play an important role as a host of the small Fox tapeworm *Echinococcus multilocularis*, which is the causative agent of a serious zoonosis (alveolar echinococcosis) on Hokkaido.

PHOTO CREDITS *Greg Miles, Shu Hui Neo (Yagizaneo Photography), Stuart Price* and *Tomoko, Hokkaido (Japan).*

Japanese Red Fox

VULPES VULPES JAPONICA

BL: 55.5-70 cm (♂), 51.5-67 cm (♀). TL: 28.5-42 cm. H: 32.2-42.3 cm. W: 4.4-6.6 kg (♂), 3.3-6 kg (♀). SL: 14.3 cm. SW: 7.9 cm. DF: 42. CN: 34. A small to medium-sized Canid, with long and slender legs and pointed muzzle, and long brush-like tail. Pelage is very variable from ochraceous buff to reddish bay, with variable amounts of white. Throat and chest are white. Underparts are white to light gray. Back of ears is black. Muzzle slender and pointed, without definite blackish stripes, white on upper lip. Legs darker than flanks, with some white hairs on their front surfaces, and usually lacking the black pattern on their anterior parts. Tail is very long, thick and bushy, white tipped. Females are slightly smaller than males. Pups are black brown in color, with the exception of the white tip of the tail.

Vulpes vulpes japonica

OTHER NAMES *French*: Renard roux japonais. *German*: Japan-Rotfuchs. *Spanish*: Zorro común japonés. *Russian*: Японская рыжая лисица. *Japanese*: Hondo-kitsune.

TAXONOMY Considered a subspecies of Red Fox (*V. vulpes*). Two subspecies occur on the Japanese islands: *V. v. japonica* on Honshu, Shikoku and Kyushu Islands, and *V. v. schrencki* on Hokkaido Island, geographically separated by Tsugaru Strait between Hokkaido and Honshu Islands, a biogeographical boundary known as Blakiston's Line.

SIMILAR SPECIES *V. v. schrencki* has larger body size than *V. v. japonica* and differs in coat color, but has a narrower cranium and shorter mandible, with long molars and premolars. The classification of the two subspecies is controversial and in need of phylogeographic investigation.

REPRODUCTION *Gestation*: 53-60 days. *Young per birth*: 3-4 (mean litter size). *Weaning*: Unknown. *Sexual maturity*: 12 months. *Life span*: Unknown. *Breeding season*: From November to late January. Most births occur from mid-March to mid-May. They use dens for residence, particularly in the breeding season in order to provide security for their litter, and for temporary visiting throughout the year, either for periodical retreat or for advertising territories. Entrance of dens measures 20-30 cm in diameter, and the burrow descends to a depth of 50-100 cm. At between 45 and 60 days the young come out of the dens and follow the mother. At 3-4 months of age the young start eating independently of the mother.

BEHAVIOR *Social behavior*: Solitary, monogamous. *Diet*: Field vole (*Microtus montebelli*) is a main source of food during all seasons, but also field mouse (*Apodemus specious*), wood mouse (*A. argenteus*), Japanese hares, and dead bodies of sika deer (*Cervus nippon*). Human activities provide a major source of food for Foxes in spring and summer; in winter, when insects and small mammals probably are less available, food derived from human activities might even increase. Mainly nocturnal. Size of home range on Kyushu is 2.8-6.3 km^2, and 0.8 km^2 on Kumamoto, without apparent differences between sexes, similar with the sizes found in other temperate farmland. As in other subspecies, scent marking is through urine, feces, anal sac secretions, the supracaudal gland and glands around the lips, jaw and the pads of the feet. Urine is the main scent marker. Facial expression can be used for communication. Vocalization is limited to simple barking and growling, although 28 sounds have been described. Vocalizations are used to communicate with both nearby and distant foxes. Red Foxes have excellent senses of vision, smell and touch.

DISTRIBUTION *Native*: Japan. Found on Honshu, Shikoku and Kyushu (Japan).

HABITAT Grasslands, sandy riversides and craggy slopes, whereas forests are usually avoided. They prefer flat and gentle slopes, and avoid slopes steeper than 30°.

CONSERVATION STATUS Least Concern.

PHOTO CREDITS *Tomoko Ichishima*, Inokashira Park Zoo (Japan); *Asante, Nayer Youakim*, Zoorasia (Japan).

Korean Red Fox

VULPES VULPES PECULIOSA

BL: 57-60 cm. TL: 35-45 cm. H: 38 cm. W: 3.5-4.7 kg. DF: 42. CN: 34. A small to medium-sized Canid, with long and slender legs and pointed muzzle, and long brush-like tail. Pelage is variable in color, from pale yellowish red to reddish brown. Underparts are white, ashy or slate. Neck and throat are white. Tip and back of ears are black. Lips are white. Lower part of the legs and feet are black. Eyes of mature animals are yellow. The nose is dark brown or black. Tail is long and bushy, with a white, sometimes black, tip. Females are slightly smaller than males.

Vulpes vulpes peculiosa

OTHER NAMES *French*: Renard roux de Corée. *German*: Korea-Rotfuchs. *Spanish*: Zorro común de Korea. *Russian*: Корейская рыжая лисица. *Korean*: Kumiho.

TAXONOMY Considered a subspecies of Red Fox (*V. vulpes*). Includes *kiyomasai* (NE population).

REPRODUCTION *Gestation*: 52-56 days. *Young per birth*: 5-6, maximum size is 13 pups. *Weaning*: Unknown. *Sexual maturity*: Unknown. *Life span*: 3 years, 12 years in captivity. *Breeding season*: Late January to late February in Korea. Mating behavior varies substantially. Often ♂ and ♀ are monogamous, but ♂ may be polygynous with multiple ♀ mates. ♂/♀ pairs use non-breeding ♀ helpers in raising their young. ♀ mated to the same ♂ may share a den. Ovulation is spontaneous and does not require copulation to occur. Mother and pups remain together until the autumn after the birth. They use a den that is excavated, an abandoned badger den, or a rocky crevice. Larger dens may be dug and used during the winter and during birth and rearing of the young. The main purpose of a den is breeding and rearing pups. Just before and after giving birth, ♀ remain in or around the den. Individuals and family groups have main earthen dens and often other emergency burrows in the home range. The same den is often used over a number of generations.

BEHAVIOR *Social behavior*: Adult ♂ and 1 or 2 adult ♀ with their associated young; they do not form packs. *Diet*: Essentially omnivorous, preying primarily on small mammals and birds, but may also eat soy, cereals, vegetables, reptiles, carrion, insects and fruits. It caches surplus food. They eat between 0.5 and 1 kg of food each day. *Main predators*: Unknown. Generally nocturnal but also coincide activities with activity patterns of prey. They are also more active in undisturbed environments. They are highly mobile, foraging over 10 km per day, and dispersal can be as far away as about 400 km. Good habitats may range between 5 and 12 km², while poor habitats are larger, being between 20 and 50 km². Partly territorial.

DISTRIBUTION *Native*: North Korea. *Regionally extinct*: South Korea.

HABITAT They prefer ecotone habitats or mixed vegetation communities, such as edge habitats and mixed scrub and woodlands from sea level to 4,500 m elevation. However, Red Foxes prefer relatively open habitats to dense forests and inhabit grasslands, cultivated fields, suburban areas, riparian habitats or forest edges with soil to dig.

CONSERVATION STATUS Least Concern. *CITES*: Not listed. *Regional status*: Endangered (South Korea). It was once very common and distributed throughout Korea, except Jeju Island and remote islands. It was extirpated from S Korea and declined in the N part in the early 1960s. Although there have been doubtful reports of Foxes, it is extirpated in South Korea. Only small populations are presumed to remain in the extreme NE part of North Korea. The cause of the extirpation of Red Foxes on the Korean Peninsula is not well known. Instead, the Raccoon Dog has taken its ecological niche. In 2011, the Korean government initiated a project to restore its population in Sobaeksan National Park, from individuals genetically and geographically close, as in North Korea, China and Russia.

PHOTO CREDITS Based on photos from *Alex Kantorovich* and *Chris Davidson*, Seoul Zoo and Sobaeksan National Park (South Korea).

Chinese Red Fox

VULPES VULPES HOOLE AND TSCHILIENSIS

BL: 61.3 cm (♀). TL: 38.7 cm. H: 35 cm. W: 3.6-7 kg. SL: 13.2 cm. SW: 7.4 cm. DF: 42. CN: 34. A small to medium-sized Canid, with long and slender legs and pointed muzzle, and long brush-like tail. A small to medium-sized subspecies of Red Fox. Pelage color is reddish brown, similar to the European Red Fox, less fulvous but duller chestnut. Flanks and thighs are bright ochraceous, mixed with gray-tipped hairs. Throat, chest and belly are buffy white, with grayish underfur. Black stripe on the front of forelegs is usually narrow, bordered by rufous, but may be broad and extend up on the shoulders. Muzzle slender and pointed, with a variable blackish area on the sides, white on upper lip. Ears relatively large, pointed, erect, black or brown backed, white inside. Tail is long and bushy, rufous to chestnut in color, buffy white below, with long hairs tipped with black and a white tip. Females are slightly smaller than males.

Vulpes vulpes hoole

Vulpes vulpes tschiliensis

OTHER NAMES Southern Chinese Fox (*hoole*), Northern Chinese Fox (*tschiliensis*). *French*: Renard roux de Chine. *German*: Südchinesischer Rotfuchs, Nordchinesischer Rotfuchs. *Spanish*: Zorro común de China del sur. *Russian*: Китайская рыжая лисица: северокитайская (*tschiliensis*), южнокитайская (*hoole*).

TAXONOMY Considered a subspecies of Red Fox (*V. vulpes*). Includes *aurantioluteus, lineiventer, huli, ognevi* and *ussuriensis*. The validity of this and other subspecies has not been confirmed by genetic analysis.

SIMILAR SPECIES Corsac Fox is smaller, and noticeably paler, and prefers the open steppe land to the forest margins and rugged terrain favored by the Red Fox.

REPRODUCTION *Gestation*: 51-53 days. *Young per birth*: 1-10, up to 13. *Weaning*: 40-60 days. *Sexual maturity*: 10 months. *Life span*: Probably 5 years. *Breeding season*: Late December to late March. The young are born from March to May. ♂ help with parental care. Dispersal occurs in the fall, with the ♂ generally dispersing farther than ♀.

BEHAVIOR *Social behavior*: Solitary, monogamous. *Diet*: Small ground-dwelling mammals, including lagomorphs and sciurids, but may also take galliformes, frogs, snakes, insects, berries and vegetables. Carrion may be seasonally important. Surplus food is buried. *Main predators*: Birds of prey, Dogs. Nocturnal. Very mobile, often covering 10 km per day, with non-overlapping territories. Territories are larger in winter than in summer.

DISTRIBUTION *Native*: China, Russia. South China Red Fox (*V. v. hoole*) is found in SW China to SE China, Szechuan, eastward to Fujian, Hunan, Guizhou. North China Red Fox (*V. v. tschiliensis*) is found in N China, Hebei, Shansi, Shensi, Gansu and Manchuria.

HABITAT Almost every habitat, farmlands, forests, high mountain tundra and semi-deserts, but they prefer brushy habitats with a mix of open areas and cover.

CONSERVATION STATUS Least Concern. *CITES*: Not listed. *Regional status*: Near Threatened (China). Once widespread in S China, its population has declined severely; it is extinct in Hong Kong.

North African Red Fox

VULPES VULPES AEGYPTIACUS, ATLANTICA AND BARBARA

BL: 46.5-64.2 cm. TL: 30.2-41.1 cm. H: 35 cm. W: 1.8-3.8 kg. SL: 12.9 cm. DF: 42. CN: 34. Ruddy to gray brown above, darker on the back of the neck. Flanks grayer, tinged buff. Throat and belly dark, even blackish, darker in winter, chin white. Forelegs brownish, marked with white and with black stripe down the rear side. Hind legs similar but with black limited to foot. Muzzle slender, beige above and reddish at the side with a dark streak running from muzzle to eye of varying distinctness. Whiskers black. Reddish brown below eyes, grayer on forehead. Ears large, inner side pale with long, whitish fringe hairs. Back of ear black. Tail full and bushy, paler below and with white tip. Juveniles paler and more uniform. In early spring, they look very shabby as they shed their winter coats.

Vulpes vulpes aegyptiacus

Vulpes vulpes atlantica

Vulpes vulpes barbara

OTHER NAMES Egyptian Red Fox, Nile Red Fox, Atlas Fox, Barbary Red Fox. *French*: Renard pâle d'Egypte, renard des Monts Atlas, renard pâle de Barbarie. *German*: Ägyptischer Rotfuchs, Atlas-Rotfuchs. *Spanish*: Zorro del norte de Africa, zorro de Egipto. *Russian*: Североафриканская рыжая лисица. *Arabic*: Tha'lab ahmar.

TAXONOMY Considered a subspecies of Red Fox (*V. vulpes*). Includes *anubis*, *niloticus*, *vulpecula*, *algeriensis* and *acaab*.

REPRODUCTION *Gestation*: 50 days. *Young per birth*: 3-5. *Weaning*: 40-60 days. *Sexual maturity*: 10 months. *Life span*: 5 years. *Breeding season*: Probably from December to February. Births occur in February and March. Dens may be burrowed in ground or it may make use of palm groves, fields, gardens, quarries and beneath walls, stables, houses, ruins and tombs. In Egypt, clay hills or karms, excavations from Roman cisterns, S of Burg el Arab are well-known burrowing sites.

BEHAVIOR *Social behavior*: Generally solitary, but larger groups can be found in winter during the mating season, where a group of ♂ may harass a ♀. Live in pairs during the rearing of the pups. *Diet*: Extremely varied, and includes invertebrates (particularly beetles, mole crickets, earthworms and crabs), small mammals (rodents, lagomorphs and weasels), birds (including game species), fishes, fruits and carrion. At Ras Muhammad, it digs for crabs. Must have daily access to water. *Main predators*: Dogs. Generally nocturnal but often seen during the day. In many areas, it excavates a den in the desert and comes down to farmland to feed at dusk. They spend the day in the den or merely lying in a scrape in the shade but also sunbathe. Hearing, smell and sight are all acute. They are most vocal during mating when the ♂ use a triple bark. They may also growl, chatter and whine. They coexist alongside feral Dogs, which are much larger; though the wild Dogs chase the them, the Foxes are much faster.

DISTRIBUTION *Native*: Algeria, Egypt, Libya, Sudan, Tunisia. *V. v. aegyptiacus* is found in Egypt along the N coast from Sallum to Alexandria, the Delta, Wadi, Natrum, the Fayoum, Cairo and its environs, including Saqqara, Abu Sir, and Gebel Asfar, Kharga, Dakhla, the N Red Sea coast, Suez, and the Nile Valley S to the Sudanese border; recently expanded into S Sinai and now resides in the Ras Muhammad National Park. It is also found in N Cyrenaica in Libya, and N Sudan toward Khartoum. *V. v. atlantica* occurs in N Africa, in Algeria (Atlas Mountains) and Tunisia. *V. v. barbara* occurs in NW Africa, along the coast of Morocco.

HABITAT It occurs in most habitats except extremely arid regions, including vegetated wadis, desert margins, gardens, hillsides, farmlands. In parts of its range, it appears closely associated with humans, as at the Step Pyramid in Egypt.

CONSERVATION STATUS Least Concern. *CITES*: Not listed.

Chinese Raccoon Dog

NYCTEREUTES PROCYONOIDES PROCYONOIDES AND ORESTES

BL: 50-58 cm. TL: 13-25 cm. H: 26-50 cm. W: 3-6 kg (6-10 kg before winter hibernation). DF: 42. CN: 54. A small, Fox-like Canid, with a stout body, short legs and a distinctive face mask like a North American Raccoon (*Procyon lotor*). Coat is long and dense, brownish gray to yellow brown in color, mingled with black tips. White morphs are common in captive-bred individuals. Forehead and muzzle are white while the eyes are surrounded by black. Cross-shaped pattern on the anterior part of the back. Chest, limbs and feet are dark brown to black. Head is short and narrow with a relatively short and pointed muzzle. Small rounded ears, edged in black, white inside. Short tail covered by shaggy hairs, blackish dorsally, lighter yellow ventrally, tipped in black. No sexual dimorphism. Neonates are covered with soft, black fur.

Nyctereutes procyonoides
procyonoides

Nyctereutes procyonoides
orestes

OTHER NAMES Yunnan Raccoon Dog, Asiatic Raccoon Dog. *French*: Chien viverrin, tanuki. *German*: Gewöhnlicher Marderhund, Festland-Marderhund, Festland-Waschbärhund. *Spanish*: Perro mapache de China. *Russian*: Китайская енотовидная собака: западнокитайская (*procyonoides*), южнокитайская (*orestes*). *Chinese*: He.

TAXONOMY Considered a subspecies of *N. procyonoides* (Raccoon Dog): *N. p. procyonoides* (Chinese Raccoon Dog), *N. p. orestes* (Yunnan Raccoon Dog), *N. p. ussuriensis* (Siberian Raccoon Dog), *N. p. koreensis* (Korean Raccoon Dog). Includes *kaliniensis* (Kalinin Raccoon Dog), *stegmanni* and *sinensis*. Japanese Raccoon Dog (*N. v. viverrinus* and *N. v. albus*) is also considered a subspecies by some authors, but here it has been elevated to full species, based on a number of karyotypic (2n=38), phenotypic, craniometric and behavioral differences.

SIMILAR SPECIES *N. p. orestes* has a whiter tail, only tinged with gray at the extreme base, and darker legs. *N. p. ussuriensis* is larger in size, with denser, longer hair. *N. v. viverrinus* is smaller, with a smaller skull and teeth, and shorter fur. The masked palm civet (*Paguma larvata*) has shorter legs and a much longer and slim tail.

REPRODUCTION *Gestation*: 59-64 days. *Young per birth*: 5-9, up to 19. *Weaning*: 45-80 days. *Sexual maturity*: 9-11 months. *Life span*: 14 years. *Breeding season*: From January to March, depending on its geographic location. Tail in ♂ forms an inverted U shape during sexual arousal, and ♂ and ♀ do not achieve the typical back-to-back tie. Probably monogamous. Both parents help out with rearing the young; ♂ bring food to the pregnant ♀. Most juveniles disperse at 4-5 months of age.

BEHAVIOR *Social behavior*: Solitary, but may live in family groups. *Diet*: True omnivores and opportunistic; small mammals, birds, eggs, fish, amphibians and invertebrates; they rely heavily on plants. *Main predators*: Wolf, marten, eagle, Dog. Mainly nocturnal. Not territorial. In northern parts of range, they hibernate from November to March, after increasing weight nearly 50%, but presumably not farther south. During hibernation their body temperature is 1.4 to 2.1°C lower than during summer. Nocturnal. Home ranges from 5 to 10 km². They can climb trees. They regularly participate in social grooming. Their vocalizations are limited to high-pitched whines and mewing sounds; they cannot bark.

DISTRIBUTION *Native*: China, Vietnam. *N. p. procyonoides* is found in W and SW China (Anhui, Fujian, Guangdong, Guangxi, Hubei, Hunan, Jiangsu, Jiangxi, Zhejiang) and N Indochina. *N. p. orestes* occurs in central and S China (Gansu, Guizhou, Shaanxi, Sichuan, Yunnan).

HABITAT Open broadleaf forests near water or open meadows, thick brushy areas, and reeds, usually associated with water. Seldom found in high mountains or dense forests. The N limit of distribution lies in areas where the mean temperature of the year is just above 0°C, the snow cover about 800 mm, the duration of the snow cover 175 days and the length of the growing season 135 days.

CONSERVATION STATUS Least Concern. *CITES*: Not listed. *Regional status*: Vulnerable (China). Once though to occur widely in China, but today it is likely to be threatened. China has well-established captive-breeding fur farms.

PHOTO CREDITS *Blickwinkel* and *Christian Schmalhofer*, based on photos from China.

Siberian Raccoon Dog
NYCTEREUTES PROCYONOIDES USSURIENSIS

BL: 50-69 cm. TL: 13-25 cm. H: 38-50 cm. W: 3.8-12.4 kg. DF: 42. SL: 12.1 cm. SW: 6.8 cm. CN: 54. A small to medium-sized, Fox-like Canid, with a stout body, short legs and a distinctive face mask. The largest subspecies of Raccoon Dog, with longer, denser hair. Coat is long and dense, especially in winter, grizzled gray to yellowish brown in color, darker and less heavy in summer. Fur of the tail and sides is tinged with cinnamon. Individuals exhibit a wide range of color from albinistic to melanistic and wholly yellowish, with white morphs being common in captive-bred individuals. Forehead and muzzle are white while the eyes are surrounded by black. Shoulder, tip of tail and legs are blackish. Head is short and narrow with a relatively short and pointed muzzle. Small rounded ears, edged in black with white inside. Short tail covered by shaggy hairs, dorsally and distally tipped in black. No sexual dimorphism. Neonates are black.

summer coat

winter coat

white morph

*Nyctereutes procyonoides
ussuriensis*

OTHER NAMES Finnish Raccoon Dog, Ussuri Raccoon Dog. *French*: Chien viverrin, tanuki. *German*: Ussuri-Marderhund. *Spanish*: Perro mapache de Siberia. *Finnish*: Supikoira. Russian: Уссурийская енотовидная собака.

TAXONOMY Considered a subspecies of *N. procyonoides* (Raccoon Dog). Includes *amurensis* (Amur Raccoon Dog).

SIMILAR SPECIES North American Raccoon is smaller in size and has larger ears, and a tail with several rings. Asian Badger also has a facial black mask, which is close to vertical (horizontal in Raccoon Dog).

REPRODUCTION *Gestation*: 63 days. *Young per birth*: 7-9, up to 16. *Weaning*: 45-80 days. *Sexual maturity*: 9-11 months. *Life span*: 16 years. *Breeding season*: From February to April, usually in March; pups are born from April to June. Climatic conditions, especially the length of the summer, and food availability influence reproductive output. Both the ♀ and the ♂ help out with rearing the young; ♂ guard the litter at the dens when ♀ are out foraging to satisfy their increased energy requirement during lactation.

BEHAVIOR *Social behavior*: Solitary, but may live in family groups and forage in pairs. *Diet:* Opportunistic omnivore, with a food niche much wider than those of most other carnivores; diet composition varies geographically: ungulate and other carcasses and amphibians in forest areas, plant material, small mammals and invertebrates in woodland and farmland mosaic, waterfowl, amphibians and plant material on marshlands, lake shores and small islands. It may potentially compete with native species such as Red Fox and badger. *Main predators*: Wolf, Dog. Underdeveloped territoriality, with high tolerance toward conspecifics, and individual home ranges that have large overlap with adjacent individuals. Monogamous, with probable lifelong pair bonds. The paired mates share their home ranges and move together throughout the year. Home-range sizes vary from 5 to 7 km², larger during August-October to feed especially in maize fields to accumulate fat reserves, and smaller during the mating season. In cold climates they hibernate during winter. In winter, they settle in shelters that protect them against cold and predation.

DISTRIBUTION *Native*: China, Mongolia, Russia. *Introduced*: Austria, Belarus, Czech Republic, Estonia, Finland, France, Germany, Hungary, Kazakhstan, Latvia, Lithuania, Moldova, Netherlands, Norway, Poland, Romania, Slovakia, Sweden, Switzerland, Ukraine. The natural range includes NE China (Hebei, Heilongjiang, Jilin, Liaoning, E Nei Mongol), E Mongolia, and SE Russia, in the Amur and Ussuri regions of Siberia and the Khankai lowland, the shores of the Sea of Japan and also areas as far inland as Komsomolsk. It was introduced as a fur game species to the European part of the former Soviet Union. Today, this subspecies is widespread in N and E Europe, thriving in moist forests with abundant undergrowth.

HABITAT Meadows and moist deciduous and mixed forests with abundant understory, river valleys, lakeshores, marshes and moist heath. They may also occupy a mosaic of woodland and agricultural areas.

CONSERVATION STATUS Least Concern. *CITES*: Not listed. Abundant in almost all its range.

PHOTO CREDITS *Manfred Meier*, Heimat-Tierpark Olderdissen (Germany); *Michelle Bender* and *Maarten de Ruiter*, Dierenrijk (Netherlands); *Ulli Joerres*, Zoodyssée (France).

Korean Raccoon Dog
NYCTEREUTES PROCYONOIDES KOREENSIS

BL: 50-58 cm. TL: 18 cm. H: 26-50 cm. W: 3.8-5.6 kg. SL: 11.6 cm. SW: 6.7 cm. DF: 42. CN: 54. A small, Fox-like Canid, with a stout body, short legs and a distinctive face mask. A medium-sized subspecies of Raccoon Dog. Coat is long, soft, and thick, brownish gray, mingled with black tips. Conspicuous dorsal black stripe, from the top of the head over the neck to the shoulders, and extending to the upper part of the body and down the tip. Head is short and narrow with a relatively short and pointed muzzle. Cheek black, darker than in other subspecies. Nose tawny olive. Forehead and part under the ear whiter than in other subspecies. Small rounded ears, rufous with dark brown margins. Chin dark slate, throat and breast dirty fawn to dark brownish. Feet are blackish slate. Tail is bushy, blackish dorsally, buff ventrally, tipped in black. There is no sexual dimorphism. Neonates with soft, black fur.

Nyctereutes procyonoides koreensis

OTHER NAMES *French*: Chien viverrin. *German*: Korea-Marderhund. *Spanish*: Perro mapache de Korea. *Russian*: Корейская енотовидная собака. *Korean*: Nurgoori.

TAXONOMY Considered a subspecies of *N. procyonoides* (Raccoon Dog). Karyotype of this subspecies is the same as that of the other continental subspecies (*procyonoides*, *orestes* and *ussuriensis*): 2n=54, whereas all those from the Japanese islands (*viverrinus* and *albus*) are 2n=38; the phylogenetic and taxonomic significance of the two distinct karyotypes within this genus is still unclear, and it is unknown whether they can produce hybrids or fertile offspring in captivity. Phylogenetic analyses indicate that South Korean populations are unique, despite being relatively close to other continental populations, with low genetic diversity.

SIMILAR SPECIES Smaller than *N. p. ussuriensis*, which may be found in N North Korea; there is no geological barrier or significant morphological differences between these two subspecies.

REPRODUCTION *Gestation*: 63 days. *Young per birth*: 7-9, up to 16. *Weaning*: 45-80 days. *Sexual maturity*: 9-11 months. *Life span*: 16 years. Probably monogamous. No specific information is given for this species, but probably similar to *N. p. ussuriensis*.

BEHAVIOR *Social behavior*: Solitary, but may live in family groups and forage in pairs. *Diet:* Opportunistic omnivore, with a food niche much wider than those of most other carnivores. *Main predators*: Feral Dogs. Crepuscular or nocturnal, spending a great deal of the day asleep hidden in vegetation. They are not territorial, with overlapping home ranges, which range from 0.37 km^2 to 0.98 km^2, similar in ♂ and ♀. Home range sizes are smaller in winter. In Korea, reduction of its predators and competitors as well as high adaptability to diverse environments has resulted in rapid growth of its population, raising concerns about its role in the ecosystem and the zoonotic transfer of various contagious diseases. It has also become a top predator despite its modest size, moderating prey densities and contributing to biodiversity in this area. It produces poor-quality fur compared to other subspecies. In several cases, it has been the core species spreading rabies and canine distemper between Domestic Dog and wild Canidae species in Korea.

DISTRIBUTION *Native*: North Korea, South Korea.

HABITAT Meadows and moist deciduous and mixed forests with abundant understory, river valleys, lakeshores, marshes and moist heath. They may also occupy a mosaic of woodland and agricultural areas. They have expanded to urban and suburban areas.

CONSERVATION STATUS *Least* Concern. *CITES*: Not listed. One of the most abundant mammals in South Korea. Most of its predators and competitors are extinct, which has resulted in rapid growth in population, raising concerns about its role in the ecosystem and zoonotic transfer.

PHOTO CREDITS *Jeon Han, Aratta Higgs* and *Jane Keeler*, Waryong-dong, Jongno-gu (Seoul).

Japanese Raccoon Dog
NYCTEREUTES VIVERRINUS VIVERRINUS (SPECIES UNCERTAIN)

BL: 29-65 cm. TL: 16-21 cm. H: 20 cm. W: 3-6.2 kg. SL: 10.9 cm. SW: 6.1 cm. DF: 42. CN: 38.
A small, Fox-like Canid, with a stout body, short legs and a distinctive face mask. The smallest
subspecies of Raccoon Dog, with fur shorter than in other subspecies. Coat color from yellow
to gray or reddish, with gray underhair. Black hairs on the back and shoulders and dorsally on
the tail. Legs, feet and chest are dark. Black facial mask. In summer, fur is thin and fat reserves
are small, so the animal looks much slimmer, while in autumn and winter, it is very fat and
has thick fur, giving an impression of a round animal with short thin legs. Small rounded ears.
Pointed muzzle. Long hair on the cheeks. Tail is fairly short, covered with thick hair. There is no
sexual dimorphism. Neonates are almost black.

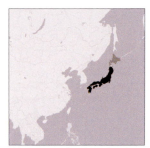

Nyctereutes viverrinus viverrinus

OTHER NAMES Tanuki. *French*: Tanuki. *German*: Japan-Marderhund. *Spanish*: Perro mapache japonés. *Russian*: Японская енотовидная собака. *Japanese*: Hondo-tanuki, mujina, anappo, kainehori, danza, tonchibo, hachimujina, banbuku, bo-zu, mameda, yomono.

TAXONOMY Considered a subspecies of *N. viverrinus* (Japanese Raccoon Dog). They have fewer chromosomes than continental Raccoon Dogs (2n=38). In addition there are a number of phenotypic and behavioral differences with continental Raccoon Dogs, such as skull and dental morphometrics, quality of fur, and physiology. Considered a subspecies of *N. procyonoides* (Raccoon Dog) by some authors.

SIMILAR SPECIES The smallest subspecies with smaller teeth and skull, and the silkiest pelt. Continental subspecies have longer fur of greater insulation value. The North American Raccoon has a shorter, fatter body, and a tail with black stripes.

REPRODUCTION *Gestation*: 62-66 days. *Young per birth*: 4-5. *Weaning*: 45-80 days. *Sexual maturity*: 9-11 months. *Life span*: 13 years. Breeding season: From April to June. Dens are often under big rocks, in tree trunks or under outbuildings. They do not construct their own burrows, and generally seek dense vegetation for diurnal cover.

BEHAVIOR *Social behavior*: Solitary, but may live in family groups and forage in pairs. *Diet:* Opportunistic omnivore, with a food niche much wider than those of most other carnivores; diet is dominated by fruit and seeds, insects and marine animals and differs considerably from that in other areas, where small rodents form the bulk of the diet. Carrion and fish are consumed during all seasons, being especially important in winter when other food sources are scarce. *Main predators*: Feral Dogs. Nocturnal, but, in contrast to earlier reports, they are also frequently active diurnally. Solitary hunters. Not territorial, with overlapping home ranges. Home range size varies greatly, from as little as 0.1 km² in an urban setting to 6 km² in a subalpine setting. Since winters are mild in Japan, this subspecies has no need to be inactive in winter and thus it does not gather large fat reserves or hibernate, although the activity level (nightly traveling speed and nightly range span) is lower in cold periods. In contrast to other Canids, they have poor vision and probably rely on olfactory senses for finding food items, and thus are less wide ranging as hunters.

DISTRIBUTION *Native*: Japan. Native to Honshu, Shikoku and Kyushu Islands of Japan (except the island of Hokkaido). Introduced to Chiburijima and Yakushima Islands.

HABITAT Mixed broadleaf-coniferous forests near lakes and rivers or the seashore, with similar habitat preferences as continental subspecies. However, it is also found in very urban areas, such as Tokyo metropolitan wards, requiring minimum vegetation cover and using gutters and underground drains for movement and resting sites. They are relatively undisturbed by human activity.

CONSERVATION STATUS Least Concern. *CITES*: Not listed. *Regional status*: Game species (Japan). Large numbers are exterminated each year, primarily as nuisance animals, but some for fur, for bristles for calligraphy brushes, or for meat. Relative abundance is high in SW parts of Japan and low in extremely urban areas. Main threats include road kills, persecution and epidemics (scabies, distemper, rabies).

PHOTO CREDITS *Niji55*, Shimane Prefecture (Japan); *Feathercollector* (Japan).

Hokkaido Raccoon Dog
NYCTEREUTES VIVERRINUS ALBUS   (SPECIES UNCERTAIN)

BL: 51-58 cm. TL: 16-21 cm. H: 26 cm. W: 3.8-5.6 kg. SL: 10.8 cm. SW: 6.2 cm. DF: 42. CN: 38. A small, Fox-like Canid, with a stout body, short legs and a distinctive face mask. A medium-sized subspecies. Coat is yellow to gray in color, with gray underhair. Black hairs on the back and shoulders and dorsally on the tail. Legs, feet and chest are dark. Black facial mask. Forehead is white. Pelage on the neck, body, tail and thighs is dense and fine, while on the lower half of each leg is scanty. Feet are very thinly haired. In winter, fur is thicker. Claws are long, slender, white or pinkish. Small rounded ears, edged in black, light brown on the back. Pointed muzzle, white on top, upper lip shows a light-colored blending of brown and white. Long hair on the cheeks. Tail is fairly short, ends abruptly at the tip, and is covered with thick hair. There is no sexual dimorphism. Neonates are almost black.

Nyctereutes viverrinus albus

OTHER NAMES White Raccoon Dog. *French*: Tanuki. *German*: Hokkaido-Marderhund. *Spanish*: Perro mapache de Hokkaido. *Russian*: Енотовидная собака острова Хоккайдо. *Japanese*: Eno-tanuki.

SUBSPECIES Considered a subspecies of *N. viverrinus* (Japanese Raccoon Dog). Raccoon Dogs of the Japanese islands (*albus* and *viverrinus*) have a reduced diploid chromosome number (2n=38), in contrast to subspecies native to the Chinese and Russian mainland (2n=54), and a different skull morphology. Hokkaido Raccoon Dog (*N. v. albus*) is sometimes considered to be a synonym of *N. v. viverrinus*, although analysis of skulls and teeth shows a clear separation between these two subspecies. Considered a subspecies of *N. procyonoides* (Raccoon Dog) by some authors.

SIMILAR SPECIES Body size and skull are larger than in *N. v. viverrinus*. The narrow postorbital constriction associated with development of temporal muscles in *N. v. albus* suggests this subspecies is more carnivorous, while premolars and molars of *N. v. viverrinus* are larger, suggesting that *viverrinus* may be more frugivorous. Naturalized North American Raccoons (*Procyon lotor*) live sympatrically with Raccoon Dogs on Hokkaido.

REPRODUCTION *Gestation*: 62-66 days. *Young per birth*: 2-5. *Weaning*: 45-80 days. *Sexual maturity*: 1-2 years. *Life span*: 13 years. *Breeding season*: From April to June. Both ♂ and ♀ participate in pup rearing, and take turns attending the den for 30 to 50 days after breeding.

BEHAVIOR *Social behavior*: Solitary, but may live in family groups and forage in pairs; they den communally during winter. *Diet*: True omnivores, seasonal food habits shift as food availability changes; small mammals, birds and fish. *Main predators*: Feral Dogs. They are mainly nocturnal, leaving their dens 1-2 hours after sunset. Mean home range size is 1.25 km². This subspecies forages intensively in autumn, resulting in the accumulation of considerable subcutaneous and intraperitoneal body fat reserves. In December, the onset of snow accumulation induces a distinct decrease in activity. They decrease their body temperature by 1.3 to 2.1°C with a transient 18-36% decrease in resting heart rate while maintaining a circadian rhythm in late February. Their vocalizations are higher in tone than those of a Domestic Dog and more or less resemble the sounds of a domestic cat. Dominant Raccoon Dogs can raise their tails in an inverted U shape.

DISTRIBUTION *Native*: Japan. Native to the island of Hokkaido, including Okushiri Island. This subspecies is separated from the main islands of Japan by Blakiston's Line, marking the transition to the subarctic climate.

HABITAT Mixed broadleaf-coniferous forests near lakes and rivers or the seashore. They tend to stay inside the forest during the daytime as well as the nighttime. Resting sites are located within woodland areas. They are rarely seen in farm fields or urban areas.

CONSERVATION STATUS Least Concern. *CITES*: Not listed. *Regional status*: Game species (Japan). Numbers appear to be stable but the recently introduced North American Raccoon may be a problem.

PHOTO CREDITS *Nobu*, Asahikawa Zoo, Hokkaido (Japan); *Tanteckken*, Singapore Zoo (Singapore); *TreviseGK*, Sapporo, Hokkaido (Japan); *Kaitlyn Fujihara*, Noboribetsu, Hokkaido (Japan).

South African Bat-Eared Fox
OTOCYON MEGALOTIS MEGALOTIS

BL: 40-66 cm. TL: 23-34 cm. H: 30-40 cm. W: 3-5.4 kg. SL: 11 cm. SW: 6.2 cm. DF: 46-50. CN: 72. A small to medium-sized Fox-like Canid, with slim long legs, a sharp, long muzzle, broad forehead, and disproportionately large ears. Coat is bushy, soft, and densely haired, gray brown to ashy gray in color, and undergoes a distinct molt once a year. Throat and underparts are pale. Lower legs are black. Muzzle is black on the top, white on the sides. Ears are white inside, black outside. Raccoon-like white facial mask, black below eyes, paler above eyes. Bushy tail with a black tip and a longitudinal black stripe on top. Females are slightly larger than males, with 2 pairs of mammae. Young have a slightly darker, glossier coat.

Young

Otocyon megalotis megalotis

OTHER NAMES Delalande's Fox. *French*: Otocyon, renard à oreilles de chauve-souris. *German*: Südafrikanischer Löffelhund. *Spanish*: Zorro orejudo sudafricano. *Russian*: Южноафриканская большеухая лисица. *Afrikaans*: Bakoorvos. *Sepedi*: Motlhose.

TAXONOMY Two subspecies recognized: *O. m. megalotis* and *O. m. virgatus*. Includes *auritus*, *caffer*, *lalandii* and *steinhardtii*.

SIMILAR SPECIES Jackals have smaller ears, a larger, less pointed muzzle, and are considerably larger. Cape Fox (*Vulpes chama*) is similarly sized, but lacks the black mask.

REPRODUCTION *Gestation*: 60 days. *Young per birth*: 2-5. *Weaning*: 28 days. *Sexual maturity*: 2 years. *Life span*: 9 years, 14 years in captivity. *Breeding season*: July-August, with most births occurring in late October to early January, with the start of the annual rains, when the insect population is at its highest. Young emerge from the den at 2-3 weeks old. Several ♀ may share a den, and the pups are cared for and suckled by all the lactating ♀. ♂ help care for and protect the young. Dispersal of young is primarily ♂-biased, although adults of both sexes also disperse.

BEHAVIOR *Social behavior*: Small groups of 1 to 12 individuals, depending on food resources and Black-Backed Jackal density, consisting of a mated pair and offspring from different years. *Diet*: Insectivorous with a marked preference for harvester termites; when termites are less abundant, it will opportunistically take a much wider range of food, including beetles, ants and other insects, scorpions, rodents, hares, birds and eggs, fruit and sometimes carrion. *Main predators*: Black-Backed Jackal, and also leopard, hyena, African Wild Dogs, lion, cheetah, and large raptors. Mainly nocturnal, except during winter when they become more diurnal due to changes in termite activity. Very social and monogamous, with lifelong pair bonds. When the pups are young, groups shelter in underground dens; otherwise they lie up under shrubs, trees, or even in the open. Not very territorial, with home ranges (2-8 km²) of neighboring groups overlapping considerably, and individuals changing groups. Their teeth are much smaller than those of other Canids, as an adaptation to their insectivorous diet. They visit termite hills, follow locust swarms or stay close to herds of zebras or antelopes in order to feed on the insects landing on their excrements. Densities from 1 to 14 per km², and may change between years based on rainfall and termite availability. Silent, communicating infrequently through soft calls, but loud barks when alarmed. Body postures, especially the raised, inverted U-shaped tail and ear positions, are used in communication.

DISTRIBUTION *Native*: Angola, Botswana, Mozambique, Namibia, South Africa, Zimbabwe.

HABITAT Short-grass plains and areas with bare ground. Also found in open scrub vegetation and arid, semi-arid or winter rainfall (fynbos) shrub lands, and open arid savanna. Its range overlaps almost completely with that of *Hodotermes* and *Microhodotermes*, termite genera prevailing in the diet.

CONSERVATION STATUS *Least Concern*. *CITES*: Not listed. *Regional status*: Least Concern (South Africa), protected in Zimbabwe. It is common in conservation areas in South Africa, becoming uncommon in arid areas and on farms in South Africa where they are occasionally persecuted. Commercial use is very limited, but winter pelts are valued and sold as blankets, and also sold as hunting trophies in South Africa.

PHOTO CREDITS *Ann and Steve Toon*, and *Blickwinkel*, Kgalagadi (South Africa); *Shumba138*, Northern Cape Province (South Africa).

East African Bat-Eared Fox

OTOCYON MEGALOTIS VIRGATUS

BL: 40-66 cm. TL: 23-34 cm. H: 30-40 cm. W: 3-5.3 kg. SL: 10.9 cm. SW: 6.1 cm. DF: 46-50. CN: 72. A small to medium-sized Fox-like Canid, with slim long legs, a sharp, long muzzle, broad forehead, and disproportionately large ears. Size and general appearance as in *megalotis* subspecies, but coat tends toward a buff pelage with dark brown instead of black, and underparts rich buff instead of whitish, brighter and more nearly a clear buff on throat, duller and more brownish between forelegs. Lower legs are black. Muzzle is black on the top, white on the sides. Ears are white inside, black outside. Raccoon-like white facial mask, black below eyes, paler above eyes. Bushy tail with black tip and longitudinal black stripe on top. No sexual dimorphism. Females with 2 pairs of mammae. Young have a slightly darker, glossier coat.

Young

272

Otocyon megalotis virgatus

OTHER NAMES *French*: Otocyon, renard à oreilles de chauve-souris. *German*: Ostafrikanischer Löffelhund. *Spanish*: Zorro orejudo de África Oriental. *Russian*: Восточноафриканская большеухая лисица. *Swahili*: Bweha masigio.

TAXONOMY Considered a subspecies of *O. megalotis* (Bat-Eared Fox). Includes *canescens* (Ethiopia and Somalia).

SIMILAR SPECIES It is distinguished from *megalotis* by its color, smaller teeth and a less inflated auditory bulla in the skull.

REPRODUCTION *Gestation*: 60-75 days. *Young per birth*: 2-5. *Weaning*: 28 days. *Sexual maturity*: 2 years. *Life span*: 13 years. *Breeding season*: June-July, with most births shortly after the onset of the rainy season, coinciding with the period of maximum dung beetle availability. Reproductive success is correlated to the density of harvester termites on their territories. Monogamous pairs, but may also breed in small cooperative groups, which form when mature daughters delay dispersal. Within cooperative groups both mother and daughter usually breed, with ♀ giving birth to litters in a communal den, and suckling one another's pups indiscriminately. After the pups are 2 weeks old, ♂ take over parental duties such as guarding, grooming, play and anti-predator defense.

BEHAVIOR *Social behavior*: Small groups of 2 to 5. Each group usually has 1 adult ♂ and 1 or 2 adult ♀. *Diet*: Insectivorous, with termites and dung beetles making up as much as 80% of their diet. Due to their diet, they have small 46 to 50 teeth, more than any other Canid; their jaw is also altered to open and close more quickly for speedy chewing. They seldom drink water as they obtain most of their moisture from their food. *Main predators*: Leopard, brown hyena, caracal, large raptors. Mainly nocturnal. Very social and monogamous, with lifelong pair bonds. Territorial in the Serengeti, urine marking and actively defending specific areas against intruding conspecifics during major parts of the year, but may be non-territorial in other areas. They are fast and good at dodging, and escape predation by fleeing to their underground dens. Size, shape and position of the ears help them to hear insects burrowing underground, and function as radiators, cooling their blood. The large, bushy tails work as a rudder when fleeing from predators in a zig-zag pattern. The alarm signal is a soft growl. Young in distress call their parents with a loud, shrill chattering.

DISTRIBUTION *Native*: Ethiopia, Kenya, Somalia, South Sudan, Tanzania, Uganda. It ranges from South Sudan, Ethiopia and Somalia down through Uganda and Kenya to SW Tanzania, and it is separated by about 1,000 km from the South African subspecies (*megalotis*).

HABITAT Open grassland and woodland boundaries. Harvester termite (*Hodotermes mossambicus*) foraging holes and dung from migratory ungulates are more abundant in areas occupied by Bat-Eared Foxes, while grass is shorter and individual plants are more widely spaced.

CONSERVATION STATUS Least Concern. *CITES*: Not included. It is common in conservation areas in E Africa. Within a circumscribed habitat, numbers can fluctuate from abundant to rare depending on rainfall, food availability, breeding stage and disease. There are no major threats, but they are subject to subsistence hunting for skins or because they are perceived as being predators of small livestock.

PHOTO CREDITS *Robert Harding*, Masai Mara (Kenya); *Stu Porter*, *Tomer Ben-Yehuda*, *Thomas Blank*, Serengeti (Tanzania); *Andrew Molinaro*, Ruaha (Tanzania).

Gray Fox-like Canids

GRAY FOX AND ISLAND FOX

RECOGNITION This small group represents the most basal clade within the extant Canidae, not closely related to any of the other Canid groups. It is represented by the monotypic North American genera *Urocyon*, which includes only two species: the Gray Fox (*Urocyon cinereoargenteus*) and the Island Fox (*U. littoralis*). Gray Fox-like Canids are small to medium-sized Canids, with relatively short and stout legs, a long tail, and a narrow muzzle, and display little color variation among individuals. Their coat is short and coarse, with a distinctive grizzled gray color, with small highlights of reddish brown on the neck, sides and legs, and some white on the ears, throat, chest, belly and hind legs. Black-tipped hairs near the center of the back form a conspicuous dark stripe that extends into a black mane of coarse hair on top of the black-tipped tail. Sexual dimorphism is minimal, with males being slightly larger than females. The skull of these species can be easily distinguished by its widely separated temporal ridges that form a U shape. They exhibit the typical Canid dental formula, I 3/3, C 1/1, P 4/4, M 2/3 = 42. The Island Fox is considered a dwarf island form of the Gray Fox. Whether the two taxa are separate species or merely subspecies of one broadly distributed and geographically variable species is open to interpretation. The karyotype of all Gray Fox-like Canids is 2n=66.

PHYLOGENY Gray Fox-like Canids diverged from other Canids during the Miocene (ca. 8-12 Ma). They evolved in North America and have been present since the end of the Hemphillian age (ca. 5 Ma) at the start of the Pliocene. *Urocyon progressus*, presumed to be an ancestral form of *U. cinereoargenteus*, is the earliest known member of the genus and lived throughout the Blancan age (ca. 5 to 2 Ma). Paleontological evidence of *U. cinereoargenteus* begins in the early Irvingtonian age (ca. 2 Ma) with fossils found in Arkansas, Florida, Maryland and Pennsylvania. Gray Foxes did not inhabit the northeastern states from the time of the last glacial maximum until as late as 900, during the Medieval Climate Anomaly. Gray Foxes probably initially reached one of the northern Channel Islands through chance by rafting or human introduction, 9,200 to 7,100 years ago, followed quickly by human translocation of Foxes from the northern to the largest southern Channel Islands. During a period of extended isolation they evolved their present small body size.

BEHAVIOR Gray Fox-like Canids are solitary hunters and opportunistic feeders, and their omnivorous diets shift seasonally and geographically with the relative abundance of foods. Social organization includes family units comprised of an adult male and female and occasionally offspring, which maintain territories separate from other family units. They are monogamous and breed only once a year. Both parents take care of their offspring. Gray Foxes are essentially nocturnal, while Island Foxes are active during daylight hours with peaks in activity occurring at dusk and dawn, probably due to the lack of natural predators. Gray Fox-like Canids have semi-retractile claws and are able to climb trees, an ability shared only with the Asian Raccoon Dog among Canids. They usually den in crevices in the rocks, in underground burrows, under rocks, in hollow logs or in hollow trees.

DISTRIBUTION The Gray Fox ranges over most of the United States, parts of southern Canada, and most of Mexico and Central America. Its distribution across a broad geographical area, coupled with the existence of barriers to gene flow, has resulted in *Urocyon* exhibiting considerable geographic variation. The Island Fox occurs only on the six largest of the eight islands off the coast of southern California, with each island presently supporting its own subspecies. Gray Fox is essentially an inhabitant of wooded areas, particularly mixed hardwood forests, while Island Fox can be found in all of the island biomes, including grassland, chaparral, temperate forest and temperate grassland.

CONSERVATION Gray Foxes are abundant throughout most areas in the lower two-thirds of North America. They have no special conservation status at this time. Although they are trapped and hunted by humans, there does not appear to be any immediate threat. Four of the six Island Fox subspecies have catastrophically declined by as much as 95% since 1994, after which they were listed as Endangered under the US Endangered Species Act. They have since recovered to or are approaching recovery to predecline population levels, and the species is being currently assessed as Near Threatened by the IUCN.

Gray Fox
Urocyon cinereoargenteus, 276

Island Fox
Urocyon littoralis, 300

Eastern Gray Fox

UROCYON CINEREOARGENTEUS CINEREOARGENTEUS

BL: 56-66 cm (♂), 52.5-58 cm (♀). TL: 30.5-38.1 cm. H: 30.5-40.6 cm. W: 2-5.8 kg. SL: 11 cm. SW: 6.9 cm. DF: 42. CN: 66. A small to medium-sized Canid, with a short muzzle, elongated and stout body, and relatively short legs. A medium to large-sized, dark subspecies. Coat color is grizzled gray above, tawny orange laterally, along the sides and from the ears ventrally, encircling the white chin and throat. Cheek, muzzle and throat are white. Underfur light tan, and some hairs with long orangish tips. Black around the eyes, encircling the muzzle. Lips and nose pad are black. Eyes with oval-shaped pupils. Tail is long, roughly triangular, not round in cross section, with a distinct black stripe along the dorsal surface, a black tip, and reddish underside. Top of feet reddish brown. There is a single molt with prime fur attained in winter. Females are slightly smaller than males, with 3 pairs of mammae. Newborns are dark brown.

Young

*Urocyon cinereoargenteus
cinereoargenteus*

OTHER NAMES Tree Fox. *French*: Renard gris. *German*: Östlicher Graufuchs. *Spanish*: Gato cervan, gato de monte, zorra gris, zorro plateado de Nueva Inglaterra. *Russian*: Восточная серая лисица.

TAXONOMY Eleven subspecies are traditionally recognized in North America (Hall, 1981): *U. c. cinereoargenteus*, *U. c. borealis*, *U. c. californicus*, *U. c. floridanus*, *U. c. madrensis*, *U. c. nigrirostris*, *U. c. ocythous*, *U. c. orinomus*, *U. c. peninsularis*, *U. c. scottii* and *U. c. townsendi*. Five additional subspecies occur in Central and South America (Cypher, 2003): *U. c. costaricensis*, *U. c. fraterculus*, *U. c. furvus*, *U. c. guatemalae*, *U. c. venezuelae*. A rigorous review of morphometric or genetic differences has not been conducted on Gray Fox, and most subspecies are probably not valid. They are assigned here on the basis of geographic distribution. Except for Foxes on the Yucatan Peninsula, there is a fairly high degree of phenetic overlap among subspecies of Gray Fox, although recent research suggests that there is a strong genetic divergence between SW and SE populations.

REPRODUCTION *Gestation*: 53-59 days. *Young per birth*: 2-6, one litter per year. *Weaning*: 45-70 days. *Sexual maturity*: 10 months. *Life span*: 6 years, 15 years in captivity. *Breeding season*: From late January to early March. ♂ probably mate with only 1 ♀ each year and may mate with the same ♀ in consecutive years. Births occur from April to the end of May, in dens in hollow logs or trees, sometimes as high as 15 m up, or underground in converted woodchuck burrows. Pups open their eyes in 10-12 days, are usually on their own by 4 months of age, and reach adult size at less than 7 months of age. They disperse as far as 80 km from the den.

BEHAVIOR *Social behavior*: Through late summer, they live in family units consisting of the paired adults and their young; in autumn they disperse. *Diet*: Small mammals (mice, rats and rabbits), but also feed on birds and insects occasionally. Native fruits such as persimmons and grapes as well as agricultural crops such as corn and peanuts are eaten more often than by other Fox species. *Main predators*: Coyote, bobcat. Typically nocturnal although they may forage during daylight hours. Good tree climbers; they grasp the trunk with their forelegs and push with their hind legs. They may climb a tree for refuge during the night and may still be in the tree at daylight. Home range size varies from 0.3 to over 24 km²; the most important factors determining the size of home ranges are habitat quality, population density and the reproductive status of individual Foxes. Areas with many different habitat types and dense populations of prey species support higher densities with smaller home ranges since Foxes are somewhat territorial.

DISTRIBUTION *Native*: Canada, United States. Found in E United States: North Carolina, N South Carolina, N Georgia, N Alabama, N Mississippi, Tennessee, Virginia, Kentucky, West Virginia, E Illinois, Indiana, Ohio, Maryland, Delaware, S Pennsylvania, Michigan, Massachusetts, New Jersey and Connecticut; and in S Ontario in Canada.

HABITAT A wide variety of forest types; they prefer woodlands and woodland-brush ecotones over open habitat. They commonly occur in E deciduous forests, but are also found in mixed and coniferous forests of the NE states.

CONSERVATION STATUS Least Concern. *Regional status*: Threatened (Canada), furbearer species (USA). *CITES*: Not listed.

PHOTO CREDITS *Virginia State Parks*, JanVa, VA (USA); *Rob Goldberg Jr.*, Greenville, NC (USA); *Kevin Council*, NC (USA).

Northeastern Gray Fox
UROCYON CINEREOARGENTEUS BOREALIS

BL: 57.2-68.7 cm (♂), 52.5-58 cm (♀). TL: 21.5-43 cm. H: 30-40 cm. W: 3.1-6.3 kg (♂), 3.9 kg (♀). SL: 11.8 cm. SW: 7.3 cm. DF: 42. CN: 66. A small to medium-sized Canid, with a short muzzle, elongated and stout body, and relatively short legs. A large-sized subspecies. Coat color is grizzled gray above, tawny orange laterally, along the sides and from the ears ventrally, encircling the white chin and throat. Cheek, muzzle and throat are white. Dorsal underfur is rather buffy, and guard hairs are buffy basally, but blackish outward, becoming white distally, sometimes with black tips. There is black around the eyes, usually encircling the muzzle. Lips and nose pad are black. Eyes with oval-shaped pupils. Tail is long, roughly triangular, not round in cross section, with a distinct black stripe along the dorsal surface and a black tip. There is a single molt with prime fur attained in winter.

Urocyon cinereoargenteus
borealis

OTHER NAMES New England Gray Fox, Tree Fox. *French*: Renard gris. *German*: Nördlicher Graufuchs. *Spanish*: Zorra gris, zorro plateado de Nueva Inglaterra. *Russian*: Северовосточная серая лисица.

TAXONOMY Considered a subspecies of Gray Fox (*U. cinereoargenteus*). This population is hypothesized to result from the post-glacial expansion of the SE population. Subspecies designations are probably invalid.

REPRODUCTION *Gestation*: 53 days. *Young per birth*: 3-7. *Weaning*: 42-84 days. *Sexual maturity*: 12 months. *Life span*: 6-8 years, 12 years in captivity. *Breeding season*: From January through March (2-4 weeks later than the Red Fox). They usually do not use an underground den but instead use dens in dense brush, cavities in stumps and trees, rock crevices or under outbuildings such as barns and sheds. They have more than one den and will readily move their young if disturbed. Young stay in the den until about 4-5 weeks of age. Both adults care for the young by bringing food and guarding the den site. In the fall, the young disperse from the family unit and will usually breed the first spring after they are born.

BEHAVIOR *Social behavior*: Solitary; mated pairs during the breeding season. *Diet*: Their favored prey is the cottontail rabbit and it is believed they have expanded into the New England area by following this prey source. They eat other small animals such as mice, voles, squirrels, birds, frogs, crayfish and insects, but may also eat corn, nuts, berries and fruit in the warm months. They may eat small pets such as cats and small dogs if the opportunity arises. *Main predators*: Feral Dog, Coyote, large raptors. Behavior similar to other subspecies of Gray Fox. They are not observed as frequently as Red Foxes due to their reclusive nature and more nocturnal habits. Active from the late evening hours until dawn. They climb trees to pursue prey, forage for other foods, and take refuge from danger; they descend the tree trunk backwards. Home ranges in Connecticut average 5 to 10 km², but may vary depending on the abundance of food. Interactions with Coyotes have not been studied, and it is unknown if Coyotes are as intolerant of Gray Fox as they are of Red Fox. Gray Fox has a voice similar to the Red Fox, but barks or yaps less often and its voice is louder.

DISTRIBUTION *Native*: Canada, United States. Found in SE Canada: SW Quebec (Sherbrooke) and SE Ontario (Windsor); and in NE United States, in New England: SW Maine, New Hampshire, Vermont, New York, NW Massachusetts, NW Connecticut, N Pennsylvania and N Ohio.

HABITAT Dense hardwood or mixed hardwood and softwood forests. Habitat is commonly located along the banks of streams and rivers. It also prefers overgrown fields for foraging.

CONSERVATION STATUS Least Concern. *CITES*: Not listed. *Regional status*: Threatened (Canada), furbearer species (USA). Canine distemper appears to be the leading mortality factor, in terms of diseases. Gray Foxes exhibit a natural resistance to sarcoptic mange. The most important limiting factor is hunting and trapping by humans. In Canada, climate, especially harsh winters, may be a limiting factor. Deforestation, which is occurring in the regions this species occupies, reduces the availability of dense cover and the variety of habitats that the species requires, and therefore may have a negative impact on the population. Neither predation nor competition with Red Foxes and Coyotes is thought to have a significant influence on population levels.

PHOTO CREDITS *Bill Amidon*, East Alstead, NH (USA); *Sally A. Leavitt* (USA); *Phil Brown*, Wenham, MA (USA).

Florida Gray Fox

UROCYON CINEREOARGENTEUS FLORIDANUS

BL: 53-76 cm (♂), 54-57.8 cm (♀). TL: 26-41 cm. H: 30-38 cm. W: 3.2-6 kg. SL: 10.3 cm. SW: 6.5 cm. DF: 42. CN: 66. A small-sized Canid, with a short muzzle, elongated and stout body, and relatively short legs. Smaller than northern subspecies, with a relatively shorter tail and ears, and harsher pelage, with a paler fulvous color on breast and belly with less white. It usually lacks the white stripe on the inside of the legs, and the rusty throat patch is longer than in northern subspecies. Coat color is grizzled silver gray above, rusty brown laterally, along the sides and from the ears ventrally, encircling the white chin and throat. Cheek, muzzle and throat are white. Breast, belly, inner surfaces of legs are pale rusty fulvous. There is black around the eyes, usually encircling the muzzle. Lips and nose pad are black. Tail is long, with a distinct black stripe along the dorsal surface and a black tip.

Young

*Urocyon cinereoargenteus
floridanus*

OTHER NAMES Tree Fox. *French*: Renard gris. *German*: Florida-Graufuchs. *Spanish*: Gato cervan, gato de monte, zorra gris de Florida, zorro plateado de Florida. *Russian*: Флоридская серая лисица.

TAXONOMY Considered a subspecies of Gray Fox (*U. cinereoargenteus*). Subspecies designations are probably invalid.

REPRODUCTION *Gestation*: 53-63 days. *Young per birth*: 3-7. *Weaning*: 42 days. *Sexual maturity*: 12 months. *Life span*: Unknown. *Breeding season*: From late January to March, with most births in April. Dens are located in hollow logs, ground burrows, beneath boulders, and even under buildings in some secluded areas or where the Foxes have become acclimated to people. Dens frequently are lined with shredded bark or leaves.

BEHAVIOR *Social behavior*: Pair bonds that last year-round. *Diet*: Small animals (rabbits, rodents, birds), fruit and insects, but they will also eat out of garbage cans and scavenge road-killed animals. Due to its climbing expertise, arboreal creatures such as squirrels are more important to its diet than to those of other Canids. *Main predators*: Dog, bobcat, owl, hawk, Coyote. Behavior similar to other subspecies of Gray Fox. Nocturnal and crepuscular, resting in dense cover during the daytime and foraging in open areas at night. They usually hunt alone. They are the only member of the Canid family that regularly climbs trees. It climbs in a scrambling motion, grasping the tree trunk with its forepaws and forcing itself higher with the long claws on its hind feet. Besides being able to leap from branch to branch in pursuit of prey, it also uses its perch to ambush victims from above. On the ground it can reach speeds of up to 17 kmph for short distances. Home ranges in this area are larger than in other areas, probably related to low biomass of available small mammal prey. Marginal overlap of home ranges of same sex adult Foxes with adjacent home range boundaries provides evidence for territoriality. Extensive overlap is observed between juveniles and adults of opposite sex. Florida home ranges average 7.7 km². It has a yapping bark.

DISTRIBUTION *Native*: United States. Found along the Gulf of Mexico: S South Carolina, Florida, S Georgia, S Alabama, S Mississippi, Louisiana and E Texas. In Florida, it occurs statewide except for the Keys. In North Carolina, they inhabit all areas of the state from the Outer Banks to the Appalachian Mountains; although viable populations are found in all of North Carolina's major habitat types, they are most numerous in the Piedmont and N Coastal Plain. In Texas it occurs E of the Balcones Fault zone (*scottii* in the W two-thirds of the state).

HABITAT Typically associated with dense woodlands and brushy areas, except in the extreme SE United States where they are more abundant in mixed woods and cultivated areas, probably due to the absence of Red Foxes, and hence competition. They are often present in large tracts of wooded areas and also thrive in open farmland. It has adapted well to urban environments, and it can be found in almost any developed area that affords some degree of vegetation cover.

CONSERVATION STATUS Least Concern. *CITES*: Not listed. *Regional status*: Furbearer species (USA). Although common, it often is inconspicuous due to its secretive habits. Its coarse, thin coat does not have much commercial value.

PHOTO CREDITS *Dave, Smith Juan,* FL (USA); *R. M. Buquoi Photographics*, Georgetown, TX (USA).

Prairie Gray Fox

UROCYON CINEREOARGENTEUS OCYTHOUS

BL: 62 cm (♂), 54-57.8 cm (♀). TL: 38 cm. H: 30-40 cm. W: 4.1-5 kg (♂), 2-3.9 kg (♀). SL: 12.6 cm. SW: 7.1 cm. DF: 42. CN: 66. A small to medium-sized Canid, with a short muzzle, elongated and stout body, and relatively short legs. A large-sized subspecies. Coat color is grizzled gray above, tawny orange laterally, along the sides and from the ears ventrally, encircling the white chin and throat. Cheek, muzzle and throat are white. Dorsal underfur is rather buffy, and guard hairs are buffy basally, but blackish outward, becoming white distally, sometimes with black tips. There is black around the eyes, usually encircling the muzzle. Lips and nose pad are black. Eyes with oval-shaped pupils. Tail is long, roughly triangular, not round in cross section, with a distinct black stripe along the dorsal surface and a black tip. Females are slightly smaller than males, with 3 pairs of mammae. Newborns are dark brown.

*Urocyon cinereoargenteus
ocythous*

OTHER NAMES Swift Gray Fox, Wisconsin Gray Fox, Maned Fox, Wood Fox. *French*: Renard gris. *German*: Prärie-Graufuchs, Central-Plains-Graufuchs. *Spanish*: Zorra gris, zorro plateado. *Russian*: Серая лисица центральной равнины.

TAXONOMY Considered a subspecies of Gray Fox (*U. cinereoargenteus*). Subspecies designations are probably invalid.

REPRODUCTION *Gestation*: 53 days. *Young per birth*: 1-7. *Weaning*: 42 days. *Sexual maturity*: 12 months. *Life span*: 6 years. *Breeding season*: From late January through February in S Illinois and from late January through March in Wisconsin. Breeding season may be heralded by fierce battles among ♂. Pups are brownish black and fully furred, but blind for the first 9 days. They stay with their parents until late summer or fall. The ♂ stays with his mate and helps care for the young. Dens are usually located in wooded areas and include underground burrows, cavities in trees or logs, woodpiles, and rock outcrops or cavities under rocks. They will use dens year-round, but predominantly when young are born.

BEHAVIOR *Social behavior*: Mated pairs during the breeding season. *Diet*: Opportunistic carnivore, with mammals composing most of its diet in the Midwest; although rabbits have been found to be one of their primary food sources, they routinely feed on small rodents and other mammals, birds and reptiles. In the summer, invertebrates have been found to be more important food items, while in the fall, it consumes more fruit and sometimes corn. *Main predators*: Coyote, bobcat. Behavior similar to other subspecies of Gray Fox. More active at night, with activity at sunrise sharply decreasing and increasing again at sunset. They are capable of climbing a tree trunk using their claws to grasp and pull themselves up or bounding from branch to branch; this behavior is used during foraging, predator avoidance, or resting. They move at a rapid trot, eyes, ears and nose alert for signs of prey. Pairs share a territory and reside close to each other during the breeding season. After this, they live disjointedly and hunt separately. In late winter and also in early spring, they will begin to live nearer and get ready for mating season. Home range size varies depending on the season and geographic location, from 0.13 to 3.1 km².

DISTRIBUTION *Native*: Canada, United States. Found in the Central Plains states: Wisconsin, Minnesota, E North Dakota, E and S South Dakota, W Illinois, Iowa, Nebraska, E Kansas, Missouri, Arkansas, E Oklahoma, N Louisiana; and in SW Ontario and extreme S Manitoba in Canada.

HABITAT Woody cover in deciduous or pine forest, but they also use edge habitat and open habitats that are transitioning from field to forest and are dominated by forbs, grass, and shrubs and small trees. They tend to select against agricultural areas. They use oak-hickory forests almost exclusively in S Missouri, and are frequently found in dense stands of young trees during the day.

CONSERVATION STATUS Least Concern. *CITES*: Not listed. *Regional status*: Threatened (Canada), Under Review (USA). Loss of preferred habitat and the increase in agricultural habitat may have caused a decline in population of this subspecies. Its fur became popular during the late 1970s for fur coats and collars and demand for its fur continues to some extent today.

PHOTO CREDITS *Geoffrey Kuchera* and *Sparky Stensaas* (ThePhotoNaturalist.com), MI (USA); *ImageBroker*, MT (USA); *Paul Boatman*, Garfield, AR (USA).

Arizona Gray Fox

UROCYON CINEREOARGENTEUS SCOTTII

BL: 58.5-64.2 cm (♂), 54-57.8 cm (♀). TL: 33-47 cm. H: 35.5-38.1 cm. W: 3-5 kg. SW: 6.4 cm. DF: 42. CN: 66. A small-sized Canid, with a short muzzle, elongated and stout body, and relatively short legs. A medium-sized, paler subspecies, purer gray, and more yellowish fulvous, with the muzzle more attenuated, and with longer ears and tail. Coat color is gray above, reddish brown laterally, along the sides and from the ears ventrally, encircling the white chin and throat. Cheek, muzzle and throat are white. Abdomen is ochraceous. There is black around the eyes, usually encircling the muzzle. Lips and nose pad are black. Eyes with oval-shaped pupils. Tail is long, roughly triangular, not round in cross section, with a distinct black stripe along the dorsal surface and a black tip. There is a single molt with prime fur attained in winter. Females are slightly smaller than males, with 3 pairs of mammae. Newborns are dark brown.

Urocyon cinereoargenteus scottii

OTHER NAMES Scott's Gray Fox, Southern Gray Fox, Desert Gray Fox. *French*: Renard gris. *German*: Arizona-Graufuchs. *Spanish*: Gato cervan, gato de monte, zorra gris de Arizona, zorro plateado de Arizona. *Russian*: Аризонская серая лисица.

TAXONOMY Considered a subspecies of Gray Fox (*U. cinereoargenteus*). Includes *inyoensis* (Inyo Mountains Gray Fox) and *texensis* (Texas Gray Fox). Subspecies designations are probably invalid.

SIMILAR SPECIES Red Fox is slightly larger, with longer legs, much lighter in color, has black feet and white tail, and its tracks show proportionally smaller toe pads and larger overall foot size.

REPRODUCTION *Gestation*: 51-53 days. *Young per birth*: 2-7. *Weaning*: 42-70 days. *Sexual maturity*: 12 months. *Life span*: 6 years, 12 years in captivity. *Breeding season*: February or March, with most births in April or May. Dens in hollow trees, into soil or in enlarged burrows of another animal. This den may be as much as 23 m long and can have 10 or more exits, and it has numerous side chambers used for food storage and for the transfer of young, once a chamber becomes too soiled to inhabit. The young venture out of the den after about 5 weeks. The ♂ provides food during this period. The family remains together until late fall, then separates. All generally remain solitary throughout the winter.

BEHAVIOR *Social behavior*: Mated pairs. *Diet*: Primarily small mammals, but will also eat eggs, insects, birds, fruits, acorns and berries. *Main predators*: Dog, cougar, eagle, owl, bobcat, hawk, Coyote (Gray Foxes killed by Coyotes are not consumed, suggesting that interference competition is the primary motivating factor). Behavior similar to other subspecies of Gray Fox. Although primarily nocturnal, it may sometimes be seen foraging during the day. Although they have a keen sense of smell, they seldom track prey species; the preferred method of hunting is to wander until a victim is heard or smelled; they will often stalk and pounce upon the prey. They can climb trees. Territorial, marking their boundaries with urine, feces, and with scent from glands on either side of the anus; the scent gland products are quite pungent, and the odor may seem reminiscent of skunk. Home range in Utah averages 1 km².

DISTRIBUTION *Native*: Mexico, United States. Found in the United States: in Arizona, New Mexico, Utah, Colorado, S half of Nevada, extreme SW Kansas, W and central Texas, California E of the Sierra Nevada; and in Mexico: in Tamaulipas, Nuevo León, Coahuila, N Chihuahua, N Zacatecas, NE Durango, N Sonora, NE Baja California, and probably N San Luis Potosí and N Veracruz.

HABITAT Generally occupies more open habitats, from low desert or lower well up into brushy and sparsely wooded, rocky slopes and canyons up to and above 2,700 m in elevation. Plant communities most often occupied include desert scrub, desert grassland, chaparral, and oak and pine woodland. It may also be seen in urban settings with ample cover.

CONSERVATION STATUS Least Concern. *CITES*: Not listed. *Regional status*: Not protected (Mexico), furbearer species (USA). It is common, and no population declines have been noted, other than short-term, local die-offs associated with disease outbreaks. The New Mexico population may have declined from over-trapping.

PHOTO CREDITS *Karen McCrorey, GaryS42* and *Glenn Seplak,* Arizona-Sonora Desert Museum, AZ (USA); *Robert Palmer,* Las Vegas, NV (USA).

Townsend's Gray Fox

UROCYON CINEREOARGENTEUS TOWNSENDI

BL: 54.6-66 cm (♂), 50.8-59.6 cm (♀). TL: 33.8-38 cm. H: 35.5-38.1 cm. W: 3.5-5.4 kg (♂), 3.4-5.4 kg (♀). SL: 11.6 cm. SW: 6.5 cm. DF: 42. CN: 66. A small-sized Canid, with a short muzzle, elongated and stout body, and relatively short legs. A large-sized subspecies. Coat color is grizzled gray, with a mid-dorsal black band extending onto the tail. Guard hairs are banded white, gray and black, producing the grizzled appearance. Throat, abdomen and inside of the legs are white. A cinnamon-rufous border to the white throat extends onto the flanks and underside of tail. Black patch on the sides of the face extending onto the lower jaw. Ears are cinnamon on the exterior and lined with long whitish hairs extending from the interior margins. Eyes with oval-shaped pupils. Tail is long, black tipped. Feet are grayish white. Females are slightly smaller than males, with 3 pairs of mammae. Newborns are gray to black.

Young

286

Urocyon cinereoargenteus townsendi

OTHER NAMES Tree Fox. *French*: Renard gris. *German*: Pazifikküsten-Graufuchs. *Spanish*: Gato cervan, gato de monte, zorra gris de Townsend, zorro plateado. *Russian*: Серая лисица Таунсенда.

TAXONOMY Considered a subspecies of Gray Fox (*U. cinereoargenteus*). Subspecies designations are probably invalid.

REPRODUCTION *Gestation*: 53-63 days. *Young per birth*: 2-5. *Weaning*: 42 days. *Sexual maturity*: 10-12 months. *Life span*: 5-7 years. *Breeding season*: February to March. Births occur in April and May. First-year mortality is in excess of 50%, and fewer than 5% exceed 4 years of age. Ground dens frequently are the modified dens of other species; hollow logs, abandoned buildings, refuse piles and rocky outcrops are used as den sites. Natal dens are commonly concealed by thick, brushy vegetation. They move to other dens about every 15-20 days especially when the pups are under two and a half months of age, possibly to keep predators off guard. Pups are gray to black, blind and deaf; within 10-12 days they attain both hearing and sight. Pups accompany adults on foraging expeditions at 2 months and forage independently at 4 months. Both ♀ and ♂ appear to be responsible for provisioning pups. Juveniles reach adult size and weight at about 210 days, and disperse at 9-10 months of age. ♂ disperse approximately 16 km from natal den home ranges and ♀ 11 km, although long-distance dispersal (over 80 km) has been reported.

BEHAVIOR *Social behavior*: Mated pairs and their offspring of the year; monogamous, with occasional polygyny. *Diet*: Lagomorphs, rodents, fruits, insects, other invertebrates and small birds, including domestic chicken. *Main predators*: Dog, cougar, eagle, owl, bobcat, hawk, Coyote. Behavior similar to other subspecies of Gray Fox. A secretive animal. Most activity is nocturnal and crepuscular, although they may be seen abroad during daylight hours. It climbs trees to escape pursuit, to forage, and to rest. It simply runs up sloping trunks or jumps from branch to branch. It runs down sloping trunks head first, but backs down vertical trunks. Ranges of adjacent family groups may overlap, but core areas appear to be used exclusively by a single family. They scent mark by depositing urine and feces in conspicuous locations. Home range size averages 1.13 km² in Oregon, and 1.02 km² in California, being similar to those of other subspecies. Home ranges of ♀ during littering and nursing season may be reduced to 20% of home ranges during prereproductive seasons. They communicate vocally via growls, alarm barks, screams, and "coos" and "mewing" sounds during greetings. Gray Foxes engage in allogrooming, with adults grooming juveniles and each other.

DISTRIBUTION *Native*: United States. Found in W Oregon, N two-thirds of California.

HABITAT Brushy vegetation in broken terrain. Plowed fields and other bare areas are avoided, but if available within home ranges, riparian areas, old-field habitats, and human-used areas may be used more frequently than expected. Gray Fox abundance is inversely related to Coyote abundance.

CONSERVATION STATUS Least Concern. *CITES*: Not listed. *Regional status*: Furbearer species (USA).

PHOTO CREDITS *Tom Ingram, v_ac_md*, Coyote Hills Regional Park, CA (USA); *Rainer Lutz Bauer*, Coyote Creek Trail, CA (USA).

California Gray Fox

UROCYON CINEREOARGENTEUS CALIFORNICUS

BL: 54.9-69 cm. TL: 33-44 cm. H: 38 cm. W: 3.2-4.5 kg. SL: 11 cm. DF: 42. CN: 66. A small-sized Canid, with a short muzzle, elongated and stout body, and relatively short legs. A medium-sized subspecies, with a bushy tail and relatively large ears. Coat color is iron gray above, rusty red laterally, along the sides and from the ears ventrally, encircling the white chin and throat. Black stripe down middle of back and along tail to tip. Cheek, muzzle and throat are white. Underfur light tan, and some hairs with long orangish tips. There is black around the eyes, usually encircling the muzzle. Lips are black. Nose pad is black. Eyes are dark with oval-shaped pupils. Tail is long, roughly triangular, not round in cross section, with a distinct black stripe along the dorsal surface, a black tip and reddish underside. Top of feet reddish brown. Females are slightly smaller than males, with 3 pairs of mammae. Newborns are gray to black.

Urocyon cinereoargenteus
californicus

OTHER NAMES Tree Fox, Coastal Gray Fox. *French*: Renard gris. *German*: Südkalifornien-Graufuchs. *Spanish*: Gato cervan, gato de monte, zorra gris de California, zorro plateado de California. *Russian*: Калифорнийская серая лисица.

TAXONOMY Considered a subspecies of Gray Fox (*U. cinereoargenteus*). Includes *sequoiensis* (Redwood Gray Fox). Subspecies designations are probably invalid.

SIMILAR SPECIES Red Fox is slightly larger, with a leaner body with longer legs, slit-shaped eyes, lighter in color, has black feet and white tail, and its tracks show proportionally smaller toe pads and larger overall foot size. Swift and Kit Foxes have black on tail only at tip. Coyote is larger and more yellowish gray.

REPRODUCTION *Gestation*: 53-63 days. *Young per birth*: 2-7. *Weaning*: 42 days. *Sexual maturity*: 12 months. *Life span*: 5 years, 10 years in captivity. *Breeding season*: February to March, with most births in April. Dens are located in natural cavities, in rocky areas, snags, logs, brush, slash and debris piles, abandoned burrows and under buildings. Nest material usually dry grass, leaves or shredded bark. ♂ helps rear the young from birth to dispersal, at 9 months of age. Pups are gray to black, blind and deaf; within 10-12 days they attain both hearing and sight.

BEHAVIOR *Social behavior*: Mated pairs during the breeding season, remaining in their home range after the young have dispersed; monogamous. *Diet*: Rabbits, mice, gophers, woodrats and squirrels; may also eat large amounts of fruits, nuts, grains, grasshoppers and crickets, beetles, moths and butterflies, carrion and small amounts of herbage. In deserts such as the Sonoran, they can get their needed water from plants, and other liquids from their prey, but they require a permanent water source near the den. *Main predators*: Coyote, bobcat, cougar, golden eagle. May carry canine distemper, toxoplasmosis, tularemia and rabies. Primarily crepuscular with the bulk of their hunting at night, occasionally active in daytime. They climb into trees that have no branches far up the trunk, and they can climb straight up. Family groups remain together until dispersal. They hunt alone. Home ranges average 1.2 km² in California. They usually travel at a rapid trot, a gait that carries them over the ground with considerable speed. May reach a speed of 69 kmph for short distances. Most common vocalizations include a rasping, hoarse bark, and a whistle.

DISTRIBUTION *Native*: Mexico, United States. Found in S California, W of Mojave Desert, N near coast at least to Ventura County, and in foothills of S Sierra Nevada, to Tulare County, San Jacinto Mountains in Riverside County; and in Mexico, in N Baja California, S at least to Vizcaino Desert District.

HABITAT Frequents most shrublands, valley foothill riparian, montane riparian, and brush stages of many deciduous and conifer forest and woodland habitats. Coyotes and bobcats may limit Gray Foxes to thicker chaparral cover. They do not use developed suburban areas.

CONSERVATION STATUS Least Concern. *CITES*: Not listed. *Regional status*: Furbearer species (USA), not protected (Mexico). Trapped for utilitarian and economic reasons, including the perceived elimination of livestock depredation, and for recreation. Recent changes in social attitudes toward trapping have resulted in lower participation in the activity and its outright ban in some states, including California.

PHOTO CREDITS *Martin Smart*, Joshua Tree National Park, CA (USA); *Steven Metidi*, San Gabriel Mountains, CA (USA); *Johnny Bovee*, Mojave National Preserve, CA (USA).

Mexican Gray Fox

UROCYON CINEREOARGENTEUS NIGRIROSTRIS AND RELATED SSP.

BL: 52.5-53.7 cm (♂), 51.3-53.5 cm (♀). TL: 34.9-43 cm. H: 30-35 cm. W: 3-5 kg. SL: 11.3 cm. SW: 6.2 cm. DF: 42. CN: 66. A small-sized Canid, with a short muzzle, elongated and stout body, and relatively short legs. Smaller than northern subspecies. Coat grizzled gray in color, with a well-defined mid-dorsal black band extending onto the tail. On the sides it is ochraceous, the abdomen is cream, and exhibits a white line throughout the hind leg. Top of head more finely grizzled gray. Cheeks, sides of muzzle, throat, inner legs and median line to base of tail are buffy white. Black patch on the sides of the face extending onto the lower jaw. Distal half of ears duller than base, inner surface buffy white. Eyes with oval-shaped pupils. Tail is long and bushy, gray, with a black dorsal stripe and tip and ill-defined ventral buffy area.

ssp. *madrensis*

ssp. *orinomus*

ssp. *nigrirostris*

*Urocyon cinereoargenteus
nigrirostris*

*Urocyon cinereoargenteus
madrensis*

*Urocyon cinereoargenteus
orinomus*

*Urocyon cinereoargenteus
peninsularis*

OTHER NAMES Colima Gray Fox, Madras Gray Fox. *French*: Renard gris. *German*: Mexiko-Graufuchs. *Spanish*: Gato cervan, gato de monte, zorro gris de México, zorro plateado de México. *Russian*: Мексиканская серая лисица.

TAXONOMY Considered subspecies of Gray Fox (*U. cinereoargenteus*). These four subspecies are assigned on the basis of geographic distribution, and they are morphologically very similar. *U. c. madrensis* differs from *nigrirostris* in having less harsh pelage and generally brighter, richer color, with a darker, more distinct dorsal stripe. Other subspecies found in Mexico include: *U. c. guatemalae* (Guatemalan Gray Fox), *U. c. fraterculus* (Yucatan Gray Fox) and *U. c. scottii* (Arizona Gray Fox), which are described in separate accounts. *U. c. colimensis* is considered a synonym of *nigrirostris*.

REPRODUCTION *Gestation*: 45-53 days. *Young per birth*: 2-7. *Weaning*: 42 days. *Sexual maturity*: 12 months (♀). *Life span*: Probably 5 years. *Breeding season*: From late February to early March. Monogamous. The ♀ is responsible for rearing the young, while the ♂ probably does not participate in this activity. Their favorite sites for construction of their shelters are hollow logs, roots of fallen trees, rocks or exposed soil and occasionally the base of living trees. The young leave the refuge in autumn, when they are 10-13 weeks old, and they become completely independent in the early winter, dispersing 20 to 80 km from the natal den. Young ♀ tend to stay in their place of origin.

BEHAVIOR *Social behavior*: Solitary, mated pairs during the breeding season. *Diet*: Opportunistic, in relation to abundance, including rodents, lagomorphs, fruits and insects. There is little information about its life history and behavioral ecology in this area, but it probably does not differ significantly from those reported by other studies elsewhere in North American temperate forests. Average home range size in Durango is 1.35 km².

DISTRIBUTION *Native*: Mexico. Colima Gray Fox (*U. c. nigrirostris*) is found in SW Mexico: Sinaloa, S Durango, S Zacatecas, Aguascalientes, Nayarit, Jalisco, Guanajuato, S Queretaro, Colima, Mexico, Morelos, Guerrero, S Hidalgo, Tlaxcala, S Puebla and W Oaxaca, ranges from sea level along Pacific coast to at least 2,500 m, on mountains bordering Valley of Mexico. Madras Gray Fox (*U. c. madrensis*) is found along the Sierra Madre Occidental mountain range in W Mexico: in S Sonora, SW Chihuahua, NW Durango and border of Sinaloa. *U. c. orinomus* is found in E Mexico, Isthmus of Tehuantepec and S Mexico: S San Luis Potosí, Veracruz, N Hidalgo, N Puebla, and central Oaxaca, ranging from 1,200 to 3,000 m. Peninsular Gray Fox (*U. c. peninsularis*) is found in S Baja California Sur.

HABITAT Semi-arid shrublands on broken terrain, and pine-oak forests. Inhabits all vegetational associations, from sea level to 3,500 m. Grassland and crop areas are less preferred.

CONSERVATION STATUS Least Concern. *CITES*: Not listed. *Regional status*: Not protected (Mexico). Very abundant; it benefits from anthropogenic disturbances. It has no conservation problems and its populations seem stable. It has been recorded in every state of Mexico. They are frequently sold illegally as pets.

PHOTO CREDITS *Arturo Morales,* Basaseachic Falls National Park (Mexico); *Arnulfo Moreno,* Tamaulipa (Mexico), *Roberto González* (Mexico).

Yucatan Gray Fox

UROCYON CINEREOARGENTEUS FRATERCULUS

BL: 48.2 cm (♂). TL: 24 cm. H: 32 cm. W: 1.8-3.5 kg. SL: 9.4 cm. SW: 5.3 cm. DF: 42. CN: 66.
A small-sized Canid, with a short muzzle, elongated and stout body, and relatively short legs. A small subspecies. Coat grizzled light gray in color, with a mid-dorsal black band extending onto the tail. On the sides, the buff becomes more conspicuous. Top of head more finely grizzled gray. Chin, upper side of muzzle and posterior half of upper lip are dusky. Cheeks, sides of muzzle, throat, inner legs and median line to base of tail are buffy white. Bases of ears, area behind ears, on sides of neck and across chest are ochraceous buff. Dark patch on the sides of the face extending onto the lower jaw. Distal half of ears duller than base, inner surface buffy white. Eyes with oval-shaped pupils. Tail is long and bushy, gray, with a black dorsal stripe and tip and ill-defined ventral buffy area. Outer sides of front legs and posterior surface of hind legs ochraceous buff.

Urocyon cinereoargenteus fraterculus

OTHER NAMES Little Gray Fox. *French*: Renard gris. *German*: Yukatan-Graufuchs. *Spanish*: Zorra de monte, gato de monte, gato cervan, zorra gris del Yucatán. *Russian*: Юкатанская серая лисица. *Maya*: W'ash, ch'amak, chomac.

TAXONOMY Considered a subspecies of Gray Fox (*U. cinereoargenteus*). Includes *parvidens* (from Merida, in Yucatan Peninsula, Mexico). This subspecies displays the greatest morphological divergence of any of the Gray Foxes, and is characterized as having inflated auditory bullae, and is smaller and darker than other subspecies in S Mexico and Central America; some authors have suggested that it may deserve full specific recognition. There is some evidence indicating that a dwarf Fox (*Urocyon* sp.) has inhabited Cozumel Island, but it has never been formally described; some authors suggest that it is phenotypically distinct from the mainland taxon, and that this population may deserve a unique species or subspecies designation based on a long history of isolation.

REPRODUCTION *Gestation*: 53-63 days. *Young per birth*: 1-7. *Weaning*: Unknown. *Sexual maturity*: 12 months. *Life span*: 5 years. *Breeding season*: Probably from February through March. There is no specific information available for this subspecies, but probably similar to the other subspecies.

BEHAVIOR *Social behavior*: Although reported to remain in family groups, single individuals are most often encountered. *Diet*: Omnivorous and opportunistic feeder; it eats large quantities of fruits when available; at other times it specializes on small mammals or insects, and it occasionally eats birds, small reptiles and carrion. During the dry season in Belize, the diet consists mainly of fruits and arthropods. Mainly nocturnal and crepuscular, spending much of the hot midday in the shade of the upper branches of the forest. It is rather easily seen and observed, trotting down wide trails or dirt roads or sitting on rocks and logs. Although almost always seen on the ground, it climbs well and sometimes dens high in trees, unlike other Canids. It is usually silent in the wild; captives may bark and whine.

DISTRIBUTION *Native*: Belize, Guatemala, Mexico. Found in San Felipe in Yucatan, Laguna Esmeralda and Quintana Roo in Mexico, and also from Uaxactun, Petén Department, in Guatemala, and in Stann Creek Valley, Camp London and Kate's Lagoon in Belize. Easily seen at night along roads in dry regions such as the N half of Yucatan Peninsula (Mexico); some have habituated to humans and may be approached closely in Tikal (Guatemala).

HABITAT Common and widespread in deciduous and semi-deciduous forest, agricultural areas and arid regions. Less common in evergreen forest. Extremely rare on Cozumel. It favors edges of forest and farmland, especially in rocky country, at low to moderately high elevations.

CONSERVATION STATUS Least Concern. *CITES*: Not listed. Not protected. Fairly common. Reports of Cozumel Gray Foxes are rare, consisting of occasional sightings or eyewitness accounts, but recent reports suggest a population may persist; this population may be extremely small and bordering on extinction, and should be considered Critically Endangered.

PHOTO CREDITS *Michael Lane* (Belize); *Pascal C.* and *Ray Wilson*, Tikal (Guatemala); Chaa Creek Belize Resort (Belize).

Guatemalan Gray Fox

UROCYON CINEREOARGENTEUS GUATEMALAE

BL: 51 cm (♂). TL: 32.7 cm. H: 34-40 cm. W: 2.5-5 kg. SL: 10.1 cm. SW: 6.0 cm. DF: 42. CN: 66. A small-sized Canid, with a short muzzle, elongated and stout body, and relatively short legs. A small subspecies, with color darker and richer. Coat color is clear gray above, tawny ochraceous laterally, along the sides and from the ears ventrally, encircling the white chin and throat. Top of head tinged with tawny. Cheek, muzzle and throat are white. Abdomen is ochraceous buff, except along median line and between hind legs, where it is dull white. Lips are black. Nose pad is black. Eyes with oval-shaped pupils. Distal half of ear thickly sprinkled with dusky hairs, inner surface of ear whitish. Tail is long and bushy, gray with a distinct black stripe along the dorsal surface, a black tip and dull ochraceous underside.

*Urocyon cinereoargenteus
guatemalae*

OTHER NAMES Tree Fox. *French*: Renard gris. *German*: Guatemala-Graufuchs. *Spanish*: Gato cervan (Honduras), tigrillo (El Salvador), zorra gris, gato de monte. *Russian*: Гватемальская серая лисица.

TAXONOMY Considered a subspecies of Gray Fox (*U. cinereoargenteus*). Subspecies designations are probably invalid.

REPRODUCTION *Gestation*: 53-63 days. *Young per birth*: 2-7. *Weaning*: 42 days. *Sexual maturity*: 10-12 months. *Life span*: 10 years, 15 years in captivity. *Breeding season*: Probably in February or March. There is no specific information available for this subspecies, but probably similar to other subspecies of Gray Fox. Dens are used year-round but are most important during whelping season. They are usually located in wooded, brushy or similarly sheltered areas, such as rock crevices or outcrops, and brush or weed piles, and in hollow logs; hollow trees are also used.

BEHAVIOR *Social behavior*: Mated pairs, monogamous. *Diet*: Opportunistic feeders and thrive on a great variety of animal and plant materials; rabbits seem to be important sources of food at all latitudes, and they are fond of fruits and plants, mice, squirrels, rats, moles, insects and even carrion. In El Salvador, plants and fruits may constitute up to 86% of its diet. Their delicate teeth prevent them from crushing large bones easily. *Main predators*: Dog, cougar, Coyote, eagle, owl, hawk. Behavior probably similar to other subspecies of Gray Fox. Their crepuscular and nocturnal habits allow them to live near human settlements practically undetected. They readily climb trees and are able to scale limbless trunks and jump from one branch to another. The long bushy tail balances it as it leaps from branch to branch. They will often seek refuge in trees when pursued and may rest or forage there as well. Unique among Canids, Gray Foxes have semi-retractile nails, a possible adaptation to their semi-arboreal life. Gray Fox tracks may be mistaken for cat tracks, as the nails do not always register as they do in all other Canids, particularly the nails on the hind feet. It has good night vision and hearing. They are slow runners on the ground and must use their camouflage to surprise their prey.

DISTRIBUTION *Native*: El Salvador, Guatemala, Honduras, Mexico. Found in southernmost Mexico, Guatemala, El Salvador, Honduras and Nicaragua.

HABITAT Dry, open country, and scrub lands. They seem to adapt fairly well to the presence of humans and the consequent disturbed habitats.

CONSERVATION STATUS Least Concern. *CITES*: Not listed. Not protected. In Central America, Gray Foxes are seldom exploited for the fur trade. They are mostly killed because of their occasional visits to poultry and other domestic animal pens. In Central America they has probably been affected also by the conversion of forested land into pastures and urban environment.

PHOTO CREDITS *William Rockey*, Calakmul (Mexico); *Elí García-Padilla*, Reserva de la Biósfera El Triunfo (Mexico); *Equal Exchange Cooperative*, Reserva de la Biósfera El Triunfo (Mexico); *Chico Sanchez*, Sierra Madre de Chiapas (Mexico).

Costa Rican Gray Fox

UROCYON CINEREOARGENTEUS COSTARICENSIS

BL: 48.3-68.5 cm. TL: 27.5-44.5 cm. H: 34-40 cm. W: 2.5-5 kg. SL: 10.3 cm. SW: 6.1 cm. DF: 42. CN: 66. A small-sized Canid, with a short muzzle, elongated and stout body, and relatively short legs. A small and very dark subspecies, less buffy, with more abundant black-tipped hairs, less white on underside and darker feet. Coat moderately long and coarse, grizzled gray in color, formed by the nearly equal mixture of black tips and white subterminal bands of the coarse hairs, with a mid-dorsal black band extending onto the tail. Top of head more finely grizzled gray. Throat, abdomen and inside of the legs are buffy white. A dull ochraceous tawny border to the white throat extends onto the flanks and underside of tail. Black patch on the sides of the face extending onto the lower jaw. Tip of ears mixed with black hairs, inner side whitish. Eyes with oval-shaped pupils. Tail is long and bushy, black on upper surface and black tipped, with cinnamon-buff underparts.

Urocyon cinereoargenteus costaricensis

OTHER NAMES Tree Fox. *French*: Renard gris. *German*: Costa-Rica-Graufuchs. *Spanish*: Gato cervan, gato de monte, zorro gris de Costa Rica, zorro plateado de Costa Rica, tigrillo. *Russian*: Костариканская серая лисица.

TAXONOMY Considered a subspecies of Gray Fox (*U. cinereoargenteus*). Subspecies designations are probably invalid.

SIMILAR SPECIES Guatemalan Gray Fox (*U. c. guatemalae*) is generally lighter in color throughout, with brighter, tawny shades about the ears and more white on underside of limbs and body. Panama Gray Fox (*U. c. furvus*) is much lighter and more buffy in color, with less abundant black-tipped hairs, underfur everywhere very much lighter; head more buffy and the limbs and feet lighter. Coyote, the only other Canid occurring in Costa Rica, is larger and mostly yellow gray in color.

REPRODUCTION *Gestation*: 50-60 days. *Young per birth*: 3-7. *Weaning*: Probably 42 days. *Sexual maturity*: 10-12 months. *Life span*: 5 years. *Breeding season*: Unknown. There is no specific information available for this subspecies, but probably similar to other subspecies of Gray Fox. They generally use burrows made by other species, including tree roots, and may be in a tunnel, in a rock pile or under a brush pile. Sometimes they have offspring in trees. Although ♀ expel ♂ from the dens after pups are born, the monogamous ♂ continues to forage for food for his family. The young are independent at 4-5 months of age.

BEHAVIOR *Social behavior*: Mated pairs, monogamous. *Diet*: Rodents, rabbits, lizards, fruits, insects and other arthropods, eggs and birds. *Main predators*: Unknown. There is no specific information available for this subspecies, but probably similar to other subspecies of Gray Fox. It is mainly nocturnal and seldom seen, although sometimes is active during the day. Territorial, marking its turf with urine. It is the only Canid that likes to climb trees, for which it is very agile, although nearly always seen on the ground. Usually travels alone, often trotting long distances on dirt roads or tracks; pairs or small groups are encountered on occasion.

DISTRIBUTION *Native*: Costa Rica. Occurs on Pacific slope at all elevations; on Caribbean slope absent at low elevations. Can become habituated to people and frequents some picnic areas (e.g., in Monteverde). It is more common in Guanacaste and in the Monteverde region.

HABITAT Found in a variety of habitats. Semi-arid fields, poor vegetation areas and scrub. In Costa Rica, it is found both in warm places (Santa Rosa, Guanacaste) and cold areas (Zarcero).

CONSERVATION STATUS Least Concern. *CITES*: Not listed. *Regional status*: Not protected (Costa Rica).

PHOTO CREDITS *Adrian Hepworth* and *Doug Greenberg*, Monteverde Cloud Forest Reserve (Costa Rica); *KFS from BKL*, Monteverde Cloud Forest Reserve (Costa Rica).

Panama and Venezuelan Gray Fox

UROCYON CINEREOARGENTEUS FURVUS AND VENEZUELAE

BL: 34 cm (♂). TL: 27 cm. H: 25-33 cm. W: Unknown. SL: 9.9 cm. SW: 5.4 cm. DF: 42. CN: 66.
A small-sized Canid, with a short muzzle, elongated and stout body, and relatively short legs.
The smallest subspecies, similar to Guatemalan Gray Fox, but paler, more buffy, and short
haired. Coat is short, grizzled gray in color, including the entire dorsal surface from between the
eyes to the root of the tail, flanks and thighs, with very little darker on the nape and mid-dorsal
area. Bases of the ears and sides of throat ochraceous. Superciliary spot whitish. Dusky brown
patch on the sides of the face extending onto the lower jaw. Tips of ears, forelegs and forefeet
paler ochraceous; hind feet grizzled grayish. Underparts and inner surface of limbs pale buffy.
Chin, upper lips, throat, a median line on lower side of neck, chest and inguinal region whitish.
Tail grizzled gray, brownish black dorsally, pale buffy ventrally.

ssp. *furvus*

ssp. *venezuelae*

ssp. *furvus*

Urocyon cinereoargenteus furvus

Urocyon cinereoargenteus venezuelae

OTHER NAMES Dusky Gray Fox, Tree Fox. *French*: Renard gris. *German*: Panama-Graufuchs, Venezuela-Graufuchs. *Spanish*: Micho de cerro (Panama), gato cervan, gato de monte, zorro gatuno, zorra gris, zorro plateado, lumba. *Russian*: Панамская серая лисица (*furvus*), Венесуэльская серая лисица (*venezuelae*). *Chibcha*: Fo, fu.

TAXONOMY Considered a subspecies of Gray Fox (*U. cinereoargenteus*).

SIMILAR SPECIES Venezuelan Gray Fox is darker than Panama Gray Fox, which is the smallest and palest subspecies, with the shortest pelage. Northern subspecies of Gray Fox are much larger. Coyote is larger and mostly yellow gray in color, and does not run with tail horizontal. Crab-Eating Fox is larger, with a shorter tail, smaller ears, and a less patterned gray-brown pelage.

REPRODUCTION *Gestation*: 53-63 days. *Young per birth*: 2-7. *Weaning*: 42 days. *Sexual maturity*: 10-12 months. *Life span*: 10 years, 15 years in captivity. *Breeding season*: Probably in February or March. There is no specific information available for these subspecies, but probably similar to other subspecies of Gray Fox.

BEHAVIOR *Social behavior*: Solitary or mated pairs and their offspring of the year; monogamous, with occasional polygyny; it is not known if breeding pairs remain together during consecutive years. *Diet*: Omnivorous, consuming primarily rabbits and rodents, insects, birds, natural fruits and nuts, and sometimes carrion; fruit and nut consumption often increases as availability of these foods increases. There is no specific information available for these subspecies, but probably similar to other subspecies of Gray Fox. More active at night than during the day. No information has been reported on specific hunting behavior. Gray Foxes are notable tree climbers, and can climb branchless, vertical trunks, as well as jump vertically from branch to branch.

DISTRIBUTION *Native*: Colombia, Panama, Venezuela, probably Peru. *U. c. furvus* is found in W Panama. *U. c. venezuelae* is found in N Colombia and N Venezuela. Subspecific status of Gray Fox recently spotted in Tabaconas-Namballe National Sanctuary, in N Peru, is uncertain; this represents the southernmost record of the species in the Americas.

HABITAT Northernmost forest montane regions. In Panama it is found in semi-arid savanna country. It may persist or even increase in areas modified by human activities.

CONSERVATION STATUS Least Concern. *CITES*: Not listed. *Regional status*: Not protected (Colombia, Panama, Venezuela); Data Deficient (Peru).

PHOTO CREDITS *Rodion Raskolnikov*, Parque Jaime Duque (Colombia)*; María José Zamora Rodriguez*, Zoológico Santacruz (Colombia); *Brian Gratwicke*, Parque Summit Municipal (Panama).

Santa Cruz Island Fox

UROCYON LITTORALIS SANTACRUZAE

BL: 41.5-46.9 cm (♂), 43.1-54.1 cm (♀). TL: 19.5-28 cm. H: 30.5-33 cm. W: 1.3-2.3 kg. SL: 9.7 cm. SW: 5.6 cm. DF: 42. CN: 66. A very small-sized Canid, the smallest Fox in North America, with similar markings as the Gray Fox but significantly smaller. The smallest subspecies of Island Fox, with shorter legs, and overall color darker and grayer than southern subspecies. Coat is short, grizzled grayish white and black. Side of the neck and limbs are cinnamon rufous in color. Abdomen is dull white with intermediate areas of pale rusty. Ears are grizzled dorsally, changing to light cinnamon rufous on the base and sides. Head is gray with black patches on the sides of the muzzle. White patches on the muzzle extending behind the lateral black patches to the cheek, which blends into the white throat. Lips are black. Tail is gray, rusty underneath, with a distinctive narrow black stripe along the dorsal surface, and a black tip. Females are smaller than males.

Urocyon littoralis santacruzae

OTHER NAMES Island Fox, California Channel Island Fox, Channel Islands Fox, Island Gray Fox. *French*: Renard gris insulaire. *German*: Santa-Cruz-Graufuchs. *Spanish*: Zorro isleño de Santa Cruz, zorro gris de la isla de Santa Cruz. *Russian*: Серая лисица острова Санта-Круз.

TAXONOMY There are six subspecies of Island Fox (Hall, 1981), each of which is native to a specific Channel Island, and which evolved there independently of the others: *U. l. littoralis* (San Miguel Island Fox); *U. l. santarosae* (Santa Rosa Island Fox); *U. l. santacruzae* (Santa Cruz Island Fox); *U. l. catalinae* (Santa Catalina Island Fox); *U. l. clementae* (San Clemente Island Fox); *U. l. dickeyi* (San Nicolas Island Fox). These subspecies are virtually identical in appearance and capable of interbreeding, but have genetic and phenotypic distinctions, such as the number of tail vertebrae.

REPRODUCTION *Gestation*: 50-53 days. *Young per birth*: 2-3, up to 5 depending on food availability. *Weaning*: 56-70 days. *Sexual maturity*: 12-24 months. *Life span*: 8-10 years. *Breeding season*: From February to March.

BEHAVIOR *Social behavior*: Monogamous pairs. *Diet*: Insects, deer mice, birds and eggs, lizards and fruits, with the proportion of each changing throughout the year as availability changes. *Main predators*: Golden eagle. Crepuscular, but may be active throughout a 24-hour period. Average home range size is 0.34 km² on Santa Cruz Island, which is the smallest home range size reported for any Canid.

DISTRIBUTION *Native*: United States. Restricted to Santa Cruz Island, the largest of the eight Channel Islands.

HABITAT Grassland, chaparral and coastal sage scrub, and woodland and forest communities, on Santa Cruz Island. The diversity of terrain and temperature, along with the availability of year-round fresh water in many canyons, supports a higher diversity of habitat types and species than any other Channel Island. Foxes on Santa Cruz Island use all these habitat types. Although Santa Cruz Island has had limited human development compared to other Channel Islands, it has nonetheless been heavily impacted by livestock grazing. The Central Valley appears to be superior habitat for Foxes on this island.

CONSERVATION STATUS Near Threatened. *CITES*: Not listed. *Regional status*: Recently delisted due to recovery (USA). Population of this subspecies dropped from 1,300 in 1993 to as low as 50 Foxes in 2001, including 10 pairs brought into captivity in 2002. Predation by golden eagles was suspected of causing this decline. Feral pigs also cause severe damage to its habitat, particularly streamside vegetation in canyon bottoms, and may impact water sources. Grazing by domestic livestock may have changed vegetation composition and structure, thereby reducing available cover and making Foxes more susceptible to eagle predation. Beginning in 2003, captive-bred Foxes were released back into the wild, and by 2016, populations had increased to 2,100 adults. This population has been brought back from near extinction, primarily through the establishment of an active program to remove golden eagles and pigs from the island, and a captive breeding program that provides a safety net for the population.

PHOTO CREDITS *Gary Kavanagh, Henri Thomassen, Laura Keene, temescal1859,* Santa Cruz Island, CA (USA).

Santa Rosa Island Fox
UROCYON LITTORALIS SANTAROSAE

BL: 44.4-47.5 cm (♂), 44.5-47 cm (♀). TL: 21.4-30 cm. H: 30.5-33 cm. W: 1.3-2.3 kg. SL: 9.9 cm. SW: 5.6 cm. DF: 42. CN: 66. A very small-sized Canid, the smallest Fox in North America, with similar markings as the Gray Fox but significantly smaller. This subspecies of Island Fox has the longest ears, but otherwise is virtually identical in appearance. Coat is short, grizzled grayish white and black. Side of the neck and limbs are cinnamon rufous in color. Abdomen is dull white with intermediate areas of pale rusty. Ears are grizzled dorsally, changing to light cinnamon rufous on the base and sides. Head is gray with black patches on the sides of the muzzle. White patches on the muzzle extending behind the lateral black patches to the cheek, which blends into the white throat. Lips are black. Tail is gray, rusty underneath, with a distinctive narrow black stripe along the dorsal surface, and a black tip. Females are smaller than males.

Young

Urocyon littoralis santarosae

OTHER NAMES Island Fox, California Channel Island Fox, Channel Islands Fox, Island Gray Fox. *French*: Renard gris insulaire. *German*: Santa-Rosa-Graufuchs. *Spanish*: Zorro isleño de Santa Rosa, zorro gris de la isla de Santa Rosa. *Russian*: Серая лисица острова Санта-Роза .

TAXONOMY Considered a subspecies of *U. littoralis* (Island Fox).

REPRODUCTION *Gestation*: 50-53 days. *Young per birth*: 2-3, up to 5 depending on food availability. *Weaning*: 56-70 days. *Sexual maturity*: 12-24 months. *Life span*: 8-10 years. *Breeding season*: From February to March. Most young are born in late April, with biparental care exhibited once the pups emerge from the den in June. When pups are born, their eyesight is limited and their pelage is dark gray to black. By the end of July or beginning of August, the adult coloration with more rust color in the pelage is achieved and the pups are close to adult size. Pups start foraging around the natal area with their parents at the beginning of the summer and dispersal begins in late September, with final dispersal from the natal area by December.

BEHAVIOR *Social behavior*: Monogamous ♂-♀ pairs. *Diet*: Diverse diet, mostly based on availability of resources, which include deer mice, beetles, Jerusalem crickets, and ice plant in addition to lizards and fruits from toyon (*Heteromeles arbutifolia*) and manzanita (*Arctostaphylos* sp.). Other items not as prevalent in the diet include crustaceans, bird eggs, ungulate and sea mammal carrion; there are rare instances of Island Foxes eating island spotted skunks (*Spilogale gracilis amphiala*), an endemic carnivore found on Santa Rosa and Santa Cruz. *Main predators*: Golden eagle; because they evolved without predators, they do not fear introduced predators, humans, cars or other potential threats. Peak activity periods follow a crepuscular pattern, although there is diurnal activity as well. Territoriality seems to be displayed only during the denning season. Foxes on Santa Rosa Island have the largest home range size reported for any Island Fox population, 3.39 km².

DISTRIBUTION *Native*: United States. Restricted to Santa Rosa Island (California Channel Islands).

HABITAT Grassland, coastal sage scrub, lupine scrub, chaparral, mixed and riparian woodland, and coastal marsh areas on Santa Rosa Island. Shrub and woodland habitats provide more cover and tend to support higher Fox densities than grassland habitats. Santa Rosa Island has more diverse habitats and terrain along with more annual rainfall than S islands.

CONSERVATION STATUS Near Threatened. *CITES*: Not listed. *Regional status*: Recently delisted due to recovery (USA). Populations on Santa Rosa declined from 1,780 animals in 1994 to only 14 individuals in 1999, all of which were brought into captivity. The primary cause of decline was predation by non-native golden eagles (prior to the 1990s, golden eagles did not occur on the Channel Islands, possibly because they were kept away by nesting bald eagles, which were extirpated). Beginning in 2003, captive-bred Foxes were released back into the wild. By 2016, the population had increased to an estimated 1,200 adults on Santa Rosa Island.

PHOTO CREDITS *Michael Field* and *Douglas Mason*, Santa Rosa Island, CA (USA).

Santa Catalina Island Fox
UROCYON LITTORALIS CATALINAE

BL: 46.5-50.8 cm (♂), 45.8-49.3 cm (♀). TL: 23.5-31.6 cm. H: 30.5-33 cm. W: 1.2-2.7 kg (♂), 1.1-2.7 kg (♀). SL: 10.1 cm. SW: 5.8 cm. DF: 42. CN: 66. A very small-sized Canid, the smallest Fox in North America, with similar markings as the Gray Fox but significantly smaller. The largest subspecies, with the longest tail, but otherwise is virtually identical in appearance. Coat is short, grizzled grayish white and black. Side of the neck and limbs are cinnamon rufous in color. Abdomen is dull white with intermediate areas of pale rusty. Ears are grizzled dorsally, changing to light cinnamon rufous on the base and sides. Head is gray with black patches on the sides of the muzzle. White patches on the muzzle extending behind the lateral black patches to the cheek, which blends into the white throat. Lips are black. Tail is gray, rusty underneath, with a distinctive narrow black stripe along the dorsal surface, and a black tip. Females are smaller than males.

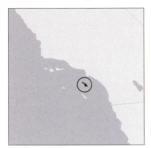

Urocyon littoralis catalinae

OTHER NAMES Island Fox, California Channel Island Fox, Channel Islands Fox, Island Gray Fox. *French*: Renard gris insulaire. *German*: Santa-Catalina-Graufuchs. *Spanish*: Zorro isleño de Santa Catalina, zorro gris de la isla de Santa Catalina. *Russian*: Серая лисица острова Санта-Катапина.

TAXONOMY Considered a subspecies of *U. littoralis* (Island Fox).

REPRODUCTION *Gestation*: 50-53 days. *Young per birth*: 2-3, up to 5 depending on food availability. *Weaning*: 56-70 days. *Sexual maturity*: 12-24 months. *Life span*: 8-10 years. *Breeding season*: From February to March. It is believed ♀ are only in estrus for 40 hours, once a year and only when a ♂ is nearby. Births occur in late April. Pups are born in simple dens. The ♀ enlarges a depression under shrubs, downed trees or large rocks by digging. While the pups are attended only by the mother in the den for the first weeks, the ♂ provides food to the ♀. By early June, pups emerge from the den and begin foraging with both parents throughout the summer. ♂ pups tend to disperse a great distance from the parental territory, while ♀ pups may stay closer even as they reach adulthood.

BEHAVIOR *Social behavior*: Monogamous pairs. *Diet*: Mice, ground squirrels, lizards, birds, berries, insects and cactus fruit. *Main predators*: Golden eagle. Crepuscular, but may be active throughout a 24-hour period. The home range size varies according to age, gender and population density. Communication between Foxes is accomplished via auditory, olfactory and visual cues. They scent mark their territories. Scat piles may be seen along roads, trails or other prominent locations. They are often heard barking and yipping to each other. They are very agile and can climb trees and cliffs easily. Acceptance of humans varies between islands. On the islands where encounters are more common, Foxes appear to be less anxious around people.

DISTRIBUTION *Native*: United States. Restricted to Santa Catalina Island (California Channel Islands).

HABITAT Coastal scrub on Santa Catalina Island, although this habitat has been heavily modified by the effects of introduced grazing animals and other human impacts. The S islands (Santa Catalina, San Clemente and San Nicolas) have greater development impacts such as naval bases and the town of Avalon.

CONSERVATION STATUS Near Threatened. *CITES*: Not listed. *Regional status*: Threatened (USA). On Santa Catalina, Island Foxes were nearly completely eliminated on the E portion of the island by a canine distemper outbreak that swept through the population in 1999, with only about 110 adult Foxes remaining on the island in 2000. Translocations from the W portion of the island, beginning in 2003, have resulted in a steadily growing population, estimated at approximately 1,852 foxes in 2013. About 80% of the Fox population now lives on the island's E end. A serious health concern is an unusual ear cancer detected, especially in older Foxes. Vehicle trauma, however, continues to be the number one cause of Fox mortalities. The outbreak of another virulent canine disease, such as canine distemper virus or rabies, continues to be the greatest threat to the long-term survival of this subspecies due to its restricted distribution and small population size, as well as the continued presence of Domestic Dogs on the island.

PHOTO CREDITS *Steve Garret* and *Kat Kiloueka*, Santa Catalina Island, CA (USA).

San Clemente Island Fox
UROCYON LITTORALIS CLEMENTAE

BL: 43.5-48 cm (♂), 42.5-47.5 cm (♀). TL: 23-29.5 cm. H: 30.5-33 cm. W: 1.3-2.3 kg. SL: 9.7 cm. SW: 5.6 cm. DF: 42. CN: 66. A very small-sized Canid, the smallest Fox in North America, with similar markings as the Gray Fox but significantly smaller. Overall appearance of this subspecies is lighter than northern subspecies, with a little less black at the tip of the guard hairs. Coat is short, grizzled grayish white and black. A brown phase may occur. Side of the neck and limbs are cinnamon rufous in color. Abdomen is dull white with intermediate areas of pale rusty. Ears are grizzled dorsally, changing to light cinnamon rufous on the base and sides. Head is gray with black patches on the sides of the muzzle. White patches on the muzzle extending behind the lateral black patches to the cheek, which blends into the white throat. Lips are black. Tail is gray, rusty underneath, with a distinctive narrow black stripe along the dorsal surface, and a black tip. Females are smaller than males.

Young

brown phase

Urocyon littoralis clementae

OTHER NAMES Island Fox, California Channel Island Fox, Channel Islands Fox, Island Gray Fox. *French*: Renard gris insulaire. *German*: San-Clemente-Graufuchs. *Spanish*: Zorro isleño de San Clemente, zorro gris de la isla de San Clemente. *Russian*: Серая лисица острова Сан-Клементе.

TAXONOMY Considered a subspecies of *U. littoralis* (Island Fox).

REPRODUCTION *Gestation*: 50-53 days. *Young per birth*: 2-3, up to 5 depending on food availability. *Weaning*: 56-70 days. *Sexual maturity*: 12-24 months. *Life span*: 8-10 years. *Breeding season*: Earlier than in other subspecies, from December to March. Parturition has been documented as early as February on San Clemente Island. Juveniles remain with their parents until about August or September, and most dispersal from natal areas apparently occurs in late fall or early winter. Dens are almost exclusively in rock crevices, contrary to the variety of locations described for other subspecies. They move litters a short distance from the natal den 4–7 weeks after parturition, similar to Red Foxes that move offspring 1 to 3 times.

BEHAVIOR *Social behavior*: Monogamous ♂-♀ pairs. *Diet*: Insects, deer mice, birds and eggs, lizards and fruits, with the proportion of each changing throughout the year as availability changes. They consume few native fruits, the exception being prickly pear cactus, which apparently is less palatable to goats and pigs, and therefore expanded considerably in abundance and distribution with the elimination of competing vegetation. This subspecies has been identified as a predator of the severely endangered race of the loggerhead shrike (*Lanius ludovicianus mearnsi*). *Main predators*: Because they evolved without predators, they do not fear introduced predators, humans, cars or other potential threats. Crepuscular, but may be active throughout a 24-hour period. They occupy relatively stable, year-round territories. Home range sizes on San Clemente Island average 0.77 km².

DISTRIBUTION *Native*: United States. Restricted to San Clemente Island (California Channel Islands).

HABITAT Coastal scrub, although this habitat has been heavily modified by the effects of introduced grazing animals and other human impacts (the island is owned and managed by the US Navy). On this island, densities appear to be higher in maritime desert scrub than in annual grasslands; ecological communities have been markedly impacted and reduced, and the distribution of woodlands and shrublands is severely restricted to certain deep canyons.

CONSERVATION STATUS Near Threatened. *CITES*: Not listed. Estimated population around 1,100 in 2011. A small area of stabilized sand dunes on the N end of the island support the highest recorded density of Foxes. Main threats include habitat loss by livestock grazing, introduction of non-native ungulates, and the spread of non-native plants and diseases. Island Foxes may lack resistance to some diseases found on the mainland, due to their geographic isolation, and may be potentially susceptible to dramatic die-offs from exposure to diseases such as rabies or certain strains of canine distemper. Population declined by over 90% during 1999-2000 due to disease most likely introduced by Domestic Dogs.

PHOTO CREDITS *Sarah Corrice, Nicole Desnoyers* and *Navy Currents Magazine*, San Clemente Island, CA (USA); *Sergey Chichagov*, Santa Barbara Zoo, CA (USA).

San Miguel Island Fox

UROCYON LITTORALIS LITTORALIS

BL: 48.8-51.5 cm (♂), 46.8-48.6 cm (♀). TL: 15.7-21 cm. H: 30.5-33 cm. W: 1.3-2.3 kg (♂), 1.1-2.7 kg (♀). SL: 10.6 cm. SW: 5.8 cm. DF: 42. CN: 66. A very small-sized Canid, the smallest Fox in North America, with similar markings as the Gray Fox but significantly smaller. Second largest subspecies, with the shortest tail (average 15 vertebrae). Coat is short, grizzled grayish white and black. Side of the neck and limbs are cinnamon rufous in color. Abdomen is dull white with intermediate areas of pale rusty. Ears are grizzled dorsally, changing to light cinnamon rufous on the base and sides. Head is gray with black patches on the sides of the muzzle. White patches on the muzzle extending behind the lateral black patches to the cheek, which blends into the white throat. Lips are black. Tail is gray, rusty underneath, with a distinctive narrow black stripe along the dorsal surface, and a black tip. Females are smaller than males.

Urocyon littoralis littoralis

OTHER NAMES Island Fox, California Channel Island Fox, Channel Islands Fox, Island Gray Fox. *French*: Renard gris insulaire. *German*: San-Miguel-Graufuchs. *Spanish*: Zorro isleño de San Miguel, zorro gris de la isla de San Miguel. *Russian*: Серая лисица острова Сан-Мигель.

TAXONOMY Considered a subspecies of *U. littoralis* (Island Fox). Genetically, it is most closely related to Foxes on Santa Rosa.

REPRODUCTION *Gestation*: 50-53 days. *Young per birth*: 2-3, up to 5 depending on food availability. *Weaning*: 56-70 days. *Sexual maturity*: 12-24 months. *Life span*: 8-10 years. *Breeding season*: From February to March.

BEHAVIOR *Social behavior*: Monogamous pairs. *Diet*: Insects, deer mice, birds and eggs, lizards and fruits. *Main predators*: Golden eagle. Crepuscular, but may be active throughout a 24-hour period.

DISTRIBUTION *Native*: United States. Restricted to San Miguel Island (California Channel Islands).

HABITAT Coastal scrub on San Miguel Island. This island has one of the windiest, foggiest and most maritime climates of all the Channel Islands. Steep bluffs line the coast, especially along the S shoreline. Domestic sheep grazing helped convert much of the island's shrub vegetation to alien annual grasslands, and many of the ravines that cut across the island are a result of erosion from years of extensive livestock grazing, military bomb testing, and agriculture; activities that no longer exist on the island. This island is owned by the US Navy, and most of the shoreline is closed to the public; there are no roads or motorized vehicles and very few developed areas. Foxes on San Miguel Island currently experience little human impact compared to Foxes on other islands.

CONSERVATION STATUS Near Threatened. *CITES*: Not listed. *Regional status*: Delisted due to recovery (USA). By 2000, this subspecies had declined to only 15 individuals, which were brought into captivity. Beginning in 2003, they were released back into the wild. By 2016, populations had increased to an estimated 700 animals on San Miguel Island. Predation by golden eagles appeared to be the primary cause of death.

San Nicolas Island Fox

UROCYON LITTORALIS DICKEYI

BL: 40-47.3 cm (♂), 46.3-50.2 cm (♀). TL: 14-32.2 cm. H: 30.5-33 cm. W: 1.3-2.3 kg (♂), 1.1-2.7 kg (♀). SL: 9.5 cm. SW: 5.6 cm. DF: 42. CN: 66. A very small-sized Canid, the smallest Fox in North America, with similar markings as the Gray Fox but significantly smaller. Lighter in color than other subspecies, with the longest legs, and the largest number of bones in the tail (average 22 vertebrae). Coat is short, grizzled grayish white and black. A brown phase may occur. Side of the neck and limbs are cinnamon rufous in color. Abdomen is dull white with intermediate areas of pale rusty. Ears are grizzled dorsally, changing to light cinnamon rufous on the base and sides. Head is gray with black patches on the sides of the muzzle. White patches on the muzzle extending behind the lateral black patches to the cheek, which blends into the white throat. Lips are black. Tail is gray, rusty underneath, with a distinctive narrow black stripe along the dorsal surface, and a black tip.

Urocyon littoralis dickeyi

OTHER NAMES Island Fox, California Channel Island Fox, Channel Islands Fox, Island Gray Fox. *French*: Renard gris insulaire. *German*: San-Nicolas-Graufuchs. *Spanish*: Zorro isleño, zorro gris de las islas. *Russian*: Серая лисица острова Сан-Николас.

TAXONOMY Considered a subspecies of *U. littoralis* (Island Fox).

SIMILAR SPECIES On average, Foxes are largest on Santa Catalina and smallest on Santa Cruz, although these differences are minor. Gray Fox is larger, with more tail vertebrae and therefore a longer tail, and somewhat darker coloration.

REPRODUCTION *Gestation*: 50-53 days. *Young per birth*: 2-3, up to 5 depending on food availability. *Weaning*: 56-70 days. *Sexual maturity*: 12-24 months. *Life span*: 8-10 years. *Breeding season*: From February to March. Births occur in late April.

BEHAVIOR *Social behavior*: Monogamous pairs. *Diet*: Insects, deer mice, birds and eggs, lizards and fruits, with the proportion of each changing throughout the year as availability changes; precipitation has a great influence on diet patterns. *Main predators*: None. Crepuscular, but may be active throughout a 24-hour period. The home range size varies according to age, gender and population density. On San Nicolas Island, home range size averages 1.81 km² during mating phase with significantly smaller home ranges, averaging 0.65 km², during post-mating, pupping and non-reproductive phases; the smaller home range size can likely be explained by activity being centralized around a den site during the post-mating and pupping seasons.

DISTRIBUTION *Native*: United States. Restricted to San Miguel Island (California Channel Islands). San Miguel Island has one of the windiest, foggiest and most maritime climates of all the Channel Islands. Steep bluffs line the coast, especially along the S shoreline.

HABITAT Coastal scrub, although this habitat has been heavily modified by the effects of introduced grazing animals and other human impacts (this island is owned and managed by the US Navy, and is used for weapons testing). They prefer the stabilized dunes and coastal sage scrub on the W end of the island, over grasslands and barren cliffs in the S and E of the island. Most trees and shrubs have been eliminated by sheep.

CONSERVATION STATUS Near Threatened. *CITES*: Not listed. In contrast to the other populations, the San Nicolas Island Fox population has remained relatively stable over the past 10 years. Since 2000, estimated population size has fluctuated from 350 to 800 individuals. Potential threats include competition with feral cats, vehicle strikes and the introduction of infectious disease.

SKULLS OF CANIDS

1- **Maned Wolf** *Chrysocyon brachyurus* (SL: 24.8 cm, SW: 13.3 cm). 2- **Bush Dog** *Speothos venaticus* (SL: 12.4 cm, SW: 7.6 cm). 3- **Southern Crab-Eating Fox** *Cerdocyon thous entrerianus* (SL: 12.2 cm, SW: 7.4 cm). Photo credits: *Phil Myers*, Museum of Zoology, University of Michigan-Ann Arbor, USA. To the same scale.

1- **Northern Pampas Fox** *Lycalopex gymnocercus gymnocercus* (SL: 14.3 cm, SW: 7.6 cm). 2- **Patagonian Culpeo Fox** *Lycalopex culpaeus magellanicus* (SL: 16.5 cm, SW: 8.9 cm). 3- **Monte Desert Chilla** *Lycalopex griseus gracilis* (SL: 14.1 cm, SW: 7.4 cm). 4- **Sechuran Fox** *Lycalopex sechurae* (SL: 11.2 cm, SW: 6.3 cm). 5- **Northern Chilla** *Lycalopex griseus domeykoanus* (SL: 11.1 cm, SW: 5.8 cm). 6- **Eastern Gray Fox** *Urocyon cinereoargenteus cinereoargenteus* (SL: 11 cm, SW: 6.9 cm). Photo credits: *Phil Myers*, Museum of Zoology, University of Michigan-Ann Arbor (1, 2, 6); *Elena Vivar*, Museo de Historia Natural, Universidad Nacional Mayor de San Marcos, Peru (3-5). To the same scale.

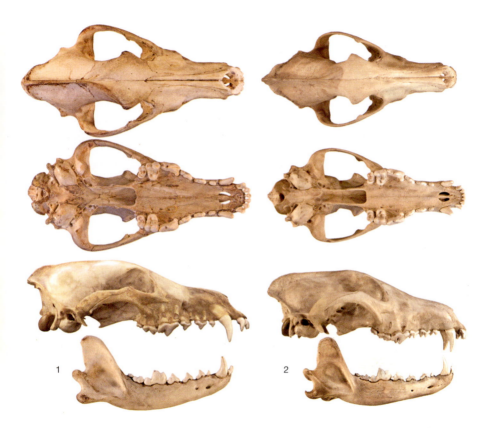

1- **Gray Wolf** *Canis lupus nubilus* (SL: 23.8 cm, SW: 13.9 cm). 2- **Red Wolf** *Canis rufus* (SL: 21.9 cm, SW: 11.7 cm). Photo credits: *Phil Myers*, Museum of Zoology, University of Michigan-Ann Arbor, USA (1, 2). To the same scale.

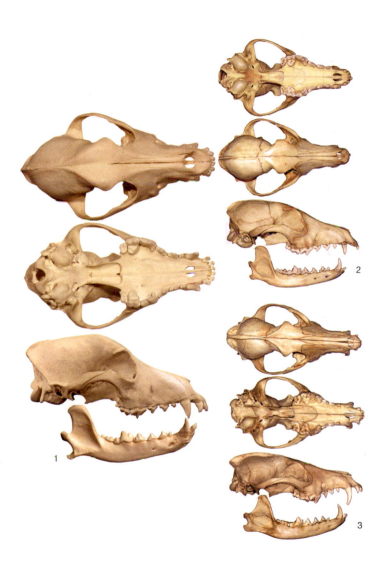

1- **Domestic Dog** *Canis lupus familiaris* (SL: 17.2 cm, SW: 9.6 cm). 2- **Black-Backed Jackal** *Lupulella mesomelas* (SL: 14.5 cm, SW: 8.6 cm). 3- **Side-Striped Jackal** *Lupulella adustus* (SL: 15.2 cm, SW: 8.0 cm). Photo credits: *Ádám Pereszlényi*, Skullbase.info (1); *Prof. Lorenzo Rook* and S*averio Bartolini*, Earth Science Department, University of Florence, Italy (2, 3). To the same scale.

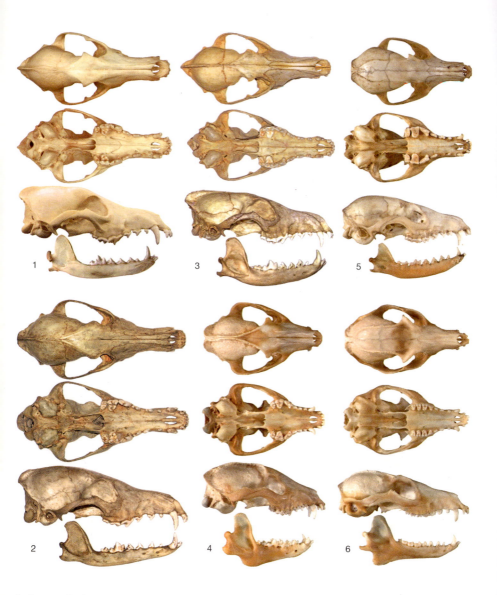

1- **Coyote** *Canis latrans* (SL: 17.5 cm, SW: 10.4 cm). 2- **Ethiopian Wolf** *Canis simensis* (SL: 18.7 cm, SW: 10.1 cm). 3- **African Wolf** *Canis lupaster* (SL: 14 cm, SW: 7.7 cm). 4- **Raccoon Dog** *Nyctereutes procyonoides* (SL: 12.1 cm, SW 6.8 cm). 5- **Indian Fox** *Vulpes bengalensis* (SL: 11.1 cm, SW: 6.4 cm). 6- **Bat-Eared Fox** *Octocyon megalotis* (SL: 11 cm, SW 6.2 cm). Photo credits: *Hideo Takahashi* (1), *Prof. Lorenzo Rook* and *Saverio Bartolini*, Earth Science Department, University of Florence, Italy (2, 3), *Phil Myers*, Museum of Zoology, University of Michigan-Ann Arbor, USA (4-6). To the same scale.

1

3

5

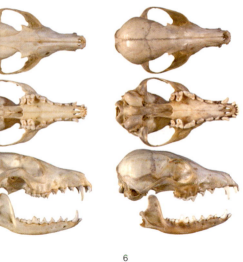

2

4

6

1- **Northern Plains Red Fox** *Vulpes fulva regalis* (SL: 14.5, SW: 8.2 cm). 2- **Swift Fox** *Vulpes velox* (SL: 11.2 cm, SW: 6.4 cm). 3- **Arctic Fox** *Vulpes lagopus* (SL: 11.7 cm, SW: 6.9 cm). 4- **Rüppell's Fox** *Vulpes rueppellii zarudnyi* (SL: 10.8 cm, SW: 5.8 cm). 5- **Fennec Fox** *Vulpes zerda* (SL: 8.3 cm, SW: 4.7 cm). 6- **Corsac Fox** *Vulpes corsac* (SL: 10.6 cm, SW: 6.3 cm). Photo credits: *Phil Myers*, Museum of Zoology, University of Michigan-Ann Arbor, USA. To the same scale.

GLOSSARY

Albinistic Absence or reduction of pigmentation, resulting in a completely or partly white animal.

Alloparenting A system of parenting in which individuals other than the parents act in a parental role.

Allopatry Occurring in separate, nonoverlapping geographic areas.

Alpha The reproductively dominant member of a social unit.

Altricial A mammal that is born with little, if any, hair, is unable to feed itself, and initially has poor sensory and thermoregulatory abilities.

Arboreal Living or active in trees.

Auditory bulla The rounded bony capsule surrounding the inner ear of many mammals. Also knows as tympanic bulla.

Baculum A rod-shaped bone that strengthens the penis in some mammalian species.

Boreal Coniferous or needle-leaf forest zone predominant between the Arctic and the temperate deciduous forest zone.

Cache A hiding place used for storing food if there is an abundance of meat from a kill.

Canine The sharp, pointed teeth, immediately behind the incisors, that carnivores use to pierce and tear the flesh of their prey.

Carnassials Pair of shearing teeth for processing meat formed by the upper fourth premolar and the lower first molar. All carnivorans possess a pair of carnassial teeth.

Carnivorous Animals whose diet comprises predominantly animal matter, including insects and crustacea as opposed to vegetable matter.

Carrion Decaying flesh of dead animals.

Cerrado A vast tropical savanna ecoregion in the center of Brazil, which includes forest savanna, wooded savanna, park savanna, gramineous-woody savanna, wetlands and gallery forests.

CITES (abbrev.) The Convention on International Trade in Endangered Species of Wild Fauna and Flora.

Clade Group of organisms with a common ancestor, often equal to a monophyletic group.

Cline A gradient in a measurable characteristic, such as size and color, showing geographic differentiation.

Color phase The color of an animal's pelage (fur), which is determined by genetics and may vary within a population.

Commensal A relationship between species in which one benefits and the other is neither benefited nor harmed.

Conspecific A member of the same species.

Crepuscular Active in twilight, including dawn and dusk, but avoiding the darkest hours of night.

Den A shelter, often a small cave or hole dug out of the ground, to protect the breeding female and her young pups from weather and other animals.

Dewclaw A vestigial digit found on the foot of most mammals, normally growing high on the animal's leg in digitigrade species, that has become functionless through evolution.

Digitigrade Walking on the toes and not touching the ground with the heels.

Disjunct Not occurring continuously over a region, but localized into widely separated populations.

Dispersal The movements of animals, often as they reach maturity, away from their previous home range.

Distal Situated away from the center of the body or point of attachment.

Diurnal Active during the day.

Dorsal On or referring to the upper side or back of an animal.

Ecosystem A community of organisms and their physical environment.

Endemic A group or taxon that is local and of limited distribution.

Estrus Period during which a female mammal is sexually receptive to the male and in which fertile mating can take place.

Extant Still in existence; not destroyed, lost, or extinct.

Extinct Refers to a species that no longer survives anywhere.

Feral Domesticated animals that have gone wild.

Forb Broad-leaved, non-woody plant.

Fulvous Tawny; dull yellow, with a mixture of gray and brown.

Gallery forest Trees and other vegetation lining watercourses, thereby extending forested habitat into savanna and arid zones.

Gestation Period of development between conception and birth.

Guard hairs The long outer hairs of an animal's coat that keep the downy underfur from getting dirty or wet.

Hibernation A deep state of reduced metabolic activity and lowered body temperature that may last for weeks or months.

Hierarchy A social structure in which the animals in a group can be arranged according to dominance.

Hock The backward-pointing joint in the hind leg of a quadrupedal animal between the knee and the foot.

Holarctic The Palearctic and Nearctic biogeographic regions combined.

Home range An area routinely occupied by an individual or group.

Hybrid The offspring of parents from two closely related species.

Inguinal Of or in the groin.

Insectivorous Animals whose diet comprises predominantly invertebrates.

Latrine A place where animals regularly deposit their excrement.

Mammae Milk-secreting organs usually arranged in pairs on the ventral surface of the body.

Maquis Dense secondary scrub dominated by heathers and strawberry trees (Mediterranean).

Melanistic Color variation in which black pigment predominates to such an extent that the pelage of the animal is partly or entirely black.

Midden A pile of dung droppings, deposited regularly to mark an individual's territory.

Miocene The geological time period that lasted from about 23.8 to 5.6 million years ago.

Molars Permanent cheek teeth near the back of the jaw in mammals. Molars are not replaced during life.

Monoestrous Having only one estrous cycle per year.

Monogamous A breeding system in which a male and female mate only with one another.

Monophyletic A group (or clade) that shares a common ancestor.

Monotypic A taxonomic category that includes only one form (e.g., a genus that includes only one species; a species that includes no subspecies).

Montane Of or inhabiting the biogeographic zone of relatively moist, cool upland slopes below timberline dominated by large coniferous trees.

Nearctic The biogeographic region that includes temperate North America.

Neotropical The biogeographic region that includes South and Central America, the West Indies and tropical Mexico.

New World A general descriptive term encompassing the Nearctic and Neotropical biogeographic regions.

Niche The role of an organism in its environment; multidimensional, with habitat and behavioral components.

Nocturnal Active during the night.

Old World A general term that usually describes a species or group as being from Eurasia or Africa.

Oligocene The geological time period occurring from about 33.7 to 23.8 million years ago.

Omnivorous Feeding on both animal material (insects or meat) and vegetable matter.

Opportunistic Referring to animals that capitalize on opportunities to gain food with the least expenditure of energy.

Pair bond The social ties that keep members of a mated pair together, usually reinforced by mutual grooming, marking, calling, aggression toward outsiders, etc.

Pelage An animal's coat of fur or hair.

Phylogeny Genealogical relationships that attempt to reconstruct historical relationships among various lineages of organisms.

Pleistocene In general, the time of the great ice ages; geological period variously considered to include the last 1 to 1.8 million years.

Pliocene The geological period preceding the Pleistocene; the last subdivision of what is known as the Tertiary; lasted from 5.5 to 1.8 million years ago.

Polyandry A breeding system in which one female mates with two or more males.

Polyestrous Having more than one estrous cycle during a specific time of the year.

Polygyny A breeding system in which one male mates with two or more females.

Premolars Cheek teeth near the front of the jaw in mammals; deciduous (milk) premolars or permanent premolars.

Protractile claws Claws passively retracted within the paw, which can be actively extended out of the paw.

Regurgitation Disgorging partially digested food as nourishment, mainly for pups and young animals.

Rendezvous site An aboveground area where pups are taken when they are old enough to leave the birth den.

Rhinarium The anterior naked part of the snout, usually in fur-covered mammals the most rugose pad surrounding the nostrils.

Riparian Occurring on the banks of a river, stream or wetland.

Rostrum The facial part of the skull in front of the orbits.

Sagittal crest A ridge of bone developed along the midline of the top of the skull, usually enabling attachment of stronger temporal muscles.

Sarcoptic mange A skin condition caused by a parasitic mite, characterized by intense itching and hair loss, resulting in hypothermia and death.

Savanna A major biome or ecological zone where annual rainfall is insufficient to support forest cover, but where grass predominates and there may be scattered xerophytic trees but no closed canopy.

Scats Solid fecal matter or feces.

Scavenger An animal that eats animals it did not kill directly but that have died from other causes such as disease, starvation or predation.

Scent mark Act of marking an area with body odor, scent from a gland, or urine or scat.

Sexual dimorphism The condition in which the two sexes of the same species exhibit different characteristics beyond the differences in their sexual organs.

Solitary Unsocial, referring to animals that do not live in social groups.

Species Basic unit of taxonomic classification that describes a group of similar organisms that share similar genes, capable of interbreeding and producing viable offspring.

Steppe A somewhat discontinuous grassland, harboring scattered shrubs or stunted trees.

Subordinate Lower ranking in power, control and privilege.

Subspecies A population that has been isolated from other populations of the same species long enough to develop genetic differences sufficiently distinctive to be considered a separate race.

Supracaudal gland A secretion gland located on the upper surface of the tail of certain mammals, including Canids, used for intra-species signaling and scent marking, and contributes to the strong odor of Foxes in particular. Also known as tail gland or violet gland.

Sympatry Condition of overlapping geographic distribution; applies to related species that coexist without interbreeding.

Tarsal Pertaining to the tarsus bones in the ankle, articulating between the leg and the foot.

Taxon (pl. taxa) Any unit of scientific classification (e.g., species, genus, family, order).

Taxonomy The science of defining groups of biological organisms on the basis of shared characteristics and organizing them into a classification system.

Terrestrial Living or active on solid ground.

Territory Any defended area. It may include the entire home range, only the area immediately around a den, or only a feeding area.

Thermoregulation An ability to regulate body temperature when the temperature of the surroundings changes.

Trenchant heel An extra-long cutting blade on the lower first molar of some Canids that allows them to more efficiently slice through flesh.

Undercoat The soft insulating underfur beneath the longer, coarser guard hairs of the outer coat.

Ventral On or referring to the underside or belly of an animal.

Vestigial Small and imperfectly formed, disappearing.

Vocalizations Calls or sounds produced by the vocal cords of a mammal, and uttered through the mouth. Vocalizations differ with the age and sex of mammals but are usually similar within a species.

Vibrissae Stiff, coarse hairs richly supplied with nerves, found especially around the snout and having a sensory (tactile) function.

Whiskers See Vibrissae.

Xerophytic A plant that shows a capacity to withstand drought.

Yearling A young animal between 1 and 2 years of age (referring to species that take at least 2 years to mature).

Zygomatic arch The narrow arched bones (cheekbones) on either side of the skull, situated below the eyes.

REFERENCES

The references listed below have been consulted during the work on this guide. Without them, this work would have been much more difficult and the end result less good. For reasons of space and to avoid repetition, references are not listed at the end of each species account.

Abe H. 1975. Winter food of the Red Fox, *Vulpes vulpes schrencki* Kishida (Carnivora: Canidae), in Hokkaido, with special reference to vole populations. Applied Entomology and Zoology, 10 (1): 40-51.

Acharya B. B. 2007. The ecology of the dhole or Asiatic wild dog (*Cuon alpinus*) in Pench Tiger Reserve, Madhya Pradesh. Thesis. Dehradun: Wildlife Institute of India.

Aggarwal R. K. et al. 2007. Mitochondrial DNA coding region sequences support the phylogenetic distinction of two Indian wolf species. Journal of Zoological Systematics and Evolutionary Research, 45 (2): 163-172.

Alderton D. 1998. Foxes, Wolves and Wild Dogs. New York: Facts on File, Inc.

Aldridge B. M. 2008. Gray fox (*Urocyon cinereoargenteus*). Mammals of Mississippi, 9: 1-7.

Allen G. M. 1923. Mammals from Darien. Bulletin of the Museum of Comparative Zoology, 65 (8): 259-274.

Allen G. M. 1923. The Pampa Fox of the Bogota Savanna. Proceedings of the Biological Society of Washington, 36: 55-58.

Allen G. M. 1938. The Mammals of China and Mongolia Vol. XI, Part 1. New York: The American Museum of Natural History.

Allen G. M. 1940. The Mammals of China and Mongolia Vol. XI, Part 2. New York: The American Museum of Natural History.

Allen J. A. 1911. Mammals from Venezuela collected by Mr. M. A. Carriker, Jr., 1909-1911. Bulletin of the American Museum of Natural History, 30 (10): 239-273.

Ambarli H., Ertürk A. and Soyumert A. 2016. Current status, distribution, and conservation of brown bear (Ursidae) and wild canids (gray wolf, golden jackal, and red fox; Canidae) in Turkey. Turkish Journal of Zoology, 40: 1-13.

Anderson R. M. 1943. Summary of the large wolves of Canada, with description of three new Arctic races. Journal of Mammalogy, 24 (3): 386-393.

André J.-M. 2008. Conservation of African Wild Dogs in Northern Mozambique. BP Conservation Programme.

Apps P. 2012. Smither's Mammals of Southern Africa: A Field Guide. 4th ed. Cape Town, South Africa: Struik Nature.

Armstrong D. M., Jones J. K. and Birney E. C. 1972. Mammals from the Mexican state of Sinaloa. III. Carnivora and Artiodactyla. Journal of Mammalogy, 53 (1): 48-61.

Arnaud G. and Acevedo M. 1990. Hábitos alimenticios de la zorra gris *Urocyon cinereoargenteus* (Carnivora: Canidae) en la región meridional de Baja California, México. Revista de Biología Tropical, 38 (2B): 497-500.

Arnold J. et al. 2012. Current status and distribution of golden jackals *Canis aureus* in Europe. Mammal Review, 42 (1): 1–11.

Atickem A. et al. 2017. Deep divergence among mitochondrial lineages in African jackals, *Lupulella mesomelas* (Schreber, 1775) and *L. adusta* (Sundevall, 1847). Zoologica Scripta, 47: 1-8.

Aubry K. B. 1983. The Cascade red fox: Distribution, morphology, zoogeography and ecology. Thesis. Seattle, WA: University of Washington. Mol Ecol. 18 (12):2668-86.

Aubry K. B. et al. 2009. Phylogeography of the North American red fox: vicariance in Pleistocene forest refugia.

Bae J.-H. et al. 2015. The distinction between *Vulpes zerda* and *Vulpes pallida* using chromosomes test in Korea. Preventive Veterinary Medicine, 39 (4): 180-184.

Bahamonde Valenzuela A. 2009. Tendencias de la abundancia del zorro gris (*Pseudalopex griseus*) en la región de Magallanes, Chile, y su relación con la propuesta de uso sustentable. Thesis. Santiago, Chile: Universidad de Chile.

Bahlk S. H. 2015. Can hybridization be detected between African wolf and sympatric canids? Thesis. Oslo, Norway: University of Oslo.

Bailey V. 1905. North American Fauna, No. 25. Washington: U. S. Department of Agriculture.

Ballard J. 2012. Wolves. Falcon Guides. Guilford, CT: Morris Book Publishing, LLC.

Bardeleben C., Moore R. L. and Wayne R. K. 2005. A molecular phylogeny of the Canidae based on six nuclear loci. Molecular Phylogenetics and Evolution, 37: 815-831.

Barja I. 2009. Prey and prey-age preference by the Iberian wolf *Canis lupus signatus* in a multiple-prey Ecosystem. Wildlife Biology, 15 (2): 147-154.

Barquez R. M., Díaz M. M. and Ojeda R. A. 2006. Mamíferos de Argentina: Sistemática y Distribución. Tucumán, Argentina: SAREM.

Barros Ferraz K. M. P. et al. 2010. Assessment of *Cerdocyon thous* distribution in an agricultural mosaic, southeastern Brazil. Mammalia, 74: 275-280.

Beisiegel B. de M. and Ades C. 2002. The behavior of the bush dog (*Speothos venaticus* Lund, 1842) in the Field: A Review. Revista de Etología, 4 (1): 17-23.

Beisiegel B. de M. and Zuercher G. L. 2005. *Speothos venaticus*. Mammalian Species, 783: 1-6.

Beisiegel B. de M. et al. 2013. Avaliação do risco de extinção do cachorro-do-mato *Cerdocyon thous* (Linnaeus, 1766) no Brasil. Biodiversidade Brasileira, 3 (1): 138-145.

Bekoff M. 1977. *Canis latrans*. Mammalian Species, 79: 1-9.

Benson S. 2009. Life and behaviour of wolves: The Arabian or desert wolf. UK Wolf Conservation Trust, 38: 12-13.

Berta A. 1982. *Cerdocyon thous*. Mammalian Species, 186: 1-4.

Berta, A. 1986. *Atelocynus microtis*. Mammalian Species, 256: 1-3.

Biben M. 1983. Comparative ontogeny of social behaviour in three South American canids: the maned wolf, crab-eating fox and bush dog: Implications for sociality. Animal Behaviour, 31: 814-826.

Bininda-Emonds O. R. P., Gittleman J. L. and Purvis A. 1999. Building large trees by combining phylogenetic information: A complete phylogeny of the extant Carnivora (Mammalia). Biological Reviews, 74: 143-175.

Blanco J. C. and Cuesta L. 1992. Distribution, status and conservation problems of the wolf *Canis lupus* in Spain. Biological Conservation, 60: 73-80.

Boser C. 2011. Santa Cruz Island Fox Recovery Program June 2009-December 2011. California Department of Fish and Game, Wildlife Branch, Nongame Wildlife Program Report 2011-12; South Coast.

Boudet C. 2016. Mammals' Planet. Retrieved from http://www.planet-mammiferes.org.

Bozarth C. A. et al. 2011. Phylogeography of the gray fox (*Urocyon cinereoargenteus*) in the eastern United States. Journal of Mammalogy, 92 (2): 283-294.

Brahmi K. et al. 2012. First quantitative data on the diet of the fennec fox, *Vulpes zerda* (Canidae, Carnivora), in Algeria. Folia Zoologica, 61 (1): 61-70.

Bray T. C. et al. 2014. Genetic variation and subspecific status of the grey wolf (*Canis lupus*) in Saudi Arabia. Mammalian Biology, 79: 409-413.

Briceño C. 2010. Assessing genetic diversity and disease susceptibility in the endangered Fueguinean culpeo fox (*Pseudalopex culpeo lycoides*) in Tierra del Fuego, Chile. Thesis. Cambridge, UK: University of Cambridge.

Brum-Zorrilla N. and Langguth A. 1980. Karyotype of South American pampas of *Pseudalopex gymnocercus* (Carnivora, Canidae). Experientia, 36 (9): 1043-1044.

Cabrera A. 1931. On some South American canine genera. Journal of Mammalogy, 12 (1): 54-67.

Caniglia R. 2008. Non-invasive genetics and wolf (*Canis lupus*) population size estimation in the northern Italian Apennines. Thesis. Italy: Alma Mater Studiorum, Università di Bologna.

Carlozzi A. 2011. Análisis filogeográfico de un cánido neotropical: El zorro de monte (*Cerdocyon thous*, Linnaeus, 1766). Thesis. Montevideo, Uruguay: Universidad de la República.

Carmichael L. E. 2007. Genetics of Northern Wolf Populations. Government of Nunavut, Department of Environment, Final Wildlife Report 21, Iqaluit.

Castillo D. F. et al. 2011. Diet of adults and pups of *Lycalopex gymnocercus* in Pampas grassland: A validation of the Optimal Foraging Theory? Annales Zoologici Fennici, 48: 251-256.

Chambers S. M. et al. 2012. An account of the taxonomy of North American wolves from morphological and genetic analyses. North American Fauna, 77: 1-67.

Clark E. L. et al. 2006. Mongolian Red List of Mammals. Regional Red List Series Vol. 1. London: Zoological Society of London.

Clark H. O. 2005. *Otocyon megalotis*. Mammalian Species, 776: 1-5.

Clark H. O. et al. 2008. *Vulpes ferrilata* (Carnivora: Canidae). Mammalian Species, 821: 1-6.

Clark H. O. et al. 2009. *Vulpes corsac* (Carnivora: Canidae). Mammalian Species, 832: 1-8.

Cockrum E. L. 1952. Mammals of Kansas. Lawrence: University of Kansas Publications.

Cohen O., Barocas A. and Geffen E. 2013. Conflicting management policies for the Arabian wolf *Canis lupus arabs* in the Negev Desert: Is this justified? Oryx, 47 (2): 228–236.

Collins P. W. 1993. Taxonomic and Biogeographic Relationships of the Island Fox (*Urocyon littoralis*) and Gray Fox (*V. cinereoargenteus*) from Western North America. In Hochberg F. G., Third California Islands Symposium. Santa Barbara, CA: Santa Barbara Museum of Natural History.

Consorte-McCrea A. G. 2011. Conservation of the maned wolf (*Chrysocyon brachyurus*): Carnivore and people relationships in the southeast of Brazil. Thesis. Canterbury: University of Kent.

Consorte-McCrea A. G. and Ferraz Santos E. 2013. Ecology and conservation of the maned wolf: Multidisciplinary perspectives. Boca Raton: CRC Press.

Coonan T. J. 2013. Recovery Strategy for Island Foxes (*Urocyon littoralis*) on the Northern Channel Islands. National Park Service, Channel Islands National Park.

Cope E. D. 1889. On the mammalia obtained by the naturalist exploring expedition to southern Brazil. The American Naturalist, 23: 128-150.

COSEWIC. 2015. COSEWIC Assessment And Status Report on the Eastern Wolf *Canis sp. cf. lycaon* in Canada. Committee on the Status of Endangered Wildlife in Canada. Ottawa.

COSEWIC. 2015. COSEWIC Assessment and Status Report on the Gray Fox *Urocyon cinereoargenteus* in Canada. Committee on the Status of Endangered Wildlife in Canada. Ottawa.

Cossios E. D. 2010. *Lycalopex sechurae* (Carnivora: Canidae). Mammalian Species, 42 (848): 1-6.

Cotterill S. E. 1997. Status of the Swift Fox (*Vulpes velox*) in Alberta. Edmonton, AB: Alberta Environmental Protection, Wildlife Management Division.

Cunningham P. L. 2009. Persecution of Rüppell's fox in central Saudi Arabia. Canid News 12 (3). http://www.canids.org/canidnews/12/Ruppells_fox_in_Saudi_Arabia.pdf.

Cunningham P. L. and Howarth B. 2002. Notes on the distribution and diet of Blanford's Fox, *Vulpes cana* Blanford, 1877 from the United Arab Emirates. Zoology in the Middle East, 27: 21-28.

Cunningham P. L. and Wronski T. 2009. Blanford's fox confirmed in the At-Tubaiq Protected Area (northern Saudi Arabia) and the Ibex Reserve (central Saudi Arabia). Canid News 12 (4). http://www.canids.org/canidnews/12/Blanfords_fox_in_Saudi_Arabia.pdf.

Cypher B. L. 2003. Foxes – Vulpes species, Urocyon species, and Alopex lagopus. In Wild mammals of North America: biology, management, and conservation: 511–546. 2nd edn. Feldhamer, G. A., Thompson, B. C. & Chapman, J. A. (Eds). Baltimore: Johns Hopkins University Press.

Cypher B.L. at al. 2014. Multi-population comparison of resource exploitation by island foxes: Implications for conservation. Global Ecology and Conservation, 2: 255-266.

Dalen L., et al. 2005. Population history and genetic structure of a circumpolar species: The Arctic fox. Biological Journal of the Linnean Society, 84: 78-89.

Dalponte J. C. 2009. *Lycalopex vetulus* (Carnivora: Canidae). Mammalian Species, 847: 1-7.

Dark-Smiley D. N. and Keinath D. A. 2003. Species Assesment for Swift Fox (*Vulpes velox*) in Wyoming. Cheyenne, WY: Wyoming State Office.

De Groot G. A. et al. 2016. Decades of population genetic research reveal the need for harmonization of molecular markers: The gray wolf *Canis lupus* as a case study. Mammal Review, 46: 44-59.

De Lavigne G. 2015. Free Ranging Dogs - Stray, Feral or Wild? San Francisco: Lulu.com.

D'Elia G. et al. 2013. A new geographic record of the endangered Darwin's fox *Lycalopex fulvipes* (Carnivora: Canidae): Filling the distributional gap. Revista Chilena de Historia Natural, 86: 485-488.

Dietz J. M. 1984. Ecology and Social Organization of the Maned Wolf (*Chrysocyon brachyurus*). Smithsonian Contributions to Zoology, 392.

Dietz J. M. 1985. *Chrysocyon brachyurus*. Mammalian Species, 234: 1-4.

Dragoo J. W. 1990. Evolutionary and taxonomic relationships among North American Arid-land Foxes. Journal of Mammalogy, 71 (3): 318-332.

Duckworth J. W. et al. 1998. A clarification of the status of the Asiatic Jackal Canis aureus in Indochina. Mammalia, 62 (4): 549-556.

Edwards J. M. 2009. Conservation genetics of African wild dogs *Lycaon pictus* (Temminck, 1820) in South Africa. Thesis. Pretoria: University of Pretoria.

Egoscue H. J. 1979. *Vulpes velox*. Mammalian Species, 122: 1-5.

Elliot D. G. 1903. A list of mammals collected by Edmund Heller, in the San Pedro Martir and Hanson Laguna Mountains and the accompanying coast regions of lower California with descriptions of apparently new species. Zoological Series Vol. III, no. 12, publication 79. Field Columbian Museum.

Ersmark E. et al. 2016. From the past to the present: Wolf phylogeography and demographic history based on the mitochondrial control region. Frontiers in Ecology and Evolution, 134 (4): 1-12.

Fan Z. et al. 2016. Worldwide patterns of genomic variation and admixture in gray wolves. Genome Research, 26: 1-11.

Farias A. A. et al. 2014. A new population of Darwin's fox (*Lycalopex fulvipes*) in the Valdivian Coastal Range. Revista Chilena de Historia Natural, 1: 3.

Ferguson W. W. 1981. The systematic position of *Canis aureus lupaster* (Carnivora: Canidae) and the occurrence of *Canis lupus* in North Africa, Egypt and Sinai. Mammalia, 45 (4): 459-465.

Ferguson W. W. and Menache S. 2002. The Mammals of Israel. Jerusalem: Gefen Books.

Fletchall N. B., Rodden M. and Taylor S. 1995. Husbandry Manual for the Maned Wolf (*Chrysocyon brachyurus*). Maned Wolf SSP Husbandry Manual.

Foley C. et al. 2014. A Field Guide to the Larger Mammals of Tanzania. Princeton, NJ: Princeton University Press.

Fox M. W. 1975. The Wild Canids: Their Systematics, Behavioral Ecology and Evolution. New York: Van Nostrand Reinhold Ltd.

Fritzel E. K. and Haroldson K. J. 1982. *Urocyon cinereoargenteus*. Mammalian Species, 189: 1-8.

Fuentes-González J. A. and Muñoz-Durán J. 2012. Phylogeny of the extant canids (Carnivora: Canidae) by means of character congruence under parsimony. Actualites Biologiques, 96: 85-102.

Funk W. C. et al. 2016. Adaptive divergence despite strong genetic drift: Genomic analysis of the evolutionary mechanisms causing genetic differentiation in the island fox (*Urocyon littoralis*). Molecular Ecology, 25 (10): 2176-2194.

Geffen E. 1994. *Vulpes cana*. Mammalian Species, 462: 1-4.

Geffen E. and Macdonald D. W. 1992. Small size and monogamy: Spatial organization of Blanford's foxes, *Vulpes cana*. Animal Behaviour, 44: 1123-1130.

Geffen E. et al. 1992. Phylogenetic relationships of the fox-like canids: Mitochondrial DNA restriction fragment, site and cytochrome *b* sequence analyses. Journal of Zoology, 228: 27-39.

Giannatos, G. 2004. Conservation Action Plan for the Golden Jackal *Canis aureus* L. in Greece. WWF Greece.

Ginsberg J. R. 1994. Conservation biology and status of the African wild dog, *Lycaon pictus*. Endangered Species Update, 11 (10): 1-4.

Ginsberg J. R. and MacDonald D. W. 1990. Foxes, wolves, jackals, and dogs: An action plan for the conservation of canids. Gland, Switzerland: IUCN Publications.

Girman D. J. et al. 2001. Patterns of population subdivision, gene flow and genetic variability in the African wild dog (*Lycaon pictus*). Molecular Ecology, 10: 1703-1723.

Goddard N. S., Statham M. J. and Sacks B. N. 2015. Mitochondrial analysis of the most basal canid reveals deep divergence between eastern and western North American gray foxes (*Urocyon* spp.) and ancient roots in Pleistocene California. PloS One, 10: 1-21.

Goldman E. A. 1937. The wolves of North America. Journal of Mammalogy, 18 (1): 37-45.

Gomes A. C. and Valente A. 2016. Cranial and body size variation in the Iberian red fox (*Vulpes vulpes silacea*). Mammalian Biology, 81 (6): 638-643.

Gompper M. E., Petrites A. E. and Lyman R. L. 2006. Cozumel Island fox (*Urocyon* sp.) dwarfism and possible divergence history based on subfossil bones. Journal of Zoology, 270: 72-77.

Gompper M. E. and Vanak A. T. 2006. *Vulpes bengalensis*. Mammalian Species, 795: 1-5.

Gonzalez Quintero E. P. 2004. Análisis taxonómico del coyote (*Canis latrans*) de la Península de Baja California, México. Thesis. La Paz: Centro de Investigaciones Biológicas del Noroeste, S. C.

Gonzalez T. 2012. The pariah case: Some comments on the origin and evolution of primitive dogs and on the taxonomy of related species. Thesis. Canberra: The Australian National University.

Goodwin G. G. 1938. Four new mammals from Costa Rica. American Museum Novitates, 987: 1-5.

Graphodatsky A. S. et al. 2008. Phylogenomics of the dog and fox family (Canidae, Carnivora) revealed by chromosome painting. Chromosome Research, 16: 129-143.

Grassman L. I. et al. 2005. Spatial ecology and diet of the dhole *Cuon alpinus* (Canidae, Carnivora) in north central Thailand. Mammalia, 69 (1): 11-20.

Greco C. 2009. Genomic characterization of the Italian wolf (*Canis lupus*): The genes involved in black coat color deterrmination and application of microarray technique for SNPs detection. Thesis. University of Bologna.

Grimwood I. R. 1969. Notes on the Distribution and Status of some Peruvian Mammals. Bronx, NY: American Committee for International Wild Life Protection and New York Zoological Society.

Grinnell J., Dixon J. S. and Linsdale J. M. 1937. Fur-Bearing Mammals of California: Their Natural History, Systematic Status and Relations to Man. Berkeley: University of California Press.

Guzmán J. A., D'Elía G. and Ortiz J. C. 2009. Variación geográfica del zorro *Lycalopex culpaeus* (Mammalia, Canidae) en Chile: Implicaciones taxonómicas. Revista De Biologia Tropical, 57 (1-2): 421-432.

Haba C. et al. 2008. Morphological variation of the Japanese raccoon dog: Implications for geographical isolation and environmental adaptation. Journal of Zoology 274: 239-247.

Habib, B., Shrotriya S. and Jhala Y. V. 2013. Ecology and Conservation of Himalayan Wolf. Wildlife Institute of India. Technical Report No. TR – 2013/01.

Hall E. R. 1981. The Mammals of North America. 2nd ed. New York: John Wiley and Sons.

Harding L. E. et al. 2016. Genetic management and setting recovery goals for Mexican wolves (*Canis lupus baileyi*) in the wild. Biological Conservation, 203: 151-159.

Hatler D. F., Poole K. G. and Beal A. M. M. 2003. Red Fox (*Vulpes vulpes*). Furbearer Management Guidelines. British Columbia. British Columbia Trappers Association Trapper Education Training Manual.

Hayssen V., Tienhoven A. and Tienhoven A. 1993. Asdell's Patterns of Mammalian Reproduction: A Compendium of Species-Specific Data. Ithaca: Cornell University Press.

Hayward M. W., Lyngdoh S. and Habib B. 2014. Diet and prey preferences of the dhole *Cuon alpinus*: Dietary competition within Asia's apex predator guild. Journal of Zoology, 294: 255-266.

Heller E. 1914. New subspecies of mammals from equatorial Africa. Smithsonian Miscellaneous Collections, 63 (7): 1-12.

Heptner V. G. and Naumov N. P. 1991. Mammals of the Soviet Union. Vol. II. New Delhi: Amerind Publishing Co. Pvt. Ltd.

Hofman C. A. et al. 2015. Mitochondrial genomes suggest rapid evolution of dwarf California Channel Islands foxes (*Urocyon littoralis*). PLoS One 10 (2).

Horowitz A. 2014. Domestic Dog Cognition and Behavior. Heidelberg: Springer.

Hunter L. 2011. Carnivores of the World. Princeton, NJ: Princeton University Press.

IUCN. 2015. IUCN Red List of Threatened Species. Version 2015-4.

IUCN / SSC Canid Specialist Group. 2011. Strategic Plan for Ethiopian Wolf Conservation. Oxford, UK: IUCN / SCC Canid Specialist Group.

Jackson H. H. T. 1949. Two new coyotes from the United States. Proceedings of the Biological Society of Washington, 62: 31-32.

Jackson S. M. et al. 2017. The wayward dog: Is the Australian native dog or dingo a distinct species? Zootaxa, 4317 (2): 201-224.

Jenks K. E. 2012. Camera trap records of dholes in Khao Ang Rue Nai Wildlife Sancturay, Thailand. Canid News. http://www.canids.org/canidnews/15/Camera_trap_records_of_dholes_in_Thailand.pdf.

Jenks K. E. 2012. Distributions of large mammal assemblages in Thailand with a focus on dhole (*Cuon alpinus*) conservation. Thesis. University of Massachusetts.

Jiménez J. E. 2007 Ecology of a coastal population of the critically endangered Darwin's fox (*Pseudalopex fulvipes*) on Chiloé Island, southern Chile. Journal of Zoology, 271: 63-77.

Jnawali S. R. et al. 2011. The Status of Nepal Mammals: The National Red List Series, Department of National Parks and Wildlife Conservation, Kathmandu, Nepal.

Johnson W. E. 1992. Comparative ecology of two South American foxes, *Dusicyon griseus* and *D. culpaeus*. Thesis. Iowa State University.

Kamler J. F. and Ballard W. B. 2002. A review of native and nonnative red foxes in North America. Wildlife Society Bulletin, 30 (2): 370-379.

Kamler J. F. and Gipson P. S. 2000. Space and habitat use by resident and transient coyotes. Canadian Journal of Zoology, 78: 2106-2111.

Kamler J. F., Gipson P. S. and Perchellet C. C. 2002. Seasonal food habits of coyotes in northeastern Kansas. Prairie Naturalist, 34: 75-83.

Kamler J. F., Klare U. and Macdonald D. W. 2012. Seasonal diet and prey selection of black-backed jackals on a small-livestock farm in South Africa. African Journal of Ecology, 50: 299-307.

Kamler J. F. and Macdonald D. W. 2006. Longevity of a wild bat-eared fox. South African Journal of Wildlife Research, 36: 199-200.

Kamler J. F. and Macdonald D. W. 2014. Social organization, survival, and dispersal of Cape foxes (*Vulpes chama*) in South Africa. Mammalian Biology, 79: 64-70.

Kamler J. F. et al. 2003. Impacts of coyotes on swift foxes in northwestern Texas. Journal of Wildlife Management, 67: 317-323.

Kamler J. F. et al. 2003. Spatial relationships between swift foxes and coyotes in northwestern Texas. Canadian Journal of Zoology, 81: 168-172.

Kamler J. F. et al. 2004. Adult male emigration and a female-based social organisation in swift foxes, *Vulpes velox*. Animal Behaviour, 67:699-702.

Kamler J. F. et al. 2004. Variation in the mating system and group structure in two populations of swift foxes, *Vulpes velox*. Animal Behaviour 68:83-88.

Kamler J. F. et al. 2007. Diets of swift foxes (*Vulpes velox*) in continuous and fragmented prairie in northwestern Texas. The Southwestern Naturalist, 52 (4): 504-510.

Kamler J. F. et al. 2012. The diet, prey selection, and activity of dholes (*Cuon alpinus*) in northern Laos. Journal of Mammalogy, 93 (3): 627-633.

Kamler J. F. et al. 2012. Resource partitioning among Cape foxes, bat-eared foxes, and black-backed jackals in South Africa. Journal of Wildlife Management, 76: 1241-1253.

Kamler J. F. et al. 2013. Genetic structure, spatial organization, and dispersal in two populations of bat-eared Foxes. Ecology and Evolution, 3: 2892-2902.

Kamler J. F. et al. 2014. Comparison of coyote diets in continuous and fragmented short-grass prairie in the Texas Panhandle. Texas Journal of Science, 66: 25-41.

Kamler J. F., Stenkewitz U. and Macdonald D. W. 2013. Lethal and sublethal effects of black-backed jackals on Cape foxes and bat-eared foxes. Journal of Mammalogy, 94:295-306.

Kasprowicz A. E., Statham M. J. and Sacks B. N. 2016. Fate of the other redcoat: Remnants of colonial British foxes in the eastern United States. Journal of Mammalogy, 97: 298-309.

Kesteren F. V. 2011. Reproductive physiology of Ethiopian wolves (*Canis simensis*). Thesis. Wildlife Conservation Research Unit, Department of Zoology, University of Oxford.

Khalatbari L. et al. 2015. First confirmed record of the corsac fox, *Vulpes corsac*, from Iran and considerations on its status (Mammalia: Canidae). Zoology in the Middle East, 61 (2): 102-108.

Kim S.-I. 2015. Evolutionary and biogeographical implications of variation in skull morphology of raccoon dogs (*Nyctereutes procyonoides*, Mammalia: Carnivora). Biological Journal of the Linnean Society, 116: 856-872.

Kingdon J. 2015. The Kingdon Field Guide to African Mammals. 2nd ed. London: Bloomsbury.

Kitao N. et al. 2009. Overwintering strategy of wild free-ranging and enclosure-housed Japanese raccoon dogs (*Nyctereutes procyonoides albus*). International Journal of Biometeorology, 53: 159-165.

Klare U. et al. 2010. Diet, prey selection, and predation impact of black-backed jackals in South Africa. Journal of Wildlife Management, 74: 1030-1042.

Klare U., Kamler J. F. and Macdonald D. W. 2011. The bat-eared fox: A dietary specialist? Mammalian Biology, 76: 646-650.

Klare U., Kamler J. F. and Macdonald D. W. 2014. Seasonal diet and numbers of prey consumed by Cape foxes *Vulpes chama* in South Africa. Wildlife Biology, 20: 190-195.

Kleiman D. G., Geist V. and McDade M. C. 2003. Grzimek's Animal Life Encyclopedia. 2nd ed. Vol. 14. Mammals III. Farmington Hills, MI: Gale Group.

Koepfli K. P. et al. 2015. Genome-wide evidence reveals that African and Eurasian golden jackals are distinct species. Current Biology, 25: 1-8.

Koler-Matznick J. et al. 2003. An updated description of the New Guinea singing dog (*Canis hallstromi*, Troughton 1957). Journal of Zoology, 261: 109-118.

Larivière S. and Pasitschniak-Arts M. 1996. *Vulpes vulpes*. Mammalian Species, 537: 1-11.

Larivière S. and Seddon P. J. 2001. *Vulpes rueppelli*. Mammalian Species, 678: 1-5.

Leite Pitman R. and de Mello Beisiegel B. 2013. Avaliação do risco de extinção do cachorro-do-mato-de-orelhas-curtas *Atelocynus microtis* (Sclater, 1883) no Brasil. Biodiversidade Brasileira, 3 (1): 133-137.

Lindblad-Toh K. et al. 2005. Genome sequence, comparative analysis and haplotype structure of the domestic dog. Nature, 438: 803-819.

Llaneza L. and Núñez-Quirós P. 2009. Distribution of the Iberian wolf (*Canis lupus signatus*) in Galicia (NW Spain): Concordance between field sampling and questionnaries. Wildlife Biology in Practice, 5 (1): 23-32.

Londeni T. 1994. An unusual fox in the Gobi, Mongolia. Bolletino di zoologia, 61: 191-194.

Los Padres Forestwatch and Center for Biological Diversity. 2010. Petition to designate critical habitat for the endangered San Joaquin Kit Fox (*Vulpes macrotis mutica*) under the Endangered Species Act.

Lucherini M. and Luengos Vidal E. M. 2008. *Lycalopex gymnocercus* (Carnivora: Canidae). Mammalian Species, 820: 1-9.

Luengos Vidal E. M. 2003. Estudio comparado de metodologías de captura y de estimación de las poblaciones de zorro pampeano *Pseudalopex gymnocercus*. Thesis. Bahía Blanca, Argentina: Universidad Nacional del Sur.

Luengos Vidal E. M. 2009. Morphometrics of pampas foxes (*Pseudalopex gymnocercus*) in the Argentine Pampas. Mammalia, 73: 63-67.

Lydekker R. 1908. The Game Animals of Africa. London: Rowland Ward, Ltd.

Lyras G. A. 2009. The evolution of the brain in Canidae (Mammalia: Carnivora). Scripta Geologica, 139. http://www.scriptageologica.nl/cgi/t/text/get-pdf?c=scripta;idno=09139a01.

MacDonald D. W. and Sillero-Zubiri C. 2004. The Biology and Conservation of Wild Canids. Oxford: UK: Oxford University Press.

MacDonald S. O. and Cook J. A. 2010. Recent Mammals of Alaska. Fairbanks: University of Alaska Press.

Maheshwari A. et al. 2013. A preliminary overview of the subspecies of red fox and Tibetan sand fox in the Himalaya (India). Journal of Bombay Natural History Society, 110 (3): 193-196.

Malcolm J. R. 1986. Socio-ecology of bat-eared foxes (*Otocyon megalotis*). Journal of Zoology, 208: 457-467.

Marino J. 2003. Spatial ecology of the Ethiopian wolf, *Canis simensis*. Thesis. Linacre College, University of Oxford.

Martin D. J., White G. C. and Pusateri F. M. 2007. Occupancy rates by Swift Foxes (*Vulpes velox*) in eastern Colorado. The Southwestern Naturalist, 52 (4): 541-551.

Martinez P. A. et al. 2013. Applications and implications of phylogeography for Canid conservation. Mastozoología Neotropical, 20 (1): 61-74.

Martinez P. A. et al. 2013. Bergmann's rule across the equator: A case study in *Cerdocyon thous* (Canidae). Journal of Animal Ecology, 82(5): 997-100.

McGrew J. C. 1977. Distribution and habitat characteristics of the kit fox (*Vulpes macrotis*) in Utah. Thesis. Logan: Utah State University.

McGrew, J. C. 1979. *Vulpes macrotis*. Mammalian Species, 123: 1-6.

Meaney C. and Beauvais G. P. 2004. Species Assessment for Gray Wolf (*Canis lupus*) in Wyoming. Cheyenne, WY: US Department of the Interior Bureau of Land Management, Wyoming State Office.

Mearns E. A. and Scott W. E. D. 1891. Description of a new species of weasel, and a new subspecies of the gray fox, from Arizona. Bulletin of the American Museum of Natural History, 3 (17): 234-238.

Mech L. D. 1974. *Canis lupus*. Mammalian Species, 37: 1-6.

Méndez E., Degádo F. and Miranda D. 1981. The Coyote (*Canis latrans*) in Panama. International journal for the study of animal problems, 2 (5): 252-255.

Menon V. 2014. Indian Mammals: A Field Guide. Gurgaon: India. Hachette Book Publishing India.

Merriam C. H. 1900. Papers from the Harriman Alaska Expedition. I. Descriptions of twenty-six new mammals from Alaska and British North America. Proceedings of the Washington Academy of Sciences, 2: 13-30.

Merriam C. H. 1900. Preliminary revision of the North American red foxes. Proceedings of the Washington Academy of Sciences, 2: 661-676.

Merriam C. H. 1902. Four new Arctic foxes. Proceedings of the Biological Society of Washington, 15: 167-172.

Michalski L. J., de Oliveira T. G. and Michalski F. 2015. New record for bush dog in Amapé State, eastern Brazilian Amazonia. Canid Biology & Conservation, 18 (2): 3-5.

Miklósi A. 2009. Dog Behaviour, Evolution, and Cognition. Oxford, UK: Oxford University Press.

Miller G. S. 1899. Descriptions of two new gray foxes. Proceedings of the Academy of Natural Sciences of Philadelphia, 51 (2): 276-280.

Miller G. S. 1912. Catalogue of the Mammals of Western Europe. London: British Museum.

Mills M. G. L. et al. 1998. Population and Habitat Viability Assessment for the African Wild Dog (*Lycaon pictus*) in Southern Africa. Apple Valley, MN: IUCN/SSC Conservation Breeding Specialist Group.

Mivart G. 1890. Dogs, Jackals, Wolves, and Foxes: A Monograph of the Canidae. London, UK.

Monroy Gamboa A. G. 2007. Uso del hábitat y ámbito hogareño del coyote *Canis latrans cagotis* en un área comunal protegida de la Sierra Madre de Oaxaca, México. Thesis. Instituto Politécnico Nacional de México.

Moore C. M. and Collins P. W. 1995. *Urocyon littoralis*. Mammalian Species, 489: 1-7.

Murdoch J. D. et al. 2008. Social interactions among San Joaquin kit foxes before, during, and after the mating season. Journal of Mammalogy, 89 (5): 1087-1093.

Murray Weston J. L. 2001. Demographics of a protected population of gray foxes (*Urocyon cinereargenteus*) in South Carolina. Athens: University of Georgia.

Nelson E. W. and Goldman E. A. 1929. A new wolf from Mexico. Journal of Mammalogy, 10: 165-166.

Nyakatura K and Bininda-Emonds O, 2012. Updating the evolutionary history of Carnivora (Mammalia): a new species-level supertree complete with divergence time estimates. BMC Biology, 10:12.

Novaro A. J. 1997. *Pseudalopex culpaeus*. Mammalian Species, 558: 1-8.

Nowak R. M. 2011. Walker's Mammals of the World. 6th ed. Baltimore: Johns Hopkins University Press.

Nowak R. M. and Federoff N. E. 2002. The systematic status of the Italian wolf *Canis lupus*. Acta Theriologica, 47 (3): 333-338.

Nurvianto S., Imron M. A. and Herzog S. 2015. Activity patterns and behaviour of denning dholes (*Cuon alpinus*) in a dry deciduous forest of east Java, Indonesia. Bulletin of Environment, Pharmacology and Life Sciences, 4 (12): 45-54.

Ognev S. I. 1926. A systematic review of the mammals of Russia. Annales Musei Nationalis Hungarici, 23: 202-233.

Ognev S. I. 1962. Mammals of Eastern Europe and Northern Asia. Vol. 2: Carnivora (Fissipedia). Washington: Smithsonian Institution.

Ojeda R. A., Chillo V. and Diaz Isenrath G. B. 2012. Libro Rojo de Mamíferos Amenazados de la Argentina. Argentina, Sociedad Argentina para el Estudio de los Mamíferos (SAREM).

Orozco M. M. 2015. El aguará guazú (*Chrysocyon brachyurus*) en Argentina. Buenos Aires: Fundación de Historia Natural Félix de Azara.

Osborn D. J. and Helmy I. 1980. The Contemporary Land Mammals of Egypt (including Sinai). Fieldiana Zoology New Series, No. 5, Field Museum of Natural History.

Özkurt S. et al. 1998. Notes on distributional records and some characteristics of five carnivore species (Mammalia: Carnivora) in Turkey. Turkish Journal of Zoology, 22: 285-288.

Palacios R. 2007. Manual para identificación de carnívoros andinos. Córdoba, Argentina: Alianza Gato Andino.

Palomo L. J., Gisbert J. and Blanco J. C. 2007. Atlas y Libro Rojo de los Mamíferos Terrestres de España. Madrid: Dirección General para la Biodiversidad - SECEM-SECEMU.

Paradiso J. L. and Nowak R. M. 1972. *Canis rufus*. Mammalian Species, 22: 1-4.

Pendragon B. 2011. A review of selected features of the family Canidae with reference to its fundamental taxonomic status. Journal of Creation, 25 (3): 79-88.

Perinio F. A., Russo C. A. M. and Schrago C. G. 2009. The evolution of South American endemic canids: A history of rapid diversification and morphological parallelism. Journal of Evolutionary Biology, 23: 311-322.

Perrine J. D. 2005. Ecology of red fox (*Vulpes vulpes*) in the Lassen Peak region of California, USA. Thesis. Berkeley: University of California.

Perrine J. D., Campbell L. A. and Green G. A. 2010. Sierra Nevada Red Fox (*Vulpes vulpes necator*): A Conservation Assessment. US Department of Agriculture (USDA).

Pia M. V., López M. A. and Novaro A. J. 2003. Effects of livestock on the feeding ecology of endemic culpeo foxes (*Pseudalopex culpaeus smithersi*) in central Argentina. Revista Chilena de Historia Natural, 76: 313-321.

Pocock R. I. 1934. LXVI.—Preliminary diagnoses of some new races of South Arabian mammals. Annals and Magazine of Natural History, Series 10, 14 (84): 635-636.

Pocock R. I. 1935. The Asiatic Wild Dog or Dhole (*Cuon javanicus*). Zoological Department of the British Museum (Natural History).

Pocock R. I. 1941. The Fauna of British India, Including Ceylon and Burma. Mammalia vol. II: Carnivora. London: Taylor and Francis.

Porini G. and Ramadori D. 2007. Estado de conocimiento sobre el manejo de zorros de interés económico en Argentina. Buenos Aires, Argentina: Secretaría de Ambiente y Desarrollo Sustentable.

Prater S. H. 1971. The Book of Indian Animals. 3rd ed. Bombay, India: The Bombay Natural History Society and Oxford University Press.

Prevosti F. J. 2010. Phylogeny of the large extinct South American canids (Mammalia, Carnivora, Canidae) using a "total evidence" approach. Cladistics, 26: 456-481.

Prevosti F. J. 2013. Revision of the systematic status of Patagonian and pampean gray foxes (Canidae: *Lycalopex griseus* and *L. gymnocercus*) using 3D geometric morphometrics. Mastozoología Neotropical, 20 (2): 289-300.

Pushpangadhan D. 2014. Irkaya. Celebrating Biodiversity in Qatar. Doha, Qatar: State of Qatar.

Queirolo D., Kasper C. B. and Beisiegel B. M. 2013. Avaliação do risco de extinção do graxaim-do-campo *Lycalopex gymnocercus* (G. Fischer, 1814) no Brasil. Biodiversidade Brasileira, 3 (1): 172-178.

Ramírez-Chaves H.E. and Pérez W. A. 2015. New record of crab-eating fox in southwestern Colombia, with comments on its distribution in Colombia and Ecuador. Canid Biology & Conservation, 18 (3): 6-9.

Rhoads S. N. 1895. New subspecies of the gray fox and Say's chipmunk. Proceedings of the Academy of Natural Sciences of Philadelphia, 47: 42-44.

Richardson J. 1829. Fauna Boreali-Americana; or the Zoology of the Northern Parts of British America. London: John Murray.

Rick T. C. et al. 2009. Origins and antiquity of the island fox (*Urocyon littoralis*) on California's Channel Islands. Quaternary Research, 71: 93-98.

Roberts T. J. 2005. Field Guide to the Large and Medium-Sized Mammals of Pakistan. Karachi, Pakistan: Oxford University Press.

Rosevar D. R. 1974. The Carnivores of West Africa. London: Trustees of the British Museum (Natural History).

Ruenes E. K. et al. 2011. The cryptic African wolf: *Canis aureus lupaster* is not a golden jackal and is not endemic to Egypt. PLoS One, 6 (1): 1-5.

Ruiz-García M., Shostell J. M. 2013. Molecular Population Genetics, Evolutionary Biology and Biological Conservation of Neotropical Carnivores. New York: Nova Science Publishers Inc.

Rutkowski R. 2015. A European concern? Genetic structure and expansion of golden jackals (*Canis aureus*) in Europe and the Caucasus. PLoS One, 10 (11).

Saavedra D. 2009. The Abune Yosef Massif. Birds and Mammals of a Hidden Jewel of Ethiopia. Barcelona, Centro de Recursos de Biodiversidad Animal, Universidad de Barcelona.

Schutz H. et al. 2009. Differential sexual dimorphism: Size and shape in the cranium and pelvis of gray foxes (*Urocyon*). Biological Journal of the Linnean Society, 96: 339-353.

Schweizer R. M. et al. 2016. Genetic subdivision and candidate genes under selection in North American grey wolves. Molecular Ecology, 25 (1): 380-402.

Schwemm C. 2014. Fact Sheet: Island Fox (*Urocyon littoralis*). Ventura, CA: Friends of the Island Fox, Channel Islands Park Foundation.

Sears H. J. et al. 2003. Landscape influence on *Canis* morphological and ecological variation in a coyote-wolf *C. lupus* × *latrans* hybrid zone, Southeastern Ontario. The Canadian Field-Naturalist, 117: 589-599.

Segura V. 2013. Skull ontogeny of *Lycalopex culpaeus* (Carnivora: Canidae): Description of cranial traits and craniofacial sutures. Mammalia, 77 (2): 205-214.

Sheikh K. M. and Molur S. 2004. Status and Red List of Pakistan's Mammals. Based on the Conservation Assessment and Management Plan. IUCN Pakistan.

Sheldon J. W. 1992. Wild Dogs: The Natural History of the Nondomestic Canidae. Caldwell, NJ: The Blackburn Press.

Shrotriya S., Lyngdoh S. and Habib B. 2012. Wolves in Trans-Himalayas: 165 years of taxonomic confusion. Current Science, 103 (8): 885-887.

Sillero-Zubiri C., Hoffmann N. and Macdonald D. 2005. Canids: Foxes, Wolves, Jackals and Dogs: Status Survey and Conservation Action Plan. Gland, Switzerland and Cambridge, UK: IUCN/SSC Canid Specialist Group.

Sillero-Zubiri C., Rostro-García S. and Burrus D. 2016. Spatial organization of the pale fox in the Termit Massif of east Niger. Journal of Mammalogy, 97 (2): 526-532.

Simcharoen S. 1998. Home range and habitat use of a male Asiatic jackal (*Canis aureus*) at Khao Nang Rum Wildlife Research Center, Thailand. Natural History Bulletin of the Siam Society. 46: 3-15.

Smith B. 2015. The Dingo Debate: Origins, Behaviour and Conservation. Clayton South, Victoria: CSIRO Publishing.

Smith C. H. and Jardine W. 1840. The Naturalist's Library. Vol. V. Mammalia. Dogs. Edinburgh: W. H. Lizars.

Soper J. D. 1944. The mammals of southern Baffin Island, Northwest Territories, Canada. Journal of Mammalogy, 25 (3): 221-254.

Soper J. D. 1970. The mammals of Jasper National Park, Alberta. Ottawa: Canadian Wildlife Service.

Soyumert A. 2013. Relative habitat use by the red fox (*Vulpes vulpes*) in Köprülü Canyon National Park, southern Anatolia. Hystrix, the Italian Journal of Mammalogy, 24 (2): 166-168.

Srinivasulu C. and Srinivasulu B. 2012. South Asian Mammals: Their Diversity, Distribution, and Status. New York: Springer.

Staham M. J. et al. 2014. Range-wide multilocus phylogeography of the red fox reveals ancient continental divergence, minimal genomic exchange and distinct demographic histories. Molecular Ecology 23: 4813-4830.

Sterndale R. A. 1884. Natural History of the Mammalia of India. Calcutta: Thacker, Spink, and Co.

Stratman M. R. 2015. Swift Fox Conservation Team: Report for 2013-2014. Brush: Colorado Division of Parks and Wildlife.

Stromberg M. R. and Boyce M. S. 1986. Systematics and Conservation of the swift fox, *Vulpes velox*, in North America. Biological Conservation, 35: 97-110.

Stuart C. and Stuart M. 2011. Field Guide to the Mammals of Southern Africa. 4th ed. Cape Town, South Africa: Random House Struik.

Tchaicka L. 2016. Molecular assessment of the phylogeny and biogeography of a recently diversified endemic group of South American canids (Mammalia: Carnivora: Canidae). Genetics and Molecular Biology, 39 (3): 442-451.

Tchaicka L. et al. 2007. Phylogeography and population history of the crab-eating fox (*Cerdocyon thous*). Molecular Ecology, 16: 819-838.

Tedford R. H., Wang X. and Taylor B. E. 2009. Phylogenetic systematics of the North American fossil Caninae (Carnivora: Canidae). Bulletin of the American Museum of Natural History, 325.

Tejera V. H. et al. 1999. Primer registro del zorro cangrejero, *Cerdocyon thous* (Carnivora: Canidae), para Panamá. Scientia (Panamá), 14 (2): 103-107.

Thoisy B. et al. 2013. Northern extension of records of the crab-eating fox in Brazil. Canid Biology & Conservation, 16 (1): 1-3.

Thomas O. 1902. LXVII. The *Lycaon* and *Pedetes* of British East Africa, and a new gerbille from N. Nyasa. Annals and Magazine of Natural History, 9 (54): 438-442.

Thomas O. 1920. X.—A new shrew and two new foxes from Asia Minor and Palestine. Annals and Magazine of Natural History, 5 (25): 119-122.

Thomas O. and Hinton M. A. C. 1921. Captain Angus Buchanan's Air Expedition. II. Mammals. Novitates Zoologicae, 28: 1-13.

Townsend C. H. 1912. Mammals collected by the 'Albatross' expedition in Lower California in 1911, with descriptions of new species. Bulletin of the AMNH 31, article 13. New York: American Museum of Natural History.

Trani M. K., Ford W. M. and Chapman B. R. 2007. The Land Manager's Guide to Mammals of the South. Durham, NC: The Nature Conservancy.

UNEP-WCMC. 2015. Overview of the Conservation Status of and Trade in Species Currently Subject to EU Reservations: *Vulpes vulpes griffithi, Vulpes vulpes montana, Vulpes vulpes pusilla, Mustela altaica, Mustela erminea ferghanae, Mustela kathiah* and *Mustela sibirica*. Cambridge: UNEP-WCMC.

Urios V. et al. 2016. The analysis of the canid mitochondrial genome studied in Morocco shows that it is neither wolf (*Canis lupus*) nor Eurasian jackal (*Canis aureus*). PeerJ PrePrints 4:e1763v1.

US Environmental Protection Agency. 2008. Analysis of the Causes of a Decline in the San Joaquin Kit Fox Population on the Elk Hills, Naval Petroleum Reserve #1, California. Cincinnati, OH: US Environmental Protection Agency, National Center for Environmental Assessment.

US Fish and Wildlife Service. 2015. Sierra Nevada Red Fox (*Vulpes vulpes necator*). Species report. USFWS.

US Fish and Wildlife Service. 2015. Species status assessment for the Alexander Archipelago wolf (*Canis lupus ligoni*). Alaska Region, Anchorage, Alaska. USFWS.

Van der Weyde, L. L. 2013. Reproductive biology of the endangered African wild dog (*Lycaon pictus*) in captive and free-ranging populations: An endocrine, behavioural and demographic approach. Thesis. University of Western Australia.

Vasco Leite J. 2012. Evolution and Biogeography of Canids (*Canis* and *Vulpes*) in North-West Africa. Porto, Portugal: Facultade de Ciéncias, Universidade do Porto.

Viranta S. et al. 2017. Rediscovering a forgotten canid species. BMC Zoology, 2: 6.

Vivar E. and Pacheco V. 2014. Status of gray fox *Lycalopex griseus* (Gray, 1837) (Mammalia: Canidae) from Peru. Revista Peruana de Biología, 21 (1): 071-078.

Volodin I. A. et al. 2013. Structure of Arctic Fox (*Alopex lagopus beringensis*) Colonies in the

Northern Extremity of Bering Island. Biology Bulletin, 40 (7): 614–625.

VonHoldt B. M et al. 2016. Whole-genome sequence analysis shows that two endemic species of North American wolf are admixtures of the coyote and gray wolf. Science Advances, 2: 1-13.

Waithman J. and Roest A. 1977. A taxonomic study of the kit fox, *Vulpes macrotis*. Journal of Mammalogy, 58 (2): 157-164.

Walton K., Gotthardt T. and Fields T. 2012. Alaska Species Ranking System Summary Report: Arctic Fox, Pribilof Island. Anchorage: Alaska Natural Heritage Program, University of Alaska Anchorage.

Walton L. R. and Joly D. O. 2003. *Canis mesomelas*. Mammalian Species, 715: 1-9.

Wang X. and Tedford R. H. 2008. Dogs: Their Fossil Relatives and Evolutionary History. New York: Columbia University Press.

Ward O. G. and Wurster-Hill D. H. 1990. *Nyctereutes procyonoides*. Mammalian Species, 358: 1-5.

Way J. G. 2000. Ecology of Cape Cod coyotes (*Canis latrans* var.). Thesis. University of Connecticut, Storrs.

Way J. G. 2013. Taxonomic implications of morphological and genetic differences in northeastern coyotes (Coywolves) (*Canis latrans* × *C. lycaon*), western coyotes (*C. latrans*), and eastern wolves (*C. lycaon* or *C. lupus lycaon*). The Canadian Field-Naturalist, 127(1): 1-16.

Way J. G. 2014. Strategies for red wolf recovery and management. Canid Biology and Conservation, 17 (2): 9-15.

Way J. G. and Lynn W. S. 2016. Northeastern coyote / coywolf taxonomy and admixture: A meta-analysis. Canid Biology & Conservation, 19 (1): 1-7.

Way J. G. et al. 2010. Genetic characterization of eastern "coyotes" in eastern Massachusetts. Northeastern Naturalist, 17(2): 189-204.

Wayne R. K. and O'Brien S. J. 1987. Allozyme divergence within the Canidae. Systematic Zoology, 36 (4): 339-355.

Weckworth B. V., Dawson N. G., Talbot S. L. and Cook J. A. 2015. Genetic distinctiveness of Alexander Archipelago wolves (*Canis lupus ligoni*). The Journal of Heredity, 106 (4): 1-3.

Weckworth B. V., Dawson N. G., Talbot S. L., Flamme M. J. and Cook J. A. 2011. Going coastal: Shared evolutionary history between coastal British Columbia and southeast Alaska wolves (*Canis lupus*). PLoS One 6(5): 1-8.

West E. W. and Rudd R. L. 1983. Biological control of Aleutian Island Arctic fox: A preliminary strategy. International journal for the study of animal problems, 4 (4): 305-311.

Weston Glenn J. L., Civitello D. J. and Lance S. L. 2009. Multiple paternity and kinship in the gray fox (*Urocyon cinereoargenteus*). Mammalian Biology, 74: 394-402.

White P. A. 1985. Social organization and activity patterns of the Arctic fox (*Alopex lagopus pribilofensis*) on St. Paul Island, Alaska. Thesis. Los Angeles: University of California.

Wilson D. E. and Mittermeier R. A. 2009. Handbook of the Mammals of the World. Vol. 1, Carnivora. Barcelona, Spain: Lynx Edicions.

Wilson D. E. and Reeder D. M. 2005. Mammal Species of the World. A Taxonomic and Geographic Reference, 3rd ed. Baltimore: Johns Hopkins University Press.

Woodroffe R., Ginsberg J. and Macdonald D. 1997. The African Wild Dog. Status Survey and Conservation Action Plan. Gland, Switzerland: IUCN / SSC Canid Specialist Group.

Wydeven A. P., van Deelen T. R. and Heske E. 2009. Recovery of Gray Wolves in the Great Lakes Region of the United States. An Endangered Species Success Story. Berlin, Springer.

Yeong-Seok Jo. 2015. Mammals of Korea: Conservation and Management. Thesis. Texas Tech University.

Zapata S. C. et al. 2008. Morfometría externa y reparto de recursos en zorros simpátricos (*Pseudalopex culpaeus* y *P. griseus*) en el sureste de la Patagonia Argentina. Mastozoología Neotropical, 15 (1): 103-111.

Zrzavý J. and Ricánková V. 2004. Phylogeny of recent Canidae (Mammalia, Carnivora): Relative reliability and utility of morphological and molecular datasets. Zoologica Scripta, 33 (4): 311-333.

Zunino G. E. et al. 1995. Taxonomy of the genus *Lycalopex* (Carnivora: Canidae) in Argentina. Proceedings of the Biological Society of Washington, 108 (4): 729-747.

INDEX

The index includes the common English and scientific names. Scientific names are in italics.